BATH SPA UNIVERSITY
LIBRARY

B.C.H.E. - LIBRARY

00083958

Food Industry and the Environment
Practical Issues and Cost Implications

Food Industry and the Environment

Practical Issues and Cost Implications

Edited by

J.M. DALZELL
Scientific and Technical Information Section
Leatherhead Food Research Association

BLACKIE ACADEMIC & PROFESSIONAL
An Imprint of Chapman & Hall

London · Glasgow · Weinheim · New York · Tokyo · Melbourne · Madras

Published by
Blackie Academic and Professional, an imprint of Chapman & Hall
Wester Cleddens Road, Bishopbriggs, Glasgow G64 2NZ

Chapman & Hall, 2–6 Boundary Row, London SE1 8HN, UK

Blackie Academic & Professional, Wester Cleddens Road, Bishopbriggs, Glasgow G64 2NZ, UK

Chapman & Hall GmbH, Pappelallee 3, 69469 Weinheim, Germany

Chapman & Hall USA, One Penn Plaza, 41st Floor, New York NY 10119, USA

Chapman & Hall Japan, ITP-Japan, Kyowa Building, 3F, 2-2-1 Hirakawacho, Chiyoda-ku, Tokyo 102, Japan

DA Book (Aust.) Pty Ltd, 648 Whitehorse Road, Mitcham 3132, Victoria, Australia

Chapman & Hall India, R. Seshadri, 32 Second Main Road, CIT East, Madras 600 035, India

First edition 1994

© 1994 Chapman & Hall

Typeset in 10/12pt Times by Acorn Bookwork, Salisbury, Wilts
Printed in Great Britain by St Edmundsbury Press, Bury St Edmunds, Suffolk

ISBN 0 7514 0031 9

Apart from any fair dealing for the purposes of research or private study, or criticism or review, as permitted under the UK Copyright Designs and Patents Act, 1988, this publication may not be reproduced, stored, or transmitted, in any form or by any means, without the prior permission in writing of the publishers, or in the case of reprographic reproduction only in accordance with the terms of the licences issued by the Copyright Licensing Agency in the UK, or in accordance with the terms of licences issued by the appropriate Reproduction Rights Organization outside the UK. Enquiries concerning reproduction outside the terms stated here should be sent to the publishers at the Glasgow address printed on this page.

The publisher makes no representation, express or implied, with regard to the accuracy of the information contained in this book and cannot accept any legal responsibility or liability for any errors or omissions that may be made.

A catalogue record for this book is available from the British Library

Library of Congress Catalog Card Number: 94-70120

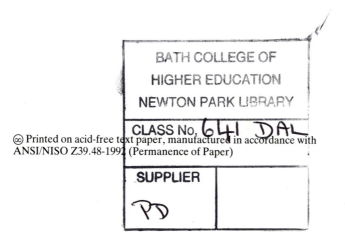

BATH COLLEGE OF
HIGHER EDUCATION
NEWTON PARK LIBRARY
CLASS No. 641 DAL
SUPPLIER
PD

∞ Printed on acid-free text paper, manufactured in accordance with ANSI/NISO Z39.48-1992 (Permanence of Paper)

Preface

All areas of industry are facing increasing pressure from governments and consumers to be more environmentally aware. The food industry is no exception, and an increasing number of companies have made the decision to implement an environmental policy. These organisations will benefit from this book, which has been written to provide a broad but detailed introduction to the topic of environmental issues and their cost implications to the food industry. Throughout the text the authors have approached the subject from a practical angle, and have borne in mind the environmental, production or site manager who is grappling with the problem of how to implement such a policy.

This book begins by considering the raw materials that are used in the food industry, whether derived from animals, fruit and vegetables, or the products of genetic engineering, as may increasingly be the case in the future. Environmental and cost considerations of food processing operations are then examined, encompassing energy conservation and the control of air, noise and water pollution; all topics that are uppermost in the priorities of the environmental manager. The finished food product also has an impact on its environment, and so the storage, distribution and packaging of foods, post food factory, is discussed in detail. Finally, the principles involved in management accounting for food industry environmental issues are highlighted.

All the authors of this book are respected experts in their chosen field, each of whom could have written a complete book on their subject. However, within a single chapter they have provided the reader with a comprehensive introduction to their topic from a practical angle, and have helpfully included insights into the future.

Although this book has primarily been written for the environmental manager, I hope that it will be of interest to all in the food industry and research establishments who are concerned about their environment. For ease of reference, a glossary of useful terms is included.

Acknowledgements

My thanks are due to all the authors for their time and co-operation, and to their families and employers, without whose support and assistance this book would not have been possible. As with any book of this type, the views expressed by the authors are their own and not necessarily the views of their employers, the publisher or indeed my own. However, all the views expressed in this book are backed-up by evidence that deserves to be considered by the reader.

My thanks are also due to my employer, Leatherhead Food Research Association, for encouraging me to undertake the editorship of this book, and for the use of their facilities that made this possible.

I also acknowledge and thank Bill Whitman, who recently retired from Leatherhead Food Research Association, for all his discussion, which helped me to 'shape' this book.

Finally, to my husband, Mark, and parents, Irene and Geoffrey Gill, for all their support and assistance, which made my task so much easier.

J.M.D.

Contributors

Dr P. Andreoli — Department of Regulatory Affairs, Royal Gist-brocades B.V., PO Box 1, 2600 MA, Delft, The Netherlands

Mrs J.M. Dalzell — Scientific and Technical Information Section, Leatherhead Food Research Association, Randalls Road, Leatherhead, Surrey KT22 7RY, UK

Mr C.V.J. Dellino — 9 Austin Street, Hunstanton, Norfolk PE36 6AJ, UK

Mr A. Gear — Henry Doubleday Research Association, National Centre for Organic Gardening, Ryton-on-Dunsmore, Coventry CV8 3LG, UK

Dr P.S. Harris — Cheriton Technology Management, St Stephen's House, St Stephen's Place, Cambridge CB3 0JE, UK

Mr G. Hazle — Exel Logistics, The Merton Centre, 45 St Peter Street, Bedford MK40 2UB, UK

Mr M. Key — Key Environmental Management, 11 Columbine Grove, Evesham, Worcestershire WR11 6LR, UK

Dr D. Praaning-van Dalen — Department of Regulatory Affairs, Royal Gist-brocades B.V., PO Box 1, 2600 MA, Delft, The Netherlands

Dr S. Roller — Food Ingredients Section, Leatherhead Food Research Association, Randalls Road, Leatherhead, Surrey KT22 7RY, UK

Dr S.E. Selke — School of Packaging, Michigan State University, 130 Packaging Building, East Lansing, MI 48824-1223, USA

Ms N.M.A. Walshe — ETSU for the Energy Efficiency Office, Harwell, Oxfordshire OX11 0RA, UK

Mr P. Walsh

P. Walsh & Associates, 45 Main Street, Sewstern, Grantham, Lincolnshire NG33 5RF, UK

Dr A.D. Wheatley

Civil Engineering Department, Loughborough University of Technology, Loughborough, Leicestershire, LE11 3TU, UK

Mr R. White

26 The Glade, Ashley Heath, Ringwood, Hampshire BH24 2HR, UK

Professor C.T. Whittemore

Institute of Ecology and Resource Management, The University of Edinburgh, School of Agriculture Building, West Mains Road, Edinburgh EH9 3JG, UK

Contents

5   Noise and air pollution in the food industry: sources, control and cost implications   106

P. WALSH and M. KEY

6   Water pollution in the food industry: sources, control and cost implications   **137**
A.D. WHEATLEY

Editorial introduction

J.M. DALZELL

Environmental issues are of increasing concern to the food industry, as consumers and legislators force manufacturers to become more aware of the consequences of their operations. The impact of a food factory on the environment is not limited to the waste materials that the processing operation generates, as consumers are only too aware. They know that the product is manufactured from raw materials, and are concerned with the methods used to produce these ingredients. For example, were excessive amounts of pesticide or fertiliser used, which may have been washed into the rivers and were calves treated with growth promoters to produce their Sunday roast? Furthermore, many consumers are increasingly concerned about what happens to packaging waste and whether it is really necessary to have so much packaging in the first place. Although some foods may be over packaged, in the vast majority of cases the packaging is there to serve a specific purpose, which is often not appreciated by the consumer. Unfortunately, consumers derive most of their environmental information from the general media, who are not always scientifically aware or in a position to provide a balanced view.

Over the past year or so, the potential consequences of genetic engineering on our environment have been highlighted. In this case, the fears of the consumer that genetically engineered plants and animals may play havoc with the gene pool and change the world irrevocably are hard to allay.

You may think that 'green' consumers are few and far between; they are not. Market survey after market survey show that consumers, particularly those in their twenties and thirties, claim to be buying more green products as the years go by; it has become desirable to be seen to be environmentally responsible. What should be of concern to the manufacturer is that children and young people are foremost in the campaign to take care of the environment, and after all these are the consumers of tomorrow. Although as they grow older and mature they may become less idealistic, their underlying concern for their environment is likely to remain. Furthermore, many parents seem to be influenced by the environmental views of their children when shopping. It is interesting that survey respondents generally claim to buy more 'green' products than is actually the case. Clearly there is some sort of social conscience at work that is locked in battle with the purse or the wallet. There is the nagging thought that, 'I really should buy the organic apples, but they are more expensive.'

Consumers may influence industry through their spending habits and legislators via the ballot box. The number of laws relating to the environment are numerous, and many of the authors who have contributed to this book have helpfully included information on legislation. This information is of great value; however, legislation is never static, new laws are introduced and amendments to existing laws are made. It is for this reason that I recommend that you check with primary sources of legislation for the current legislative position.

The food factory manager may ignore the views of consumers at risk of loss of sales, but he ignores the views of the legislators at risk of prosecution. The laws that are foremost in the mind of the site manager are those relating to pollution, particularly regulations dealing with pollution of the air, water or land, and regulatory limits for noise pollution. Each sector of the food industry produces its own unique mixture of waste materials; the dairy industry for example is a major source of industrial effluent in Europe. Dairy waste may have a drastic effect on the chemical oxygen demand of a waterway, and the cleaning agents that are used to remove the fat and protein deposits from processing equipment are highly alkaline, and may raise the pH to toxic levels. It is in the interests of the manufacturer to treat waste to such a standard that it is clean enough to release to the waterways or sewers, as this avoids paying large sums of money for the waste to be treated by the local water company.

Money is also to be saved by conserving energy, additionally this preserves the earth's natural stock of fuels and cuts down on emissions of carbon dioxide, a gas that has been linked to global warming. An environmental audit of virtually any food factory will almost certainly identify areas where energy use may be reduced. Energy conservation is often the first step a company takes on the road to becoming more environmentally aware, as small inexpensive measures can result in vast savings in energy and fuel bills.

The number of companies having an environmental policy who are committed to producing food in an environmentally friendly way has grown over the years, reflected by the appointment of Environmental Managers. There are still some companies that have not come to terms with environmental issues; this book should provide a practical and comprehensive introduction to this topic.

Glossary

Adsorption costing: A term used in accounting to describe the way that costs are allocated to activities and products to ensure that these costs are recovered through the product pricing mechanism.

Activity based costing: A system of allocating costs on the basis of the activities that generate the costs.

Alumina: Purified aluminium oxide.

Armitage Norton problem: The low priority given to investment in energy efficiency or environmental protection in organisations, because it is discretionary business maintenance capital expenditure, specifically to reduce a revenue cost.

Bauxite: Aluminium ore, consisting of 40–60% aluminium oxide.

BOD: Biological oxygen demand, biochemical oxygen demand, the oxygen consumed by aerobic microorganisms to degrade organic matter in the effluent.

BOD5: Five-day biological oxygen demand.

Btu: British thermal unit, 1 Btu = 1054.8 joules.

Capital return budget: A table that compares the reduction in revenue costs through discretionary capital investment.

COD: Chemical oxygen demand, a measure of the amount of potassium dichromate needed to oxidise reducing material in a water sample. It is expressed as the concentration of oxygen gas in parts per million chemically equivalent to the amount of dichromate consumed.

Control chart: A chart of the differences between the actual value of some measured quantity and the expected based on an established historic pattern immediately before the measurement, plotted against time.

Co-transformation: Simultaneous introduction and assimilation of different DNA molecules from one organism to another via uptake of naked DNA.

CNG: Compressed natural gas.

Cullet: Recycled glass used as a feedstock for glass production.

CUSUM: A statistical technique used for measuring bias in equal interval sequential data. CUSUM is an acronym for CUMulative SUM deviation. There are three forms of CUSUM: univariant measures changes in a single variable; parametric measures the changes in the relationship between one variable and another; and recurrent, which measures the changes in a variable that repeats over a cycle in time.

Degree day: A measure of the cumulative difference between the outside temperature and a base temperature in a period of time for all occasions when the outside temperature is below (heating degree day) or above (cooling degree day) the base temperature. There are two definitions of the degree day. One is a summary indicator of the weather and uses a formula based on the daily maximum and minimum outside temperatures. The formula used in the United Kingdom for this purpose is different from that used in other countries. The other definition, recognised only since 1984, is a coefficient derived from the physical law of cooling for a building. These are often used interchangeably but care needs to be exercised in assuming that they are identical.

Dioxins: A group of chemicals with the chemical name polychlorinated dibenzo-*p*-dioxins, which are ubiquitous environmental contaminants.

DMT: Dimethyl terephthalate.

Energy audit: An examination of, and expression of an opinion on, the use of energy in an enterprise and the systems in place to manage the energy use.

Energy survey: An examination of a building or site to identify areas of energy use which give rise to unnecessary energy waste, to identify energy using equipment inappropriate to its task or to identify equipment that is not functioning as intended.

Energy balance: An examination of a building or process to identify the energy outputs and equate them with the energy inputs, as required by the first law of thermodynamics.

Eutrophication: The process of nutrient enrichment of an aquatic system.

EVOH: Ethylene vinyl alcohol.

Gauss Markov conditions: A set of conditions which data must meet in order for regression to be a valid procedure for finding the best fit line through the data. These conditions are that the expectation of the relationship between the variables is linear and the data are homoscedastic.

Gene: The fundamental physical and functional unit of heredity. The portion of a DNA molecule that is made up of an ordered sequence of nucleotides that produce a specific product or have an assigned function.

Gene-replacement: Technology used to replace or to substitute a gene from the genome of an organism.

GWP: Global warming potential.

Heterologous: Recombination of DNA sequences originating from different species.

HDPE: High density polyethylene.

Homologous: Recombination of DNA sequences originating from the same species.

IPC: Integrated pollution control.

Intron: A portion of a gene that is transcribed but does not appear in the final messenger RNA transcript.

Kaplan problem: The tendency of organisations to require other aspects of management to use the information systems developed for financial control in preference to setting up purpose designed information systems.

Kraft pulping: The most common pulping process for packaging papers, a chemical process using sodium sulphate.

LDPE: Low density polyethylene.

LLDPE: Linear low density polyethylene.

LNG: Liquefied natural gas.

LPG: Liquefied petroleum gas.

MAC: Maximum admissible concentration.

Monitoring and target setting: A term used in energy management for the routine collection of information on energy use and its conversion to consumption targets.

NO_x: Oxides of nitrogen.

NSSC: Neutral sulphite semi-chemical pulping.

ODP: Ozone depleting potential.

PE: Polyethylene.

PET: Polyethylene terephthalate.

PG: Polygalacturonase.

POM: Particulate organic matter.

PP: Polypropylene.

PS: Polystyrene.

PVC: Polyvinyl chloride.

PVDC: Polyvinylidene chloride.

Procaryotic: cells having no membrane surrounding the nuclear material and no organelles, e.g. bacteria and blue-green algae.

Promoter: A DNA sequence to which RNA polymerase binds, and then initiates transcription.

Prophylactic: Tending to prevent or to protect against disease, especially infectious disease.

Recombination: The process of joining pieces of DNA.

Reverse transcriptase: An enzyme that can synthesise a single strand of DNA from a messenger RNA, the reverse of the normal direction of processing genetic information within the cell.

Scedasticity: A statistical term used to describe the structure of the scatter in an $x-y$ graph. Homoscedastic describes random scatter with no structure.

Self-cloning: The removal of nucleic acid from a cell of an organism, followed by re-insertion of all or part of that nucleic acid (with or without further enzymic, chemical or mechanical steps) into the same cell type, or into phylogenetically closely related species which can naturally exchange genetic material with the donor species.

Sour gas: Natural gas containing more than 0.25 grains of hydrogen sulphide per 100 standard cubic feet.

SO$_x$: Oxides of sulphur.

Terminator: A DNA sequence at the end of a transcriptional unit that signals the end of transcription.

TOC: Total organic carbon.

TPA: Terephthalic acid.

Transgenic: Used to describe animals that are derived from embryos into which isolated genomic DNA from another species has been introduced at an early stage of development.

Transcription: Formation of the ribonucleic acid (RNA) from the DNA template.

Translation: The process in which the genetic code contained in the nucleotide sequences of messenger RNA directs the order of amino acids in the formation of a peptide.

TSP: Total suspended particles.

TSS: Total suspended solids.

VOC: Volatile organic compound.

1 Food from animals: environmental issues and implications

C.T. WHITTEMORE

1.1 Introduction

The world's population of 5 000 000 000 is estimated to use annually some 600 000 000 000 kg of meat, milk and eggs from animals (Table 1.1). An increase in per capita income brings about an increase first in the consumption of crop products, but soon after, an increase also in more costly animal products; this is a positive relationship which is maintained until the highest income levels are attained, at which point the consumption rate for animal product plateaus (Figure 1.1). It is not surprising, therefore, that animal production output is predicted to stabilise in many countries of the developed world but to expand in developing countries. Relative national desires to increase and cheapen animal production on the one hand, and to control and proscribe on the other, are closely reflected in the attitudes of each society to environmental and ethical issues related to the consumption of meat, milk and eggs. Thus it is that consideration of the environmental aspects of the production of human food from animals tends to be a science which is both recent in origin and the privilege of the nutritionally satisfied. The average European consumes 80 kg of meat per capita annually. However, animal production, if allowed to become unbalanced, may also induce environmental problems in developing countries; extensive farming of herbivorous stock has led in some areas to overgrazing and land erosion. These occurrences are particularly distressing where the food product is destined for export out of the area of its primary production.

1.2 Disposal of animal excreta

Farmed animals consume feedstuffs, usually farmed crops and crop by-products (and sometimes also animal products), to create food for consumption by humans. This process may be considered as one of biochemical enrichment. The feedstuffs used by animals are often inappropriate for human consumption (grass), unwanted by humans (lower quality seeds and grains, or grains grown in excess of human requirement), or by-products of human food manufacture (brans, starches, oilseed residues). Such a

Table 1.1 Estimated annual world consumption of farmed animal product

	Millions of tonnes
Milk and milk products	400
Pig meat	65
Beef meat	50
Poultry meat	35
Eggs	20
Farmed fish	10
Sheep and goat meat	5

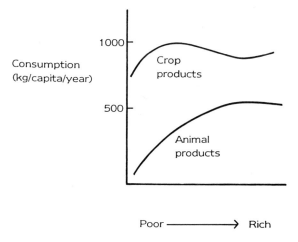

Figure 1.1 Consumption of crop and animal products according to income.

notion of enrichment is limited, of course, to those circumstances where animals are not perceived to be competing with people for crop products in limited supply.

The wide difference in nutrient concentration between crop plants and animal products results in substantial returns of ingested materials to the environment. Digestibility by ruminants of plant forages, rich in structural carbohydrates, is usually between 0.3 and 0.7; this value being inversely related to plant fibre content. Cattle, consuming some 15 kg of dry matter daily of a forage with a digestibility coefficient of 0.5, will therefore excrete nearly 3 tonnes of dry matter as faecal material annually, or some 20–30 tonnes of fresh faeces. Faecal and urinary excreta may be returned to the land directly, as in the case of the grazing animal, or stored for spreading later, as in the case of housed animals. In many parts of the world, animal dung is a highly valued fuel material; both for domestic fires and for use by power stations. The return of animal excreta to the land from which it originates was always an environmentally positive and ancient cycle; but now it is seen as sensitive, due to the potential for eutrophication and water contamination. Sustainable mixed farming systems require the effective return of excreta to the land, but this very process is currently identified as problematic and requiring control by legislation. The reasons for this are twofold: (a) the addition of artificial manures represents a nett input to the system which has increased the output of crops per unit of land, allowing more animals to be fed per unit of land area, and (b) intensive pig, poultry and dairy farming systems have caused the crop outputs to be transported to, and concentrated in, limited areas distant from the point of primary crop production. The ability of a small area of land within transport distance of an intensive farming unit to accept excreta which has originated from a greater area of land is now a primary environmental issue, involving limitation by legislation in Northern Europe.

The pig may serve as an appropriate example of the environmental implications of the animal excreta output from intensive livestock units. The world's pig meat is produced from about 850 000 000 animals, more than 30% of which are in China. Of the total, 20% of pig meat is produced in the European Community. European pigs are found clustered especially densely in localities such as north-west Germany, the Low Countries, east England, Brittany, Catalonia and the Po Valley. A 500-sow pig breeding and rearing unit will produce around 25 tonnes of wet (10% dry matter) mixed faeces and urine daily. Animal excreta are rich in the elements nitrogen, phosphorus and potassium, all of which may be considered valuable as fertilisers in moderation and pollutants in excess. Some 30% of the N and some 10% of P and K is lost during storage. Wet excreta contains 4.0–4.5 g N/kg, 1.5–2.0 g P/kg and 2.5–3.0 g K/kg. Guidelines to possible permissible application levels of N and P are given in Table 1.2.

The amount of nutrient usable by farmland, which can be applied without run-off and excessive loss through the soil, is highly dependent upon crop and soil type. Good agricultural practice indicates a maximum application rate for organic manures of 250 kg N/ha, although lower limits are more appropriate in zones vulnerable to nitrate excess. Zones in which intensive livestock units are concentrated are considered vulnerable. EC recommendations are likely to suggest 170 kg N/ha as a general purpose guideline for an upper limit. If 150 kg N/ha were to be considered a

Table 1.2 Guide to possible permissible application levels of N and P (kg/ha per year)

	N	P
Arable land	150	60
Grassland	300	100
Particularly rapid-growing and demanding crops	400	120

completely safe annual application rate, then a land area of 250 ha is required to handle the output of excreta from a 500-sow pig production unit. Nearly half of all meat consumed by Europeans is pig meat, and at the rate of 35 kg of pig meat per year, an annual output of 570 tonnes, such as might be expected from a 500-sow breeding and production unit, would supply 16 000 persons. There is no special embarrassment in these quantities other than where the available land area is determined to be inadequate to cope with the excreta output of local animal production units, as may sometimes unfortunately be the case. Pressure in these circumstances would be for (i) extensification, (ii) integration of intensive animal production units with extensive crop farming systems, and, *in extremis*, (iii) the treatment of animal waste and/or its transportation outwith the local area.

The calculation of land area required per productive animal unit is sensitive not only to crop and soil type (see Table 1.2) but also to the rate of animal excretion itself. The average daily output of nitrogen by the pig can be reduced by restraining nitrogen inputs and by increasing the efficiency of dietary nitrogen use through improvement of amino acid balance. Particular circumstances of land type, crop type and nutrient utilisation may cause the estimation of land area requirement per livestock unit to vary by a factor of up to four. This potential for variation is especially unhelpful to legislators, and has stimulated detailed study, not only of crop and soil acceptability rates for farmyard manures but also of how the rate of excretion of nitrogen from animals can be minimised. It should not be immediately assumed, however, that the minimisation of nitrogen excretion is necessarily to be considered wholly beneficial in efficiency terms. An important purpose of meat-producing animals is the conversion of low-grade vegetable proteins which are relatively deficient in essential amino acids into high-grade animal proteins which are relatively rich in balanced essential amino acids. As this process is essentially one of concentration, there is a necessary excretion, mostly in the urine, of non-essential and unbalanced amino acid nitrogen. The animal's role as an upgrader of nutrient sources is therefore in conflict with a policy of excretion minimisation. The closer the amino acid spectrum of the animal diet is to the amino acid spectrum of the human protein requirement, then (i) the more efficiently will the animal use that protein and the less will be voided in faeces and urine, but (ii) the less useful will the animal be in terms of creating, from low-grade vegetable proteins, high-grade animal proteins for human consumption. It is also the case that reducing the protein content of animal diets so that they become protein-limiting will reduce nitrogen excretion rates, and there is some pressure for this to happen where intensive animal production units are considered an environmental threat. Unfortunately, creating protein-deficient diets will have the consequence of depressing animal performance, reducing efficiency, possibly increasing the overall rate of nitrogen excretion per unit of meat produced, and may even be ethically dubious.

The principles outlined for farmed livestock also relate to farmed fish. Temperate farmed fish, usually salmonid sea-caged salmon and fresh-water ponded trout, are less efficient than tropically farmed tilapia and carp. First, fish growth rate is highly influenced by water temperature. More important, however, are the diverse nutrient requirements of these different fish types. The salmonids require to be fed a diet high in animal protein, usually comprising fish derivatives and other animal wastes. Certain tropical species, on the other hand, may be gathered together in ponds of polycultures and the pond is then fed with a wide variety of relatively low-grade materials, such as vegetable matter and carbohydrates, and even excreta from pigs, poultry and cattle. In the case of sea-caged salmon and fresh-water ponded trout, feed wastage and excreta from the fish is a significant problem leading to pollution in sea lochs and eutrophication of fresh-water systems, these being significantly challenged already by phosphates and nitrates emanating from the land. River Authorities have now set upper limits on phosphorus and nitrogen levels in natural water systems.

1.3   Energetic efficiency

Energy losses through the inefficiency of transfer of feed energy to edible animal product is an important element of any discussion of environmental impact and the efficient use of scarce resources in sustainable production systems. Figure 1.2 shows the amounts of energy required to produce 1 kg of meat protein from various domestic livestock species. The energy costs of supporting the breeding female are substantial in the case of the larger

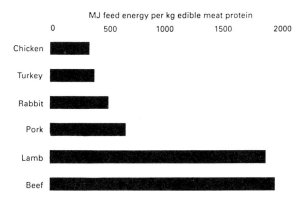

Figure 1.2 Efficiency of transformation of animal feedstuffs to human food in the form of meat.

herbivores (cattle and sheep) but less so in the more prolific pig and rabbit, and especially in poultry. The maintenance costs of the marketed meat-producing animal itself also comprise a significant inefficiency in the transfer of animal feedstuff to human food. Maintenance costs may be reduced and efficiency increased by enhancing growth rate and reducing the number of days taken to reach market weight. Figure 1.2 shows the feed energy costs per kg edible meat protein to be less than 500 MJ for poultry, some 700 MJ for pigs and 2000 MJ for beef.

A further element of meat production efficiency is the yield of edible product from the primary live animal. This will depend upon the content of inedible offals and bone, and the amount of (waste) carcass fat present. Beef and sheep carcasses may contain 25–30% of fat, those of poultry and pigs 10–20%. Of the total animal product entering abattoirs, only a little over 50% leaves as appropriate for human use; the remainder is usually rendered and returned usefully to the system by recycling into animal feed. This cycle is not only a highly efficient use of resources but it also solves what would otherwise be a severe problem of disposal of vast quantities of animal tissue waste in an environmentally appropriate manner. However, in the absence of stringent process control the very act of recycling allows the possibility of the transfer of infective agents, such as salmonellae and that for bovine spongiform encephalopathy.

For her 8 years of productive life, a dairy cow may eat 1 000 000 MJ of gross energy and produce with exemplary efficiency 50 000 kg of milk containing 1500 kg of protein, not to mention 2000 kg of milk fat and as much again of milk sugar. The modern high-yielding dairy cow is arguably the most metabolically stressed of our farm animals, and it is possible that her role as a producer of human food may require to be curtailed on animal health and welfare grounds. Trends in milk production are now towards improved efficiency through the use of a larger proportion of cheaper, lower quality feed roughages, and a smaller proportion of expensive feed grains. This has led to the introduction of sustainable low input/lower

Table 1.3 Performance and efficiency of selected[a] and control dairy cows given diets of high and low nutrient concentration

	High nutrient concentration		Low nutrient concentration	
	Selected cows[a]	Control cows	Selected cows[a]	Control cows
Milk yield (kg/lactation)	7569	6537	6327	5360
Protein (%)	3.1	3.2	3.1	3.1
Fat (%)	4.2	4.2	4.5	4.4
Energetic efficiency (MJ/MJ)	0.42	0.38	0.44	0.37

[a]Genetic selection over 15 years, from the control base level, was for the yield of fat plus protein.

output dairy farming systems. The drive for the introduction of high forage systems of dairying has come primarily from the demand by society for minimum welfare standards and, equally as important, legislators placing quotas on absolute levels of farm output in order to limit production, which in Europe has become excessive. However, genetic selection for high performance genotypes remains beneficial, as indicated by the results of a trial comparing two genotypes (genetically selected and control) each on two feeding systems (high and low diet nutrient concentration). These results are shown in Table 1.3. The improvements in performance and efficiency of selected cows are evident, on either the high or the low concentrate diets.

1.4   Environmental influences upon perceptions of quality in food from animals

1.4.1   Flavour

The notion that the circumstances of production may influence the nutritional content and organoleptic properties of meat, milk and eggs is one of long standing. This is not to suggest, however, that substantial changes in the nutritional content of animal products, or their tastes, are readily achievable through environmental manipulation. The biochemical forces prevailing in the animal's body ensure transformations within and between nutrient components which preclude such possibilities. Variations in flavour and texture of pork and beef meat are never so great that the difference between them do not remain evident. It is relatively easy to manipulate the ratio of fat to lean in meat, and possible to alter the ratio of lipid to protein in milk, but it is more difficult to alter the endogenously synthesised amino acid composition of muscle and milk proteins.

Flavours may be transferred from animal feedstuffs through to animal products. Milk may change its taste according to summer and winter feeding regimes, and according to the presence or absence of individual feedstuffs in winter rations (such as root crops). Dietary fatty acids may, in particular, be transferred directly to animal lipid and impart particular flavours and characteristics. Dietary unsaturated fatty acids produce softer body fat in monogastrics. Body fats of sheep, cattle and goats are not so susceptible to this process due to rumen hydrogenation. Off-flavours may be found in the fat of pork and chicken given diets containing high levels of fishmeal and/or containing fats tending to rancidity. Chickens fed high levels of white maize will tend to have white fat, whereas those fed high levels of yellow maize will tend to have yellow fat. It is possible also that the development of the unpleasant odour, skatole, in pork may have a dietary component relating to tryptophan degradation in the hind gut.

Not surprisingly, it is difficult to alter to any great extent the composition of an egg (avian or mammalian) by dietary means. The proposition that the nutrient composition of a hen's egg may be related to the way the hen is farmed is difficult to substantiate, although yolk colour is readily influenced by the addition to the diet of natural or artificial colour (carotines and xanthins). It is equally hard to demonstrate important organoleptic differences between wild and farmed fish, despite very different nutritional and environmental circumstances. Again, the colour of salmon flesh derived naturally from the consumption of prawns may be produced artificially by the addition of xanthins to the diet.

1.4.2   Fatness

Food quality as determined by the ratio of lipid to lean in an animal product can be manipulated by control of the ratio of energy to protein in the diet. Protein deposition in lean meat requires provisions of adequate dietary protein; diets of high protein/energy ratio predispose to the production of lean meat, and vice versa. The demand for lean and protein (rather than fat) in meat has led to an increase in the protein content of animal diets. The composition of milk is rather more intransigent but the type of energy-yielding feed given can alter butterfat levels. Fibrous foods will alter the rumen volatile fatty acid ratio in favour of acetate, which in turn favours the production of milk fat. High-level feeding of cereal grains to dairy cows may depress milk fat. Advances in knowledge of nutritional requirements of livestock have led to large reductions in the fat content of meat and improvements in the efficiency of production of lean.

Genetic selection for specific heritable characters has allowed some alteration to the nutritional composition of animal products, especially the fat protein ratio, but not greatly to their flavour. Targets for genetic selection have tended to be: (i) level of production, (ii) efficiency of production, (iii) fat: lean ratio in the product and (iv) product quality, invariably measured in terms of tenderness. All these forces have led to selection of genotypes which mature larger and which therefore grow faster and more efficiently. At any given market weight, larger maturing breeds of cattle, sheep, pigs and poultry will be physiologically less mature and therefore leaner, more tender and possibly also carrying less flavour.

1.4.3   Freedom from undesired characteristics

The public perception of quality in meat and milk products is probably firstly in terms of their fatness, secondly in terms of organoleptic qualities, thirdly in terms of absence of harmful constituents, and lastly in terms of the circumstances in which the product was derived. However, in some sectors of industrialised communities, the absence of fat is taken for granted, the perception of natural flavour is becoming a lost sense, and freedom from additives and undesired characteristics are becoming paramount.

The efficiency of production of food from animals, and therefore its cost to the purchaser, can be helped by the prevention of animal disease (utilisation of prophylactic medicines and antibiotics), the enhancement of appetite and growth response to nutrients (feed flavours and enzymes, growth promoters and probiotics) and the exogenous encouragement of endogenous systems (natural and artificially manufactured hormone preparations). It is superfluous to state in retrospect that some of these substances, used with the best of intentions, have been found to be unsafe, or to argue that, learning from past experience, legislators can now ensure that only unimpeachable products are allowed to be used by farmers to improve the efficiency of their operations and maintain low-cost high-quality food production. Where pressure is upon agriculture to provide more food from animals at a low cost which can be afforded by the populations of developing countries, the positive attributes of aids to efficiency need no rehearsal. In contrast, where assurance and perception of food quality is more important than price, the arguments are irrelevant. In many developed countries of the world, the first requirement of an animal product upon the supermarket shelf is that it is derived from animals reared free of unnatural dietary additives, prophylactic medicines, hormone treatments and the like. Where food commands a low proportion of society's disposable income, the costs of electing to forego improvements in efficiency are considered trivial.

Such shifts in consumer demand are well understood by the agricultural community who are now entering into a plethora of local and national farm-quality-assured schemes whereby production processes are independently monitored and guaranteed to have abided by stated criteria. The extreme position of this movement may be seen as the rise of public interest in organic farming. Organically farmed meat is stated not only to be free of artificial aids to production but also the crops upon which the animals are fed are grown without the aid of 'artificial' fertilisers, insecticides and weed control agents. The evidence for organic beef to be of higher eating quality is equivocal. The extra costs are substantial, especially if the cereals consumed by the cattle are also disposable onto the human food market where a 20–40% premium can prevail. However, if the cattle are reared as part of an integrated farming system involving extensive low-input pastures, then the extra costs of organic beef production can be covered by a 15–20% premium on the value of the beast at market. The prognosis for provision of animal products up to full organic specification is poor due to the difficulty in meeting the severe regulations imposed by governing bodies; and the majority of a population may not share the same rigour of approach. More likely is the growth of consumer demand for lower input extensive and sustainable farming systems which do not deny an opportunity to maintain efficiency by some degree of regulated assistance and enlightened management for pest control and health enhancement practices, provided these do not endanger the environment or cast doubt on the integrity of the product. Rather than draconian insistence on absolute purity and freedom from artificiality, the consuming public is more likely to ask for guarantees of safety relating to farming practice, and to ask for farming systems to be acceptable, responsible and sustainable.

Bovine and porcine somatotrophins, growth hormones, are naturally occurring endogenous products which, as the name suggests, enhance anabolic activities such as growth and lactation. Faster-growing animals, and those which yield greater quantities of milk, have a more effective somatotrophic system. Encouraging the presence of somatotrophin in the body will therefore enhance productivity. Somatotrophic hormones may be synthesised through the use of recombinant DNA technology, and the injection of the synthesised product into animals has been seen as attractive, increasing growth rate, reducing fatness, enhancing milk yield, and improving efficiency, all by some 10–20%. Its use has been stalled, however, by objections on grounds of (i) perceived over-supply of meat and milk in European countries, (ii) negative welfare, and (iii) the natural (but subjective) concern of customers that meat and milk from treated animals may not be as wholesome as that from untreated ones. The latter two objections may be overcome by the artificial insertion of gene sequences for growth hormone, or by the immunisation of animals against that part of the endocrine complex which limits endogenous somatotrophin production. There can be objections here on account of recombinant DNA-created somatotrophin being qualitatively different (if quantitatively similar) to the natural product. Somatotrophin-producing bacteria have been engineered, rather than occurring in nature.

The safety of consumption of transgenic animals is presently under consideration, although *prima facie* the judgement is likely more to be one of moral value than of objective science. The product is less likely to be faulted than is the method of its production. Objectivity is not necessarily the primary basis upon which to make judgements on the eating quality of food. In addition, it appears that there may be unexpected consequences for transgenic animals with elevated blood somatotrophin levels, including diminished health as evidenced, for example, by increased susceptibility to arthritis in pigs. This may be a result of the manipulation of only one part of a highly complex system which has caused an imbalance. The benefit of genetic selection for growth rate and milk yield by conventional means has the advantage of each small step forward, generation by generation, being achieved whilst at the same time there is an opportunity for a balance of the genetic make-up of the whole animal to be maintained.

By definition, the transgenic has involved a dramatic enhancement of one small part of its fundamental constitution. It remains to be seen whether biotechnology has more to offer than has breed improvement by selection; but at present transgenic animals created by genetic manipulation and gene insertion are perceived by some sectors of some societies to be less environmentally correct than animals that have been chosen by conventional selection from naturally occurring populations. In countries where food from animals is plentiful, moral judgements concerning the ethics of the creation of more efficient transgenic animals may well differ from those in countries where food is scarce.

1.4.4   Animal welfare perceptions

A perception of quality in terms of the way the customer feels about an animal product, rather than its nutritional content or organoleptic properties, has led those concerned with the welfare of farmed animals to include within the description of product value a definition of the level of animal welfare pertaining in the system of production under which the animal was kept. Attention has so far been directed at the intensive pig and poultry industries, and has led to European-wide guidelines, *inter alia*, on minimum space requirements for laying hens kept in cages, on stocking densities for pigs and on the abolition of tethers and stalls for pregnant sows. A sector of both the poultry and pig industries have opted for extensification as exemplified by the outdoor breeding of pigs and free-range egg production systems for poultry.

Outdoor pig production also makes low demands upon capital building costs and now comprises some 15–20% of the UK pig breeding herd, but is less common as a commercial practice elsewhere in the world. Comparison of an intensive housed system with a semi-intensive (straw-based) housed system and an outdoor system for keeping breeding sows has led to the interesting conclusion that it is the middle course which is most likely to be optimum. Capital costs for the semi-intensive and outdoor systems were respectively some 85% and 50% of the intensive system. Productivity on the intensive and semi-intensive systems was similar but there was a 10% reduction in productivity on the outdoor system. Feed costs were similar for the two housed systems but were 10% higher on the outdoor system. Energy expenditures for the semi-intensive and outdoor systems were 70% and 20%, respectively, of the intensive housed system (mostly through the cost of heating), but in the latter two cases there were expenditures on straw bedding which did not exist in the fully intensive system. Overall profitability was found to be highest for the semi-intensive housed system, and the profitability for the intensive and the extensive outdoor system was similar. With regard to the keeping of growing and finishing pigs, a similar comparison of intensive (slatted floors), semi-intensive (increased space allowance and straw-bedded pens), and outdoor pig huts showed that daily gain and feed conversion efficiencies were best for the fully intensive system but the capital costs for the semi-intensive and outdoor systems were only 70% and 60%, respectively, of those for the intensive system. Profitability of the semi-intensive and outdoor growing and finishing systems was only 70% and 80%, respectively, of that for the intensive finishing system. Overall it was concluded that the outdoor system was particularly susceptible to fluctuations in performance, whilst the housed systems were particularly sensitive to the costs of finance for the initial capitalisation. However, it is quite evident that some sectors of society perceive the semi-intensive system to be more acceptable than the intensive system, and this difference in perception is likely to yield, in some sectors of the market, an adequate product price premium to cover the difference in profitability between the intensive and semi-intensive systems. With regard to the fully extensive outdoor pig production systems, it should also be noted that the working environment for people is harsh, and the presumptive association of extensification with improved animal welfare may be unsafe.

Egg production has traditionally been almost totally fully intensive, with birds confined in cages in groups of 3 and 4. However, semi-extensive and extensive systems are now being used by some poultry farmers and the egg-buying public is offered freedom of choice to support extensive, semi-extensive or intensive production systems. In semi-extensive systems, the birds are usually housed in barns in flocks and have a greater degree of freedom than those in cages; they also have access to dust baths and nesting boxes and may therefore express a wider range of natural behavioural activities. The ultimate in high-welfare egg production is (probably wrongly) considered to be the fully extensive free-range system in which the birds have access from their house to extensive outdoor activity areas. Table 1.4 shows that this extensive system is not only more expensive in terms of costs of production (labour, capital and recurrent expenditures such as feed usage) but may also have less to offer in terms of hen welfare. The remarkable efficiency of the cage system is evident from the dramatic egg price premiums that are required to cover the extra expenditures of the semi-extensive and extensive systems of production. There is interest, therefore, in the possibility of increasing the welfare of caged birds by provision of perches and nesting arrangements, and further improving the efficiency of barn-based production systems. It is likely that the fully extensive free-range system will continue to target only a specialist niche market rather than providing a substantial proportion of the general public's requirement for eggs.

Poultry manure from egg production is a particularly rich source of fertiliser which has been 'rediscovered' by crop farmers. Given access to sufficient land area through effective distribution of egg production units

Table 1.4 Comparison of three systems of egg production

	Space available (m^2 per bird)	Mortality (birds per year) (%)	Egg price premium to cover cost of less intensive system (%)
Intensive (caged)	0.045	3–5	–
Semi-extensive (barn-housed)	0.060–0.125	5–10	30
Extensive (free-range)	–[a]	15–20	60

[a]The definition of free-range is fraught. Full free-ranging requires upward of 10 m^2 per bird.

within crop farming localities, the recycling of poultry excreta to crop production is biologically, economically and environmentally judicious.

1.5   Conclusion

The environmentally sensitive nature of animal production systems will cause food from animals to be subject to national and local product quality assurance schemes. These will favour integrated and sustainable farming systems, mixtures of enterprises on farms, judicious use of aids to efficient and effective management, and movement away from very intensive production systems for dairy cattle, pigs, fish and poultry. One of the aspects of the assurance will be that the production system is part of a lower pressure environment which, although not denying the proper and controlled application of modern technologies, will provide a guarantee of high-quality and safe food from animals farmed in an environmentally acceptable way. The cost of such assured systems of production and excreta management will undoubtedly result in a price premium on food from animals. In comparison to fully intensive systems using all available technological aids and free from legislative proscription, that premium is likely to be some 15–50%; the major and most dramatic increases in price being in those aspects of livestock production which are now the most efficient and most intensive, and which provide the best value animal foods, namely eggs, poultry meat, pig meat and, to a lesser extent, milk and milk products. The lower premium prices will be appropriate for the already expensive and less intensive beef and sheep meet. Over all, foods produced from animals, pressures relating to the return of animal excreta to the land, the demand for higher product quality in terms of safety, and concerns for animal welfare bring about an average cost increase required to be borne by the consumer of around 15–20%. Given a willingness on the part of the consumer to pay these premiums, there is no reason why the agricultural community should not espouse more environmentally conscious production systems. In addition, as only 18% of total household expenditure in Northern Europe is currently on food, it is reasonable to assume that a significant sector of the general public may indeed be ready to pay such a premium for the benefits that ensue. Such readiness might not be so evident, however, amongst the lower income groups of the developed nations, nor amongst all income groups of the developing nations.

2 Organic and non-organic agriculture
A. GEAR

2.1 Background

During the first half of the 20th century, indeed for most of the period when the United Kingdom was a major economic power, Government policy towards food was simple, it should be available at the cheapest possible price. Farming suffered as food, much of it capable of being grown in the United Kingdom, was imported from the Empire, where it could be produced at a much lower cost. Consequently, the United Kingdom entered the Second World War with its domestic agriculture in a seriously weakened state; a point driven home by the calamitous 'U'-boat attacks on the Atlantic convoys that were its lifeline. Thanks to a combination of military successes and a drastic plan for home production, the country was not starved into submission. Nevertheless, the experience proved cathartic for government planners. The maintenance of an adequate food supply, through agricultural self-sufficiency, became a primary objective during the ensuing years of the Cold War.

The main vehicle for this policy, coordinated in England by the Ministry of Agriculture, Fisheries and Food (MAFF), and in the rest of the United Kingdom by similar government bodies, was a complex series of financial incentives that encouraged output. These included support of the market price, subsidies towards the cost of fertilisers and capital grants for farm improvement. With no fear of temporary gluts driving prices down, it is hardly surprising that farmers responded enthusiastically.

Farmers were urged to specialise, backed by an ever-increasing effort invested in research and development. Gradually the mixed family farm of pre-war years was replaced by all-arable or all-livestock enterprises. Nitrogen fertiliser use was to expand sevenfold during the next 40 years. Completely new types of animal husbandry such as large-scale indoor pig and poultry units came into being, superseding their more extensive outdoor counterparts.

During hostilities, the Germans had been working on organophosphate-based chemicals, for use in biological warfare. It was found that these nerve gases could, with little modification, be pressed into service as insecticides. Similarly, DDT, which had been used extensively by front line troops, for controlling lice infesting their uniforms, found a ready and expanding market as a novel pesticide. Other insecticidal organochlorine compounds, Dieldrin, Aldrin, BHC, quickly followed, whilst new chemical substances were also developed to kill diseases and weeds.

Given such financial and technological support, output rose accordingly. Yield increases for cereals, for example, more than doubled. Although fertilisers played a major part in this success story, the role of the plant breeder in developing a succession of hybrid wheat varieties that responded positively to such chemical inputs, was no less significant.

When, in 1973, the United Kingdom joined the European Community (EC), domestic farming support was replaced by the Common Agricultural Policy (CAP). Little changed, however, since Brussels' policy was also to encourage output throughout the territory of its European members. This was achieved by price support of the market, albeit in a somewhat different form.

By the mid 1970s, the US-inspired model of agricultural production, involving intensive use of chemical inputs, factory livestock systems and crop specialisation, had become the dominant world model. Not only was it applied extensively in the developed Northern economies, it had also taken root in many Third World countries. In the case of the latter, the spur had been not so much fear of food security in time of war, but more the spectre of failing to feed rapidly rising populations. If food supply was to keep pace with the birth rate, it was argued, output must rise accordingly. The outcome was Norman Borlaug's *Green Revolution*, involving strains of high-yielding grains that responded to a diet of chemical fertilisers with improved irrigation and intensive use of pesticides. It, too, achieved impressive results but, ironically, overall levels of hunger, if anything, got worse.

However, by the end of the 1970s, questions were being asked about the thrust of agricultural policy. Concern over possible food shortages in the northern hemisphere had been replaced by anxieties over what to do about burgeoning surpluses. In the United States, this resulted in productive farmland being taken out of cultivation, whilst in Europe, immense sums of money were being expended to pay for the production, storage and disposal of cereals, milk, wine and other commodities produced to excess.

More alarming to some was the ensuing environmental damage caused by industrialised farming. As early as 1962, the American biologist Rachel Carson had warned, in her book *Silent Spring*, against the indiscriminate use of pesticides. It was not long before such warnings became reality in the United Kingdom, as birds of prey went into serious decline because of the use of organochlorine insecticides.

Better environmental monitoring throughout the 1980s revealed the widespread pollution of inland watercourses and underground aquifers, by fertiliser run-off and pesticides. Many people lamented the destruction of the traditional English landscape, particularly in the Midlands and Eastern counties, with its patchwork of small fields and hedgerows. These no longer made economic sense in an agriculture dominated by intensive cereal monocultures. The new landscape, sporting vast open prairie fields, gave little delight to the eye. It simultaneously deprived much of the United Kingdom's wildlife of its habitat.

Consumers, too, began to be concerned about the potential harmful effects of food contaminated by pesticide, hormone or antibiotic residues on human health. A rise in vegetarianism, especially amongst the young, warned of a seachange in attitudes towards the exploitation of animals kept under indisputably inhumane conditions.

By the end of the 1980s, the pressure to reform the CAP was irresistible. Something had to be done to curb the crippling financial burden caused by supporting surpluses, which in 1990 amounted to over 28.5 billion Ecus (£20 billion), 95% of the total CAP budget. Of this, more than 13 million Ecus (46% of the total) was spent on the destruction and disposal of unwanted produce (EC, 1991). Dairy quotas, to limit milk production, had already been introduced a few years earlier, but the problem of over-production of cereals still posed a major headache. Pressure, especially from the United States, to bring European food prices more into line with world prices, meant attacking the price support underpinning of the CAP. The method chosen to achieve this by the then EC Farm Commissioner, Ray MacSharry, during negotiations over the Uruguay GATT round, was to simultaneously take land out of production and to reduce the guaranteed price paid for commodities. Farmers received alternative compensation via 'Set Aside', arable area and livestock payments, respectively.

At last the deleterious environmental consequences of the previous policy were officially acknowledged, and new measures were proposed. Some individual schemes, such as management agreements for 'Sites of Special Scientific Interest' (SSSIs), or 'Environmentally Sensitive Areas' (ESAs), had already been introduced by the UK Government. In early 1992, the EC formally endorsed such policies under the 'Agri-Environment Programme' and, for the first time, financial support was made available for environmentally friendly organic farming. Although tiny, at £1 million for 1993–1994, compared with the £800 million allocated to the Set Aside Programme, at last a path, as yet indistinct and uncharted, had been opened towards a more sustainable agriculture.

2.2   What is organic farming?

Throughout the last 40 years, the agricultural paradigm just described was enthusiastically promoted by Government advisors and agrochemical interests and was taken up by virtually all farmers, except for a handful who chose to do things differently.

Inspired by the writings of agriculturalists like Sir Albert Howard (1940) and Lady Eve Balfour (1943), they took issue with the neo-orthodoxy that reduced plant nutrition to a mere consideration of supplying soluble nutrients in precise amounts, at the correct time, or that saw pest and disease control as a continual battle against nature. For such organic farmers, as they were to be called by the pioneering American agriculturalist, J.I. Rodale, attention to the well-being of the soil, as a prerequisite to plant growth, was paramount. Upon its vitality depended the health of plants, and of the animals and humans that depended in turn on them for food. Or, as Lady Eve Belfour put it more eloquently, the health of soil, plant, animal and man is one and indivisible.

In 1946, she founded the Soil Association, an organisation dedicated to promoting a holistic vision of agriculture which, eschewing synthetic fertilisers and pesticides, sought to work in harmony with natural processes. Membership remained small during the ensuing decades with little organic produce finding its way onto the market. Indeed, throughout the 1960s and 1970s, it was nigh impossible to buy organic food, apart from the organic flour and cereals that were sold by wholefood shops, specialist outlets or direct from the farm. If you wanted to eat organic fruit and vegetables you had little choice but to grow them yourself!

That a significant number of people opted to do just this was evidenced by the, then largely gardening, membership of The Henry Doubleday Research Association, which from its beginnings in 1954 grew steadily to number around 6000 by 1980. In that same year, The Organic Growers Association was founded by a group of mainly young vegetable producers, many of whom had settled in West Wales. The market for organic vegetables grew rapidly, particularly after its take-up by the supermarkets, Safeway plc being the first to sell an organic range. To this day, a large proportion of domestic vegetable production still derives from West Wales (although regrettably the vast majority is now imported), and the country's largest wholesaler is still based on an industrial estate in Lampeter, Dyfed.

Other multiples have followed the lead set by Safeway and although during the recent recessionary years some have stopped selling organic produce, it is now possible to buy a reasonable range of organic items from most supermarkets; meat and certain dairy products are still rarely found, however. A similar situation exists in many European countries, although the market is better developed in Germany, Scandinavia and many parts of the United States.

For all that organic produce has been available for the best part of a decade, through outlets accessible to most people, there is still considerable public misunderstanding about organic food. Survey after survey confirms a public preference for organic produce (at the right price), although the term 'organic' is at best understood hazily. Most people assume that food from organic farms is entirely free from pesticide residues, whereas there can be no guarantee that it does not contain unwanted pesticide residues that may have come via the soil, water or even the surrounding air. Others believe that it is tastier and more nutritious than conventionally grown food, and indeed a case for this, albeit inconclusive, can be made. Some assume that all organic food must be suitable for vegetarians, misunderstanding the crucial role that livestock play in organic farming.

Before proceeding further, therefore, it is worth turning to two definitions of what constitutes organic farming. The first is supplied by the International Federation of Organic Agriculture Movements (IFOAM). It should be noted that these principles encompass a far wider brief than is usual when food production is considered; involving equity, environmental sustainability and social justice.

IFOAM states that organic farming seeks to:

- produce food of high nutritional quality in sufficient quantity;
- work with natural systems rather than seeking to dominate them;
- encourage and enhance biological cycles within the farming system, involving microorganisms, soil flora and fauna, plants and animals;
- maintain and increase the long-term fertility of soils;
- use as far as possible renewable resources in locally organised agricultural systems;
- work as much as possible within a closed system with regard to organic matter and nutrient elements;
- give all livestock conditions of life that allow them to perform all aspects of their innate behaviour;
- avoid all forms of pollution that may result from agricultural techniques;
- maintain the genetic diversity of the agricultural system and its surroundings, including the protection of plant and wildlife habitats;
- allow agricultural producers an adequate return and satisfaction from their work including a safe working environment;
- consider the wider social and ecological impact of the farming system.

A rather more concise description of organic practices has been framed by the United States Department of Agriculture, as follows:

'Organic farming is a production system which avoids or largely excludes the use of synthetically compounded fertilisers, pesticides, growth regulators and livestock feed additives. To the maximum extent feasible, organic farming systems rely on crop rotations, crop residues, animal manures, legumes, green manures, off-farm organic wastes, and aspects of biological pest control to maintain soil productivity and tilth, to supply plant nutrients and to control insects, weeds and other pests.'

How organic principles are applied in practice is, perhaps, most easily understood by comparing a hypothetical organic farm with its non-organic counterpart.

One obvious difference is the absence of a large stack of chemical fertiliser sacks for, on an organic farm, fertility is derived not from a bag but by mobilising soil microorganisms. These, of which there can be as many as 5 billion in a few grams of soil, break down animal and plant wastes and, in the process, make the resulting nutrients available to plants. Organic fertilisers such as hoof and horn, bonemeal and seaweed meal are occasionally bought in, but these are supplementary to, rather than a substitute for, on-farm derived fertility.

This leads naturally on to another significant difference, the presence of animals as an integral part of the farm, both as a source of income from livestock products and as recyclers of nutrients. An organic enterprise is almost invariably a mixed farm, employing a rotation of crops and livestock. Whereas the manure derived from conventional, intensive livestock units is viewed as a polluting waste product, which incurs disposal costs for the farmer, to the organic farmer it represents the foundation of the farm's fertility.

Because organic regulations prohibit the intensive rearing of livestock, most animals are kept under free-range conditions, mostly outdoors. This necessitates the upkeep of stock-proof hedges and other field boundaries. In addition to their usefulness in preventing livestock from straying, hedges and accompanying grass headlands play an invaluable role in providing a habitat for many beneficial insects and predators. Consequently, ponds, hedges, woodland and other conservation features are much more likely to occur on an organic farm, because they are such an essential part of a natural pest controlling strategy. Although pesticides may be used occasionally, most organic farmers tackle pests, diseases and weeds by environmentally benign alternative methods.

A fundamental yet less obvious difference lies within the soil itself. It is only when you closely examine the soil of most conventional arable farms that you realise how 'lifeless' they have become. Depleted of organic matter, the countless microorganisms, previously described, have all but disappeared. Worms, for instance, which are highly sensitive to most agrochemicals, are generally conspicuous by their absence; organic matter levels are lower than on the soils of their organic neighbours. This has important implications for soil erosion.

On organic farms, animals are not subjected to the same degree of stress that conventionally reared livestock have to endure. Organic farmers rely on a preventive approach to health and therefore aim to keep their livestock in ways which are compatible with their innate behavioural needs.

There are other major disparities between organic and conventional livestock husbandry. Chief is the prophylactic use of antibiotics and other drugs, which is the norm on intensive livestock units, because of the high risk of disease. By adopting lower stocking rates, which eliminates overcrowding, diseases are much less likely to arise. Use of prophylactic medicines is, in any case, forbidden under organic standards, although veterinary treatment with modern drugs is allowed to treat serious illness and to alleviate genuine distress. Similarly, no growth-promoting substances may be added to organic livestock rations, although they are frequently used in conventional feeds.

There are, of course, other differences which are covered later, but it should be noted that the organic farm of today is not a throwback to its pre-war antecedents. Whilst it is true that organic agriculture is rooted in the traditional wisdom of the past, the organic movement does not eschew modern scientific research. The last few years have seen rapid strides in the development of modern organic techniques, especially mechanical and thermal methods of weed control. Despite the near total neglect of research and development relating to organic agriculture during the past half century, the performance of many modern organic farms is in line with the average for farms as a whole, a fact that may surprise many.

2.3 Organic husbandry techniques

It is frequently assumed that organic farming involves little more than substituting manure for artificial fertilisers, and 'organic' sprays in place of potentially more toxic pesticides. This explanation is wide of the mark.

Whilst manure is important to organic farmers, its primary role lies in enhancing the soil, unlike artificial fertilisers that feed plants direct. Crop rotations are also an important key to fertility in organic systems. They provide a balance between feeding the soil on the one hand and exploitational cropping on the other. In the United Kingdom, this chiefly involves what is known as ley farming.

At any one time, organic farmland will be split approximately into 60% grass and 40% crops. Most of the land which is growing grass will be of a temporary nature, known as a ley, although some will usually be classed as permanent, i.e. pastures that are never ploughed. During the period that the land is sown to grass, it will be grazed by cattle and/or sheep, and so enriched by the manure deposited as they feed. During the winter, when the livestock are taken into the farmyard and bedded on straw, piles of 'muck' build up which are then spread on the land the following year. Typically, the ley will be grazed for 3–5 years, before being ploughed in. The accumulated fertility is then released, for the benefit of the ensuing cash crops, usually wheat, barley or other cereals. This land is then returned, after 2 or 3 years of such cropping, to grass again.

Although grass is the predominant component of a ley, nitrogen fixing clovers and other legumes play a key role. Bacteria living in the vicinity of the roots of such plants enjoy a symbiotic relationship, simultaneously converting atmospheric nitrogen which can be exploited by the plant, in return for advantageous secretions from its roots. This is, in effect, free fertiliser and can be equivalent to as much as 150–200 kg of nitrogen per hectare per year.

Legumes are also introduced into the cropping phase of a rotation in the guise of green manures, non-cropping plants grown specifically to enhance soil fertility. Although green manures may be grown at any time of the year to exploit a gap in cropping, they are usually sown in the autumn immediately after harvest. They are allowed to grow through the winter before being dug in or incorporated into the soil prior to drilling the new year's crop. As they decay, nitrogen and other nutrients are released, which can then be utilised by the succeeding food plants.

By such methods, the major field crops of wheat, barley and oats can be grown almost indefinitely, without recourse to outside inputs. Although minerals are constantly being taken out of the land in the food that is destined for animal or human use, the biological activity of soil microorganisms stimulated by applications of organic matter is continuously making available nutrients from the reservoir in the soil. There is evidence to support this from a long running experiment on a Suffolk organic farm. It indicated that the topsoil alone contained sufficient quantities of the major plant nutrients potassium and phosphorus to allow for a thousand years of exploitation, not counting the reserves in the subsoil (Milton, 1975). Where deficiencies do exist, however, a remedy is sought by application of rock minerals such as rock phosphate and magnesian limestone.

Organic vegetables, such as potatoes, carrots and brassicas, are produced on a field scale, by introducing them into the farming rotation as an alternative to cereals, and by specialist horticulturalists, operating from individual holdings. Clearly the type of system appropriate for a farm of several hundred hectares is inappropriate for a plot of ten hectares or less, for which the use of livestock would prove uneconomic. Under such circumstances, fertility will usually need to be brought in by way of imported animal manures. This, unfortunately, is usually from non-organic farms, and so it must be composted before use. However, manures are not allowed from conventional farming enterprises that involve battery egg, broiler, or other intensive livestock units.

With regard to pest control, a large proportion of the pesticides used on conventional crops is applied as a direct result of the adoption of monoculture practices, which actively encourages the build up of specific diseases and weeds. Crop rotations break such cycles and as such are one of the key ways in which organic farms deal with pest problems. Weeds, such as wild oats and blackgrass, for example, which flourish in cereal crops, quickly succumb, once the field is turned over to grass and grazed by livestock. Similarly, populations of soil-borne fungal organisms, such as clubroot disease of cabbages and other brassicas, will, if deprived of host plants during the rotational cycle, decline significantly.

Growing crops on a horticultural scale has traditionally relied on cultivations, involving a combination of hand weeding and hoeing, for the elimination of weeds. Although these methods are still employed, a range of labour-saving weeders has come onto the market in recent years. These include mechanical devices which pass between crops, tear out weeds and a set of revolving brushes 'sweeps' them up. Thermal weeders, which pass over the land at a precise number of days after the crop has been sown, apply an instantaneous burst of intense heat, exploding the cell walls of any weeds in their path. A day or two later, the crop germinates in a field virtually devoid of weed competition.

Insect pests are dealt with using a variety of strategies. A great deal of emphasis is placed on encouraging natural enemies, such as insect predators and parasites, insectivorous birds, frogs, toads and other predating creatures, through the provision of suitable habitats, trees, hedgerows, ponds, 'wild' areas and the specific cultivation of beneficial insect attractant plants. In horticulture, a range of porous synthetic fabrics has been developed to cover crops during seedling stages. Such 'fleeces' provide highly effective physical barriers to many flying pests.

Biological pest control, involving a controlled and deliberate release of beneficial insects, has a long history of use in commercial glasshouses for the control of pests on tomatoes and cucumbers. Red spider mite and glasshouse whitefly are just two of the pests that are successfully controlled by such methods. However, the problems associated with pesticide resistance and the cost of developing new compounds has made biological control a more attractive option for all farmers and growers. In recent years, new biological control agents have been developed to deal with pests in the field, such as vine weevil of ornamentals, codling moth of apples and field slugs. Similarly, the breeding of disease-resisting crop varieties offers an attractive, non-chemical solution to disease attack, for organic and non-organic growers alike.

It would be untrue to say that organic growers have reliable alternatives to pesticides in all cases and, whilst sprays are almost never employed on cereal crops, they are used on vegetables and fruit. Such sprays are usually derived from plants and are of low toxicity and persistence, hence unlikely to cause any significant environmental problems, except perhaps in exceptional cases such as the continued use of copper fungicides on vines. The types of spray allowed to be used in organic systems are listed as part of the organic standards (Table 2.1).

Even so, there are crops that are extremely difficult to grow organically because of pest and disease problems. Apples, pears and other 'top fruit' are a case in point. The cosmetic standards demanded by today's market

Table 2.1 Inputs allowed by EC Regulation No. 2092/91 for use in organic agriculture

Allowable fertilisers and soil conditioners	Allowable pest and disease control products
Farmyard and poultry manure	Preparations on basis of pyrethrins
Slurry or urine	extracted from *Chrysanthemum*
Straw	*cinerariaefolium* containing
Peat	possibly a synergist
Composts from spent mushrooms and	Preparations from *Derris elliptica*
vermiculture substrates	Preparations from *Quassia amara*
Composts from organic household refuse	Preparations from *Ryania speciosa*
Composts from plant residues	Propolis
Processed animal products from	Diatomaceous earth
slaughterhouses and fish industries	Stone meal
Organic by-products of foodstuffs and	Preparations based on metaldehyde
textile industries	containing a repellent to higher
Seaweeds and seaweed products	animal species and as far as
Sawdust, bark and wood waste	possible applied within traps
Wood ash	Sulphur
Natural phosphate rock	Bordeaux mixture
Calcinated aluminium phosphate rock	Burgundy mixture
Basic slag	Sodium silicate
Rock potash	Sodium bicarbonate
Sulphate of potash	Potassium soap (soft soap)
Limestone	Pheremone preparations
Chalk	*Bacillus thuringiensis* preparations
Magnesium rock	Granulose virus preparations
Calcareous magnesium rock	Plant and animal oils
Epsom salt (magnesium sulphate)	Paraffin oil
Gypsum (calcium sulphate)	
Trace elements (boron, copper, iron,	
manganese, molybdenum, zinc)	
Sulphur	
Stone meal	
Clay (bentonite, perlite)	

require near-continuous prophylactic spraying of pesticides by conventional growers, which can amount to 30 or 40 applications in a season. Organic growers have yet to find a reliable alternative to this spray programme and so, unless consumer attitudes to the outward appearance of fruit change, little organic fruit is likely to be grown in the foreseeable future.

2.4   The environmental impact of agriculture

Agriculture necessarily disrupts the environment, since it replaces indigenous plants with cultivated crops. Different types of agriculture impact differently on the surrounding ecosystem, both within the confines of the farm and in the immediate countryside. Similarly, farming systems differ in their dependency on external inputs, which in turn may cause environmental damage in their manufacture and supply. Some aspects of farming, such as pesticide contamination, may even involve a risk to human health. The consideration of these issues will help us determine to what extent a farming system may be described as 'sustainable'.

Whereas in the past farms were largely self-sufficient, today's farmers are highly dependent on the purchase of fertilisers, pesticides, fuel, heavy machinery, animal feedstuffs and other off-site derived inputs. The benefit, in terms of high yields is obvious, but at what cost to the environment?

2.4.1 Pesticides

Of all the aspects of modern farming, the role of pesticides is the most controversial. Now almost universally accepted as being integral to crop production, their use has grown phenomenally. In 1950, there were just 15 types of insecticide and fungicide in common use. By 1960, worldwide sales had increased to 850 million dollars, but over the ensuing three decades, this went up by 3100% to over 26 000 million dollars in 1990.

During that period, many pesticides were withdrawn from sale having subsequently proven to have adverse side effects. Examples include DDT, Aldrin, Dieldrin and many of the other organochlorine compounds which caused significant damage to wildlife. It was discovered that these substances are stored in the fatty tissue of animals and hence as one type of organism is eaten by another and they move up through the food chain, they accumulate at ever higher concentrations. Such is the persistence of such compounds, and their ability to travel the world on wind and water currents, that they even threaten creatures such as polar bears, who live far away from any agricultural activity.

As a species at the top of a food chain, humans are at the most potential risk from poisoning by pesticides. The fear is not that of acute poisoning, although regrettably this does occur, but more for the possible long-term adverse effects brought about by continually eating food contaminated with low levels of pesticide residues. Many pesticides are known to cause cancer, genetic damage and other disorders in laboratory animals. Of the pesticides evaluated by the Environmental Protection Agency in the United States, 92 are listed as possible, probable or known carcinogens (EPA, 1992).

The agrochemical industry dismisses such fears on the basis that any residues present in food are in such minute quantities as to be harmless. However, it is worth considering the practice of homoeopathic medicine, whereby beneficial effects on human health are produced by taking potions diluted to concentrations several orders of magnitude less than that of most pesticide residues. As yet, in part to the difficulty of devising effective epidemiological trials, there is no substantive body of scientific opinion proving the case one way or the other. In effect, most of the population are unwitting guinea pigs in a long-term experiment.

However, there is considerable evidence as to the acute toxicity of pesticides. According to the World Health Organization, more than 3 million people suffer acute severe pesticide poisoning, of which 20 000 may die, worldwide each year (The Pesticides Trust, 1992). Many of these occur in the developing world which is now the fastest growing market for pesticides (Jeyaratnam, 1990). Such tragedies frequently arise when agricultural workers, many of whom are illiterate, fail to take any precautions, or use any protective clothing, when spraying chemicals, many of which are banned in the developed world.

Much of this food is grown for export, however, and so the pesticides return in the form of toxic residues, the so-called 'Circle of Poison'. Although the more persistent pesticides have now been superseded by newer compounds, environmental problems continue to build up. Elimination of pesticide residues from drinking water in order to comply with the EC legal limit is set to cost over 900 million dollars in the United Kingdom alone (DOE, 1991). Accidents such as the loss of 5 tons of lindane in the English Channel in 1989, the pollution of the River Rhine in 1986 following the fire at the Sandoz warehouse, or the explosion at Bhopal, India, in 1984, are but the most dramatic examples of the damage that these toxic substances cause when they enter the environment.

Pesticides can also exert harm in ways that are unlikely to be detected during the complex and costly evaluation process. For example, fungicides sprayed against diseases affecting wheat and other cereals also kill harmless fungi living in the soil. These fungi represent an important part of the diet of predatory insects that eat cereal insect pests. Consequently, predator numbers decline, pest numbers soar and farmers are forced to use yet more pesticides.

The same pesticide used time and again against a particular pest species eventually, through elimination of susceptible individuals, leads to the evolution of a race of pests that are immune. This has now become a major problem with more than 650 species of fungi, insects and weeds recorded as being resistant to pesticidal sprays (Georghiou, 1986). According to Pimentel (1978), while insecticide use in the United States increased tenfold during the period from 1945 to 1978, crop losses to insects actually increased from 7 to 13%.

Latterly, there has also emerged a potential threat to the ozone layer from pesticide use. Fumigation with methyl bromide, a widely used soil sterilant, is estimated to be responsible for as much as 10% of observed atmospheric ozone loss (UNEP, 1992).

2.4.2   Nitrates

In November, 1992, the United Kingdom was convicted in the European Court of Justice for breaching the legal EC nitrate limit of 50 mg/l for drinking water, as set out in directive 80/778 issued in July 1985. According to the Drinking Water Inspectorate, around 5.1 million people in 1990 consumed water that was above the legal limit for nitrates (The Guardian, 1992).

That the UK's water supplies are so badly polluted is an inevitable consequence of the high chemical input policy adopted by post-war agriculture. Although nitrate contamination arises from the discharge of untreated sewage into rivers, and the ploughing up of grassland, the major factors are the routine use of artificial fertilisers plus spillage of animal slurry from intensive livestock units. According to the Royal Commission of Environmental Pollution (RCEP, 1979), agriculture accounts for 50–60% of the nitrate load of surface waters, and may be as high as 80% in certain cases (Moss, 1978).

It is estimated that at least half of all nitrogen fertiliser applied to the soil is wasted (Cooke, 1979). Nitrate nitrogen dissolves easily in water. Once in the soil, any nitrogen not taken up by the crop finds its way into the field drainage system and hence either to surface waters or, by percolating down through the soil, eventually gets into deep underground aquifers. Any remaining is bound up with soil particles or alternatively lost to the atmosphere, to return ultimately as acid rain.

What are the health hazards from nitrate polluted drinking water? At high concentrations this can produce methaemoglobinaemia or 'blue baby syndrome' in newborn infants, although this is unlikely to occur at levels below 100 mg/l. There is also a theoretical hazard, whereby nitrates which are changed by enzyme action into nitrites, on cooking and/or on ingestion, then react with secondary and tertiary amines to form nitrosamines, which are known cancer-producing agents. Although each of these links has been demonstrated, and stomach cancers have been produced in laboratory animals, there is no firm evidence that this is yet happening in humans. Indeed, paradoxically, the incidence of stomach cancer appears to be less in areas having high nitrate levels in the water supply.

Nevertheless, the official decision, which has been to peg nitrate levels at 50 mg/l, has imposed a considerable cost burden on water authorities. Strategies for reducing nitrate levels include blending high level and low level sources, the installation of nitrite elimination technology at treatment works and, in extreme cases, the issuing of bottled water to lactating mothers. The cost of taking nitrates out of the UK's water supplies has been estimated to be of the order of £1600 million overall (The Royal Society, 1983). With borehole supplies, the problem is likely to remain for many years, since nitrate-contaminated rainwater can take decades to percolate down through rock before reaching the aquifer.

Although most public attention has focused on nitrate contamination of drinking water, an even greater public health threat exists in the form of nitrate levels in food. Four-fifths of the nitrate entering our bodies comes from food rather than from water. Of this, the nitrate in vegetables exceeds the total for all other food sources (The Royal Society, 1983). Salad vegetables such as lettuce and spinach are most susceptible. Interestingly, analytical comparisons between organic and conventionally grown lettuces shows significantly less nitrate accumulation in the organic crop, except during winter months (Vogtmann, 1984).

A further complication occurs where crops have been treated with any of the fungicidal dithiocarbamate (DTC) sprays. Nitrites are capable of reacting with the breakdown products of these sprays to form powerful cancer-producing chemicals, further illustrating the difficulties of assessing potential hazards of pesticides under laboratory conditions. This so-called 'cocktail effect', and the synergy or enhancement of toxicity which frequently accompanies it, is extremely worrying, since it can occur without our realising it, with totally unknown consequences.

Human health apart, pollution from livestock slurry and, to a lesser extent, uncontrolled fertiliser run off, present a considerable threat to the integrity of inland waterways. In this instance it is phosphorus, rather than nitrogen that is the main culprit. Excess phosphorus produces rapid algal and plant growth, leading to the choking of lakes and rivers. This process, known as eutrophication, causes fish and other aquatic wildlife to die, either as a result of oxygen starvation brought about by decaying plants, or directly from ammonia toxicity.

Under organic regimes, or previously, when animal manure was valued as a resource, this was rarely a problem as the manure would either have been composted or dealt with safely by other means. However, modern intensive animal units, in which thousands of head of livestock are confined in high density housing, all too frequently has a surfeit of waste and an insufficiency of land on which to dispose of it.

This is not to say that organic farms are incapable of causing pollution from excess nutrients. Manure, badly handled on an organic farm, can be just as dangerous. Also, the ploughing in of a temporary grass/clover ley, especially if done in late autumn, can lead to a nitrate flush as the foliage decomposes. However, given the importance of such nutrients to organic farmers, great care will usually be taken to minimise losses. Non-hardy winter green manures, for instance, may be sown with the following cereal crop immediately after turning in a ley in order to mop up nutrients that might otherwise leach away. Overall, current evidence suggests that nitrate loss from most organic farms, taken over the entire crop rotation, is likely to be considerably less than that from conventional farms (Lampkin, 1990).

2.4.3   Wildlife

Wildlife has undoubtedly been the loser in the post-war drive to intensify agriculture. A number of forces have been at work. The attractive prices paid to cereal producers throughout the 1970s and early 1980s made it economic to cultivate land which, although valuable to wildlife, would otherwise have been unsuitable for such crops. Fertiliser use by livestock farmers on grassland, by encouraging the growth of vigorous ryegrasses, has resulted in the demise of many pasture wildflowers.

The 1984 report from the erstwhile Nature Conservancy Council charts the changes affecting specific habitats that occurred between 1945 and 1984 (NCC, 1984). It makes grim reading:

- 95% of the UK's wildflower-rich meadows destroyed;
- 30–50% of ancient lowland woodlands destroyed;
- 80% of lowland grasslands on chalk and limestone destroyed;
- 50–60% of lowland heaths destroyed;
- 50% of lowland fens destroyed or damaged;
- 50% of upland grasslands, heaths and mires destroyed.

Most noticeable of all has been the loss of hedgerows, some 140 000 miles in total, of which all but 20 000 miles is directly attributable to farming.

Needless to say, such a wholesale removal of unique habitats has taken its toll on wildlife numbers and although extinctions are still, thankfully, rare, the status of a considerable number of animals and plants has been altered to rare or vulnerable. Table 2.2 is derived from figures supplied by the Department of the Environment and is contained in the report *Organic Farming and the Countryside*, edited by Mark Redman for British Organic Farmers (Redman, 1992).

Table 2.2 Species lost or endangered

	Total no. of species	No. extinct	No. of endangered, rare or vulnerable
Dragonfly since 1953	43	1	12
Butterfly since 1950	55	1	24
All insects current	22430	–	1685
Plants since 1930	1423	10	149
Breeding birds current	215	–	51
Mammals breeding on land current	51	–	25

It is impossible to estimate the direct impact of pesticide poisoning on wildlife but in view of the fact that more than 90% of insecticides may never reach the target (Pimentel and Levitan, 1986), the remainder will frequently kill flora and fauna in the immediate vicinity of the crop. Paradoxically, this in many cases includes beneficial insects (predators and parasites) which might otherwise exert a controlling influence on the pests in question. As there is no official monitoring of wildlife losses, poisoning of smaller birds, mammals, amphibians and reptiles goes unreported.

Apart from the direct poisoning of wildlife, there is an indirect relationship that has already been touched on earlier in Section 2.4.1. The best documented example has been that of the decline of the grey partridge across much of the southern area of the United Kingdom. This has been found, by the Game Conservancy, to be due to starvation of the newly hatched chicks (Potts, 1986). The young birds depend, during the first few weeks of their lives, on a plentiful supply of insects. Such insects in turn depend on there being weeds present in the crop. With the advent of cereal herbicides, which virtually ensure clean fields, there are no weeds and hence no insects; the food chain collapses. Indeed, according to Potts (1986), the use of chemicals on cereals has seriously depleted or threatens 800 species of insects, 90 species of flowering plants and 14 bird species. This is backed up by the British Trust for Ornithology's Common Bird Census which reports that, in just two decades since 1970, partridge numbers have decreased by 67%, linnet 36%, lapwing 59%, bullfinch 58%, song thrush 55%, corn bunting 69% and swallow 40% (Marchant *et al.*, 1990).

These trends are now being somewhat addressed by conventional farmers. Techniques such as integrated pest management (IPM), in which predator numbers are monitored and taken account of before spraying takes place, or the sowing of grass strips which act as 'beetle banks' and habitats for other beneficial species, are beginning to be adopted. Nevertheless, for the United Kingdom to lose more than half of its commonest farmland bird species in just 20 years is a shocking indictment of modern farming methods.

Are organic farms more beneficial to wildlife? As mentioned in Section 2.2, conservation features such as hedges, ponds and woodland are an essential part of the organic strategy of combatting pests and diseases, by enlisting the help of natural enemies. However, in addition, desirable environmental and conservation requirements are incorporated into the Soil Association organic standards, prohibiting farmers from ploughing unimproved pastures, hedge-trimming between the end of March and the beginning of September, the ploughing of species-rich grassland and any new or improved drainage affecting wetlands of significant conservation value.

There have been but a few studies to date in which European organic farms have been compared with matched conventional farms, to compare densities of flora and fauna, but in almost all cases the organic farms had significantly greater abundance and diversity (Redman, 1992).

In Nebraska, bird population densities on fields managed organically were six times those on conventional farms (Ducey *et al.*, 1980). This is backed up by a study in the mid-west by Gremaud and Dahlgren (1982), who found population increases of between six and eight times conventional levels on organic farms.

2.4.4   Soil erosion

In any discussion of the deleterious effects of conventional farming methods, soil erosion barely rates a mention yet it is perhaps the single most serious environmental problem.

Reserves of top soil, which takes thousands of years to form, are being squandered at an alarming rate. Worldwide an estimated 25 million tonnes of top soil are lost from croplands every year (Brown and Wolf, 1984). This is not confined to obviously susceptible areas, such as the Himalayas or the Ethiopian Highlands. The United States loses 1.7 billion tonnes of top soil annually and each year in the former Soviet Union, more than a million acres are abandoned because they are so severely eroded that they are no longer worth farming (Brown and Wolf, 1984).

In the United Kingdom, the Government's own research group reported that 44% of the country's arable land was at risk from erosion (Soil Survey of England and Wales, 1986) and on the Sussex Downs erosion rates of 200 tonnes per hectare, representing 10% of the soil in the field, have been documented (Boardman, 1986).

The soil loss on the Downs typifies the land most at risk; slopes where the cultivation of winter cereals leaves the land exposed to the effects of rainfall that washes the soil downhill. This type of land should be permanently grassed, as indeed it was prior to the advance of the CAP regime when the Downs were famous for their sheepwalks. Other aspects of conventional farming, such as hedgerow removal, soil compaction by heavy machinery leading to permanent tractor runnels (which are ideal for carrying away silt-laden water), and a general reduction in soil organic matter content, all contribute to the problem.

Nor should the problem of soil erosion be thought of purely in the context of degraded farmland. Streams and rivers also deteriorate as channels silt up with a consequent loss of aquatic habitats. Wildlife may be further exposed to the additional pesticide load from contaminated soil particles.

To an extent, the declining fertility of soil is disguised by increased applications of artificial fertilisers, and higher yielding plant varieties. However, it is imprudent, to say the least, to be moving towards a position where land is incapable of producing a crop without the addition of imported fertilisers.

By contrast, organic farmers with their 60:40 mixture of grass and arable cropping, greater density of hedgerows and enhanced soil organic matter (produced as a result of decomposing grass leys), and use of green manures and cover crops, are intrinsically less prone to soil erosion. This was borne out in a post-War study (Reganold *et al.*, 1987) of two neighbouring farms, one conventional, one organic, which found that 5 cm of soil had been eroded from the organic fields, compared with 21 cm from the non-organic fields. In the case of the conventional farm, the soil loss represented one-third of the total top soil present in 1948.

2.4.5   Energy and non-renewable resources

Proponents of the farming status quo in the United Kingdom never tire of referring to the superior 'efficiency' of conventional farming, over its much derided 'inefficient' continental partners in the EC. What is usually meant by efficiency, when thus expressed, is output per acre, per livestock unit or, indeed, per agricultural worker.

However, if efficiency is instead defined by comparing the energy content, or calorific value, of the crop with that required to produce it, a very different picture emerges. More energy goes in than is produced, such is the energy demand of modern farming in terms of fuel to run and manufacture machinery, and to make fertilisers and pesticides.

By contrast, organic agriculture consistently uses up to 60% less fossil energy per unit of food produced than conventional agriculture (Lampkin, 1990).

Opinion differs as to the availability of oil reserves but as they become scarce, probably during the next century, such energy inefficiency might well be a determining factor in making organic farming more competitive.

Other resource shortages will confront future generations. Current estimates put phosphate reserves at 400 years and potassium reserves somewhat less. As both are indispensable to conventional producers, it is clear that alternatives must ultimately be found. It is likely that recycling of waste products, especially household rubbish and human sewage, will feature significantly in the solution to this problem.

2.5   Physical and financial performance of organic farms

Because of the price premium attached to organic food, many commentators regard organic production as merely a niche market, catering only for the relatively well off consumer. This belies the fact that a majority of people would choose to buy organically produced food if the price differential were lowered; typically from a 50–100% premium to one nearer 10–20% (Mintel, 1989).

A more serious accusation is that, because of the lower yields, a widespread switch to organic farming would be the quickest route to mass starvation. There would be little likelihood of organic agriculture becoming a major policy objective if such was the case. Where is the evidence to support this?

2.5.1   Yields

It is only in the last few years that there have been sufficient organic farms from which statistically valid data could be extracted, consequently the evidence on comparative yields is patchy. The earliest study, conducted by Vine and Bateman in 1981, indicated that organic yields average between 10 and 30% less than would have been expected if conventional methods had been used. However, they did find significant individual variations between farms so that for winter wheat production, for example, organic yield varied from 3.0 to 5.3 tonnes/hectare, compared with conventional yields of 4.6–5.7 tonnes/hectare.

Much of the credit for present day conventional high crop yields must go to plant breeders who have produced a succession of high yielding seed varieties. These have been bred to respond to high fertiliser inputs and it cannot be assumed that such varieties will perform as well when grown under an organic regime, where nutrients are made available much more slowly and in a less concentrated form.

Another difficulty when comparing organic and conventional yields is the variability in farmland location. In the case of field vegetables, for example, where much of the organic production is concentrated in West Wales, the yields cannot be expected to equal those of crops grown in the rich fen soils of the east of England.

Because organic farmers rely to a large extent on fertility derived from the rotational system of farming, the yield from any particular crop will depend to a large extent on its position in the rotation. A winter wheat crop, exploiting the abundance of nutrients following the ploughing in of a temporary ley, would reasonably be expected to outperform a similar crop sown prior to the field returning to grass. It follows that any proper comparison of organic and conventional yields needs to be aggregated over the entire rotational period of 7 years or more.

A recent review of most of the comparative studies that have been done to date confirmed that the average yield reduction on UK organic farms ranged from 10 to 20%, with a mean of 9% (Stanhill, 1990).

Comparisons of relative outputs of livestock under organic and conventional systems are also difficult to evaluate because of their very different natures, which is, perhaps, why little data exist. Organic livestock is managed extensively with stocking rates generally 20% or so less than those reared conventionally. Feedstuffs are in the main home produced, relying heavily on forage from the grass/clover ley element of the rotation plus cereal legumes, such as field peas and beans. This compares with conventional production which is centred around the feeding of high protein concentrates, much of which, as in the case of soya beans, is imported. Indeed, from the point of view of national self-sufficiency and food security, it is worth reflecting on the annual consumption of cereals for livestock feed which, at 8.1 million tonnes in 1987, accounted for 45% of all cereals grown in the United Kingdom during that year, with a further amount imported equivalent to 50% of domestic production used for this purpose (MAFF, 1988).

Thus, the evidence to date indicates that, whilst yields would decline under an organic regime, these would not be catastrophic; indeed, in the context of a European oversupply of cereals and other agricultural commodities, it could be seen as a positive advantage. It should also be remembered that, for the past 40 years, organic agriculture has been effectively starved of Research and Development and that, with an increasing effort in this area, productivity gains would be expected.

2.5.2   Prices

Prior to the recession of the early 1990s, the strong demand for organic produce, coupled with an undersupply in the market place, allowed for significant premiums to be charged. According to Redman (1991), typical farmgate premiums were as follows: 30–80% for vegetables, 35–100% for cereals and 15–20% for livestock products.

Although obviously attracted by such price premiums, there has been a reluctance on the part of many farmers to accept that they would hold forever, particularly as the market grew. This fear was borne out by cereal prices, which declined markedly in 1991–1992 from £240/tonne to £190/tonne, mainly as a result of large quantities of organic grain grown in France being diverted onto the UK market. This was brought about because of the contraction of French exports to Germany, which occurred as a direct result of Government supported organic farm conversion in Germany, significantly stimulating its home production.

Prices will continue to come down as the market expands, and although there will obviously be some marketing gains and economies of scale, it is doubtful whether these will be sufficient to compensate for the reduction in premiums. At present, the demand for organic food across much of northern Europe appears to have levelled out and many existing organic producers are currently without a premium market (Redman, 1992).

2.5.3   Costs

It is hard to be specific about costs, other than in general terms. On organic farms, there is clearly a significant reduction in outgoings as a result of not having to buy in artificial fertilisers and pesticides. However, this is offset to an extent by the increased number of mechanical cultivations that are required, particularly for weed control. In certain cases, seed costs are also higher due to the higher density sowing rates required to crowd out weeds.

Contrary to popular belief, organic farming is not intrinsically more labour intensive than non-organic farming, except in specialised circumstances such as the intensive growing of vegetables which may require a considerable amount of hand weeding. The main proviso to this occurs when an all-arable conventional farm converts to an organic mixed farm, since the additional livestock enterprise, which must be developed for fertility building reasons, frequently requires additional labour.

However, it is the cost of conversion that is the main stumbling block for many farmers contemplating change. Capital costs, particularly where livestock must be purchased, buildings and stockproof fencing erected, new machinery obtained, etc., can be enormous. Lampkin (1993b) has estimated the reduction in income during the typical 5-year conversion period of a UK all arable farm to be in the region of £200 per hectare per year.

2.5.4   Profitability

Given the combination of generally lower yields and variable costs, although higher labour costs and a price premium over conventional produce, what is the overall effect on profitability? Again the evidence is scant.

Vine and Bateman (1981) found that the price premiums obtained were not sufficient to compensate for lower yields and that the majority of farms in their survey could have obtained a better return had they farmed conventionally. The main weakness of the study was that it only dealt with 30 farms and 1 year's figures, and that, at the time, commercial organic farming was in its infancy.

Other figures from continental Europe show a different picture. Chief of these is a study from West Germany, in which 57 organic farms are compared with 223 conventional farms, although again only over a single year, 1987–1988 (West Germany Federal Ministry of Agriculture Annual Report, 1989). The overall finding was that profitability was the same for both groups, even though the output of the organic farms averaged 18% less. This was mainly because costs were less, by 23% on average. A more recent report (Lampkin, 1993a), covering the years 1985–1986 to 1990–

1991, reinforces these results with the organic farms, if anything, out-performing the conventional farms.

A similar conclusion was reached in a detailed study of 14 paired organic and conventional farms in the United States cornbelt for the period 1974–1976. This was repeated in 1977–1978 with 20 farms, again with the finding that net returns for both sets of farms were more or less equal, mainly because costs incurred by organic farms were 25–50% less than the average for the conventional farms (Lockerton *et al.*, 1984).

Also in the United States, the National Research Council, reporting in 1989 on a 4-year study of 'alternative agriculture' that included organic farms and other low input systems, concluded that well-managed alternative farms 'use less synthetic chemical fertiliser, pesticides and antibiotics without necessarily decreasing per acre crop yields and productivity of livestock systems. Wider adoption of proven alternative systems would result in even greater economic benefits to farmers and environmental gains for the nation.'

The most recent study in the United Kingdom (Murphy, 1992) paints a much more dismal picture. It was conducted by Cambridge University on behalf of the three Government agriculture departments and surveyed the results from 238 organic farms and smallholdings for the period 1989–1990. The conclusion that more than half of the farms were losing money and one in eight was technically insolvent led to numerous banner headlines in the press dismissing organic farming as a viable option for farmers.

What the study failed to take into account was that, during the year in question, many conventional farms also failed to make money. Indeed, the data for 38 farms in Wales have since been re-analysed and compared against published acreage figures for conventional Welsh farms (Lampkin and Bateman, 1993). The authors conclude that 'if farms are distinguished into full and part time types, the organic mixed and dairy farms perform as well, or better, than their conventional counterparts, despite smaller than average farm size'.

Nevertheless, the overall picture, incomplete as it is, indicates that if profitability for organic farmers is dependent primarily on the existence of premium over conventional produce, the market is unlikely to grow substantially. Furthermore, if, through a temporary production stimulation such as conversion grants, the market does grow, the inevitable reduction in price premium which would result would almost certainly lead to a subsequent contraction.

It would seem that for there to be any long-term expansion of organic farming there either has to be a deterioration in the competitive position of conventional farming, perhaps through a recognition of the polluter pays principle, a rise in input costs or both, which pushes up the price of all food. Alternatively, Government recognises the environmental benefits of organic agriculture such as the reduction in pollution of air, land and watercourses, protection of diversity and maintenance of landscape features, amelioration of soil erosion and so on, and pays accordingly, sufficient to reduce the dependence on a price premium.

2.6   Standards for organic food and farming

Although an increasing number of consumers indicate in surveys that environmental considerations play a part in their food purchasing decisions, it would appear that health reasons are the predominant motive for buyers of organic products. In particular, it is concern over the presence of harmful contaminants, such as pesticide residues, which routinely occur in most conventionally produced food, and the likelihood of traces of growth-promoting agents and prophylactic drugs, still widely used in animal husbandry, turning up in meat and animal products.

Organic food is perceived by many people as a safe alternative. Yet how valid is this assumption and what guarantees are there that organic produce is, in fact, genuine?

Standards for organic production have been in place for many years, having been first developed in the 1960s by the Soil Association. It retains a pre-eminent position today responsible for approximately 70% of UK organic acreage (Redman, 1991).

Farmers belonging to the Soil Association's Symbol Scheme have first to undergo an initial 2-year conversion period, in order to rid the soil of pesticide residues and to begin to re-establish the soil micro and macro flora and fauna. During this period, and subsequently, they have to adhere to a well-defined set of requirements. This is backed up by an inspection procedure which includes at least one annual visit, scrutiny of the farm's production returns and access to all of the farm's financial records. Farmers who successfully comply with the set of standards are entitled to use the Soil Association logo on their produce.

During the 1970s, another organic symbol scheme was set by Organic Farmers and Growers Ltd, a marketing cooperative catering primarily for cereal producers in the east of England.

There was nothing in law during this period to compel anyone to join either of these schemes, hence produce could be sold as organic without any check being made on its validity, subject always, of course, to the possibility of action by Trading Standards Officers (TSOs).

2.6.1   EC regulations

All of this changed on 1 January, 1993, with the implementation of the EC Regulation on Organic Food (No. 2092/91). It is now illegal to market crops and plant derived foods as organic unless they have been properly inspected and certified by an approved certification body. This covers not only the growing of the crops but also all processing, packing, wholesaling and, in some cases, retailing; in the latter cases to guard against unwanted contamination and/or substitution of conventionally grown food. Meat and animal products do not at the present time fall under this legislation but they will eventually.

Each member state has the obligation of policing the regulations, which in the United Kingdom is shared between the TSOs and The United Kingdom Register of Organic Food Standards (UKROFS), an organisation set up in 1987 under the auspices of 'Food from Britain', which produced unified standards in May 1989. Although farmers and food processors may register direct with UKROFS, the preferred route is via one of the approved certifying bodies, which at the present date are:

- Soil Association Organic Marketing Company Ltd
- Organic Farmers and Growers Ltd
- Scottish Organic Producers Association
- BioDynamic Agricultural Association

The EC regulation enshrined the principle, already followed by the Soil Association and the International Federation of Organic Agricultural Movements, that organic food should be defined in terms of the production process and not by reference to an analysis of the end product. The latter approach was felt to be unworkable, not least the problem of defining acceptable residues of pesticides in organic food for, despite their absence during cultivation, stray contamination via air and water pollution makes any claim of freedom from pesticide residues virtually impossible to justify.

This has not stopped actions being brought in the past by TSOs against companies selling organic food that was considered to contain unacceptably high pesticide residues. Except in the case of post-harvest pesticides, which are much less likely to arise through accidental contamination, these actions have all failed. Processed organic food has a much more subscribed list of non-agricultural ingredients that may be added than its conventional counterpart (Table 2.3). Post-harvest chemicals, ethylene gas for ripening, chemical and synthetic agents used for preparation, presentation and preservation are all banned, as are irradiated products. Successful prosecutions based on finding such products, based on analytical methods, should not be ruled out.

The rules governing organic production throughout the EC also apply to imported produce from third countries. From January 1995, in order to qualify for admission into EC countries, the importer or certifying body overseas must satisfy the Commission that the standards and inspection and certification scheme comply with the EC regulation. Until then, six countries, Argentina, Australia, Austria, Israel, Sweden and Switzerland, have been given a temporary derogation, whilst organic products from

Table 2.3 Permitted substances used in organic food processing: Annex VI to EC Regulation 2092/91 at 29 January, 1993

Section A: Ingredients of non-agricultural origin

E170 Calcium carbonates	E413 Tragacanth gum
E270 Lactic acid	E414 Arabic gum
E290 Carbon dioxide	E415 Xanthan gum
E296 Malic acid	E416 Karaga gum
E300 Ascorbic acid	E440(i) Pectin
E322 Lecithins	E500 Sodium carbonates
E330 Citric acid	E501 Potassium carbonates
E334 Tartaric acid	E503 Ammonium carbonates
E335 Sodium tartrate	E504 Magnesium carbonates
E336 Potassium tartrate	E516 Calcium sulphate
E400 Alginic acid	E938 Argon
E401 Sodium alginate	E941 Nitrogen
E402 Potassium alginate	E948 Oxygen
E406 Agar	Natural flavourings
E410 Locust bean gum	Drinking water
E412 Guar gum	Salt
	Microorganism preparations

Section B: Processing aids and other products that may be used for processing of organically produced ingredients of agriculture origin

Water	Gelatin
Calcium chloride	Isinglass
Calcium carbonate	Vegetable oils
Calcium hydroxide	Silicon dioxide gel
Calcium sulphate	Activated carbon
Magnesium chloride	Talc
Potassium carbonate	Bentonite
Carbon dioxide	Kaolin
Nitrogen	Diatomaceous earth
Ethanol	Perlite
Tannic acid	Hazelnut shells
Egg white albumen	Beeswax
Casein	Carnauba wax
	Preparations of microorganisms and enzymes

Section C: Ingredients of agricultural origin which have not been produced organically

Unprocessed vegetable products	Pumpkin seed
Coconuts	Pine kernels
Brazil nuts	Radish seeds
Cashew nuts	Edible spices and herbs (except thyme)
Dates	Millet
Pineapples	Wild rice (Zizania plauspra)
Mangoes	Sesame seed
Papayas	Algae, including seaweed
Sloes	Olive oil
Cocoa	Sunflower oil
Maracujas (Passion fruit)	Cane and beet sugar
Colanuts	Starches produced from cereals and tubers
Peanuts	Rice paper
Rosehips	Gluten
Swallowthorns	Lemon juice
Blueberries	Vinegar from fermented beverages other than wine
Maple syrup	Honey
Quinoa	Gelatin
Amaranth	Milk powder and skimmed milk powder
Horseradish seed	Edible aquatic organisms, not originating from aquaculture

other countries are considered by the UKROFS board individually on their merits.

2.6.2 Labelling

The EC regulation prescribes exactly how organic food may be defined. Only food that has been produced to authorised organic standards may be described as such, although in the case of products containing a number of ingredients, up to 5% of the total can be of non-organic origin. This remaining 5% must still come from an approved list of ingredients (Table 2.3). Those products that contain between 50 and 95% organic ingredients may refer to their organic origin only as part of the ingredients list and not especially highlighted in any way. Where organic ingredients make up less than 50% of the total, the fact that they are organically produced must not be referred to anywhere on the label.

There are a number of ambiguities concerning the labelling rules which, at the time of writing, have not been satisfactorily resolved. It is unclear, for instance, whether 'organic potatoes' may be defined as such, since the regulations state that unprocessed crop products should show that they relate to a method of production. They may instead have to be marketed as 'organically grown potatoes' or 'potatoes from organic farming'. There is also concern that the 'less than 50% rule' will drive organic preserves off the market because of the absence of supplies of organically grown sugar.

2.6.3 Other schemes

The 1980s witnessed the development of a whole range of 'green' or 'environmentally friendly' foodstuffs, representing a 'halfway house between organic and conventional food'.

Of these, the most established is the Guild of Conservation Food Producers' 'Conservation Grade'. This evolved out of the secondary conversion standard originally developed by Organic Farmers and Growers Ltd, and differs from organic food in allowing a restricted range of artificial fertilisers and pesticides which are claimed to have less environmental impact than other conventional inputs. Examples include the herbicides glyphosate and asulam, and fertilisers such as Chilean nitrate and superphosphate. Current non-livestock products bearing the Conservation Grade label are entirely restricted to cereals. A published set of standards is available from the Guild and all farms are independently inspected.

The 'Conservation Grade' also includes production standards for livetock husbandry which cover aspects such as welfare, the prohibition of routine and prophylactic use of drugs and restrictions on the use of feed additives.

Livestock schemes comprise all of the other halfway house labels on the market. Most of them address the issue of animal welfare, in particular the abuses of intensive livestock systems, and have been introduced as own-brand initiatives by supermarkets. The Cooperative Wholesale Society, however, has announced a 'Farm to Family' pesticide use policy in which pesticides will be ranked by the company, on grounds of safety, into 'preferred', 'qualified approval' and 'not preferred'. These distinctions will determine purchasing policy although they will not show up on product labels as such. An analysis of all existing schemes has been carried out by the Soil Association (Soil Association, 1991).

Before leaving this section, it is worth referring to the products of biodynamic farming marketed bearing the Demeter trademark or, for farms in conversion, the Biodyn symbol. Although not widely practised in the United Kingdom, there is a significant number of biodynamic farms on the continent. Biodynamic farming does not differ significantly from organic farming in that the basic premises are the same. However, it goes further inasmuch as it attempts to work more closely with subtle forces such as lunar and planetary influences acting on the whole farm environment. This leads to practices such as undertaking cultivations by reference to an astronomical calendar (Thun, 1993) and the use of sprays, derived from animals and plants and diluted to homoeopathic levels, in crop production and on compost and manure heaps. For a full account of biodynamic farming, the reader is referred to *Biodynamic Farming Practice* by Sattler and von Wistinghausen (1992).

2.7 Future trends

To devise and implement systems of financial support that encourage maximum production was, for 40 years, official agricultural strategy. That this policy proved successful is without doubt. Indeed it can be said to have been too successful, inasmuch as Europe currently produces more food, over a range of staple commodities, than it needs to feed its own population. Surplus food is either stored, destroyed or sold onto world markets, at considerable cost to the European taxpayer.

Other agricultural exporters elsewhere in the developed world, producing food at prices way below European levels, are simultaneously denied access to the EC market, whilst having to compete against heavily subsidised European exports to third countries. Commodities are frequently dumped on Third World countries, destabilising or destroying the fragile local markets of farmers who are unable to compete with blatantly unfair competition.

Two factors, the spiralling cost of supporting surpluses, and the insistence of the United States and Cairns group of agricultural exporters, that

EC commodity support prices must be brought down, as a prerequisite to any GATT deal, have led to reform of the Common Agricultural Policy.

The lynchpin of this reform is the 'Set Aside' scheme. In order to qualify for financial support, farmers must undertake not to grow crops on 15% of their land each year, for which lost output they are compensated. In addition, the market support prices for cereals will be progressively reduced each year, in order to bring them closer to world levels. Farmers' incomes will still be protected by a new flat rate payment, based on the acreage.

The big question is, will it succeed? At present the answer given by most commentators is a resounding 'No!'. The likelihood is that, although 15% of land will no longer be producing food, farmers will attempt to make up for this loss by intensive use of agrochemicals on the remainder. If this assumption is correct, then any saving will be less than anticipated and is likely to be more than offset by the cost of implementing the new scheme. The sheer bureaucratic administration involved on the farmer's part in vastly complicated form-filling in order to prevent fraud, is already proving to be a nightmare, as well as horrendously costly.

Other, undesirable outcomes of the reform are likely to include yet more pruning of the agricultural workforce, an increasing number of smaller farms going out of business, or being amalgamated with larger farms, as farmers seek to reduce fixed costs and spread overheads. The profitability of intensive livestock units, for which concentrated feedstuffs are a major variable cost, should improve as cereal prices drop.

Picture the scenario, therefore, a few years hence, of a sixth of the country's arable acreage assuming a permanent air of dereliction, increasing use of fertilisers and sprays on the rest, more factory farming, not less, and a CAP budget even greater than it is now, with some farmers showing every appearance of receiving huge sums of taxpayers' money for doing absolutely nothing. Set against the public desire for more consideration for issues like animal welfare in livestock husbandry, decreased use of agrochemicals and the production of 'healthier' food, it is hard to see where the political support will be found to sustain the status quo.

2.7.1   Towards a sustainable agriculture

The conclusions of the Rio Summit of 1992 include a clear commitment by the participating governments to encourage more sustainable forms of agriculture. It is difficult to see how conventional high-input agriculture, with its over-dependency on fossil fuels and agrochemicals and deleterious environmental consequences, such as increased soil erosion, pollution of air, land and watercourses by pesticides and nitrates, could possibly be considered in the sustainability stakes. It is true that work is underway to modify existing systems in order to devise low-input models for agriculture but this research is in its infancy and there is no guarantee of success. It is also clear from a number of surveys of farmers' attitudes that they are unhappy with present directions in farming and would prefer to reduce their reliance on agrochemicals.

Organic farming, is, by contrast, sustainable, both by nature and by definition. Because of the more limited use, and restricted range of fertilising materials, plant protection products and other inputs, a more widespread adoption of organic farming would confer significant environmental benefits as discussed earlier. There would also be cost savings attaching to a reduced need for activities such as nitrate and pesticide clean-up of water supplies, costs which are not currently borne by agriculture. Equally, the reduction in crop yields would provide further savings on storage and disposal costs.

Currently the organic sector, although growing fast, is still tiny when compared with conventional agriculture (see Table 2.4 and Figure 2.1). Thirty-nine percent of Soil Association symbol holders farm land of less than ten hectares. If the market is to expand to become a mass market, it must be capable of delivering a price premium over conventional food at an acceptable, affordable level, of the order of 10%. In order to do so, farmers will require alternative financial support from the Government.

2.7.2   Environment first: a new concept for agriculture?

Farmers have traditionally been looked on by city dwellers as custodians of the countryside. It is only during the last decade or so that this view has changed, in response to the major landscape alterations, environmental pollution and destruction of wildlife which have accompanied latter day food production policies. The farming community tries to improve its image through good PR but it will take radical change in farm practices to alter people's poor perception of farmers.

Agriculture requires a new way forward, which seeks to minimise the market distortions inherent in price support, whilst rewarding farmers for producing food in ways that meet environmental criteria. To an extent, this already happens, but the approach is piecemeal, with seven schemes currently in operation in the United Kingdom (Environmentally Sensitive Areas, Farm and Conservation Grant Scheme, Nitrate Sensitive Areas, Countryside Premium Scheme, Countryside Stewardship Scheme, Sites of Special Scientific Interest, Farm Woodland Premium Scheme) receiving only 3% of that spent on market support on 1990–1991.

Consumer dissatisfaction with the failure of EC farming policy could, within a few years, force a further reform that could elevate environmental sustainability to a prime role. This would require the Agri-Environment Programme, currently a 'bolt-on' extra to Set Aside, to become the centrepiece of a new strategy. By integrating the disparate existing

Table 2.4 Extent of organic agriculture and food production[a]

Organically managed land area (certified and in conversion) in western Europe, 1985–1993									Estimated	Forecast	Utilisable agric. area	
	1985	1986	1987	1988	1989	1990	1991	1992	1993	1994	×10³ ha	% organic
Germany[b]	**29100**	**24800**	**25700**	**32850**	**42365**	**59734**	**76133**	**98733**	197136	**288090**	17727	1.11
France	45000	50000	55000	57000	60000	65000	72000	90000	90000		**30710**	0.29
Sweden	4000	5500	7500	8000	12000	**28424**	**37000**	**42000**	**44000**		2700	1.63
Austria	10000	12000	15000	17000	20000	22500	26000	**30951**	50000			–
United Kingdom	6000	7000	**8500**	11000	**18500**	25000	30000	34000	37000		**18031**	0.21
Denmark	4340	4800	5035	**5881**	9553	**11581**	**17963**	**18653**	**19000**		**2809**	0.68
Italy	5000	5500	**6000**	7500	9000	11000	**13218**	**16850**	17000		**17297**	0.10
Netherlands	**2450**	**2724**	**3384**	4800	**6544**	**7469**	**9227**	10000	11000		**2019**	0.54
Finland	1000	1200	1500	1800	2050	11000	15000	10000	20000		–	–
Switzerland	3000	3500	4000	**5031**	**7990**	9000	10000	10500	11000		–	–
Other[c]	4690	5550	6468	7195	7920	13250	17350	26909	27725		44569	0.06
Norway	500	600	750	900	1000	3000	5000	7000	7000			–
Belgium	500	700	**972**	1000	1000	1200	1300	1400	1500		**1363**	0.11
Luxembourg	350	400	**412**	425	450	550	600	**634**	700		**126**	0.56
Ireland	1000	1100	**1300**	1400	1500	3700	3800	**4500**	5000		**5697**	0.09
Greece	0	0	0	100	250	300	400	500	500		**5741**	0.01
Portugal	**200**	250	**320**	370	420	550	1000	2000	2000		**4532**	0.04
Spain	**2140**	2500	**2714**	3000	3300	**3650**	**4700**	**6850**	7000		27110	0.03
Estonia								500	500		–	–
Poland						300	550	**1025**	1025		–	–
Czech Rep								**15371**	15500		–	–
Slovakia								**12000**	12000		–	–
Hungary								**2500**	2500		–	–
Total	114580	122574	138087	158057	195922	263958	323891	398596	523861		135862	0.39
EC12	96080	99774	109337	125326	152882	189734	230341	284120	387836		133162	0.29
EFTA	18500	22800	28750	32731	43040	73924	93000	110451	132000		–	–
Central/Eastern								31396	31525		–	–

Source: N. Lampkin (1993c).

[a]Bold type indicates confirmed values. All other values are estimated.
[b]Germany 1993 data: 127/240 AGOel certified; 150/546 other (1992 extensification entrants); 160/850, Koenig.
[c]Countries with less than 10 000 ha in 1992.

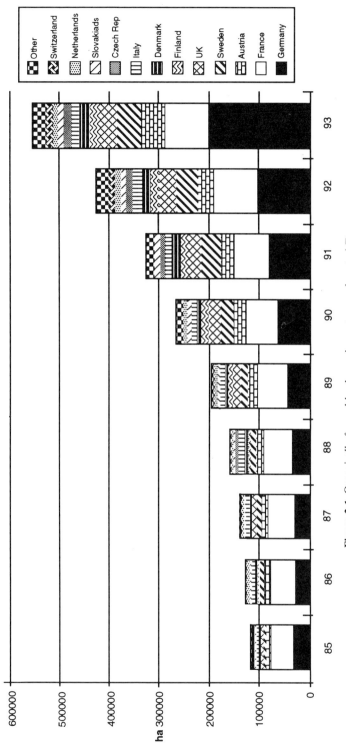

Figure 2.1 Organically farmed land area in western and central Europe.

environmental schemes into a unified coherent approach, the economic underpinning that has favoured high-input chemical farming would be replaced by a more sustainable biological approach. Such a scenario would provide a much more amenable climate in which organic farming could operate and might well be sufficient to bring about the evolution of the mass market which is desired by many consumers and practitioners alike.

Further reading

For a comprehensive, fully referenced textbook of organic agriculture, the outstanding work is *Organic Farming* by Nicolas Lampkin, Farming Press, 1990. A more personal and philosophical account has been written by H.R.H. The Prince of Wales in conjunction with Charles Clover, *Highgrove, Portrait of an Estate*, Chapman, 1993. *Thorsons Organic Consumer Guide*, by Mabey, Gear and Gear, Thorsons, 1990, gives a basic introduction to organic food and farming and lists outlets in the United Kingdom.

References

Balfour, E.B. (1975) *The Living Soil and the Haughley Experiment*, Faber and Faber, London (first published as *The Living Soil* in 1943).
Boardman, J. (1986) The Context of Soil Erosion *SEESOIL*, **3**, 2–13.
Brown, L.R. and Wolf, E.C. (1984) *Soil Erosion: Quiet Crisis in the World Economy*, Worldwatch Paper 60, Worldwatch Inst, 1776 Massachusetts Avenue, N.W., Washington DC 20036, USA.
Cooke, G.W. (1979) Some priorities for British soil science. *J. Soil Sci.* **30**, 187–213.
Department of the Environment (1991) News report. *The Guardian* **5 October**, 1991.
Ducey, J. *et al.* (1980) *A Biological Comparison of Organic and Chemical Farming*, University of Nebraska, Lincoln.
EC (1991) The Agricultural Situation in the Community 1990 Report, Commission of European Communities.
EPA (1992) *List of Chemicals Evaluated for Carcinogenic Potential*, Office of Pesticide Programs, Washington, DC.
Georghiou, G. (1986) *Pesticide Resistance: Strategies and Tactics for Management*, National Academy Press, Washington DC.
Gremaud, J.K. and Dahlgren, R.B. (1982) Biological farming: impacts on wildlife, in *Workshop in Midwest Agricultural Interfaces with Fish and Wildlife Resources*, ed. R.H. Dahlgren, Iowa State University, pp. 38–39.
Howard, A. (1940) *An Agricultural Testament*, Oxford University Press, Oxford.
Jeyaratnam, J. (1990) Acute pesticide poisoning: a major global health problem. *World Health Statist. Q.* **43**, 139–144.
Lampkin, N. (1993a) The economic implications of conversion from convention to organic farming systems. PhD Thesis, Department of Economics and Agricultural Economics, University of Wales, Aberystwyth.
Lampkin, N. (1993b) Farm level physical and financial impacts of conversion to organic farming. Discussion Paper Series 93/4. Centre for Organic Husbandry and Agroecology, University of Wales, Aberystwyth.
Lampkin, N. (1993c) The growth of organic farming in Europe, 1985–1993. Discussion Paper

Series 93/7, Centre for Organic Husbandry and Agroecology, University of Wales, Aberystwyth.

Lampkin, N. and Bateman, D. (1993) *The Economies of Organic Farming in Wales, 1989*, Department of Economics and Agricultural Economics, UCW, Aberystwyth.

Lampkin, N. (1990) *Organic Farming*, Farming Press Books, Ipswich.

Lockerton, W. *et al.* (1984) Comparison of conventional and organic farming in the corn belt, in *Organic Farming: Current Technology and its Role in a Sustainable Agriculture*, eds. D. Bezdicek *et al.* American Society of Agronomy, Special Publication No. 46, Madison, WI.

MAFF (1988) *Output and Utilisation of Farm Produce in the United Kingdom, 1981–1987*. HMSO, London.

Marchant, J.H., Hudson, R., Carter, S.P. and Whittingham, P. (1990) *Population Trends and British Breeding Birds*, British Trust for Ornithology, Tring, Herts.

Milton, R.F. (1975) The Haughley Experiment – some unsolved problems, their significance and suggested methods for investigation, in *The Living Soil and the Haughley Experiment*, ed. E.B. Balfour, Faber and Faber, London.

Mintel (1989) *The Green Consumer*, Mintel, London.

Moss, B. (1978) The ecological history of the medieval man-made lake Hickling Broad, Norfolk. *Hydrobiologia* **60**, 23–32.

Murphy, M. (1992) *Organic Farming as a Business in Great Britain*, Agricultural Economics Unit, University of Cambridge, Cambridge.

National Research Council (1989) *Alternative Agriculture*, National Academy Press, USA.

NCC (1984) *Nature Conservation Review of Great Britain*, Nature Conservancy Council.

Pimentel, D. *et al.* (1978) Benefits and costs of pesticide use in US food production. *Bioscience* **28**, 772–784.

Pimentel, D. and Levitan, L. (1986) Pesticides: amounts applied and amounts reaching pests. *Bioscience* **36**, 86–91.

Potts, G.R. (1986) *The Partridge*, Collins, London.

Redman, M. (1991) *The Organic Fact File: A Guide to the Production and Marketing of Organic Produce in the UK*, British Organic Farmers, in conjunction with Safeway plc, 86 Colston Street, Bristol BS1 5BB.

Redman, M. (ed.) (1992) *Organic Farming and the Countryside*. A Special Report from British Organic Farmers in conjunction with the Soil Association.

Reganold, J.P., Elliott, L.F. and Unger, Y.L. (1987) Long term effects of organic and conventional farming on soil erosion. *Nature* **330**, 370–372.

RCEP (1979) *Agriculture and Pollution, 7th Report of the Royal Commission on Environmental Pollution*. HMSO, London.

Sattler, F. and von Wistinghausen, E. (1993) *Biodynamic Farming Practice*. Biodynamic Agricultural Association, Stourbridge, West Midlands.

Soil Association (1991) *Green Tokenism or The Real Thing? An investigation of 'Animal Welfare' and 'Environmentally Friendly' Food Labelling Schemes and Related Farming Systems*. The Soil Association, 86 Colston Street, Bristol BS1 5BB.

Soil Survey of England and Wales (1986) *Soil Erosion in England and Wales*.

Stanhill, G. (1990) The comparative productivity of organic agriculture. *Agric. Ecosystems Environ.* **30**, 1–26.

The Guardian, 26 November 1992, p. 3.

The Pesticides Trust Report (1992) The Pesticides Trust, 23 Beehive Place, London SW9 7QR.

The Royal Society (1983) *The Nitrogen Cycle of the United Kingdom*.

Thun, M. (1993) *Working with the Stars – a Biodynamic Sowing and Planting Calendar*. Lanthorn Press, East Grinstead.

UNEP (1992) *Synthesis Report of the Methyl Bromide Interim Scientific Assessment and Methyl Bromide Interim Technology and Economic Assessment*. UNEP, Nairobi.

Vine, A. and Bateman, D.I. (1981) *Organic Farming Systems in England and Wales – Practice, Performance and Implications*, Department of Agricultural Economics, UCW, Aberystwyth.

Vogtmann, H. *et al.* (1984) Accumulation of nitrates in leafy vegetables grown under contrasting agricultural systems. *Biol. Agric. Hort.* **2**, 51–68.

3 The environmental implications of genetic engineering in the food industry

S. ROLLER, D. PRAANING-VAN DALEN
and P. ANDREOLI

3.1 Introduction

Since the end of World War 2, insect and pest control in agriculture has been heavily dependent on the use of chemical insecticides and pesticides. However, several of these synthetic compounds accumulated in the environment, in the food chain and sometimes in human adipose tissue and had acute or chronic side-effects in non-target organisms. Further-more, due to the intensive use of pesticides, resistance developed in some pest populations. Consequently, and as a result of the high cost of biotechnological development, the first wave of research in food-related biotechnology was instigated and supported by the large seed and agro-chemical industries. This has resulted in a preponderance of novel plant, animal and microbial strains genetically engineered for the benefit of the farmer or fertiliser/pesticide producer. For example, transgenic plants carrying the traits of pest and disease resistance have already been devel-oped. The products of this technology, one of the first and most successful practical applications of the new biotechnology, are already on the market.

Whilst the early developments in agricultural biotechnology may ulti-mately lead to reductions in the usage of agrochemicals and consequently to a less detrimental effect on the environment, they are unlikely to impinge directly on the food processor or consumer. Yet, the technology of genetic engineering offers a great deal more than just a method for improving agronomic traits. Recombinant DNA technology provides an opportunity to develop genetic traits which are beneficial to the food processor, e.g. an increase in the solids content of fruit and vegetables, and ultimately to the consumer, e.g. nutritional composition, flavour, colour, texture and extended shelf-life of many foods. However, relatively little work has been reported in the literature on the genetic manipulation of crop traits that control the functional properties of a food plant, compared to the massive amount of work carried out on agronomic traits. This lack of activity is partly due to a dearth of knowledge about the physiological, biochemical and molecular basis of important functional traits in foods, such as flavour, texture and chemical composition.

It has been suggested that the new biotechnology has the potential to

Table 3.1 Current and emerging products of gene technology of interest to the food processing industry

Product name	Quality attribute	Company[a]	Status
Bovine somatotropin (BST)	Increased milk yields	Monsanto, Eli Lilly, Upjohn, Cyanamid	EC moratorium to end of 1993; all-out ban proposed FDA approval sought
Chymosin	Replacement for animal rennet	Gist-brocades Pfizer Genencor	SCF clearance FDA-approved 1992 FDA-approved 1990 FDA approved 1993
Bakers yeast	Improved dough characteristics	Gist-brocades	UK-approved 1990
Canola (rapeseed)	High content of unsaturated fatty acids	DuPont/DNAP	Commercial plants available
	High content of hydrogenated oil for margarine	Calgene/P&G	Commercial production of oil planned for 1995
Fresh tomato	Longer shelf-life, better taste	Calgene	FDA approval sought Planned launch date: Late 1993 for FLAVR SAVR
Fresh tomato	Longer shelf-life, improved taste	Zeneca	Field trials and tasting assessments complete
Fresh tomato	Longer shelf-life	DNAP	Plans to market VineSweet by 1995
Processing tomato	Higher solids	Petoseed (ICI/ Zeneca)	Product launch planned for mid-1990s
Processing tomato	Higher solids	Calgene ESCAGenetics	Field trials underway A few years from market
Tomato	Tolerance to freezing	DNAP	Field trials conducted in 1991
Corn	Improved amino acid profile	BioTechnica International	Applied for field trials
Corn	Enhanced sweetness	DNAP	Applied for field trials
Potato	Increased starch content, lower moisture for low-fat chips	Monsanto	Lab trials complete
Potato	Reduced sugar content	Maribo Seed (Danisco)	Field tests planned for 1993

[a]DNAP, DNA Plant Technology; P&G, Procter & Gamble.
Compiled and adapted from: Anon (1992); Anon (1993b, e, f); Duxbury (1993); Elkington, 1993; Miller and Morrison, 1991; Scher (1993a,b); Simon-Moffat, 1993.

ensure environmentally sustainable supplies of safe, nutritious, affordable and, above all, enjoyable food (Fraley, 1992). As shown in Table 3.1, the edible products of recombinant DNA technology have yet to make a significant impact on the market. Of the products shown in the table, the chymosins are known to have achieved good market penetration already. Since its approval by the FDA in 1990, the genetically engineered chymosin from Pfizer (trade name CHY-MAX®) has reportedly been used to make more than 13 million kg of cheese in 17 countries (Barbano and Rasmussen, 1991; Scher, 1993a,b). More detailed accounts of another genetically engineered chymosin, MAXIREN® from Gist-brocades, is presented later in this chapter. However, none of the other products listed in Table 3.1 have yet entered the markets. Therefore, we can only look to the future for evidence of the realisation of the potential of the new biotechnology. In the meantime, we have attempted to examine some of the edible products of recombinant DNA technology that are about to enter the markets and to anticipate their environmental impact. In the following chapter, we discuss the more general issues of legislation and consumer acceptability, followed by more detailed analyses of three recombinant food products: the tomato, chymosin and bakers yeast.

3.2   The regulatory climate

With the gradual adoption of genetic engineering techniques by the food sector and with an almost complete absence of quantitative experimental studies on the ability of transgenic organisms to survive in or invade the environment, the regulatory authorities have been obliged to formulate new legislation on a case-by-case basis. Results of ecological studies on the risks of the use of genetically engineered plants are only just beginning to be reported. For example, in a recent landmark paper, Crawley et al. (1993) from Imperial College, London, have reported on the invasiveness of transgenic oilseed rape in three climatically distinct sites and four habitats (wet, dry, sunny and shady). The results were reassuringly clear; under no environmental or experimental conditions did the transgenic cultivars exhibit different rates of population growth to those of their unmodified counterparts.

The history of regulation of food biotechnology is characterised by many obstacles and delays. For example, in 1987 the first court hearing regarding field tests of genetically altered bacteria (Frostban, designed to protect against frostbite) took place but it was not until 4 years later that the trials of Frostban were finally allowed to proceed in a California strawberry field (Gorner and Kotulak, 1991). As another example, the FDA and Monsanto have compiled some 500 volumes of approximately 400 pages each of data on the genetically engineered bovine somatotrophin (BST) or bovine growth hormone. However, in spite of receiving clearance from its own advisory panel of experts (Veterinary Medicine Advisory Committee) in March 1993, the FDA has still not issued regulatory approval for the product (Fox, 1993a). On the contrary, in May 1993, the FDA convened a meeting of its Food Advisory Committee to advise on the need to label BST-derived foods, thus prolonging the approval process even further (Fox, 1993b).

Following concern about the competitiveness of the US economy in biotechnology, the American regulatory authorities appeared to adopt a less restrictive view of food biotechnology in 1992. Thus, the USDA and FDA adopted the policy that genetically engineered foods that are similar to those which could have been obtained by cross-breeding need not be regulated. Calgene's FlavrSavr tomato fitted into this category and is discussed in more detail later in this chapter. On the other hand, if a new substance (for example, from another species) was introduced by genetic engineering, that food would be treated as a novel food additive. Again, Calgene have provided the lead with a recent application for approval for use as a food additive for their gene marker enzyme, present in the FlavrSavr tomato. In 1992, there appeared to be a new willingness among US regulators to assess risk relative to benefit rather than arbitrarily setting the risk level to zero as exemplified by the unpopular Delaney clause (van Wagner, 1993). By mid-1993, however, and in response to public opinion, the FDA was re-examining its non-restrictive policy on genetically modified plants particularly in relation to labelling issues. Additional data have been requested to clarify under what circumstances labelling may be necessary. Scientific opinion on the potential allergenicity of genetically engineered foods is also being sought (Fox, 1993b). It is this latter issue that may well prove to be a considerable obstacle as there are at present no validated methods either *in vivo* or *in vitro* to predict the allergenicity of new proteins in the diet (Kok *et al.*, 1993).

The apparent lack of innovation in some food companies has been blamed by some observers of the food industry on restrictive regulations governing the introduction of any novel food or food ingredient. Nevertheless, in spite of potentially restrictive legislation, progress in moving the products of biotechnology from the laboratory to the supermarket shelf is being made. For example, in the United States, more than 370 permits for field trials of 21 different genetically engineered crops and 2 microorganisms have already been issued and completed at 1000 sites (Harlander, 1993; Kareiva, 1993). In 1993, the USDA published new guidelines for completing applications for transgenic field trials; the guidelines require firm evidence that the phenotype of the transgenic crop poses no greater risk than does the unmodified plant from which it was derived (US Federal Register, 1993).

In Europe, there are as yet no community-wide procedures for field testing or for full commercialisation of the food-related products of gene technology. The European Community is still struggling with council regulations that cover recombinant DNA products as food or components of foods (Miflin, 1993). In 1993, proposals for regulation of marketing of genetically modified farm animals and of genetically engineered plant protection products were still at the drafting stage (Lex, 1993). New EC directives on contained use and deliberate release of genetically modified organisms have been released but their implementation has not been completed by all the Member States (EEC 219 and 220, 1990). In the United Kingdom, the environmental aspects of recombinant DNA technology are only beginning to be addressed by politicians and the EC directives were implemented into national legislation in 1993 (Anon, 1993a; Lex, 1993).

3.3   Consumer acceptability

Consumers are receptive to improvements in food quality, but the application of biotechnology may encounter resistance if public concerns are ignored. The public is generally ill-informed about biotechnology and suspicious of some of the examples sometimes highlighted in the media. On the other hand, industry and large businesses rarely consult consumer or environmental organisations before embarking on programmes that are likely to affect them both. This situation will have to change if a backlash of the kind now experienced against food irradiation is to be avoided.

The early efforts of the agri/food industry to commercialise the products of gene technology have not been very successful largely due to consumer resistance. For example, Monsanto's transgenic bovine somatotrophin (BST) has met with fierce opposition from consumer groups on both sides of the Atlantic. The arguments produced against the product have been far from irrational. When used to augment milk production by about 20%, BST has been reported to increase the incidence of mastitis, an inflammation of the cow's milk glands caused by infection. This could, in turn, lead to increased usage of antibiotics and consequently to increased risk of antibiotic residues in milk, posing a human health hazard. Although the FDA's advisory panel had concluded in early 1993 that the degree of increase in mastitis was within manageable limits for farmers, the agency has still not issued regulatory approval for the product. Vociferous anti-biotech groups have succeeded in launching a boycott of all foods containing milk from BST-treated cows and have received the backing of several food companies including an ice-cream maker and a manufacturer of infant formulas. Opponents have also argued that BST would increase production of a commodity already in surplus (Fox, 1993c). In Europe, the

College of Commissioners has recently proposed an all-out ban on the use of BST, perpetuating the current moratorium imposed on the product. Approval of BST in Europe has been under consideration for 6 years and the Commission is still awaiting the results of studies on the social and economic impact of BST on the EC agricultural policy. Meanwhile, Monsanto have closed down the company's animal health care business in Europe whilst Pitman Moore have halted research on their recombinant porcine somatotropin (Ward, 1993).

In 1990, the approval by the UK government for the use of a genetically engineered baker's yeast without the requirement to label those products made with the new yeast provoked negative reactions from consumer and environmentalist groups (Anon, 1990a). It has been suggested that an unhelpful press release from the Ministry of Agriculture has led to newspaper stories of 'mutant' bread and to accusations of undue secrecy from Friends of the Earth and the London Food Commission (Anon, 1990b). Because yeasts used as starter cultures in bread-making are difficult to contain, the Government clearance was viewed by lobbying groups as a *de facto* clearance for the deliberate release of all genetically engineered organisms.

In 1992, the FDA announced that labelling of genetically engineered foods would not be made mandatory in the United States. The announcement provoked nearly 3000 complaints from the public. Consequently, the agency issued a request in April 1993 for scientific advice on which foods should be labelled and what the labels should say, suggesting that a review of the policy may be forthcoming in the future (Anon, 1993c).

3.4   A case study: the genetically engineered tomato

One of the major technological obstacles to improvement of fruit and vegetable quality has been the difficulty of defining molecular targets that correlate with desirable functional properties. As pointed out by Wasserman (1990), if quality improvements in fruit and vegetable products are to be realised, a balanced perspective between molecular biology and postharvest physiology must be maintained. Nevertheless, given sufficient time and investment in R&D, there is no reason to believe that these obstacles are insurmountable from the technological point of view. Indeed, by the early 1990s, over 70 crops have been reported to be under development by biotechnology companies worldwide. Of these, the two plants that have received most R&D attention to date have been the tomato and the potato. These two crops represent approximately 60% of all the vegetables processed worldwide and 73% in the United States alone (Addy, 1991).

The application of recombinant DNA techniques to the humble tomato has received much impetus from industry due to a number of business incentives. Firstly, consumers have traditionally been dissatisfied with the quality of the fresh tomato, often perceived as mealy in texture and lacking in flavour. This loss in perceived quality has arisen from the need to pick green, hard tomatoes to survive shipping, followed by treatment with ethylene gas to turn them red. The practice of picking green tomatoes for transport followed by ethylene treatment to initiate ripening and start development of colour is already carried out regularly in the United States and Australia. Secondly, total tomato production has been reported at a level of over 11 million tonnes in 1991 in the United States alone, of which about 2 million tonnes were marketed fresh and were worth about $5 billion at the retail level (Scher, 1993a,b). Worldwide, it has been reported that production exceeded 47 million tonnes in 1986 alone (Addy, 1991). Thus, a very modest penetration of this size of market would bring substantial profit to the successful company.

3.4.1   The techniques of genetic subtraction

The genetic engineering of foods has proceeded along two principal lines of approach. In the first approach, single-trait genes have been added to otherwise acceptable commercial plants, animals and microorganisms. Recombinant chymosin and the genetically engineered baker's yeast, described later in this chapter, are examples of this approach. However, the number of single-trait genes that could be added in this way to plants has been limited and in the mid- to late 1980s, the concept of inhibition of gene expression emerged. The blocking of undesirable effects was achieved by antisense technology. This involved the insertion of a gene constructed in reverse orientation to the normal gene (the 'sense' gene). In this way, the reverse gene coded for antisense RNA which would bind to the 'sense' RNA thereby preventing normal protein synthesis (Kidd, 1993).

Using antisense genes, the activity of polygalacturonase, pectin methylesterase, aminocyclopropane carboxylate synthase (also known as the ethylene-forming enzyme) and phytoene synthase have all been down-regulated in a variety of transgenic tomatoes. Of these, the long-life fresh tomato has come nearest to entering the consumer market. Calgene have announced plans to launch their FlavrSavr tomato late in 1993 in the United States. This new tomato is claimed to soften less rapidly than other tomatoes, enabling the fruit to ripen on the vine until its natural flavour is fully developed, resulting in a superior taste, less stringent transport requirements and an extended shelf-life at the retail level. This has been achieved by the application of antisense technology to inhibit the 'softening enzyme', polygalacturonase (PG).

3.4.2 Metabolic studies of the recombinant tomato

In competition with the Calgene team in the United States, a long-life tomato has also been under development by Professor Grierson's team at Nottingham University in collaboration with Zeneca (formerly ICI Seeds) in the United Kingdom. Grierson's team demonstrated that the expression of antisense RNA inhibited polygalacturonase activity by 90% whilst having no effect on other aspects of ripening, such as, for example, pigmentation (Bridges *et al.*, 1988; Smith *et al.*, 1988; Sheehy *et al.*, 1988; Bryant, 1989). However, it was discovered that the reduction in PG activity failed to reduce the softening rate in transgenic tomatoes. It was suggested that the remaining 10% of PG activity may need to be eliminated from the plant by increasing the dose of the antisense gene. Alternatively, antisense technology would also have to be applied to enzymes other than PG which may play small but very important roles in fruit softening. Furthermore, a tomato cultivar in which the PG enzyme was hyper-expressed failed to soften (Giovannoni *et al.*, 1989). These reports have called into question the entire issue of correct molecular targeting.

3.4.3 Field trials of the recombinant tomato

Several semi-commercial trials at the Horticultural Research Institute in the United Kingdom have confirmed that the new genetic system developed by Zeneca is now stable. Although low PG fruit was not firmer than its normal counterpart, it was more resistant to deterioration. Thus, PG was again shown not to be the only enzyme involved in softening (Hobson, 1993). In a comprehensive review of tomato softening, Gross (1990) has concluded that in addition to the important role of endopolygalacturonase, mechanisms regulating the net loss of cell wall neutral sugar components, hemicellulose modifications, wall biosynthesis and non-enzymatic deaggregation may all be of importance in understanding the fruit ripening process.

The transgenic tomatoes produced by the Zeneca team have been tested under conditions designed to prevent any release of the experimental material to the environment. Tasting trials have been overseen by an ethical panel external to Zeneca and established for the express purpose of overseeing the trials. In line with the UK's Environmental Protection Act of November 1990, the tomatoes were grown in sealed greenhouses to prevent pollen escaping and all seeds were removed from the tomatoes before eating to avoid the risk of release into sewers. The tasting trial was approved by the Advisory Committee on Novel Foods and Processes (Anon, 1991a).

3.4.4   Ethylene production in recombinant tomatoes

Another target that has attracted the attention of the genetic engineers has been the enzyme system involved in the production of ethylene, a plant hormone responsible for initiating the complex cascade of steps (including the activation of the PG enzyme) that lead to ripening of many fruits (Bleecker, 1989; Miller and Morrison, 1991). Although chemically relatively simple, ethylene production is controlled by a complex array of genes, many of which have yet to be identified. Recently, the isolation of the gene coding for aminocyclopropane carboxylate synthase, the key enzyme in the biosynthetic pathway of ethylene in tomato, has been reported (Bleecker *et al.*, 1986; Bleecker, 1989; Anon, 1990a; Hobson, 1993). Tomato cultivars in which ethylene production has been reduced to about 4% of normal using antisense technology are already being tested in field trials in the United Kingdom and the United States (Anon, 1992; Hobson, 1993). However, even this small amount of activity has been reported to allow near-normal ripening (Hobson, 1993). Nevertheless, it has been found that the engineered fruit had a longer shelf-life than the normal tomato. Trials in the United States have shown that the genetically engineered tomatoes could be left on the vine for as many as 120 days, developing sweetness and enhanced flavour without the fruit softening or changing colour. When harvested and exposed to ethylene gas, the fruit softened and developed additional colour normally, producing a tomato with superior taste and texture.

3.4.5   The engineering of processing tomatoes

Tomato varieties used currently to manufacture sauces and pastes contain only 5% solids, a valuable commodity in the production of thick tomato paste, ketchup and soup. Furthermore, once the fruit has been chopped up in readiness for processing, the enzyme PG tends to degrade the long pectin chains responsible for imparting viscosity. As a result, typical production lines include a heating step (the hot break process) to inactivate the enzyme in the comminuted fruit. If the tomato were to contain reduced or inactivated PG, this energy-intensive step could be omitted, resulting in significant cost savings for the processor. Consequently, companies such as the Campbell Soup Company have shown considerable interest in the antisense tomato.

In collaboration with Campbell's, Calgene have successfully transformed processing varietals of tomato with antisense polygalacturonase constructs, followed by field trials in Florida, California and Mexico. Tomatoes in which enzyme activity was reduced to less than 1% of normal were used to produce juices and pastes with significant increases in viscosity and consistency relative to the non-recombinant controls. Interestingly, recombinant fruit was also observed to be more resistant to certain common fungal infections of ripening tomato (Kramer *et al.*, 1992). Tomatine and ascorbic acid levels remained unchanged.

Having funded tomato work at both Calgene and DNAP for a number of years, Campbell's have recently reversed their policy on using products of gene technology and have sold their exclusive rights to grow the FlavrSavr tomato for processed products (Elkington, 1993).

3.4.6   *Regulatory approval of the recombinant tomato*

Calgene have submitted to the FDA data on the FlavrSavr tomato from several comprehensive compositional, nutritional and safety studies conducted by the company over a period of 8 years, including the results of more than 4 years of field trials (Redenbaugh *et al.*, 1992; Anon, 1993; Miflin, 1993). Some of the analyses carried out by the company have included the determination of vitamin A and C content and levels of the natural toxin, tomatine. In addition, expression levels of the antibiotic resistance marker genes were determined and compared to the acceptable daily intake. Finally, the company has also submitted the results of trial on the technological performance of the recombinant tomato, such as acidity, viscosity, consistency and pH. And finally, a homogenate of the tomatoes was fed to laboratory animals in an acute oral toxicity study (Redenbaugh *et al.*, 1992). The value of this last test has been questioned by others as the concentrations in the diet of the constituent compounds would be too low to detect potential adverse reactions (Kok *et al.*, 1993). However, at the time of writing (Summer 1993), full FDA approval for the FlavrSavr tomato had not been granted. Although the agency had indicated earlier in 1993 that the FlavrSavr tomato was a non-regulated food item and could be marketed without special labelling, opposition by consumer groups prompted a review of this policy, resulting in further delay.

In Europe, the regulatory situation has been more problematic than in the United States with procedures for full approval yet to be established. Therefore, it is quite likely that the appearance of recombinant tomatoes or any other fruit or vegetables on European supermarket shelves will lag behind the American equivalent by several years.

3.4.7   *Legal dispute*

The right to exploit antisense DNA technology and its application to tomatoes is currently in legal dispute between Calgene, Enzo Biochem and Zeneca. Enzo Biochem have claimed that their patent on antisense technology was sufficiently broad to cover its application to all species, including Calgene's FlavrSavr tomato. However, in 1986 and 1989, ICI (now Zeneca) and Calgene, respectively, were granted patents for the specific use of antisense technology to inhibit the polygalacturonase gene in tomato. In June 1992, the US Patent and Trademark Office notified Zeneca and Calgene of the interference between the patents granted to the two companies (Anon, 1993d). The results of the legal proceedings now underway may not become public for 2 years and may have a profound effect on the status of the genetically engineered tomato (Simon-Moffat, 1993). It would appear that years of legal wrangling are possible and this, in addition to the regulatory difficulties, may well slow down the appearance of recombinant tomatoes on our dinner tables.

3.5   A case study: chymosin produced by genetic engineering

The coagulation of milk by rennet is one of the most important steps in cheese manufacture. The fourth stomach of suckling calves has been the traditionally preferred source of rennet due to its high content of the active ingredient, the proteolytic enzyme chymosin. Due to its specific activity, chymosin is considered by manufacturers as the best proteolytic enzyme for cheese production. However, the availability of rennet with a high chymosin content has decreased during the past decades, due to the continuous decline in the slaughter of suckling calves. At the same time, cheese production has continued to grow to an annual output of 13.7 million tonnes, requiring 50 000 kg of chymosin. The increasing gap between supply and demand for high quality calf rennet has forced industry to search for alternative solutions.

One alternative to extracting rennet from suckling calves is to use the stomachs of older animals. However, due to their reduced chymosin and increased pepsin content, these alternative rennets have several disadvantages, including reduced cheese curd yield and adverse flavour development. Other alternative sources were developed in the 1960s, when various microorganisms which produced milk-clotting proteases were identified and used to produce microbial rennet by fermentation. The microbial rennets had drawbacks such as less desirable flavour development. Recombinant DNA technology has offered the possibility of genetically modifying microorganisms in such a way that calf chymosin could be produced by a fermentation process. The principal attraction in this approach was that a constant supply of high-quality rennet containing pure chymosin that had properties identical to calf chymosin could be produced.

3.5.1   *The biosynthesis of mammalian chymosin*

In the calf, chymosin is produced as an inactive precursor, preprochymosin, by the secretory cells of the fourth stomach. During secretion into the stomach, the preprochymosin is converted into prochymosin. In the acid environment of the stomach, this prochymosin is converted by an autocatalytic process into mature or active chymosin. The mature chymosin consists of a polypeptide chain of 323 amino acid building blocks, compared to 381 amino acids for preprochymosin.

In mammals, the transcription of genes into corresponding mRNA is a complex process. The genes often contain several DNA nucleotide sequences, called introns, which are not found in the mature mRNA. Introns do not contain information for the final gene-product and constitute inhibiting factors for expression of mammalian genes in microorganisms. Therefore, it was not until the discovery of the enzyme reverse transcriptase (Baltimore, 1970) that it became possible to obtain a mammalian gene without introns by reversing the transcription process, starting with isolated mRNA. This genetic engineering technique has been used to obtain the DNA encoding for preprochymosin. For a detailed account of techniques employed, the reader is referred to papers by Maat and Smith (1978), Maxam and Gilbert (1977), Balbas *et al.* (1986) and Sambrook *et al.* (1989).

The cloning of the calf chymosin DNA was carried out by investigators at the Unilever Research Laboratories in Vlaardingen, The Netherlands (Maat *et al.*, 1983). A plasmid harbouring prochymosin DNA was used for the construction of the prochymosin-producing *Kluyveromyces lactis* strain.

3.5.2   The choice of host organism

In the late 1970s, many genetic engineering techniques were developed using the bacterium *Escherichia coli*. Proteins like insulin and human growth hormone were produced using this bacterium as host. The choice of this host organism was mainly based on the availability of DNA transformation procedures and an extensive available knowledge of the genetics and biochemistry of *E. coli*. However, *E. coli*, an organism frequently associated with poor hygiene in food processing plants, was not considered a suitable host for the expression of a protein destined for use in foods (van Leen *et al.*, 1991). Therefore, at Gist-brocades, the yeast *K. lactis* was chosen as it excreted no toxins; was not pathogenic to man; failed to grow on skin, mucous membranes or intestines of mammals; occurred naturally in many fermented food products such as Kefir, Koumiss, yoghurt and several cheeses (Roquefort, Camembert, Cheddar, etc.); was affirmed as safe by the FDA for the production and application of lactase in the food industry (FDA, 1984) and was a strain for which an industrial process already existed. Finally, basic recombinant DNA techniques were becoming available for this organism and it offered an opportunity to obtain a unique patent position.

3.5.3   Construction of the genetically engineered K. lactis

To produce a protein in a foreign host, the DNA encoding this protein, the so-called structural gene, must be localised in such a way that the regulatory signals allow the correct protein to be made. Furthermore this 'expression construct' must be introduced into the selected host cell. Usually, an 'expression construct' is made *in vitro*, containing the structural gene in proper orientation between the essential regulatory elements: the promoter (a nucleotide sequence responsible for starting transcription into a mRNA) and the terminator (a nucleotide sequence responsible for stopping the transcription process at the end of the gene).

A prochymosin copy-DNA plasmid was used for the construction of a set of different expression-cassettes in *E. coli* K12 strains by standard recombinant techniques (Sambrook *et al.*, 1989). A typical example of one of the expression vectors is shown in Figure 3.1.

Several signals or leader sequences to direct the secretion of prochymosin by *K. lactis* were tested (Van den Berg *et al.*, 1990). The best prochymosin secretion was obtained when the signal sequence of the yeast

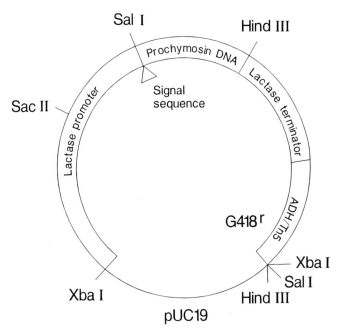

Figure 3.1 Expression vector for mammalian chymosin. The expression vector contains the promoter of the lactase gene (*lac*4), the prochymosin encoding DNA and the optional signal sequence, the lactase transcription terminator, the *E. coli* plasmid pUC19 and the Tn5 gene conferring resistance to kanamycin (G418[r]) under the direction of the *S. cerevisiae* ADHI promoter (ADH/Tn5). Important restriction endonuclease sites are indicated.

Saccharomyces cerevisiae alpha-factor was fused to prochymosin DNA in an expression cassette as depicted in Figure 3.1, resulting in a plasmid named pKS105. To transform the host *K. lactis*, the yeast cells were treated with lithium salts and incubated with pKS105 DNA. The transformants were selected by conferring resistance to the antibiotic kanamycin. Southern-blot DNA analyses were performed to prove that the expression cassette was integrated at the lactase gene of *K. lactis*, *lac*4 (Sambrook *et al.*, 1989). The amount of prochymosin produced by the selected transformants was quantified using a milk-clotting assay (Van den Berg *et al.*, 1990). The *K. lactis* transformant with the best production performance designated CHY1, was selected for large scale production of prochymosin.

3.5.4   Production of chymosin

The production of chymosin from the genetically engineered yeast consisted of three successive steps: aseptic fermentation, product recovery (downstream processing), and formulation of the end product, chymosin. When the desired prochymosin titre in the fermenter was achieved, the fermentation was stopped by adding 0.5% sodium benzoate and lowering the pH to 2 with sulphuric acid to kill the yeast cells and inactivate proteolytic enzymes other than chymosin. The low pH also induced the conversion of prochymosin to chymosin, comparable to the situation in the calf stomach.

As the enzyme was excreted by the organism into the medium, separation of cell material from the enzyme was achieved by simple filtration, followed by ultrafiltration to concentrate the product. Depending on the market requirements and the type of cheese, the product was further formulated with either food grade NaCl, glycerol, propyleneglycol or sorbitol to obtain a liquid stream which was filter-sterilised. Powdered formulations were obtained by using suitable carriers. All formulating agents were chosen from those normally used in the cheese industry. The formulated product is sold under the trade name MAXIREN®.

3.5.5   Safety of production

The microbial and environmental safety aspects of the recombinant DNA process has received special attention. Firstly, selection of the host organism was made on the basis of its known safety. Furthermore, the chymosin gene was incorporated into the chromosome thereby conferring genetic stability to the organism. Therefore, transfer of the newly acquired genes from the recombinant yeast into the environment was as unlikely as for all the other natural genes of the yeast.

Normally, about 25 generations of yeast are produced during a chymosin fermentation. The stability of the chymosin-producing trait was followed for 66 generations and no significant change in productivity was observed. In addition, it was shown by DNA analysis that the integrated gene remained unchanged after 100 generations.

The emission of yeasts via the exhaust pipe of the production plant was monitored during production. An average of 700 colony forming units (cfus) per cubic metre of air were detected. Clearly, dilution in air was very high and local emission thus extremely low when compared to the 10^{12} yeasts per litre in the fermentation medium. Even more importantly, the recombinant yeast could not be isolated from soil samples taken from the production site in France, suggesting that the organism had very limited ability to survive in soil. When tested under laboratory conditions, a reduction factor of 10 000 to 1 million was determined in non-sterilised soil whilst in sterilised soils, the reduction factor was lower (100–1000). No active growth was observed in these soils.

With regard to the liquid wastestream, the biomass was routinely inactivated at the end of the fermentation by the combined action of low pH and sodium benzoate. Together with the operation of hygienic standards expected in the modern food industry, it was concluded that the precautions and safety measures taken have been sufficient to ensure a safe and stable industrial fermentation process.

3.5.6 The chemical and functional properties of chymosin produced by the genetically engineered K. lactis

The chymosin from *K. lactis* is a clear liquid with a slight odour and taste characteristic of fermentation. The product is completely soluble in water and has a pH ranging between 5.5 and 6.0.

The biochemical properties of the chymosin were shown to be identical to those of calf-derived chymosin by several methods. The molecular sizes of mammalian chymosin and chymosin from *K. lactis* were found to be the same using high performance size exclusion chromatography. The molecular weights of both forms of chymosin were 36.3 kDa, as determined by polyacrylamide gel electrophoresis. Using monoclonal antibodies against calf chymosin and Western immuno-blotting, it was shown that both chymosins reacted in the same way (Sambrook *et al.*, 1989). The first 10 N-terminal amino acids and the total amino acid composition for both chymosins were also identical.

The enzymatic activity of the *K. lactis* preparation was compared with standard animal rennet from INRA-Poligny, France. Both enzymes showed similar sensitivity to temperature (optimum at about 45°C) and pH. The stimulating effect of calcium on both preparations was very similar although the chymosin from the genetically engineered yeast was stimulated slightly more than the animal rennet. As with animal rennet, the coagulation time on raw milk for chymosin from *K. lactis* was inversely proportional to the enzyme concentration.

Table 3.2 Cheese trials lasting 1 month or longer carried out using chymosin from genetically engineered *Kluyveromyces lactis*

Cheese type	Duration of trial in months	Institute/production plant
Appenzell	1	FAM, Liebefeld (Switzerland)
Camembert	1	Université de Nancy (France)
Cheddar	6	University of St Paul (US)
Cheddar	6	Department of Agricultural Development, Irene (US)
Cheddar	12	University of Cork (Ireland)
Cheddar	12	AFRC Institute of Food Research, Reading (UK)
Edam	2.5	Milchforschungsanstalt, Kiel (Germany)
Edam	6	Food Research Institute, Jokioinen (Finland)
Emmental	2	Institute Technologique de Gruyère, La Roche sur Foron (France)
Emmental	3	FAM, Liebefeld (Switzerland)
Emmental	3	FAM, Liebefeld (Switzerland)[a]
Emmental	6	Food Research Institute, Jokioinen (Finland)
Gouda	3	Bundesanstalt für Milchwirtschaft, Wolfpassing (Austria)
Gouda	6	Department of Agricultural Development, Irene (US)
Gouda	12	NIZO, Ede (Netherlands)
Hispanico	2	INIA, Madrid (Spain)
Italico	2	Instituto Sperimentale Latteriero-Caseario, Lodi (Italy)
Kashar	6	Marmara Research Center, Gebze-Kocaeli (Turkey)
Manchego	6	INIA, Madrid (Spain)
St Paulin	1	Université de Nancy (France)
Tilsit	2.5	Milchforschungsanstalt, Kiel (Germany)
White pickled	3	Marmara Research Center, Gebze-Kocaeli (Turkey)

[a]Large scale trials were carried out at three independent factories.

In cheese trials, milk coagulation, curd-firmness, ageing profiles, flavour development and organoleptic qualities were identical with both sources of chymosin. The chymosin from *K. lactis* was tested at a number of institutes, involving a wide variety of cheese types, as shown in Table 3.2. In all cases, *K. lactis* chymosin proved to be an excellent coagulant for a wide variety of cheeses.

3.5.7 Safety of recombinant chymosin

The health aspects of animal rennet as a food ingredient were evaluated by the FAO/WHO in 1972 (WHO, 1972). It was concluded that the establishment of an acceptable daily intake (ADI) for rennet was not necessary. Another evaluation was performed by the Federation of American Societies for Experimental Biology under contract with the FDA of the United States in 1977 (Anon, 1977). The conclusion of this evaluation was that rennet represented no hazard to the public when used at levels that are now current or that might reasonably be expected in the future. As a consequence, animal rennet has maintained its previously obtained GRAS (generally regarded as safe) status.

Although all compositional data strongly suggested that the *K. lactis* chymosin was identical to the active component of animal rennet, several toxicological tests have been commissioned by the manufacturer. No signs of acute oral toxicity were observed for 14 days following the administration of a single 5 g/kg chymosin dose to rats. A short-term toxicity study was also performed in rats fed on cheese prepared with the *K. lactis* chymosin; the results from the experimental and control groups were identical, indicating absence of systemic toxicity. No abnormalities were observed in a 91-day subchronic toxicity study on rats fed with *K. lactis* chymosin alone as well as with cheese prepared with the chymosin. No indication of mutagenic activity of *K. lactis* chymosin was obtained in three different *in vitro* mutagenicity tests. Allergenicity tests showed that, in contrast to animal rennet, *K. lactis* chymosin was not a sensitiser of guinea pig skin. In all these studies, no indications of toxic effects with the *K. lactis* chymosin were obtained.

3.5.8   Regulatory position of MAXIREN®

MAXIREN®, the trade name for chymosin isolated by Gist-brocades from genetically modified *K. lactis*, has been approved for use in foods in 24 countries including 7 member states of the European Community (EC). The Scientific Committee for Food (SCF) of the EC has evaluated MAXIREN® safety and has agreed that this product is acceptable for use in the manufacture of cheese. Furthermore, MAXIREN® has been affirmed as GRAS (generally recognised as safe) by the FDA on 25 February 1992. MAXIREN® was evaluated and declared safe by the FAO/WHO and it was concluded that the determination of an acceptable daily intake (ADI) level was not necessary. An overview of the regulatory position of MAXIREN® and how this was achieved, has been published (Praaning-van Dalen, 1992).

It can be concluded that a safe process has been developed for the production of calf chymosin by the yeast *K. lactis* using recombinant DNA techniques. The *K. lactis* chymosin or MAXIREN® has been confirmed as structurally and functionally indistinguishable from chymosin isolated from calf stomachs. The *K. lactis* chymosin offers a number of advantages over animal rennet:

- a standardised coagulant of the highest quality and purity;
- an unlimited supply of pure chymosin, thereby making the practice of mixing with low grade coagulants obsolete;
- a more stable price than calf rennet;
- a vegetarian, Kosher and Hallal product that reduces our dependence on the slaughter of young calves.

3.6   A case study: the genetic engineering of a food-grade organism

The leavening activity of yeast in dough is the result of an anaerobic fermentation of sugars to ethanol and carbon dioxide. In lean dough (no added sugar), most of the sugar available to yeast is maltose, derived from starch. The first step in the metabolism of maltose by yeast is the transport of the sugar molecules across the plasma-membrane, mediated by the enzyme maltose-permease. After entering the cell, maltose is hydrolysed to glucose by the enzyme maltase. Glucose is subsequently converted to carbon dioxide and ethanol via the Embden–Meyerhof pathway.

Maltose fermentation by *Saccharomyces* species requires the presence of one of a series of five unlinked MAL-loci on the genome (Celenza and Carlson, 1985). A typical MAL-locus consists of at least three genes encoding maltose permease, maltase and a regulatory protein (Needleman *et al.*, 1984). Expression of the genes encoding maltose transport and maltase activity is catabolite-repressed by glucose and in many *Saccharomyces cerevisiae* strains, induced by maltose.

Several studies have been published investigating the possible correlation between maltose fermentation and leavening activity of baker's yeast. In some cases, a positive correlation between the rate of maltose fermentation and maltose-permease and maltase activities has been reported. Therefore, an attempt was made to increase carbon dioxide production of commercial baker's yeast strains by increasing their capacity to ferment maltose. The research was specifically focused on improving gas production of existing commercial strains in lean doughs. Therefore, the aim of applying recombinant DNA technology to baker's yeast was to produce a strain able to ferment maltose instantly in a lean dough, resulting in immediate production of carbon dioxide. All the other characteristics of the new strain had to be identical to the existing commercial strains.

3.6.1   Construction of a yeast strain with altered maltose fermentation

Using gene replacement and co-transformation procedures, modified maltose permease and maltase genes were integrated into the genome of baker's yeast. The natural MAL-gene promoters were replaced by strong constitutive promoters. For details of the techniques employed, the reader is referred to papers by Gottlin-Ninga and Kaback (1986), Rothstein (1983) and Gatignol *et al.* (1990). This ultimately yielded transformant 352 Ng which contained altered promoters in front of the maltase and the maltose-permease genes. This 352 Ng transformant has been designated the MAL-yeast (Osinga, 1992). It is stressed that this final recombinant MAL-yeast contained only homologous yeast DNA and no heterologous DNA from other organisms.

3.6.2   *Performance of the genetically modified baker's yeast*

Carbon dioxide production of the parent and recombinant strains were compared experimentally at 28°C. It was demonstrated that the MAL-yeast produced between 18 and 28% more carbon dioxide than the parent strain at 60, 100, 120 and 165 min following addition of the yeast to the dough. The improvement in carbon dioxide production was also demonstrated in a model system consisting of a synthetic dough-like medium without flour. The results of the model system experiments are shown in Figure 3.2.

As shown in Figure 3.2, the parent yeast showed a characteristic 'dip' in carbon dioxide production rate between 40 and 90 min as a result of a lag-time in the induction of maltase and maltose-permease. Both enzymes were fully induced in the parent strain after about 100 min. The modified yeast had higher activities of both enzymes at the beginning of the process, resulting in rapid gas production. The modified yeast lacked the 'dip' in gas production.

Extensive testing showed that all the other properties of the MAL-yeast were unchanged in comparison to the parental strain (van der Wilden,

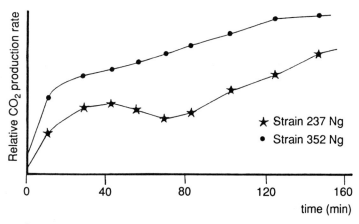

Figure 3.2 Gas production in lean dough by the genetically modified baker's yeast (strain 352 Ng) and its parent strain (strain 237 Ng).

1990). It is important to note that the rate of gas production of the modified yeast in lean dough was not superior to some other already existing commercial strains, selected by classical breeding. However, the advantage of the modified yeast was that it could be applied in a broad range of products including lean and high-sugar doughs.

3.6.3   Survival of the genetically modified yeast in the environment

On the basis of previous experience with industrial microorganisms, there was no reason to expect that the modified baker's yeast would grow or survive better than the parent strain in either the natural environment, dough, bread, the fermentation vessel or the effluent. Industrial strains in general are rarely, if ever, found in natural substrates. In order to survive in the environment, an industrial strain as a newcomer has to multiply at a rate comparable to that of the indigenous flora and to build up sufficient energy reserves to survive the next period of famine when an essential substrate becomes exhausted. Experience has shown that industrial strains are not able to do this.

In the case of baker's yeast, *S. cerevisiae* strains have been developed by classical mutation-selection procedures for more than a century. These procedures, which were aimed at improving the dough-rising capacities, have resulted in yeast strains that are specifically adapted to grow optimally under the rich, non-competitive conditions in dough and in fermentation media. When compared to the wild type strains, these adapted baker's yeast strains have lost their ability to survive in their original ecological niche, the external surfaces of fruits and other parts of plants (Do Carmo-Sousa, 1969).

In Delft, The Netherlands, where baker's yeast has been produced for more than 110 years, no growth and/or survival of baker's yeast, released from the production plant, has ever been recorded in the surrounding environment. There was no reason to suspect that the recombinant baker's yeast would behave any differently. The instantaneous maltose response would not alter the inability of the new strain to survive in its parent's ecological niche. There was no indication that the genetic modifications had any influence on the sporulation behaviour of the yeast. The modified MAL-strain, exactly like the parent strain, was aneuploid and sporulated very poorly, resulting in much lower spore numbers compared to the wild-type organism.

Nevertheless, survival studies on the recombinant yeast have been carried out. Under standard bakery conditions, two batches of bread were prepared using the modified and the parent strain according to a standard recipe and process. In order to determine heat susceptibility of the organism during the breadmaking process, samples were taken from the dough just prior to baking and from the centre of the bread 1 h after the loaves

Table 3.3 Survival of the parent and genetically modified yeast strains in the environment (cfu's)

Test material	Strain	Day 0	Day 1	Day 2	Day 5	Day 9
Control sample	Parent	4.8×10^5	1.5×10^6	1.0×10^6	nd[a]	nd
(peptone water)	Modified	3.6×10^5	1.5×10^6	1.6×10^6	3.4×10^6	2.4×10^6
Domestic sewage	Parent	5.3×10^5	3.3×10^5	1.5×10^5	7.3×10^2	1
	Modified	4.1×10^5	3.0×10^5	9.5×10^4	1.6×10^2	8
Sea water	Parent	5.3×10^5	3.9×10^5	2.5×10^5	9.7×10^4	4.3×10^4
	Modified	3.4×10^5	4.5×10^5	2.4×10^5	8.9×10^4	4.3×10^4

[a]nd, not determined.

had been taken out of the oven. The temperature of these samples was measured and the number of viable cells was determined. It was found that there were fewer than 10 cfu per g bread present in the centre of the bread after baking. This is not surprising, since the temperature in the centre of the bread, measured immediately after baking, was 95°C. No differences in the viability of the two yeast strains tested under these conditions were observed.

In the fermentation vessel, where the yeasts are traditionally grown on a sugar-rich, maltose-free medium, the advantage of the recombinant strain over its parent was eliminated. During research and development, a great number of labscale fermentations (10 l) with both the modified and parental strain had been carried out. During these fermentations, a number of characteristics such as growth rate, oxygen consumption, ethanol production and molasses consumption were measured on line. No differences between the two strains were observed.

The survival of the parent and recombinant yeast strains in domestic sewage and sea water was also determined. Samples of domestic sewage, sea water and peptone water (control) were inoculated with a fresh culture of the modified and parent strain, respectively, to give a final concentration of approximately 10^5 cfu per ml. The inoculated samples were incubated for 9 days at 25°C and the viability of the yeast cells was monitored. The results, shown in Table 3.3, indicated that under the conditions of the experiment, there was no difference in the survival of the two strains. Viability in peptone water remained at a constant level, whereas in domestic sewage viability was reduced by a factor of at least 10^4–10^5. A moderate reduction in viability was observed in sea water.

3.6.4   Risk of genetic transfer

The MAL-yeast did not contain any procaryotic, heterologous DNA. The modification concerned exclusively the integration of homologous yeast DNA from other yeast strains. Moreover, the insert was stably inherited.

The risk of DNA transfer from the modified yeast would therefore not be any different from that of transfer from the parent yeast strain.

The risk of DNA transfer from baker's yeast in general is very low. When yeast cells die (after vegetative propagations, for instance) the process of autolysis (self-destruction) begins. During autolysis, the DNA is degraded before the thick cell wall is destroyed. Therefore, release of free yeast DNA in such a form as to allow uptake by other organisms is unlikely. The species *S. cerevisiae*, to which baker's yeast belongs, does not mate or normally exchange DNA with any known bacterial or fungal pathogen. Furthermore, the species harbours no known DNA viruses which might easily transfer yeast DNA to other organisms (Fink *et al.*, 1978).

Transfer of DNA between closely related *S. cerevisiae* strains is possible via formation of zygotes; the yeast cells sporulate, mate and form a zygote. The sporulation frequency of both the recombinant and the parent baker's yeasts was very low. Both were aneuploid, producing a limited number of ascospores. A high concentration of viable cells would therefore be needed to obtain crossing between strains. In natural environments, such high cell concentrations are not found, due to the very low survival ability of baker's yeast. Even if the modified baker's yeast could survive, sporulate, mate and form a zygote outside the laboratory, it was unlikely that the behaviour of the modified strain would be different from that of the parent.

As no genetic transfer or survival of the modified yeast in the environment were expected, no special control or elimination measures other than those normally used in industrial fermentations or in baking were deemed necessary.

3.6.5   Consumer safety

The recombinant yeast is a strain of conventional baker's yeast belonging to the species. *S. cerevisiae*. Yeast strains from this species are known not to be pathogenic for humans or for animals. Baker's yeast strains have never been known to cause infections or illness, either to bakers or to consumers. Kappe and Müller (1978) have reported experiments in which 130 g of good quality baker's yeast was administered orally to healthy volunteers without any adverse effects.

Baker's yeast is consumed regularly by humans in bread and other fermented products. In addition, yeast is consumed directly in huge amounts (as much as 10^{10} living cells per dose) by many people as vitamin supplements, with no ill effects. Substantial levels of viable yeast are also present in certain types of popular ale.

S. cerevisiae is occasionally found on human and animal skin but there are no indications of proliferation. In an extensive review of safety procedures in laboratories and of biotechnology processes, Frommer *et al.*

(1989) have reported *S. cerevisiae* as a harmless organism that has never been identified as a causative agent of disease in man and that offers no threat to the environment. *S. cerevisiae* has been classified as a harmless microorganism by the OECD (1986).

In general, the pathogenicity and potential toxicity of a genetically engineered organism is governed by the pathogenicity or toxicity of the host organism, unless genes coding for virulence or toxin production have been used in the process of modifying the organism. By this definition, the recombinant yeast described in this chapter could not in any conceivable way exhibit pathogenicity.

Saccharomyces species are known to be rich in vitamin B. It is not anticipated that the genetic rearrangement in the recombinant yeast would in any way affect the nutritional qualities of the yeast or of the bread made with it. Since the parent strain also produces the two enzymes involved in maltose fermentation (only less efficiently), the biochemical reactions occurring during the leavening process are still the same when using the modified strain. The products formed during leavening are the same as before, leading to an end-product (bread) which has the same composition as bread prepared in the conventional way.

Following review of the modified MAL-yeast, the UK Advisory Committee on Novel Foods and Processes (ACNFP) has declared that there are no consumer safety reasons why the use of the genetically modified yeast should not be permitted in foods.

3.6.6   Regulatory position of the genetically modified baker's yeast

Many new technologies evoke feelings of fear (fear of the unknown) in society. Although yeast experts were convinced that the genetically modified MAL-yeast was as safe as any other baker's yeast, at Gist-brocades, it was decided not to introduce the new yeast on the market prior to assessment and approval by regulatory authorities. In 1986, Gist-brocades notified the former Dutch ad hoc Recombinant DNA Advisory Committee of the existence of the project on recombinant yeast. Based on the fact that the recombinant yeast did not contain heterologous DNA, the Advisory Committee declassified the project in a way comparable to obtaining 'exempt' status by the National Institute of Health in the United States. The experimental protocol matched the 'self-cloning' category in Annex I B of the Council Directive 90/219 EEC on contained use.

The first petition for production of the recombinant yeast was filed in the United Kingdom where one of the main Gist-brocades production plants was located. Since yeasts cannot be contained in bakeries, the use of the MAL-yeast would result in the release into the environment of a genetically engineered microorganism. The implications of this release for workers and consumers were evaluated by the authorities. In a joint announcement by MAFF and the Department of Health on 1 March 1990, the UK Government declared the recombinant baker's yeast safe for use by bakers. Copies of the ACNFP advice on the MAL-yeast are available from the Department of Health, Eileen House, 80–94 Newington Causeway, London, SE1 6EF.

In conclusion, the application of recombinant DNA technology has led to the successful development of a commercial baker's yeast in which the synthesis of two enzymes, maltose-permease and maltase, was no longer repressed by the presence of glucose. As a result, the new yeast had gas production ability in lean doughs comparable to that of sugar-rich doughs. The use of the MAL-yeast in the manufacture of bread has been cleared by the regulatory authorities in the United Kingdom. Nevertheless, the modified baker's yeast has not been introduced to the market for commercial reasons.

3.7   Conclusions and future prospects

In the preceding paragraphs, we have described three edible products of the new biotechnology: a tomato in which the softening process has been halted by 'switching off' a specific gene; a cheese-making enzyme secreted by a yeast containing a mammalian gene; and a baker's yeast which has been made more versatile by genetic engineering. Of the three products examined, only one, the recombinant chymosin, is currently on the market.

The major technological hurdle to progress in the future will come from insufficient knowledge of the genetic make-up of food raw materials, particularly plants and animals. Effort needs to be committed to chromosome mapping of those genes responsible for coding of important quality parameters. However, technical feasibility is unlikely to be the most important concern for the food industry. Advances in the laboratory and the pilot plant will continue in the next 10–15 years but future emphasis will be shifting from technical feasibility to the regulatory arena.

In terms of future regulation of food biotechnology, the prospect looks bleak. If successful, an innovator will face heavy costs and delay while safety evaluation takes place. Because of cost, biotechnological innovation on a large scale tends to be an activity for big companies only. The enactment of simplified legislative procedures common to North America, Europe and Japan would make it easier to carry out the necessary testing to assure farmers, food processors and the public that recombinant foods perform as desired and pose no additional safety or environmental risks over those derived from traditional sources.

The consumer's innate conservatism with respect to food means that changes will have to be introduced in small, careful steps. It will be important to keep consumer organisations well informed of the changes that are introduced so that they can be critically evaluated. If the edible products of biotechnology are to make any impact at all in the future, industry will have to do a much better job of addressing public concerns than has been evident to date.

Acknowledgements

The authors wish to thank their colleagues at Gist-brocades and the Leatherhead Food RA for their advice in preparing this chapter. We also thank Mrs W. Braadbaart for critical reading of this chapter.

References

Addy, N.D. (1991) Impact of biotechnology on vegetable processing, in *Biotechnology and Food Ingredients*, eds. I. Godberg and R. Williams. Van Nostrand Reinhold, New York, pp. 307–316.
Anon (1977) Federation of American Societies for Experimental Biology, National Technical Information Service PB-274 668.
Anon (1990) *Biotechnol. Bull.* **May.**
Anon (1990a) Antisense genes for long-life fruit. AFRC Annual Report, 1989–90, AFRC, Swindon, pp. 14–15.
Anon (1990b) *Food Proc.* **April.**
Anon (1991) *Biotechnol. Newswatch* **11** (6), 6.
Anon (1991a) ICI Corp. *Abstracts in Biocommerce* **13** (14), 8.
Anon (1992) DNA plant technology gets patent for antifreeze proteins. *Food Technol.* **August,** 72.
Anon (1993) Data on genetically engineered tomato submitted to FDA. *Food Technol.* **May,** 36.
Anon (1993a) Dispute over GMO registers could land government in hot water. *Biotechnol. Bull.* **March,** 2.
Anon (1993b) Transgenic potatoes. *Agro-Food Industry Hi-Tech* **March/April,** 44.
Anon (1993c) FDA considers labelling of bio-engineered foods. *Biotechnol. Bull.* **June,** 3.
Anon (1993d) Calgene files suit against Enzo Biochem. *Biotechnol. Bull.* **February,** 6–7.
Anon (1993e) Calgene receives brassica transformation patent. *Biotechnol. Bull.* **March,** 6.
Anon (1993f) Rennet substitute affirmed as GRAS. *Food Technol.* **July,** 72.
Bains, W. (1990) Antisense technology can have substantial impact in several novel application areas. *Genet. Eng News* **Nov./Dec.,** 4.
Balbás, P., Soberon, X., Zurita, M., Comeli, H., Valle, F., Flores, N. and Bolivar, F. (1986) Plasmid vector pBR322 and its special-purpose derivatives – a review. *Gene* **50,** 3–40.
Baltimore, D. (1970) RNA-dependent DNA polymerase in virions of RNA tumour viruses. *Nature* **1209,** 11.
Barbano, D.M. and Rasmussen, R.R. (1991) Cheese yield performance of fermentation-produced chymosin and other milk coagulants. *J. Dairy Sci.* **75,** 1–12.
Bleecker, A.B. (1989) Prospects for the use of genetic engineering in the manipulation of ethylene biosynthesis and action in higher plants, in *Biotechnology and Food Quality*, eds. S.-D. Kung, D.D. Bills and R. Quatrano. Butterworths, Boston, pp. 159–165.
Bleecker, A.B., Kenyon, W.H., Somerville, S.C. and Kende, H. (1986) Use of monoclonal antibodies in the purification and characterisation of ACC synthase, an enzyme in ethylene biosynthesis. *Proc. Natl. Acad. Sci.* **83,** 7755–7759.

Bridges, I.G., Schuch, W.W. and Grierson, D. (Assignee: ICI) (1988) Tomatoes with reduced fruit-ripening enzymes. European Patent Application 0 341 885.

Bryant, J.A. (1989) Antisense RNA makes good sense. *TIBTECH* **7** (2), 20.

Celenza, J.A. and Carlson, M. (1985) Rearrangement of the genetic map of chromosome VII of *Saccharomyces cervisiae*. *Genetics* **109**, 661–664.

Crawley, M.J., Hails, R.S., Rees, M., Kohn, D. and Buxton, J. (1993) Ecology of transgenic oilseed rape in natural habitats. *Nature* **363**, 620–623.

Do Carmo-Sousa, L. (1969) Distribution of yeast in nature, in *The Yeast*, eds. A.H. Rose and J.S. Harrison. Academic Press, London, pp. 79–106.

Duxbury, D.D. (1993) Genetic researchers boost plant starch yields. *Food Proc.* **February**, 66.

EC (1990) Council Directive on the contained use of genetically modified microorganisms, 90/219/EEC. *Off. J. Eur. Commun.* **L117**, 1–14.

EC (1990) Council Directive on the deliberate release into the environment of genetically modified organisms, 90/220/EEC. *Off. J. Eur. Commun.* **L117**, 15–27.

Elkington, J. (1993) Campbell in the soup? *Biotechnol. Bull.* **12** (1), 1.

Federation of American Societies for Experimental Biology (1977) National Technical Information Service PB-274 668.

Fink, G. R. *et al.* (1978) Yeast as a host for hybrid DNA, in *Genetic Engineering*, 2, eds. H. W. Boyer and S. Nicosia. Elsevier/North-Holland, Amsterdam, pp. 163–171.

FDA (1984) Lactase from *Kluyveromyces lactis*, GRAS affirmed, 21 Code of Federal Regulations (CFR) 184.1388. 49, Federal Register 47387, December 4.

FDA (1992) Chymosin from *Kluyveromyces lactis*, GRAS affirmed, 21 Code of Federal Regulations (CFR) 184.1685 57, Federal Register 6476–6479, February 25.

Fox, J.L. (1993a) FDA advisory panel moves Monsanto's BST. *BioTechnology* **11**, 554–555.

Fox, J.L. (1993b) FDA panel ponders labels for BST-derived foods. *BioTechnology* **11**, 656–657.

Fox, J.L. (1993c) FDA reexamines biotech policy. *BioTechnology* **11**, 656.

Fraley, R. (1992) Sustaining the food supply. *BioTechnology* **10**, 40–43.

Frommer, W. *et al.* (1989) Safe biotechnology. III. Safety precautions for handling micro-organisms of different risk classes. *Appl. Microb. Biotechnol.* **30**, 541–552.

Gatignol, A., Dassain, M. and Tiraby, G. (1990) Cloning of *S. cerevisiae* promoters using a probe vector based on phleomycin resistance. *Gene* **91**, 35–41.

Giovannoni, J.J., DellaPenna, D., Bennett, A.B. and Fischer, R.L. (1989) Expression of a chimeric polygalacturonase gene in transgenic rin (ripening inhibitor) tomato fruit results in polyuronide degradation but not fruit softening. *Plant Cell* **1**, 53.

Goodman, R.M., Hauptli, H., Crossway, A. and Knauf, V.C. (1987) Gene transfer in crop improvement. *Science* **236**, 48.

Gorner, P. and Kotulak, R. (1991) Gene splicers putting new food on the table. *Food Technol.* **August**, 46–103.

Gottlin-Ninga, G. and Kaback, C.B. (1986) Isolation and functional analysis of sporulation-induced transcribed sequences from *Saccharomyces cerevisiae*. *Mol. Cell Biol.* **6**, 2185.

Gross, K.C. (1990) Recent developments in tomato fruit softening. *Postharvest News Inf.* **1** (2), 109–112.

Harlander, S.K. (1987) Biotechnology: Emerging and expanding opportunities for the food industry. *Nutr. Today* **22** (4), 21–29.

Harlander, S.K. (1993) Food biotechnology: toward the twenty first century, in *Recent Advances in US Food Technology*, *Proc. IFT Conf.*, Wallingford, UK, 1992.

Hobson, G. (1993) The transgenic tomato, the story so far. *Grower* **January**, 14.

Kappe, R. and Müller, J. (1978) Cultural and serological follow-up of two oral administrations of baker's yeast to a human volunteer. *Mykosen* **30**, 357–368.

Kareiva, P. (1993) Transgenic plants on trial. *Nature* **363**, 580.

Kidd, G. (1993) DNAP takes the lead in genetic subtraction. *BioTechnology* **11**, 874.

Kok, E.J., Reynaerts, A. and Kuiper, H.A. (1993) Novel food products from genetically modified plants: do they need additional food safety regulations? *Trends Food Sci. Technol.* **4**, 42–48.

Kramer, M., Sanders, R.A., Bolkan, H., Waters, C., Sheehy, R.E. and Hiatt, W.R. (1992)

Postharvest evaluation of transgenic tomatoes with reduced levels of polygalacturonase: processing, firmness and disease resistance. *Postharvest Biol. Technol.* **1**, 241–255.

Lex, M. (1993) Letter from Brussels. *BioBulletin* **14** (1), 10.

Maxam, A.M. and Gilbert, W. (1977) A new method for sequencing DNA. *Proc. Natl. Acad. Sci. USA* **74**, 560–565.

Maat, J. and Smith, A.J.H. (1978) A method for sequencing restriction fragments with dideoxynucleoside triphosphates. *Nucleic Acids Res.* **5**, 4537–4546.

Maat, J., Verrips, C.T., Ledeboer, A.M. and Edens, L. (1983) DNA molecules comprising the genes for preprochymosin and its maturation forms and microorganisms transformed thereby. European Patent Application 077109.

Miflin, B.J. (1993) Bringing plant biotechnology to the market – the next steps. *Agro-Food Ind. Hi-Tech* **January/February**, 3–5.

Miller, P. D. and Morrison, R. A. (1991) Biotechnological applications in the development of new fruits and vegetables, in *Biotechnology and Food Ingredients*, eds. I. Godberg and R. Williams. Van Nostrand Reinhold, New York, pp. 13–29.

Needleman, R.B., Kaback, D.B., Dubin, R.A., Perkins, E.L., Rosenburg, N.G., Sutherland, K.A., Forrest, D.B. and Michels, C.A. (1984) Mal 6 of *Saccharomyces cerevisiae*: a complex genetic locus containing three genes required for maltose fermentation. *Proc. Natl. Acad. Sci. USA* **81**, 2811.

OECD (1986) *Recombinant DNA Safety Considerations*, OECD, 2, rue André-Pascal, 75775 Paris Cedex 16, France.

Osinga, K.A. (1992) Genetische Verbesserung vom Backerhefestammen. *Getreide, Mehl Brot* **3**, 73–75.

Praaning-van Dalen, D.P. (1992) Application and regulatory position of Maxiren. *Bull. Int. Dairy Fed.* (IDF) **269**, 8–12.

Redenbaugh, K., Hiatt, W., Martineau, B., Kramer, M., Sheeay, R., Sanders, R., Houck, C. and Emlay, D. (1992) *Safety Assessment of Genetically Engineered Fruit and Vegetables: A Case Study of the Flavr Savr Tomato*. CRC Press, Boca Raton, FL.

Rothstein, R.J. (1983) One-step gene disruption in yeast. *Methods Enzymol.* **101**, 202.

Sambrook, J., Maniatis, T. and Fritsch, E.F. (1989) *Molecular Cloning: A Laboratory Manual*, 2nd edition. CSHLP, Cold Spring Harbor, NY.

Scher, M. (1993a) Biotechnology's evolution spurs food revolution. *Food Proc.* **January**, 36–43.

Scher, M. (1993b) The human factor. *Food Process.* **April**, 117.

Sharp, W.R., Evans, D.A. and Ammirato, P.V. (1984) Plant genetic engineering: Designing crops to meet food industry specifications. *Food Technol.* **February**, 112.

Sheehy, R.E., Kramer, M. and Hiatt, W.R. (1988) Reduction of polygalacturonase activity in tomato fruit by antisense RNA. *Proc. Natl. Acad. Sci. USA* **85**, 8805.

Simon-Moffat, A. (1993) ICI demerger signals new direction in biotech world. *Genet. Eng. News* **13** (10) 1, 36.

Smith, C.J.S., Watson, C.F., Ray, J., Bird, C.R., Morris, P.C., Schuch, W. and Grierson, D. (1988) Antisense RNA inhibition of polygalacturonase gene expression in transgenic tomatoes. *Nature* **334**, 724.

US Federal Register, Part X. Department of Agriculture, 7 CFR Part 340, Final Rule, March 31 1993.

Van den Berg, J.A., van der Laken, K.J., van Ooyen, A.J.J., Renniers, T.C.H.M., Rietveld, K., Schaap, A., Brake, A.J., Bishop, R.J., Schultz, K., Moyer, D., Richmann, M. and Shuster, J.R. (1990) *Kluyveromyces* as a host for heterologous gene expression: expression and secretion of prochymosin. *BioTechnology* **8**, 135–139.

Van der Wilden, W. (1990) Recent developments in yeast technology, in *Proc. 71st Conf. British Soc. Baking*, pp. 20–26.

Van Leen, R.W., Bakhuis, J.G., van Beckhoven, F.W.C., Burger, H., Dorssers, L.C.J., Hommes, R.W.J., Lemson, P.J., Noordam, B., Persoon, N.L.M. and Wagemaker, G. (1991) Production of human interleukin-3 using industrial microorganisms. *BioTechnology* **9**, 47–52.

Van Wagner, L.R. (1993) Foreseeing the death of Delaney. *Food Proc.* **February**, 31–32.

Ward, M. (1993) European Commission proposes ban on BST. *BioTechnology* **11**, 869.

Wasserman, B.P. (1990) Expectations and role of biotechnology in improving fruit and vegetable quality. *Food Technol.* **44** (2), 68.

Whitaker, R.J. and Evans, D.A. (1987) Plant biotechnology and the production of flavour compounds. *Food Technol.* **September**, 86.

Whitaker, R.J. and Evans, D.A. (1990) Biotechnology and the production of food ingredients, in *Biotechnology and Food Safety*, eds. D.D. Bills and S.-D. Kung. Butterworth-Heinemann, Boston, pp. 291–310.

WHO (1972) 15th Report of the Expert Committee, FAO Nutrition Meetings Report Series 50. WHO Technical Report Series 488.

4 Energy conservation and the cost benefits to the food industry

N.M.A. WALSHE

4.1 Introduction

The food and drink industry is one of the larger energy users in the United Kingdom, consuming approximately 10% of the energy used in manufacturing industries. In 1992, the sector's delivered energy consumption was 176 PJ at a cost of £793 million, approximately 268 PJ per annum in primary energy terms. The industry is made up of a large number of consortia although, due to rationalisation, the number has been gradually falling for some time in most sub-sectors. In general, the top five organisations in each sub-sector are responsible for between half and two-thirds of gross output.

New products are continually being introduced to take account of changing markets due to shifting attitudes towards diet and health, as well as technical developments, economic factors and the generally keen competition within the industry. In addition, food hygiene issues are currently being reviewed in some parts of the industry. These factors make for a continually shifting and developing market.

Energy consumption only represents 2–3% of the production costs, and, hence in general, has received a relatively low priority in many organisations. Even where there is a good awareness of energy efficiency, uptake of energy efficient technology is often slow. The transient nature of the market together with over-capacity in many parts of the industry and the resultant rationalisation mean that the lowest capital cost option is often preferred when new plant is installed. This tendency is accentuated in large companies where capital funding is supplied by head office, with the individual sites being responsible for plant running costs.

The most important energy saving measures applicable to the food and drink industry are those involving low capital expenditure. Thus, monitoring and targeting shows particular potential for energy saving, and is viewed in some parts of the industry as being the most favourable option. Retrofit technology also offers good opportunities for improvements in energy efficiency, and the rate of uptake by the industry will be markedly greater for any measures that can be achieved by means of a 'bolt on' extra to improve existing equipment, avoiding the greater capital expenditure of new-bought plant.

Material in this chapter is used with the permission of the Energy Efficiency Office, part of the Department of the Environment, London, UK, who retain the copyright.

While it is true that energy costs form a small part of overall production costs in most food and drink industries, energy may be one of the larger *controllable* costs. Looking at energy costs compared with profits can give a radically different picture. In many sectors of the food and drink industries, profits and energy costs are about the same proportion of total costs. This means that a 10% reduction in energy costs, which is realistically achievable in many cases, will give a 10% increase in profits, as energy cost savings go direct to the bottom line. It is interesting to consider just what investment would be required to bring about the same increase in profits through increased sales.

A concept often used in the food and drink industry is that of 'giveaway'. Poor control of the weight of bags of crisps resulting in a 30-g bag containing 33 g represents a 10% giveaway. Manufacturers spend much time and effort in trying to reduce giveaway while still being confident that the product is not underweight. In the search for total quality, it is worth widening the concept of giveaway, so that it does not simply cover putting too much product into the package, but includes putting too much of anything into producing the product. In this way, a high wastage rate through poor control of product quality is a form of giveaway. So too is the use of more energy than is required to manufacture the product. Here energy is regarded as another of the raw materials needed to manufacture the product. Sometimes this excessive use of energy can have a direct impact on product quality, as would be the case with poor oven controls, leading to some biscuits being over-baked. It might also have no effect on product quality, but a strong effect on yield for a given input of raw material. For example leaving the oven on when it is not baking is as wasteful as spilling flour on the floor instead of using it for baking.

Improved energy efficiency gives several direct environmental benefits. Firstly, through the reduced use of fuel or electricity, emissions of carbon dioxide are reduced. The use of combined heat and power (CHP) to generate heat and electricity in a single process offers especially large reductions in CO_2 emissions compared with the central generation of electricity and local production of heat. Secondly, reduced burning of fossil fuel, whether on-site or at central power stations, reduces emissions of both sulphur and nitrogen oxides. The use of heat recovery schemes can have a double benefit. In addition to the benefits already mentioned of reducing the use of primary fuels, there will be a reduced level of local thermal pollution, whether airborne or of local watercourses. Improved effluent quality or reduced effluent volumes is often an indirect benefit of energy conservation. While this will give good cost benefits, it is also an environmental benefit, even if it may be at the level of the local sewage treatment works rather than at site level. Finally, improved energy efficiency offers the opportunity of reduced wastage through improved product quality arising from better control.

4.2   Energy monitoring and targeting

Better control of energy is possible only if decisions are based on accurate information. Monitoring and targeting (M&T) is a disciplined approach to energy management which ensures that energy resources are used to the maximum economic advantage. It has two principal functions:

- the on-going control of energy use;
- planned improvements in the efficiency of energy use.

The use of M&T can be likened to the approach taken by the accountant of a company to control financial expenditure. Just as the accountant keeps track of where money is spent (and on what), and sets budgets for the next financial year, so the M&T system is used to monitor how much energy is used and where in the process it is used. Targets can then be set in the same way as financial budgets.

Currently over 1000 industrial sites are known to be using M&T. These sites have achieved energy savings representing between 5% and 25% of their annual energy bill. The important feature of these savings is that they have mainly been achieved with little or no capital investment. Savings have resulted from improved practices, plant adjustments, operator training, etc. In addition to energy cost savings, the systematic investigation of energy use through M&T can lead to improved product quality and yield, reduced maintenance and reduced or deferred capital expenditure.

The implementation costs of M&T comprise installation costs and operating costs. Installation costs include:

- an initial site audit to identify energy accountable centres (EACs);
- the supply and installation of meters;
- computers and software;
- manpower to set up the system;
- training;
- consultancy, if required;

while operating costs include:

- meter reading and data collection costs;
- hardware/software maintenance;
- manpower to operate the system.

The total expenditure will depend on a number of factors such as the type and complexity of system being implemented, the amount of metering already present, and the method of data collection. Not all of the items listed above will be applicable to all systems.

All sites should be able to save 5% of their annual energy bill by implementing M&T. If this is linked to a 1 year payback, it allows up to 5% of the energy bill to be spent on M&T. This gives an initial guideline for expenditure. Further expansion of the M&T system can then be funded from energy cost savings.

The number of meters involved is a key factor in the cost of any M&T system. More meters give more readings, more data to analyse, more reports to produce, more data to store, all of which can increase the costs. To make M&T more cost effective, it can be necessary to optimise the design of the system, by applying it to the most significant energy users first. These areas can also act as pilots, to ease the implementation of full M&T in gradually.

4.2.1   Types of system

At its simplest, monitoring involves the systematic and regular measurement and recording of the energy consumption of the whole organisation. The target set might be the average energy consumption for a given output. For many companies this approach is too simplified to give accurate results, and it becomes necessary to sub-divide the energy use on the site into suitable EACs.

Small companies may only have a single site at which to implement M&T, but larger companies may wish to implement M&T at all sites across the company. However, it is often worth running a pilot M&T system at one site and only extending it to the whole company once it is running smoothly and generating savings at that site.

As the amount of data to be analysed increases, so does the need for a greater level of sophistication in the system. At the most basic level, with only a small number of meter readings to be dealt with, the data can be both collected and analysed manually. With a more complex system, the data can still be collected manually, but it becomes useful to input the data to a personal computer via the keyboard for data analysis and report production. At the highest levels of complexity, automatic input of the data from meters to the personal computer becomes cost effective. At this stage, the system can be very closely tied in with production control systems, and M&T can be integrated with other site information systems. It is worth noting that the automatic input of data from the refrigeration system in a meat plant, for example, could provide a clear 'due diligence' defence if it were required, by proving that the temperatures specified by

Table 4.1 Applicability of M&T systems

	Single site			Multi-site		
	Invoice	Main meters	Sub-meters	Invoice	Main meters	Sub-meters
Manual	√	√	√	√	?	×
Keyboard input	√	√	√	√	√	√
Automatic input	×	?	√	×	√	√

regulations had been met. The suitability of the different types and applications of M&T systems is illustrated in Table 4.1.

4.2.2   System implementation

A prerequisite of the successful implementation of M&T is high level management commitment. Without this, the system may run well while its champion is pushing for its acceptance, but is likely to fall into disuse if this key person is absent from the site for any length of time, for whatever reason. An M&T system can survive in the event of the person responsible for its day-to-day management leaving the company, but it will only do so if there is high level management commitment to the principles of M&T, which has resulted in the M&T system being integrated into the ordinary site and production management.

It may be that the senior management need to be convinced of the benefits of M&T. This could be done by monitoring energy use for the site as a whole over a period of time and relating it to production output. Showing the variability of the specific energy consumption, and the savings that would be achieved if the current average energy use were not exceeded, would in most cases provide a strong argument for the implementation of M&T.

The introduction of M&T requires careful consideration. Its adoption must form part of the overall strategic plan. It may be that a computer-aided solution is inappropriate. Whatever system is specified, it is more important that it is utilised to the full than that it uses the latest computer software. It must be appreciated that the M&T system itself does not save energy costs; it only provides the information to enable these savings to be made. An effective M&T system should operate for many years, so it is worth taking the time to set it up properly. As with any management tool, an M&T system will only be as successful as the time, effort and thought that went into its implementation allow it to be.

Training forms an important part of the implementation of an M&T system. The training does not have to be a formal course, but it is important that all staff who will have dealings with the M&T system understand what is required of them and what they can expect of the system. A computer aided M&T system works at two levels: routine and investigative. Routine operation involves the input of data and the production of standard regular reports. This function can be carried out by relatively low level staff. Investigative operation involves the detailed examination of the M&T results to look at performance anomalies, or investigate process changes, 'what if' calculations, etc. This requires more experienced management skills and is best carried out by relatively high level staff such as the engineering manager or accountant.

The two key strategic parameters in any M&T system are the reporting period and the number of meters. Too long a reporting period and the system will have high inertia and a slow response; too short and there can be an excess of data associated with high operating costs and problems with data analysis. The optimum reporting period depends on the M&T system as a whole. The most common reporting periods are the week and the month, but they can be mixed or varied on computer-aided systems. Weekly reporting is often used for single sub-metered sites, complex sites, and high energy sites or processes. Monthly reporting is appropriate for large multi-site, utility-based applications. The frequency with which different people receive the reports can also be varied; the chief executive of a multi-site company will probably only want quarterly and annual reports, while the manager of an EAC is likely to receive weekly reports and an annual summary. It is important to remember that the function of the reports is not merely to inform; reports initiate action and show results.

The choice and location of meters can be of critical importance influencing whether the system is unwieldy and over-complex or easy to use, giving appropriate data. There is nothing wrong with starting with a small number of meters and installing more later in those locations where more detailed data would be useful. Meters can be calculated meters, where the consumption is given by the difference between two meter readings, for example, the difference between a main meter and a sub-meter. Care must be taken here as any losses such as those on a water or steam line will be attributed to the calculated meter.

A properly implemented M&T system provides the following benefits:

- better control of energy use, an increased awareness of energy costs, and a greater commitment to improving the efficiency of energy use;
- good energy cost information for making manufacturing and commercial decisions and for forecasting future energy budgets;

- reductions in energy costs, typically of about 10% and, exceptionally, as high as 25%, achieved by improvements in the use of energy, without significant capital expenditure and within existing workloads;
- better information on the ways in which the efficiency of energy use can be increased, and on the cost savings that can be made through improvements in working practices or through capital investment;
- further reductions in energy bills through cost-effective capital investment in measures which improve the energy efficiency of buildings, plant or manufacturing processes;
- more reliable procedures for measuring actual energy cost savings achieved and evaluating the return on energy-saving investments.

Indirect benefits from the introduction of M&T systems include the more satisfactory control of environmental conditions within buildings and, in manufacturing industry, improvements in output, products of higher and more consistent quality, and lower reject rates. In manufacturing industry, M&T can be the key to achieving substantial energy cost savings; it provides the motivation for an improvement in performance and persuades senior management of the value of investment in improved energy efficiency.

4.2.3 Case study

Table 4.3 shows an energy monitoring sheet from a small bakery. Energy use is read from the main site meters on a monthly basis and correlated with the production in kg of flour used. At this level, the data can be analysed either manually, building up the graph shown in Figure 4.1 month by month, or on the same computer used for the bakery accounts. This then allows an easy comparison of any time period with another, e.g. May this year with May last year.

The energy data could be taken from the bakery invoices, but these invoices are often for an estimated energy use, and even if meters are read, it is rarely on the same day each month. By taking the trouble to read the meters themselves, the bakery can be sure that the energy use and flour use do relate to the same time period. If it becomes apparent that it would be useful, the frequency of monitoring can easily be increased from monthly to weekly, either permanently, or for a short period to help sort out a particular problem.

By comparing the data shown in Figure 4.1 and Table 4.2, it can be seen that while the energy use was lower in August than in any other month, the production was also low. Thus, the specific energy consumption, or performance indicator, was high. The plant could have operated more efficiently if oven loading had been improved and waiting time had been cut. In May and April the production levels were very similar, but the

Table 4.2 Example of an energy monitoring sheet for a bakery

	Gas (00s) (cubic feet) A	Gas (kWh) A × 30.3 = B	Electricity (kWh used) C	Total energy use (kWh) B + C = D	Total product (kg of flour) E	Performance indicator (kWh/kg) D/E = F
Jan	51.5	1560	14400	15960	5100	3.13
Feb	68.1	2063	14050	16113	5400	2.98
Mar	46.6	1412	14642	16054	5700	2.82
Apr	33.4	1012	13950	14962	6100	2.45
May	24.4	739	12220	12959	6000	2.16
June	46.6	1413	11748	13161	5100	2.58
July	33.3	1009	12079	13088	4600	2.85
Aug	37.4	1133	10440	11573	3500	3.31
Sep	50.9	1542	12487	14029	5100	2.75
Oct	38.1	1154	13616	14770	5400	2.74
Nov	43.0	1303	14274	15577	5800	2.69
Dec	47.1	1427	12945	14372	6400	2.25
Total		15778	156851	172629	64200	2.69 (average)

specific energy consumption was 14% better in May than in April. This was because the mix of products allowed a better scheduling of the oven.

It is important to recognise that seasonal effects may produce a variation in the specific energy consumption. There could be a natural fluctuation in the level at which the plant operates at different times of the year; in many food and drink industries it is simply not possible to operate at 100% capacity all year round because of the timing of the agricultural production output. Some processes require more energy as the ambient temperature

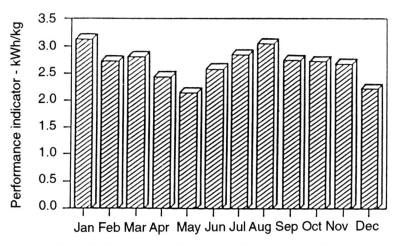

Figure 4.1 Graph of monthly energy performance for a bakery.

drops, and there will be an increased demand for space heating in winter. In summer, the electricity use may increase as a result of a need for more refrigeration. There are many statistical methods that can be used to try and isolate the 'true' variations in energy use from the variations caused by the above factors. One of the simplest is to look at the running total specific energy consumption over the last twelve months. If this increases on a month-by-month basis, then there has been a real increase in energy use.

4.3   Steam/hot water systems

4.3.1   The heating medium

Why use steam? The simplest explanation is that it is a convenient means of transporting heat from the fuel being burned in the boiler to the point in the process where it is required. The alternatives are to use water or some other liquid to carry the heat. Each method has advantages and disadvantages.

4.3.2   Hot water

Water is a relatively poor means of transporting heat. It can carry only a limited amount of heat and the heat transfer is restricted by the temperature drop, which is usually only 10–20°C. Its ability to carry heat is increased slightly if the water is pressurised, but again only a relatively small fraction of this is available in practice. Nevertheless, water can be the most appropriate heat transfer medium for low temperature processes (up to 120°C) where some temperature variation can be tolerated, and is generally the preferred choice for space heating applications. Many food and drink sites have no requirement for steam. There is always, however, a fairly large requirement for hot water to meet strict hygiene regulations on washing down and cleaning. Hot water can be supplied in several ways:

- by a conventional gas- or oil-fired boiler which is also used in winter for space heating;
- by a point-of-use water heater;
- by using off-peak electricity to heat water in a storage tank.

Generally the use of a gas- or oil-fired boiler will be the most efficient and, in the long term, cost effective option. However, if a boiler is used only for water heating in summer, standing losses can be high because of the low load. Rather than using the boiler in these circumstances, it may be more economic to use a point-of-use water heater.

Under some circumstances it may be economic to heat the water electrically; however, on energy efficiency grounds the case is less clear cut.

4.3.3   Thermal fluids

Thermal fluids such as mineral oils have a much higher heat carrying capacity, up to five times that of water. This reduces the volume required for the same heat transfer, and so gives lower installation costs. However, thermal fluids are expensive, and tend to become acidic during use, so requiring replacements at regular intervals.

4.3.4   Steam

Steam has three main advantages as a heat transfer medium. Firstly, most of the heat is carried in the form of the latent heat required to evaporate the water. This is much greater than the sensible heat carried by hot fluids, and also means that the heat transfer occurs at constant temperature. Secondly, the temperature of the steam is dependent on the steam pressure, giving a simple method of temperature control. Thirdly, as a result, steam has a high heat carrying capacity, leading to simpler piping systems.

4.3.5   Raising steam

When raising steam, the water temperature must first be raised to its boiling point by adding sensible heat. Supplying the latent heat of evaporation then turns the water into steam. For a kettle operating at normal atmospheric pressure, 419 kJ of sensible heat would be needed to raise the temperature of 1 kg of water from freezing point (0°C) to boiling point (100°C). To convert 1 kg of water at 100°C into steam, a further 2258 kJ are required. It is this large quantity of latent heat that is recovered by the process at the point of use.

If the pressure is increased, the water will no longer boil at 100°C but at a higher temperature. As can be seen in Figure 4.2, the total heat content of steam increases with pressure, but the useful latent heat content decreases as more of the input is required as sensible heat, shown as heat in the condensate. Because the boiling point increases as the pressure increases, the process heat requirement can be exactly matched. If, for example, a material being processed undergoes a certain chemical change at 170°C, it can be seen from Figure 4.2 that a pressure of at least 7 bar is required. At this pressure, less latent heat is available from each kilogram of steam, as shown in Figure 4.3, so proportionately more steam is required. For greater accuracy, the relationship between sensible and latent heat content of steam at different pressures has been established experimentally and these data are tabulated in the form of steam tables.

4.3.6   Steam distribution and pressure

For the optimum performance of steam-using equipment, a supply of steam of the right quantity and quality is vital. The right quality means

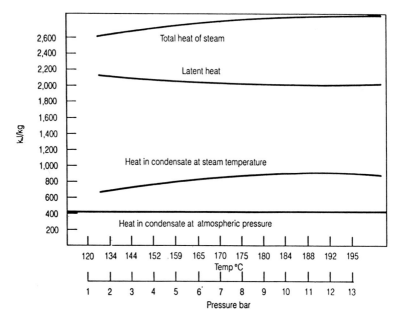

Figure 4.2 The properties of steam. (All pressures are gauge unless otherwise stated.)

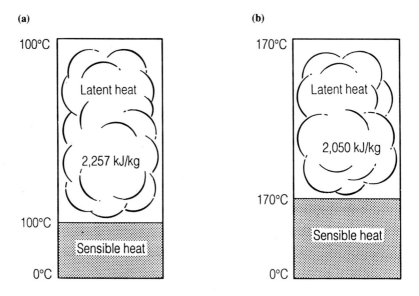

Figure 4.3 Latent heat content of steam at (a) atmospheric pressure and (b) 7 bar.

that the steam is at the correct pressure to satisfy process temperature requirements, for example to give a specific rate of heating within a process. The ideal steam distribution system would take the shortest possible route from the boiler to the process, and use the smallest possible pipework consistent with acceptable friction losses and pressure drop. This minimises heat losses in the system. The final design of a practical steam distribution system is a compromise between this ideal and practical constraints.

Steam should be generated at the pressure necessary to meet the maximum required by the equipment in the system. In practice, the pressure chosen is a balance between capital costs and the overall efficiency of the system. High pressure distribution minimises the size of pipework required, so reducing capital costs. As the pressure increases, the specific volume of steam decreases. At atmospheric pressure, 1 kg of steam occupies 1.67 m^3 but at 7 bar it only occupies 0.24 m^3 so a smaller pipe can be used to carry the same quantity of steam. The smaller pipe diameter leads in principle to reduced quantities of insulation, but the higher temperatures associated with the high pressure steam reduce these benefits. The heat loss per m^2 at 10 bar is about 15% more than at 5 bar. Steam leakage losses are also higher, being twice as much at 10 bar as at 5 bar. The use of higher pressures may entail the use of thicker-walled, more expensive pipework and fittings. There is also a greater potential for producing flash steam, by reducing the pressure of the hot condensate, and this is wasted unless there is a requirement for low pressure steam. The optimum pressure for the system is determined by the balance between these factors. It may be better to have two separate small systems than to have long pipework runs serving steam needs at different pressures.

4.3.7 Pipework

While new steam installations usually have well thought out distribution systems, modifications are often made over the years, and it can be worthwhile reviewing the system to try and eliminate redundant pipework. This will reduce heat losses, and the costs involved can usually be recovered quickly through the reduced steam requirement. This is also a good opportunity to renew the pipework insulation where necessary. The pipework must be correctly sized for the system pressure. If the pipe diameter is too small, insufficient steam at a high enough pressure will get through to the process. If, on the other hand, the pipe diameter is too large, surface heat losses will be increased. Proper sizing of the steam lines means selecting a pipe diameter that gives the minimum acceptable pressure drop between the boiler and the user.

The simplest method involves calculating the steam velocity in a pipe for a given flow rate. The specific volume of steam for the chosen distribution pressure can be obtained from steam tables. The only other factor that needs to be known is the quality of the steam, whether it is wet or superheated. Wet steam contains water droplets which can cause damage and erosion when they hit the pipe walls at bends or at valves and fittings. Superheated steam, which has been heated above its boiling point at the given pressure, contains no water droplets, nor are any likely to condense out in the pipe; the danger of water droplet damage is therefore negligible and higher pipe velocities can be used.

The practical guidelines are as follows:

- superheated steam velocity: 50–70 m/s;
- saturated steam velocity: 30–40 m/s;
- wet steam velocity or exhaust velocity: 20–30 m/s.

A number of charts and computer programs have been developed over the years to aid in sizing pipework. In almost all cases, the results fall within the velocity bands given above.

4.3.8   Drain points and condensate

As steam cools it reverts to water, and the condensate produced in a steam line is a nuisance and can be potentially disastrous. At least, the condensate lying at the bottom of a pipe effectively reduces the pipe cross-sectional area, so requiring increased velocities and causing higher pressure drop. In the worst case, the condensate layer becomes deep enough to be picked up by the steam and forced down the pipe as a plug. These high velocity plugs have difficulty passing round bends and through fittings. The resulting water hammer can lead to damage to the system and even failure of the pipe or of fittings such as valves. It is important that there is provision for removing condensate from the distribution before it can cause a problem. This is a part of good system design, and for these drain points to be effective, the pipework must be installed so that the condensate flows towards these points.

When the steam gives up its latent heat to the process being heated, it condenses. This condensate still contains about 20% of the original heat content put in by the fuel. If it is thrown away, this represents a considerable waste, so it is preferable to either use it in another process or retain it within the steam system for return to the boiler. Condensate that has not been in direct contact with the process is chemically pure and therefore needs little water treatment apart from pH adjustment. Both water treatment costs and blowdown losses can therefore be reduced. Where it is uneconomic to return the condensate to the boiler house, for example because of the length of pipe run that would be required, another use for it should be sought. If there is any doubt as to the purity of the condensate it must not be directly returned to the boiler feedwater. The consequences of returning contaminated condensate to the boiler can be serious, even resulting in the failure of the boiler itself.

4.3.9   Feedwater treatment and blowdown

Any water, regardless of its source, contains some impurities. These occur mainly in solution, but may include suspended organic and mineral matter. The dissolved minerals causing the greatest problems are calcium and magnesium salts. These do not remain in solution as the water is heated; they become less soluble and eventually precipitate out. Water treatment is designed either to prevent this occurring or to make sure that the precipitate does not form a scale on the metal heat transfer surface and is in a form that can easily be removed from the boiler by blowing down. This treatment is usually achieved in one of two ways:

- external pre-treatment methods remove or modify the problem mineral salts;
- chemicals are added directly to the boiler water to prevent scale formation and corrosion.

External treatment consists either of converting the calcium and magnesium (or temporary hardness) salts into non-scale forming compounds of almost infinite solubility, or of removing the temporary hardness salts altogether. The first approach is the most common and is known as base-exchange softening, while the second process is called demineralisation. Over the past 10 years, reverse osmosis has sometimes been used in place of demineralisation. The process used will depend on the type of boiler installed, the quality of the raw water, the boiler rating and the amount of condensate returned to the boiler house.

Internal water treatment regimes can be very complex, depending on the type of boiler, the chemical composition of the raw water and whether or not the steam will be in direct contact with the process. The basic rule is never to use more of these chemicals than absolutely necessary, as not only are they expensive, but they also add to the total dissolved solids (TDS) of the boiler water, which means that more blowdown is necessary.

To maintain TDS concentration below the recommended level, water at the steam temperature must be blown down from the boiler and replaced with cooler low TDS feedwater. This process must take into consideration not only the cost of the energy used to heat the blowdown water to the steam temperature, but also the cost of buying the water, treating it and pumping it into the boiler. Too much blowdown represents a considerable waste of both energy and money. Even when demineralisation is the method of water treatment used, some blowdown is still necessary to control the build-up of other chemicals injected into the boiler to prevent oxygen corrosion, etc. Blowdown should be kept to the minimum required to maintain the boiler manufacturers design limits for TDS. A regular sampling and testing routine will keep this under control. It is possible to recover about 50% of the heat in the blowdown using equipment which is readily available.

4.3.10   Improving energy efficiency: what to do first

There are many ways in which the energy consumption and costs of boiler plant can be significantly reduced. The approach is the same, whether one is dealing with an old system that has been altered and developed over the years, or considering the proposed design for a brand new installation.

If combustion efficiency alone is considered, a quick assessment of the system performance can be made provided both the exit temperature and the O_2 or CO_2 content of the flue gases is known. This does not represent the total extent of the losses, however. Boiler shell losses, blowdown losses

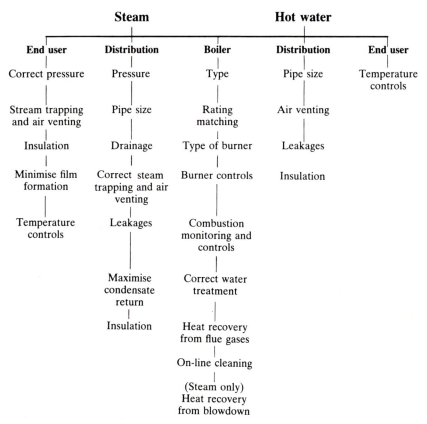

Figure 4.4 Improving energy efficiency: what to do first.

and possible losses from combustibles remaining in ash must also be considered.

Figure 4.4 shows the options when maximising the system energy efficiency. It should be noted that this does not start at the boiler house, but with the end user. Poor control or use of heat at this point is potentially the biggest threat to thermal efficiency. The distribution system is the next most likely to be poorly designed and to incur high losses. Only when these two areas have been rectified, should attention be paid to making the overall boiler plant as efficient as possible. Even at this stage, the first objective is to maximise the efficiency that the boiler manufacturer has built into the unit. Here consideration should be given to implementing combined heat and power. The final step involves improving the original design by upgrading controls or improving heat recovery. Several standard texts are available on this subject, and some sources of further information are given in Section 4.6.

4.4 Refrigeration

Refrigeration is used in industry for cooling and freezing of products, condensing vapours, maintaining environmental conditions and for cold storage. There is a vast number of different applications, and the sizes and types of plant can vary greatly. The food and drink industries account for some 32% of industrial refrigeration use. Refrigeration systems can represent a large fraction of an individual site's electricity costs; up to 70% in some cases. Yet it is common to find systems in service that are using up to 20% more energy than they should be. Most of the 'faults' can be easily rectified, requiring little or no capital expenditure.

Major barriers to maintaining good plant efficiency can be the relative complexity of refrigeration systems and plant operators' lack of understanding of efficiency issues. Most engineers have a good understanding of the operational and maintenance aspects of boiler plant and consequently, it is rare to find large boiler installations operating substantially below expected levels of performance. However, the converse can be true for refrigeration plant. Many refrigeration engineers concentrate on obtaining maximum reliability. In some cases, an inefficient operating mode is more convenient to the operator. Full management commitment to improved efficiency is essential if these problems are to be overcome.

Acquiring an awareness of the cost of refrigeration for a site under investigation is an important first step towards creating a more efficient and cost-effective plant. It is not only operating costs that need to be carefully considered. An industrial refrigeration system represents a significant capital expense and can be a vital part of the production process. Effective refrigeration is required for good food quality and hygiene.

There are also environmental effects, in particular the use of CFC refrigerants (chlorofluorocarbons) which have been identified as having a depleting effect on the ozone layer. Excessive use of energy contributes to global
warming, acid rain, increased nuclear power requirements, etc.

4.4.1   Refrigeration cycles

It is important that the basic principles of refrigeration are fully understood
if a refrigeration plant is to be effectively operated and maintained. The
majority of refrigeration systems are driven by a machine that compresses
and pumps refrigerant vapour round a sealed circuit. Heat is absorbed and
rejected through heat exchangers. These systems work on what is called a
vapour recompression cycle. There are other types of plant that can be
used to obtain a cooling effect, but these are not in common use.

Figure 4.5 shows a simple, single stage, vapour compressor refrigeration
system. Low pressure refrigerant enters the compressor where its pressure
is raised. The high pressure vapour then passes to the condenser where it
is cooled and liquefied. The heat extracted in the condenser is released to
the environment. High pressure liquid passes from the condenser through
the expansion valve, where its pressure is lowered, and into the evaporator. The low pressure liquid in the evaporator boils to produce low
pressure vapour and the cycle is repeated. The heat required to boil and
vaporise the liquid in the evaporator is taken from the substance that
requires cooling, e.g. air, water, alcohol, process fluids, or foodstuffs.

Figure 4.6 shows the same cycle on a diagram of refrigerant pressure
against enthalpy (the total heat content of the refrigerant). The difference

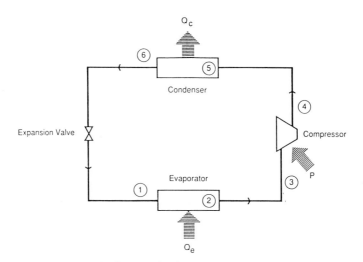

Figure 4.5 Schematic diagram of a simple single-stage refrigeration system.

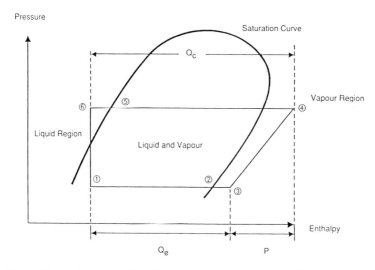

Figure 4.6 Single-stage refrigeration system on a pressure enthalpy diagram.

in enthalpy between two points in the cycle represents the energy absorbed or liberated. The energy input to the evaporator (cooling achieved) and the compressor (power consumed) and the energy liberated in the condenser (condenser heat load) are illustrated in the diagram. The sum of the energy absorbed by the refrigerant at the evaporator and the power consumed by the compressor is equal to the heat extracted in the condenser.

To appreciate how a refrigeration system works, it is necessary to understand how boiling points of refrigerants vary with pressure. At a low pressure (e.g. in the evaporator), the refrigerant will boil at a low temperature and do useful cooling. This is referred to as the evaporating temperature. At the higher pressure in the condenser, the boiling point is much higher and the refrigerant can be cooled and liquefied by air or water at or near ambient temperatures. This is referred to as the condensing temperature.

Condensing and evaporating temperatures are very important in refrigeration. Since liquid is changing phase in the evaporator and condenser, the conditions are saturated and the temperatures correspond to particular pressures. Condensing and evaporating temperatures are normally measured using pressure gauges at the compressor suction and discharge. The gauges are often calibrated in temperature for the particular refrigerant concerned.

Figure 4.7 shows the 'heat pulley analogy', which is a useful aid to help understand refrigeration efficiency. Refrigeration systems are like pulley systems. In refrigeration, the objective is to lift a 'packet of energy' from

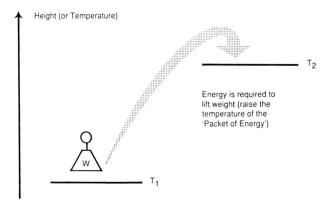

Figure 4.7 Heat pulley analogy.

a low temperature to a higher temperature. This is like lifting a weight from a low level to a higher level. Energy is required to lift the 'energy packet' to the higher temperature, and the greater the 'distance' between the two temperature levels, the more energy is required. It follows that energy requirements are increased, and therefore efficiency decreased, by lower evaporating temperatures and higher condensing temperatures.

The single-stage cycle is the most commonly encountered in industrial refrigeration. However, for larger applications at temperatures below −20°C, two- and three-stage systems are used to achieve higher efficiencies. In a single-stage system, there are four major components:

- evaporator;
- condenser;
- compressor;
- expansion valve.

These components are available in a variety of types. Evaporators may be shell and tube, finned coil units, plate exchangers, etc. Condensers include shell and tube air cooled and evaporative types. Compressors may be screw, reciprocating, centrifugal or rotary, and expansion valves include thermostatic, float and electronic types. Different combinations of components are appropriate for different applications.

4.4.2   Auxiliary equipment

Auxiliary equipment can be a significant consumer of electricity in a refrigeration system. This equipment includes:

- evaporator pumps and fans;
- condenser pumps and fans;
- secondary refrigerant distribution pumps and fans;

- oil pumps;
- defrost heaters.

Auxiliary equipment should be taken into consideration when looking at costs. Auxiliaries can greatly affect the efficiency of systems running at part-load, or add to the cooling load that the refrigeration has to cope with as well as using electricity themselves, effectively meaning that they have to be paid for twice.

4.4.3   Coefficient of performance

The coefficient of performance is probably the most useful parameter for assessing efficiency, and is defined as the ratio of cooling achieved to power used by the compressor.

$$COP = \frac{\text{Cooling achieved}}{\text{Power required by the compressor}}$$

A high COP implies that a refrigeration plant is achieving more cooling for a given power input, i.e. the system is more efficient. A lower COP means the plant is less efficient.

Unlike most efficiency parameters (e.g. boiler efficiency), COP is not expressed as a percentage and it is not usually less than 1. For most industrial applications, COPs can be expected to range from about 2 (for plants at around $-40°C$ evaporating temperature) to 5 (for plants at around $0°C$ evaporating temperature). COP can vary quite considerably as the ambient weather conditions and process requirements change.

The definition of COP given above is the one most commonly used in industry. However, it is not always the best parameter to use when evaluating a complete system. Energy is required not only by the compressor but also by auxiliary equipment such as evaporator and condenser fans and pumps. System COP is defined as the ratio of cooling achieved to the total power input to the system.

$$\text{System COP} = \frac{\text{Cooling achieved}}{\text{Total power used (incl. auxiliaries)}}$$

4.4.4   Factors affecting efficiency

It is important to understand the factors that affect efficiency and therefore operating costs. Savings can be achieved by effectively controlling these factors.

- *Cooling loads*: The importance of cooling loads on the running costs of refrigeration plant cannot be overstressed. If the cooling load is higher than necessary, then more cooling is needed, and the operating costs are higher. There are two main categories of cooling loads: process loads and auxiliary loads. Process loads include the removal of sensible heat in the cooling or chilling of fluids or solids such as beer or meat, latent cooling in the condensing of vapours, and temperature control for a reaction such as the fermentation of beer. Auxiliary loads include heat gains from poorly maintained insulation, lights and fans in cold spaces, heat ingress from open doors, pumps for the circulation of chilled fluids and excessive defrosting.

- *Evaporating temperature*: The higher the evaporating temperature the higher the COP and the lower the running cost. Raising the evaporating temperature by 1°C reduces operating costs by 2–4%. Higher evaporating temperatures can be achieved using good control systems and set points, and by making best use of available evaporator surface by avoiding fouling, frosting, excessive superheating, poor heat transfer, etc.

- *Condensing temperature*: A lower condensing temperature means lower operating costs. A 1°C drop in condensing temperature reduces operating costs by 2–4%. Lower condensing temperatures can be achieved with good controls and by making best use of condensing surface by avoiding fouling, blocking, poor heat transfer, etc.

- *Compressor efficiency*: A higher compressor efficiency means lower operating costs. Isentropic efficiency is the best measure of compressor efficiency. With most types of compressor, particularly screw and centrifugal, efficiency falls dramatically at part-load operation. The compressor motor efficiency is also important. In general, high efficiencies can be maintained by avoiding part-load operation, using the best compressors at any given time, and by good compressor maintenance. An increase in costs of 20% or more can result from incorrectly controlled compressors.

- *Auxiliary power*: The auxiliary power requirement of a refrigeration system can account for 25% of the total consumption, and even more when systems are operated at part-load. Reducing auxiliary power can dramatically increase efficiency. Good use of controls to avoid excessive operation of auxiliaries, avoidance of flow blockages, and good maintenance of pumps, fans and lights are specific good practice which can be explored. Poor control of auxiliaries can increase costs by 20% or more.

- *Part-load operation*: One of the most common reasons for poor refrigeration plant efficiency is part-load operation. Most plants spend less than 20% of the year at, or close to, the nominal design point. During the rest of the year, cooler ambient temperatures allow lower condensing temperatures and reduced cooling duties alter the required compressor capacity. Unless these part-load conditions are properly taken into account it is likely that the system COP will be poor, even if the COP at the nominal design point is good.

4.4.5   Calculating annual costs

It is important to develop an awareness of the annual cost of energy for refrigeration, as this helps quantify the effects of poor maintenance and operation. The best method of calculating the annual cost of refrigeration systems is to use electricity meters to measure the consumption in relevant areas. Remember to include:

- central plant (i.e. the compressors);
- main auxiliaries, including condenser and evaporator fans and pumps, and secondary refrigerant-air distribution pumps and fans;
- 'secondary' auxiliaries, i.e. other equipment which is not directly associated with the refrigeration plant but which affects its performance such as lights in cold stores, defrost equipment in cold rooms, etc.

It is useful to break down the use of energy as far as possible. This may highlight some surprises such as very high auxiliary loads or baseloads. If the results are suspect, but the costs are clearly high, then it becomes easy to justify the installation of further meters to establish costs more accurately.

4.4.6   Case study: cooling from too high a temperature

Figure 4.8a shows a prawn processing line where prawns are 'cooked' in hot water and then leave the cooker at around 70°C on a conveyor. They are then cooled with mains water at about 10°C, followed by chilled water at about 2°C and finally they are frozen with liquid nitrogen.

During site work, it was discovered that prawns were entering the final stage of cooling (liquid nitrogen) at 40°C. This temperature is very high. In general, the highest temperature refrigerant is the cheapest, i.e. cooling with chilled water is much cheaper than cooling with nitrogen. Similarly, the 'free' cooling with mains water is cheaper than chilled water cooling. In this case, it was found that increasing the mains and chilled water flow rates, together with minor adjustments to spray nozzles to improve heat transfer, could reduce the prawn temperature at the inlet to the nitrogen section by 30°C, giving significant cost savings. The new conditions are shown in Figure 4.8b.

4.4.7   Other issues

The factors discussed above will help to achieve the efficiency that was 'designed in' when the refrigeration system was specified and installed. Good design of the system will optimise this 'designed in' efficiency, aid good maintenance and operation and so maximise the working efficiency of the refrigeration plant. Design of refrigeration systems is complex and

(a)

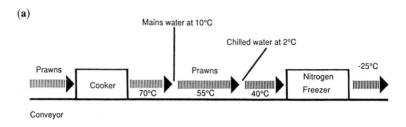

(b)

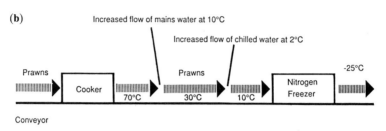

Figure 4.8 Prawn processing. For explanation of parts (a) and (b) see text.

the best solutions are almost always site-specific. Several good standard texts are available on this subject, and some sources of further information are given in Section 4.6.

An issue of increasing relevance is the choice of refrigerant. In the past, refrigerants were selected on the basis of cost, performance of the resulting cycle, toxicity, flammability and pressure constraints. Now ozone depletion potential has to be added to the list and global warming potential may also feature as a consideration. A number of refrigerants are being phased out (R11, R12, R502), some replacements have been developed to take their place (R123, R134a), and some refrigerants that have been well known for some time are receiving renewed attention (ammonia). Some of the new refrigerants are blends, designed as transition substances, to be used until long-term replacements for conventional fluids are developed. This is an area in a rapid state of change, and it is recommended that up-to-date expert advice is sought before a refrigerant choice is made.

4.5 Combined heat and power

Producing heat from fuel is generally an efficient process with modern boilers achieving fuel efficiencies of around 80% and condensing boilers over 90%. However, the conversion of fuel to electricity in the conventional power station is more wasteful, with even the most efficient modern power stations losing around 50% of the input energy as waste heat. With

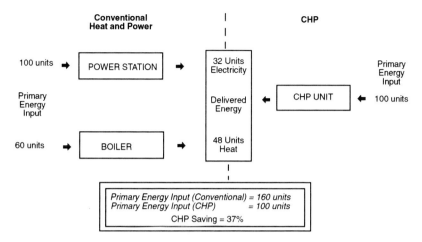

Figure 4.9 Comparison of conventional heat and power with CHP.

most traditional power stations the overall efficiency drops to around 30%, once transmission and distribution losses are included.

However, overall energy savings of between 20 and 40% are achievable if the power generation is located where the heat produced is also used. This is the combined heat and power (CHP) concept, illustrated in Figure 4.9.

4.5.1   CHP plant

CHP, or cogeneration, is the on-site generation of heat and power as a single process. The engineering principles behind this process have long been understood, and the technology has been refined and developed over the years, so that now, modern CHP systems can achieve efficiencies of up to 90%.

A typical CHP plant consists of a reciprocating engine, gas turbine or steam turbine driving a generator which produces the electricity; the exhaust gases pass through a recovery unit which provides the heat in the form required by the site (as steam, for example). A schematic is shown in Figure 4.10. Any fuel can be used, subject to environmental constraints. However, some wastes and by-products may be more suited to CHP based on an incinerator/boiler and steam turbine.

A CHP installation may supply part or all of the site requirements for heat and part or all of the electricity with little or no export of either heat or power. The optimum size of a CHP scheme is a function of the local heat and power requirements. The electrical output of installed schemes varies from 15 kW to more than 20 MW. The proportions of heat and power (heat/power ratio) may vary from less than 1:1 (reciprocating engine

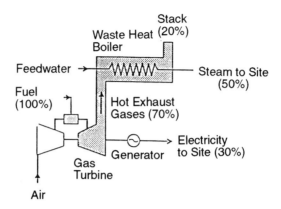

Figure 4.10 CHP schematic.

based and combined cycle cogeneration schemes) to more than 10:1 (steam turbine based schemes). There is thus no standard CHP kit; each installation must be tailored to the particular site requirements. Intensive developments over the past decade have ensured a wide variety of generator drives and heat conversion equipment, enabling the best match of CHP package to site requirements. CHP schemes offer a large amount of flexibility, so that there is usually a combination of plant and fuels that can match most individual requirements.

The installed cost of the CHP plant will be approximately £500/kWe or £2.5 million for a 5 MWe CHP scheme. A scheme may be entirely self-financed, with all profits accruing to the company, or it may be partly or wholly taken over by a contract energy management company. This would of course entail an appropriate profit-sharing element.

In general, total energy costs can be reduced by up to 40%, which is equivalent to annual savings of up to £150 000 for each MWe installed. Correctly applied, CHP will show a profitable return on the considerable capital outlay involved, plus the intangible but valuable benefit of enhanced security of supply. Financial savings quickly offset the additional costs incurred, giving a payback within as little as 3 or 4 years.

CHP, because of its unique energy benefits, can use primary energy nearly three times as effectively as conventional power stations. By using less fuel, CHP significantly reduces emissions, particularly of carbon dioxide. It is predicted that if the present trend towards high efficiency gas-fired CHP continues and accelerates, it could in time lead to reductions of as much as 10% in UK carbon dioxide emissions. CHP's inherently greater efficiency makes it a proven and cost-effective solution to combating global warming.

In the food and drink industry, energy consumption only represents 2–3% of the production costs, and hence in general has received a

Table 4.3

Cogeneration equipment	No. of sites	Cogeneration capacity (MWe)
Back pressure steam turbine	19	168
Gas turbine	7	50
Reciprocating engine	4	3
Compression ignition engine	0	0
Total	28	221

relatively low priority in many organisations. Despite this, a number of the larger food and drink sites have cogeneration installations. These tend to be in the parts of the sector where the process is continuous and/or energy intensive and reminiscent of the chemicals sector. Current installed capacity of cogeneration in the sector as a whole is over 200 MWe.

Table 4.3 gives a breakdown of the type of cogeneration equipment used in the food and drink industry. It can be seen that 81% of schemes are based on steam turbine plant and 18% on gas turbines. These are generally used on the bulk processing sites, especially sugar processing. It is estimated that a doubling of this capacity is the realistic economic potential for cogeneration in this sector with a payback period of between 3 and 5 years.

4.5.2   Suitability for CHP

A detailed appraisal of the site will indicate whether CHP is a viable proposition. It is recommended that the appraisal of CHP should be undertaken in two stages:

- *Stage 1*: Initial appraisal to determine if it is worth committing the resources necessary to undertake a detailed technical appraisal.
- *Stage 2*: If Stage 1 shows that CHP is viable in principle, a detailed technical appraisal should be undertaken. This involves analysing a significant amount of accurate load and site data, to enable an efficient and cost effective CHP unit to be specified. It will also determine if the overall plant performance can be enhanced by plant optimisation, export of electricity, heat dumping and integration of CHP with the existing standby plant. In most cases, it is necessary to use the services of a specialist consultant to undertake the detailed sizing and evaluation.

Although the profitability of CHP generally results from its cheap electricity, its success hinges on using by-product heat productively and the prime criterion is a suitable heat requirement. If there is a site demand for heat for at least 5000 h in the year, a base load and a simultaneous heat and power requirement, CHP is a likely proposition. CHP can be installed on existing sites where boiler plant is adequate. However, the case for CHP can be significantly improved when:

- existing boiler capacity needs to be replaced;
- new facilities are being planned;
- the electrical infrastructure, switchgear or site supply point need upgrading;
- CHP can also be designed to supply standby power when public supply fails.

For steam-related processes of 3 MW or more thermal input, gas turbines and large reciprocating engines of 1 MW are the best size of plant. Steam processes with an input of less than 2 MW are unlikely to raise steam from CHP; however, CHP systems are available for low temperature hot water applications. In these cases, packaged CHP should be considered. The CHP decision tree in Figure 4.11 enables a rough assessment to be made of whether the site is a good candidate for CHP.

4.5.3   Case study

United Biscuits manufactures a range of biscuits at its Levenshulme works. It is one of five factories operated by McVitie's Group, a division of United Biscuits (UK) Ltd, that manufacture biscuits and snacks. The site includes a range of processes which include mixing, baking, conveying, cooling and wrapping. Operation is based on a 24-h day, 6 days a week for more than 48 weeks per year. The site's energy bill is approximately £1 million per year with an average weekday imported electrical load of 4 MW. The steam demand varies between 2 tonnes/h in summer and 5 tonnes/h in winter and was supplied by three boilers.

The CHP scheme involved the replacement of two of the three existing boilers on site with a 1 MWe Turbomeca Makila TI gas turbine and a Beel composite boiler. The cogeneration system was installed in the boiler house with a number of modifications that included acoustically cladding the enclosure. The turbine, which can be fuelled on either natural gas or gas oil, has an electrical output of 1000 kW, with a generation efficiency of 26% (net calorific value basis). The composite boiler is rated at 5.9 tonnes of steam per h at 10 bar(g). It comprises two sections that can be fired independently. The heat recovery section produces 2.3 tonnes/h of steam, while the direct fired section can produce up to 3.6 tonnes/h. The direct fired section can be fuelled by either natural gas or gas oil via a dual fuel burner.

The cogeneration scheme was installed by the INENCO Group as part of a site wide Contract Energy Management (CEM) contract to supply

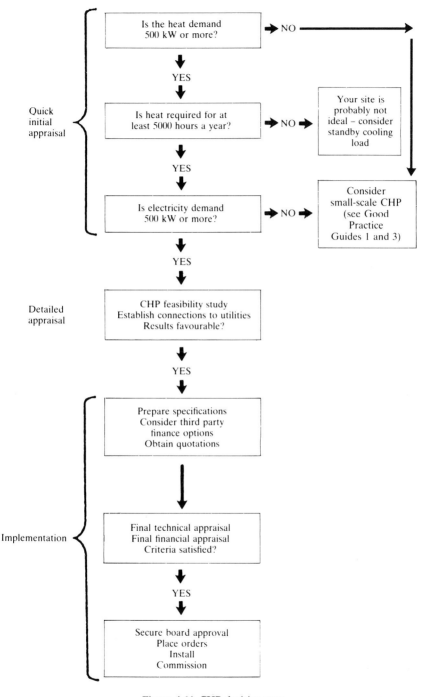

Figure 4.11 CHP decision tree.

utility services to United Biscuits. INENCO have undertaken a comprehensive range of energy efficiency measures of which the small scale gas
turbine cogeneration scheme forms a major part. INENCO own and
supervise the operation of the plant, supplying electricity and steam to
United Biscuits under contract at predetermined prices for 11 years. The
plant then becomes the property of United Biscuits.

The installation and commission of the cogeneration system was completed by early 1992 and the project was monitored for 12 months from
July 1992.

At 6700 annual operating hours (93% availability) the project results in
an annual primary energy saving of 27 000 GJ/year (25 700 therms/year).
The project reduces the emissions of carbon dioxide by some 4500 tonnes/
year, a 65% reduction, and sulphur dioxide by 115 tonnes/year, compared
with the generation of the CHP electrical output in a coal-fired power
station.

Had the CHP system been installed as an in-house project, the net
annual project benefit, after allowing for CHP maintenance costs, would
be £163 400. The installed cost of the project in 1991 was £797 000, which
is equivalent to £860 000 at 1993 prices. Additional savings resulting from
the avoidance of replacing the site boiler plant within the contract period
are worth £160 000. The simple payback would therefore be 4.3 years.
However, the scheme is part of a CEM contract and the capital costs for
the installation are financed through the 11-year contract with INENCO.

4.6   Further information

There are many publications which give further detail and guidance on the
technologies discussed in this chapter. Those given below are available free
from the Energy Efficiency Office (Tel 0235 436747).

Good Practice Guides:

   No. 1   Guidance Notes for the Implementation of Small Scale Pack-
           aged CHP
   No. 3   Introduction to Small Scale CHP
   N6. 18 Reducing Energy Consumption Cost by Steam Metering
   No. 30 Energy Efficient Operation of Industrial Boiler Plant
   No. 31 Computer Aided Monitoring and Targeting for Industry
   No. 36 Commercial Refrigeration Plant: Energy Efficient Operation
           and Maintenance
   No. 37 Commercial Refrigeration Plant: Energy Efficient Design
   No. 38 Commercial Refrigeration Plant: Energy Efficient Installation
   No. 42 Industrial Refrigeration Plant: Energy Efficient Operation and
           Maintenance

No. 43   Introduction to Large Scale CHP
No. 44   Industrial Refrigeration Plant: Energy Efficient Design
No. 64   Reducing Energy Consumption and Costs in Small Bakeries

Fuel Efficiency Booklets:

No. 1   Energy Audits for Industry
No. 2   Steam
No. 11   The Economic Use of Refrigeration
No. 14   Economic Use of Oil-fired Boiler Plant
No. 15   Economic Use of Gas-fired Boiler Plant
No. 17   Economic Use of Coal-fired Boiler Plant

5 Noise and air pollution in the food industry: sources, control and cost implications

P. WALSH and M. KEY

Part 1 Noise pollution

5.1 Sources

Noise is defined as undesired sound, and sound is a sensation produced in the ear caused by small variations of air pressure. There are many sources of generation of the air pressure changes; the following is a list of the main ones:

- air excited by the vibration of a surface;
- air turbulence generated by a moving surface, such as a fan;
- air turbulence generated by mixing of gases, such as a flue or exhaust port;
- the flow of air over a discontinuity, causing turbulence, for example a whistle.

All the above sources of noise exist in the food industry in one form or another. The cause of vibration of a surface can be obscure, but some simple examples are:

- material being dropped onto a plate;
- impacts between parts in a machine;
- out of balance forces from a motor;
- electromagnetic excitation;
- turbulent fluid flow within a pipe.

5.2 Effects on health

There are two aspects to noise pollution, the effects of relatively high noise levels on people's hearing, and the disturbance to people's concentration, enjoyment or sleep, from lower levels of noise.

In most cases, the effects on people's hearing takes place in the work place, fairly close to the source of noise. On initial exposure people may notice a slight dullness in hearing or a faint ringing in the ear, when they are away from the noise, rather as experienced from a cold or flu. These effects are usually short-term after first exposure, lasting perhaps only minutes or hours. With prolonged exposure, the dullness of hearing and in some cases the ringing, lasts longer and longer, until eventually it is there until the next day when the process begins again. As the effect is very slow to build up it is not readily noticed by most people, and they often claim that they 'have got used to it'. It is not until after many years of exposure that the reduced ability to understand speech becomes clearly apparent.

The short-term effect is called temporary threshold shift and the long-term, permanent threshold shift (TTS and PTS). It is called threshold shift since this is the effect that can be measured. The threshold being the lowest level of sound that can be heard. As the names imply, TTS is a reversible phenomenon, whereas PTS is the condition of permanent irreversible impairment.

As is the case for other exposure generated effects on the body, high noise levels do not produce equal results on different people. Some workers seem to have the ability to be exposed to high noise levels for their entire working life and suffer little if no reduction in hearing ability, whereas others suffer PTS after comparatively short-term exposure. This difference in susceptibility cannot be measured before exposure, and thus everyone needs to be considered at risk from high noise levels and prolonged exposure.

Very high noise levels, in excess of 140 dB re 20 μPa, can cause instantaneous damage to the ear. Fortunately, such levels do not occur too often in industry, mainly being generated from explosive devices such as explosive cartridge operated tools or very heavy impacts. Noise induced hearing loss mostly occurs due to prolonged exposure, and can be assessed in terms of the exposure to a certain energy per day. Since the ear can in general recover from short-term exposure, then if day-long exposure is limited, PTS can be avoided.

Noise levels that are low enough not to be considered hazardous can have other effects on workers that are difficult to quantify. Noise can induce fatigue and irritability that can result in reduced efficiency. Conversely extremely quiet environments can also lead to reduced efficiency since any sound not produced as a consequence of your own actions becomes a disturbance.

Noise emitted from a factory to residential areas often leads to complaints. Whilst this noise is rarely directly hazardous, it can make the receiver extremely annoyed or lead to disturbance to sleep and thus produce adverse medical effects.

5.3   Legislation

5.3.1   Noise at work

In the United Kingdom, since 1975 employers have had a general obligation under the Health and Safety at Work Act 1974 etc. to safeguard
workers' health. From January 1990 the law also requires specific steps
under the Noise at Work Regulations 1989. The regulations are based on
a European Community (EC) Directive requiring similar basic laws
throughout the Community on reducing the risk of hearing damage as far
as is reasonably practicable. Thus, in general, the limits on noise levels
and actions required by employers that will be outlined, apply to most of
Western Europe with detailed differences from one country to another. In
the United States, there is some difference in the way noise exposure is
assessed but the principles are the same.

The Noise at Work Regulations 1989 deal only with people at work, and
with risks to hearing, not other aspects of health, safety and welfare. The
HSW act is more general and can require employers to take action if noise
creates risks other than hearing damage, or creates risks to persons other
than workers. An example of such action is if noise reduces the audibility
of a warning sound, the warning sound may need to be made louder or
the noise level reduced.

There are three action levels of noise given in the Noise at Work
regulations:

- First action level: a daily personal noise exposure of 85 dB(A);
- Second action level: a daily personal noise exposure of 90 dB(A);
- Peak action level: a peak sound pressure of 200 Pa (140 dB re
  20 μPa).

Every employer must, when any of his employees is likely to be exposed
to the first action level or above or to the peak action level or above, ensure
that a competent person makes a noise assessment. This assessment must
cover the following:

- identify which employees are likely to be exposed;
- provide sufficient information to enable appropriate action to be
  taken.

If you are not sure if an assessment is necessary, then a simple guide is
that it will be required wherever people have to shout or have difficulty
being heard clearly by someone about 2 m away.

It is not usually necessary to measure the noise level at the position of
every worker in a factory; the noise can often be assessed in an area where
there are a number of people by taking a typical case. Measurements can
often be made for a relatively short sample period and then calculated for

a full working day. Where exposure is to widely varying noise levels over a working day, then special equipment can be used to assess the day-long level.

Reassessments should be undertaken at periods of not more than 2 years or when ever any change has taken place that may effect noise levels, such as the installation of new machinery, or after a programme of noise reduction has been undertaken.

The employer should ensure that the person undertaking the assessment is competent to do so. This may mean sending someone from the company on a suitable course to learn how to undertake noise measurements, or employing an outside consultant who has the necessary equipment and knowledge to undertake the work.

All assessments should be kept at least until a new one is taken, but most companies are wise to keep all records so that long-term trends can be monitored, or in case there is some dispute in the future concerning individual noise exposure levels.

The assessment of noise levels should only be seen as a start, as the regulations require every employer to reduce the risk of damage to the hearing of his employees from exposure to noise to as low a level as possible. Although the first action level is set at 85 dB(A), there is a small risk to some people from noise less than this. Thus, if it is reasonably practical, noise levels should be reduced to as low a level as possible.

Where it is found from the assessment that employees are exposed to noise levels greater than the second action level, 90 dB(A), or to the peak action level or above, then the employer must take action to reduce noise levels, so far as is reasonably practical (by means other than the supply of ear protectors).

There are clearly many sources of noise for which at the present time there are no practical means of reducing to a safe level. In these cases, until means are found, then ear protection must be used. At the first action level or above, but below the section action level, every employer must provide employees, if they request, with suitable ear protectors. At or above the second action level or the peak action level, every employer shall ensure that not only are ear protectors provided but that they are worn.

As many factories have some noisy and some quiet areas the regulations require that ear protection zones be clearly marked where workers are likely to be exposed to the second action level or above or to the peak action level or above.

Any equipment installed to reduce noise levels or ear protection devices provided to workers must be kept in good order by employers. The regulations also require workers to cooperate in all noise assessments and to use all noise control measures provided.

Employees have the right to know what levels of noise they are likely to be exposed to, and should be provided with adequate knowledge concerning the risks and consequences of noise exposure.

A factory inspector can insist on an assessment of likely noise exposure levels. If he finds particularly high noise levels, he can issue an enforcement notice requiring an employer to undertake such work as is necessary to reduce noise to a safe level.

If an employer is ignorant of the consequences of high noise levels, or ignores the legislation, he may find at some time in the future that an existing or past employee makes a claim against the company for compensation for loss of hearing. The costs of contesting such claims or payment of compensation can be several thousands of pounds per employee. To prevent this eventuality a good employer should undertake all the requirements of the Noise at Work Regulations. In addition, to protecting themselves, as well as finding people with existing hearing defects, use of screening audiology tests for new workers is sensible.

5.3.2   Neighbourhood noise

Complaints of noise nuisance due to noise emitted from a factory are usually investigated by a local council agency; in the United Kingdom this would be the Environmental Health Department. A noise may be determined as a nuisance according to the professional opinion of an Environmental Health Officer. This is necessarily a somewhat subjective appraisal and the officer relies on his experience with similar problems, the concept of 'public nuisance' as formally held, and a British Standard, BS 4142: 1990 – Method of Rating Industrial Noise Affecting Mixed Residential and Industrial Areas. This latter document is used as a guide when deciding if a given noise will excite complaint, i.e. a predictive technique, and is not meant as a technical substitute if complaints have actually been received. However, to determine the 'reasonableness' of complaint, some recourse is necessary for assessing a problem against average noise susceptibility and a standardised situation. Thus despite the above comments, BS 4142: 1990 is widely used as a criterion for rating an existing situation.

There is no absolute threshold on noise nuisance; rather the sound complained of is compared with the background level existing in the absence of the noise, and depending on the level difference, the tonal character of the noise, or its impulsive nature, the probability of complaint may be determined and the complaint deemed reasonable or otherwise. If it is not possible to measure the background sound level in the absence of the offending sound, a 'notional' level may be deduced. If the noise measured from the factory together with any additions due to tonal or impulsive nature of the noise exceeds the background noise by more than 10 dB(A), it is generally accepted that there is a justified nuisance.

The powers of a local authority in these matters are potentially very strong. At first, a notice can be issued giving the owners of a factory a certain time period to undertake such work as is necessary to abate the nuisance. If this is not adhered to, fines can be imposed, and ultimately a factory could be closed down. However, if the owners of a factory can show that they have undertaken all practical means of abating the nuisance, this can be a defence, 'best practical means'.

5.4   Methods of measurement

As previously described, sound is as a result of fluctuations in the pressure of air. To quantify this, one can measure the pressure fluctuations, and in addition the rate of change of fluctuations can be determined, commonly known as the frequency.

The frequencies of interest for the effects on man are those to which the human ear responds, from about 30 cycles per second or hertz (abbreviated Hz) to 20 000 Hz, although only young people can hear the very high frequencies. Frequencies above 10 000 Hz are not usually a problem and are usually ignored.

The range of sound pressures to which the ear responds is very large although the pressures themselves are very small. Pressures are measured in terms of the Pascal (abbreviated Pa) which is 1 Newton/m^2.

At the frequencies at which the ear is most sensitive (about 2000–4000 Hz), the threshold of hearing occurs at a sound pressure level of about 0.00002 to 0.00003 Pa, whilst at the other end of the scale at the pressure at which the ear begins to hurt, the pressure is about a million times greater, 20–30 Pa.

In comparison, the atmospheric pressure is about 100 000 Pa. It can be seen that if sound pressure were described in terms of Pascals it would be a large and awkward range of numbers to deal with. An added complication is that subjective changes in loudness are not equal for uniform changes in sound pressure. The ear would hear the same relative difference in sound levels between 0.0002 Pa and 0.002 Pa as between 2 Pa and 20 Pa, although the actual changes in sound pressure are widely different. Thus, a scale is required that is based on ratios, which is the basis of the decibel scale.

It should be noted that the decibel is not an absolute measure but always a relative one, and is not only used for measurement of sound, it gives the ratio of one thing to another. In the case of sound, it is the ratio of two pressures and is defined as 20 times the logarithm (to the base 10) of the ratio of the two pressures, i.e.

$$\text{decibel ratio} = 20 \log(p_1/p_2)$$

where p_1 and p_2 are the two pressures being compared. For example, if the pressure is doubled the decibel ratio is $20\log(2/1)$ which is 6 decibels (abbreviated dB).

To enable everyone to work to the same standard, it is useful to have a reference pressure; this has been agreed internationally as 0.00002 Pa (which corresponds approximately to the average persons threshold of hearing at the ear's most sensitive frequencies). If the sound pressure level produced by say a pneumatic drill is 2 Pa, this is 100 000 times the reference pressure. The noise can then be described as 100 dB greater ($20\log 100\,000$) than the reference level, usually written as 100 dB re 20 μPa.

The ear does not hear all frequencies equally well; it is developed to hear and understand speech and is thus optimised to work best at those frequencies containing the intelligibility content of speech, about 1000–4000 Hz. Thus, the perceived loudness of a sound depends on both its pressure and frequency.

The basic equipment used to measure sound consists of a microphone, which converts the fluctuating air pressure into a voltage, an amplifier, and an indicating device. These are usually combined into one piece of equipment, the sound level meter.

There is a wide range of sound level meters on the market today offering different combinations of signal processing. All sound level meters should have a 'weighting network' (an electrical circuit arranged to attenuate different frequencies by different amounts) built in, which causes the meter to mimic the frequency response of the human ear. This is called 'A' weighting, and decibel readings on a sound level meter using this weighting are called dB(A). Use of the (A) after the reading also implies that the standard decibel reference pressure level of 20 μPa has been used.

To measure noise levels for the purpose of assessing the noise in a factory, many sound level meters incorporate an integrating function. This continuously adds the energy incident on the microphone and divides it by the time during which the measurements have been taken. The reading is called the equivalent continuous level, abbreviated L_{eq}. Where it is not practical to assess the noise level over a sufficiently long period of time because a worker is moving from one position to another or the noise is greatly varying, he can be fitted with a dose meter which will measure the equivalent continuous noise level over a complete working day.

To help with the investigation of noise problems, more sophisticated equipment can be used that will measure the levels in various frequency bands or will show the noise level variation with time. To monitor the background noise level in cases of neighbourhood noise, it is usual to use a statistical meter that gives the level of noise exceeded for 90% of the time (abbreviated as the L_{90}).

Measurement and analysis of vibration levels on machinery can sometimes be used to help solve noise problems. Most sound level meters can be adapted for this purpose.

As stated previously, the decibel scale is a relative one and thus it is essential that all noise measuring equipment is calibrated regularly. A simple calibration can be made before each measurement using a calibrator coupled to the microphone.

5.5   Methods of reduction

5.5.1   Ear defenders

Ear protection devices come in two basic forms, those that fit in the outer ear passage (often called ear plugs) and those that cover the outside of the ear (ear muffs). Use of either of these as a protection against high noise levels should only be made if no other means of reducing noise levels are possible, or until other means are undertaken. In many sections of the food industry, there are particular problems in wearing ear protection devices due to the high temperatures and humidities involved. Sweating inside an ear muff can lead to ear infections. Ear plugs can be a problem where there is a danger of them falling into food to be processed, although there are some on the market that are linked to a cord that can be attached to clothing, or to a flexible rod that can be placed around the head.

If ear protection has to be used, then advice should be sought on the suitability of the particular types, to ensure that they afford sufficient protection to the noise levels present, that they suit the working environ- ment, and they fit the wearer.

Dispensers for the supply of disposable plugs can be placed at the entrances to noise hazardous areas.

It is a good idea to insist that supervisory and management staff should wear ear protection when they enter noise hazardous areas, even if it is only for a short period, to encourage other workers to wear them.

5.5.2   Reduction of noise at source

This is the best but the most difficult way of solving noise problems. It can usually only be done at the design stage of a new machine, but users can encourage this process by insisting on lower noise levels when they are purchasing machinery. In the food industry, there are particular problems due to hygiene requirements with the use of certain materials. This often leads to machines being covered in large panels of stainless steel or aluminium which act as good radiators of sound.

Noise is typically a waste of energy so a noisy gearbox or squeaking conveyor belt should be seen as something wrong. A common source of noise in many food processing factories is leaking compressed air. Compressed air seems to be treated by some people as free whereas it is expensive as well as being a source of unnecessary noise. Noise from air exhaust ports can be reduced by the fitting of a pneumatic silencer costing less than £3.

The operation of plant can be changed in some cases to reduce noise levels. For example, the impacts between cans on a conveyor line could be reduced if the line speed was continuously changed to match the supply of cans to the line, rather than running at fixed speed.

5.5.3   Noise enclosures

With existing machines, acoustic enclosures can sometimes be used, consisting usually of a metal box around the machine with controls mounted externally. Careful design of any necessary openings in the enclosures are called for. It is usual for the inside of an enclosure to be covered in a sound absorbing material (mineral fibre or cellular foam plastic); for many applications in the food industry this is not possible for hygiene reasons, and thus the enclosure needs to be built especially well. Costs of enclosures range from £1000 to £10 000 per machine and make noise reduction exercises very expensive. A full noise survey of a factory should include measurements of the noise from individual machines thus enabling the noisiest machines to be tackled first. In many cases, however, satisfactory noise levels are not achieved until all noisy machines are enclosed.

In some cases, it may be possible to enclose the operator in a refuge rather than enclose the machine.

5.5.4   Reduction of reverberation

Food factories are often very reverberant as a result of the use of tiled or hard plastered surfaces for hygiene requirements. This leads to higher noise levels than might otherwise be present. In some cases, a reduction in reverberation is worthwhile and there are now available sound absorbing materials that can be used on the ceilings and upper walls of food processing plants or hung in panels. These materials can be subjected to the normal washing processes used in food processing plants and will not support the growth of bacteria, etc. Typical material costs are of the order of £50 per square metre for flat ceilings. Before embarking on the installation of acoustic treatment, one should be sure that it will be worthwhile. In most instances, the level of noise that workers are subjected to is as a result of direct noise from machinery rather than reflected noise from the building.

5.5.5   Reduction of the time exposure

Not only are the levels of noise important but the length of time exposed to them is as well. One way of reducing the 'total' exposure of individuals to noise is thus to reduce the time of exposure. This must be done on a per day basis; it is not acceptable to be exposed one full day to noise and then not on another day. The legislation assumes an 8-h working day; if exposure to noise is reduced to 4 h per day, then the limits can rise by 3 dB(A), reduced to 2 h per day, the limits can rise by 6 dB(A) and so on, each halving of time allowing a 3 dB(A) increase.

5.5.6   Reduction of noise to neighbours

If this is a problem, first one should undertake a detailed study of the noise sources. Where possible noise measurements should be made with individual items of plant running at the time of day or night that complaints have been made. This should be done near the complainants houses or it may be necessary to do it closer to the factory so that the measurements are clearly discernible above the background noise level.

Reduction of noise at source or enclosure of machines will reduce the noise emitted from a factory, but this is often not practical or cost effective. In some cases, the sound insulation of the building needs to be improved, this may mean filling in holes in the walls, bricking up or double glazing windows, building lobbies to doors, etc.; if all such work does not reduce the level of noise emitted sufficiently, then it may be necessary to build a false wall inside or outside the existing walls.

In many instances the source of noise nuisance from food processing factories is ventilation or cooling fans. Attenuators can usually be fitted to these to reduce noise to an acceptable level.

Screening a factory from houses by building an earth bund or wall can be a useful noise reduction measure. It is necessary to screen the line of sight from windows in the affected houses and any potential sources of noise. The screen is most effective if it is close to the source of the noise or the potential receivers, and will give a 10 dB(A) reduction if line of site is just broken, more if the screen is considerably higher than the original line of site.

Part 2   Air pollution

5.6   Air pollution sources and effects

5.6.1   Introduction

This section will concentrate primarily on 'chemical' emissions from food processing operations. In general, food processing operations are not considered to be major sources of emissions into the air, in comparison with other industrial sectors such as the metal or chemical industries. However, although emissions from food processing may be of less significance, several important emission sources are responsible for polluting discharges.

The emission profile in terms of pollutant type and loading is dependent upon the process materials and process operations. It is possible to identify typical processes within food processing operations, such as handling dusty raw materials, cooking and grinding/milling, and to characterise emissions from such sources. In addition there are potential emissions from utility operations such as heat or power production at the food processing site. The main types and sources of emissions into the air can be summarised as follows:

- particulate matter and combustion gases (carbon dioxide, sulphur dioxide and nitrogen oxides) from combustion processes;
- particulate matter from process operations such as size reduction, raw materials handling and transfer, and from cooking and heating processes;
- volatile organic compound (VOC) and chemical emissions (i.e. ammonia, hydrogen chloride, sulphides) from processes involving the use of organic solvents or potentially volatile chemical species;
- VOC and chemical emissions from processes involving the heating or cooking of food, or from fermentation processes;
- halogenated VOC and other chemical emissions from leaks from refrigeration systems;
- VOC emissions from packaging printing and manufacture.

5.6.2   General effects of emissions

Emissions into the air can result in a wide range of environmental effects. In order to consider these effects further, it is perhaps necessary to consider what the term pollution means. There are several proposed definitions; however, the most recent definition used in the UK Environmental Protection Act 1990 defines pollution in terms of the capability of a substance to cause harm to man or other living organisms supported by the environment. The term harm can be defined further as:

> harm to the health of living organisms, interference with ecological systems of which they form part, or offence caused to any sense of man or harm to his property.

The range of possible effects of substances emitted include:

1. chronic and acute toxicity to humans, flora or fauna;
2. impairment of health or disfunction of humans, flora or fauna;
3. dry deposition leading to building and other surface soiling and possible toxic effects due to ingestion of deposited materials;
4. wet deposition of soluble materials leading to building material damage and effects in water such as acidification;
5. induced changes in environmental systems due to atmospheric chemistry, such as ozone depletion, climate change and photochemical ozone production.

These effects are considered in greater detail in the following sections, which also detail the potential emission control and minimisation techniques available for the various pollutants.

5.7   Legislation affecting emissions into the air

5.7.1   Introduction

The legislation affecting emissions into the air is specific to the country of operation of the process, although there are similar principles underlying most of the international air pollution control legislation. This section will consider the general principles; however, reference must be made to the relevant legislation in the country of operation of the process.

5.7.2   Legal framework

In most countries, the environmental protection legislation developed considerably in the 1970s and 1980s, the principles used in these developments being to produce a system which is:

- precautionary;
- preventative;
- pre-emptive.

This results in a system which: (1) relies on scientific evidence but does not require absolute proof that a certain emission produces environmental damage (precautionary); (2) is based upon prevention of pollution; and (3) is pre-emptive (requires the issue of licences, permits or authorisations). In addition, there is an important international approach to pollution control which is central to most legal systems, that is *the polluter pays principle*. The central theme to the principle is that environmental resources are limited and, as their use is not given a direct value, the misuse of such resources is not reflected in the market. It therefore seems reasonable to expect that the cost of pollution prevention and control measures should be reflected in the cost of goods and services which cause the pollution either in production or consumption, in order that the rational and careful use of environmental resources is encouraged.

5.7.3   Responsibilities for enforcement

Most countries have a two-tier system for air pollution control from industry. This usually results in certain listed processes falling under the control of State/Regional authorities requiring the issue of a licence containing specified operating conditions. The second tier of control concerns the non-listed processes, which are usually controlled by a reactive regulation system that responds to nuisance or environmental effects after they have occurred. The latter approach is expanded further in section 5.10.

In addition, air pollution control is usually divided between State/ Regional authorities and National Government Agencies. The responsibilities of these bodies varies from country to country, for example in the United States, the national Environmental Protection Agency (EPA) sets standards of control and oversees the enforcement responsibilities of the State Governments, although the States are responsible for setting the conditions in the licences issued. In Australia, the State authorities specify the industries which require licensing and set their own emission limits. This can lead to processes requiring licensing in some States but not in others and the industries may also be subject to differing emission limits. It is usual for National Government Agencies to establish standards and guidelines for the operation of processes subject to licensing by the State/ Regional authorities.

In most cases, food processing operations are not included in National lists of processes requiring licensing or authorisation, although there may be some local variations in State regulations. The main operations which may be carried on at food processing sites and which could be listed for permit-type control are power or heat production by combustion processes, waste incineration, product drying and certain processes involving the use of organic solvents or hazardous chemicals.

5.7.4   Air pollution control standards

In most countries, emissions from processes are controlled by setting conditions on licences requiring the installation of control equipment. The level of control is often determined by taking account of the environmental benefits and costs of the control equipment, the legal standards requiring the installation of best technology at reasonable cost. The term used varies between countries, but the basis of the approach is similar. Section 5.7.5 outlines the principles behind the United Kingdom's approach of best available techniques not entailing excessive cost (BATNEEC).

There are basically three methods of establishing the performance standards that may be applied to processes and used to establish conditions on licences/authorisations/permits:

1. establishing technologies which must be fitted to process plants to control emissions into the air;
2. establishing emission concentration limits for discharges from processes which effectively set the level of control required;
3. establishing ambient air quality standards used to determine the effect on air quality of emissions from individual processes.

In many cases, the strategy used will be a combination of these. The use of emission limits and quality standards is discussed further in section 5.7.6.

5.7.5   Best available techniques not entailing excessive cost

Best available techniques not entailing excessive cost (BATNEEC) is an approach implemented in the United Kingdom. The European Communities Directive on the combating of air pollution from industrial plants (84/360/EEC), the so called 'Framework Directive', required that member states took all necessary measures to (1) require operators of certain categories of industrial processes to seek prior authorisation; and (2) use all appropriate preventive measures against air pollution, including the application of the best available technology not entailing excessive cost.

In the United Kingdom the requirement was implemented slightly differently: that processes use the best available *techniques* not entailing excessive cost (BATNEEC) for preventing the release of substances to any environmental medium or, where it is not practicable by such means, for reducing the release of such substances to a minimum and for rendering harmless any substances that are released.

The accepted definition of the term BATNEEC is that:

- *Best* should mean the most effective in preventing, minimising and rendering harmless polluting emissions. There may be more than one set of techniques which can be termed 'best'.
- *Available* should mean procurable by any operator of the class of process in question. It should not imply that the technique is in general use but it does require general accessibility.

- *Techniques* include the process and how the process is operated, including the concept and design of the process, and staff numbers, supervision, training and working methods.
- *Not entailing excessive cost* needs to be taken in two contexts depending upon whether it is applied to a new or an existing process. The presumption will be that the best available techniques will be used, although this can be modified by economic considerations where the cost of applying the best available techniques would be excessive in relation to the environmental protection achieved.

The principle in the application of BATNEEC is therefore the use of the most efficient pollution control technique having regard to a balance between the economic costs and environmental costs. This approach is common to most countries, although the term used is likely to be different to BATNEEC.

5.7.6   Establishing the level of control required

As there are obvious difficulties in establishing the BATNEEC requirement, it is more usual for Governments to establish emission limits or ambient air quality standards to effectively reflect the level of control they require.

In determining what particular control strategy will fulfil the objective, a systematic and analytical approach must be taken. Once the pollutant produced by a process has been identified, it is relatively simple to produce a list of available control techniques. The next step is then to systematically assess each of these control techniques and examine how efficient and effective they are in relation to control of the particular pollutant in the particular circumstances of its production in the process concerned. The next stage is then to consider the relative cost of each of these control techniques, including both capital and running costs, and then to compare how the efficiency of pollution control and costs correlate. The difficult stage is then to determine where the balance lies between the cost and the environmental protection achieved. This should relate to a number of parameters including:

- any air quality guidelines that exist for the pollutant concerned;
- the ecotoxicity of the pollutant concerned;
- whether the pollutant concerned has any nuisance potential, for example odour;
- any additional environmental problems and supplementary costs incurred by particular arrestment equipment, for example the production of liquid waste or solid waste which will then require further treatment and disposal.

It can be seen that the effect of the pollutant on air quality is important, and most countries now have statutory air quality standards. These can be used to measure the effectiveness of the process-specific controls, an approach used by the EPA in the United States, or can be combined with emission limits to establish dual controls on emissions, an approach used in Australia.

In the European Community, the Directives issued indicate a similar dual approach; there are Directives which:

1. set statutory air quality standards, including 80/779/EEC on sulphur dioxide and suspended particulates, 822/882/EEC on lead in air and 85/203/EEC on nitrogen dioxide in air;
2. set control standards for certain types of industrial process, for example 88/609/EEC on large combustion plant.

5.7.7   Best practicable environmental option (BPEO)

As referred to in section 5.7.6, the installation of air pollution control equipment often converts the pollution to a liquid or solid waste for disposal. Internationally, there has been developed an approach to integrate the control of emissions to air, water and waste generation at each process, to ensure that pollution problems are not simply transferred from environmental media to another.

This has resulted in the promulgation of the *best practicable environmental option* (*BPEO*) concept. The UK Royal Commission on Environmental Pollution twelfth report issued in 1988 entitled *Best Practicable Environmental Option*, proposed the following explanation of the term:

> A BPEO is the outcome of a systematic consultative and decision making procedure which emphasises the protection and conservation of the environment across land, air and water. The BPEO procedure establishes, for a given set of objectives, the option that provides the most benefit or least damage to the environment as a whole, at acceptable cost, in the long term as well as in the short term.

The aim is to consider the environment as a total system; any proposals to reduce pollution to one part of that system should not adversely affect another part of that system.

5.7.8   Development planning control

One common theme amongst all pollution control activities is the importance of planning. In terms of development control, the considerations made when a new process is proposed should include environmental hazards. One of the more recent initiatives in the planning field was the development of the Environmental Impact Assessment for larger proposals, particularly industrial processes with significant pollution potential.

Environmental assessment, also known as environmental impact assessment, is a systematic procedure for collecting, analysing and presenting environmental data to ensure that the likely effects on the environment of a new development are fully understood and taken into account before the development is commenced. The requirements for carrying out environmental assessment are different in each country; however, it is likely that any large food processing operation may require an environmental assessment.

5.8   Emissions, effects and controls

5.8.1   Introduction

As indicated in section 5.7, most air pollution control legislation is based upon the concept of preventing emissions from the process. This can usually only be achieved by changing the process operations or the raw materials used. For example, it is possible to prevent the emission of volatile organic compounds (VOCs) from processes by ceasing the use of organic solvents. However, in most cases the option of process change is limited by the process technology and therefore 'end-of-pipe' pollution abatement equipment is utilised to minimise emissions.

5.8.2   Combustion process emissions

There are two main methods of using energy within food processes:

1. *Indirect usage* where the gases arising from combustion are used to heat the process or product through heat exchange not involving contact with the product.
2. *Direct usage* where the steam or hot waste gases are passed directly into the process equipment and involve contact with the product.

The majority of combustion process emissions from food processes arise from indirect energy usage, via the production of heat or steam on-site. However, some drying and cooking processes may involve the direct injection of steam or direct use of combustion gases. The emissions will be different from direct and indirect heat usage, although the emissions arising from direct energy use in the process are considered in section 5.8.4.

The combustion process releases a range of pollutants, the most important being particulate matter and smoke, carbon dioxide, sulphur dioxide, nitrogen oxides and organic compounds.

The emissions produced from combustion processes are largely dependent upon the fuel used in the combustion process. The following summarises the emission potential of different energy sources:

Coal. Coal has a relatively high sulphur content and will produce quite large quantities of particulate matter (smoke, grit and dust).

Oil. The sulphur content of oil varies with quality, but is generally relatively high. Good combustion should ensure that smoke is minimised.

Gas. Gas has a very low sulphur content and produces hardly any particulate matter or smoke.

Waste. Waste can be used but the emission profile depends upon the waste origin and may include large quantities of heavy metals, organic compounds and toxic pollutants such as arsenic and mercury.

Particulate matter

Effects. This is a term used to cover a range of particles which may be released and includes smoke, grit, dust and fume. The effects of particulate matter depend upon the particle size and chemical nature. The primary health effect is respiratory dysfunction. Particulate matter can act as a vehicle for gaseous substances to enter the respiratory system, which may then be very harmful, particularly if the particulates are of respirable size. In combustion gas emissions, particulate matter often shows a synergistic effect with sulphur dioxide, causing mucous membrane irritation. The effects of particulate matter inhalation are especially problematic to persons already suffering respiratory problems. Other effects of particulate matter are soiling of building materials and personal property, possible interference with plant photosynthesis due to deposition on leaves, and visible nuisances.

Control equipment. If combustion is not complete, unburned carbon-based particulate matter may produce visible smoke emissions from the process. Emissions of smoke are prevented by adequate secondary combustion of the gases. Emissions of particulate matter can be reduced by the use of simple low-cost techniques such as (i) momentum separators where gas expansion reduces velocity and solids 'fall-out'; or (2) cyclones where the emissions are passed into a chamber and subjected to centrifugal force by inducing a 'swirling' motion in the waste gas flow, encouraging particulate separation by inertia. Such systems typically have a low cost in the region of less than £10 000. On larger combustion processes more extensive equipment may be required as detailed in section 5.8.3. In the case of smaller processes, where it is necessary to control particulate matter, wet scrubbing techniques may also be appropriate; these may be able to deal simultaneously with acid gases and particulate matter in the same equipment. There are various types of wet scrubber but the basis of the technique is to pass the dust-laden air into a tower and provide contact with water either by spray or by a combination of spray and packing material. Table 5.1 in section 5.8.3 summarises the options available.

Acid gases

Effects. These are due primarily to sulphur dioxide (SO_2) and oxides of nitrogen (NO_x). Exposure to SO_2 can lead to acute effects such as bronchitis, and to chronic pulmonary effects, especially in persons susceptible to lung dysfunction such as asthma. Exposure to NO_x results in similar effects. In addition, both these gases can lead to acidification of rain, soil and waters, and to building material damage. Acid gases can also lead to leaf collapse in plants. Finally, oxides of nitrogen are implicated in photochemical oxidation reactions (see section 5.8.5).

Control equipment. It is necessary to prevent as far as possible the release of acid gases from the process. This is achieved by the incorporation of absorption (scrubbing) equipment in the flue gas cleaning plant. A variety of scrubbing techniques is in use, essentially divided into:

1. wet scrubbing, where the acid gases are absorbed into a liquid medium;
2. dry or semi-dry scrubbing equipment, where lime is injected into the flue gases either as a solid or as a slurry with water. The dry techniques rely on subsequent control of particulate matter.

Wet scrubbing has the disadvantage of producing a liquid effluent which may require treatment prior to discharge to a sewer or watercourse, and also has the potential to create a visible steam plume from the chimney. The cost of this equipment is dependent upon the waste gas flow but can cost from £10 000 to £250 000. Further information is included in Table 5.2 in section 5.12.2.

Nitric oxide is produced in any combustion process using air, and is influenced by the temperature of the combustion gases (typically temperatures below 1200°C have an insignificant formation rate). In many cases it is possible to reduce the emission of nitrogen oxides by conversion to low-NO_x burners.

Carbon dioxide

Effects. Carbon dioxide (CO_2) is a product of complete combustion and an important gas in respiration reactions. CO_2 is a greenhouse gas, i.e. it is implicated in climate change (global warming). This phenomenon occurs because the gas allows light from the sun to pass through it and warm the earth. The earth itself then radiates heat, but at a different wavelength. This is absorbed by the greenhouse gases, thus trapping the heat and leading to a surface temperature increase, which in turn may cause significant changes in climatic conditions. CO_2 is an important pollutant which is subject to considerable international controls to cut back emissions and to reduce the potential for climate change.

Control equipment. Whilst techniques for the abatement of carbon dioxide are under development, the only effective method of reducing emissions is to minimise fuel use by energy efficiency.

5.8.3   Particulate matter emissions from processing

There are many potential sources for the emission of particulate matter from process operations. These include size reduction, raw materials handling and transfer of raw materials and products. These emissions are generally dry, and the principal effect is possible nuisance due to deposition and soiling of buildings and other property. Many food processing operations will include processes which generate particulate matter and therefore require the installation of abatement equipment to control emissions.

Table 5.1 is a comparative list of the different particulate matter arrestment options, detailing approximate arrestment efficiencies and typical particle size collection range.

Table 5.1 Comparison of particulate matter control equipment

Equipment	Efficiency (%)	Particle size (μm)	Cost
Settling chamber	>50	>50	Low
Cyclone	>80	>10	Low
Fabric filter	>99	>1	Medium
Electrostatic precipitator	>99	>1	High
Fibrous scrubber	>90	>1	Medium
Impingement scrubber	>90	>1	Medium
Moving bed scrubber	>90	>1	Medium
Plate scrubber	>90	>1	Medium
Spray tower	>90	>2	Medium
Venturi scrubber	>98	Submicron	Medium

There are several drawbacks with this equipment which should be considered:

1. dry collection systems produce a solid material for disposal;
2. wet systems produce a slurry effluent for treatment or disposal;
3. the dry materials have to be carefully handled from the collection equipment to ensure continued containment;
4. with dry systems there is the possibility of re-entrainment of the dust;
5. there needs to be regular inspection and maintenance of the equipment, and it is essential that adequate spare parts are held.

5.8.4 Chemical emissions from food processing

Sources and effects. There are several other potential emissions from food processing operations. However, the range of process variations undertaken make it impossible to cover all process options. A number of food processes utilise acids in the processing operations. As discussed in section 5.8.2, emission of acid gases can lead to acidification of rain, soil and waters, building material damage, and leaf collapse in plants. Other processes may involve the use of sulphides and similar chemicals, the effects of these primarily being odour generation.

Control equipment. The principal equipment used for the control of acid gas emissions is based upon absorption (scrubbing) technology. Scrubbers rely on the absorption of the gas into a liquid (usually water). The liquor can then be treated to remove the acid simply by pH adjustment. There is a wide range of scrubber variations, the main two types being (1) spray towers where the liquid is sprayed counter current to the gas flow; and (2) packed towers where the liquid is sprayed onto a packing material which effectively increases the surface area of contact between the gas and the liquid. In general, packed towers are the more efficient technique for this application. Further information is contained in Table 5.2 in section 5.12.2.

5.8.5 Emission of volatile organic compounds

Sources and effects. The potential sources of emissions of volatile organic compounds (VOCs) are many. They include heating and cooking operations where organic material present in the food may be volatilised (although usually in this case odour is the main concern). A significant number of food processing operations use organic solvents in the process operations (often for extraction processes) or may emit VOCs as a by-product of reaction (for example brewing/distilling and bread baking). Sources of VOC emissions in the food industry are currently under investigation in the European Community as part of a major programme to review the emission and control of VOCs.

VOCs are currently one of the most important group of pollutants, and have the potential for transboundary pollution effects (damage is caused at a distance, possibly in a different country, from the emission source). The major problems caused by the emission of VOCs are (1) photo-chemical oxidation in the presence of sunlight and nitrogen oxides to produce ground level ozone; and (2) the risk of perceptible odour at ground level. Whilst there is concern at the loss of ozone in the strato-sphere, the ozone which exists at ground level (known as tropospheric ozone) is a pollutant which causes eye, nose and throat irritation, chest discomfort, coughing and headaches. People who exercise or who already suffer from asthma or bronchitis are most at risk. The environmental chemistry involved in photochemical oxidation has a timescale of tens of hours and therefore it is most unlikely that there will be any adverse effects on local air quality.

Control equipment.   The available techniques for the control of VOC emissions are very similar to the techniques available for odour control and are addressed in detail in section 5.12.2.

5.9   Monitoring of air pollutants

5.9.1   Introduction

There are three options available for the monitoring and assessment of emissions into the air:

1. monitoring of emissions at the point of discharge from the process;
2. monitoring of ambient air quality;
3. monitoring of process equipment or abatement equipment efficiency.

The third option is an indicative method of determining the continued operating effectiveness of control equipment and is a critical process management technique but does not give quantitative data for assessing the effects of emissions.

5.9.2   Emission monitoring

The measurement of the concentration of pollutants in waste gases is central to most legal emission control systems. The establishment of emission concentration limits provides a performance standard, against which the operation and effectiveness of control measures can be assessed.
   There are two options for emission monitoring:

1. continuous monitoring involving the installation of a monitoring device in the chimney or discharge point;
2. extractive testing where a measurement of emission concentration for a given pollutant is performed over a discrete time period.

In both cases there is a very wide range of measurement equipment and methodologies available (in many cases the technique used for continuous and extractive measurement is the same). Often the methods are specified or recommended by regulatory agencies in support of the air pollution control standards. In relation to the measurement of gaseous emissions, there has been a rapid move over the last decade away from techniques involving wet chemical analysis, towards instrumental methods which often provide direct read-out of emission concentrations. The techniques used for particulate matter are usually light-based measurement systems for continuous analysis, and extractive sampling with gravimetric analysis for non-continuous methods.

There are several central factors concerning emission monitoring techniques:

1. the method of sampling is critical to ensure that representative samples of the whole have been collected or measured;
2. the technique chosen must be sensitive to the pollutant concerned and must have a resolution capable of measuring accurately at the concentrations likely to be encountered;
3. all sampling and analysis systems must be provided with calibration facilities, particularly in the case of continuous monitoring devices;
4. any monitoring must take account of normal process variations and should involve testing over the range of possible processing options;
5. the technique chosen should minimise the possible interference from cross sensitivity to other species in the gas flow.

5.9.3   Ambient air monitoring

Many countries have combined systems which specify emission concentration limits from process equipment and also establish air quality guidelines or standards for determining the effects of emissions on local air quality. This approach is used in the United States and, in some states, the severity of the emission limits on process emissions depends upon the local air quality and the anticipated effects of emissions from the process on the ambient air standards.

Consideration of the effects of emissions on air quality raises the important issue of dispersion of residual emissions from the process via the chimney or stack. The aim of a chimney is to ensure that natural dispersion in air occurs, resulting in maximum ground level concentrations below critical levels. If the emission rates from a process are known, it is possible to model the expected effect of these emissions on ground level ambient air quality.

The methods of measurement for ambient air are often based upon similar principles to the methods used for emission monitoring. The main variation is that the levels of pollutants will be considerably lower than in process discharges and therefore the technique used must have lower resolution. Also, as the rate of variation is of less concern in ambient air, monitoring concentrations are typically based on daily averages rather than 30 minute means. In the absence of national standards, it is usual to compare measured values to the guideline values specified by the World Health Organization.

Most countries have a network of ambient air quality monitoring, although currently only the United States use the results of this monitoring to determine routinely the permitted discharges from process equipment.

5.10   Odours: sources, nature and effects

5.10.1   Introduction

Assessment of odour emissions and the effect of such emissions is more complex than general air pollutants. The following are some of the reasons:

1. odour effects are generally not caused by a single pollutant or chemical species; odour is a 'cocktail' of chemical species emitted from a process;
2. in the case of odours, perception by the nose is the detection method and the nose is extremely sensitive; it can respond to small variations in concentration over periods of a few seconds, and to concentrations of fractions of a part per billion;
3. the assessment of odour nature is subjective and varies with the receptor;
4. dispersion of odour, and hence ambient concentrations of potentially odorous substances, are very dependent upon meteorological conditions;
5. the generation of odour from the process can vary with raw material variations and cycle operations in the process.

Odour is often a substantial potential problem in respect of emissions from food processing operations by virtue of the nature of the raw materials handled and the processing operations undertaken.

Whilst there are several potential odour sources, the most common sources of odours that may lead to complaint is from processes involving the cooking, heating or drying of food. The components of emissions which lead to odour complaints commonly comprise significant quantities of volatile organic compounds, such as natural oils, the exact chemical species often being complex and varied.

5.10.2   Odour sources

There are numerous potential sources of odour emissions from food processing operations. These include:

1. odours associated with raw materials, such as fish products;
2. odours associated with cooking processes;
3. odours associated with heating or drying processes;
4. odours arising from waste and effluent handling and treatment at food processing factories.

The odours can be from point sources such as chimneys and vents, as well as from fugitive sources such as building, process vessel and pipework leakage. It is possible to measure odour from point sources quantitatively (section 5.13), although fugitive emission sources are extremely difficult to characterise and monitor.

5.10.3   Effects of odour emissions

As detailed in section 5.11, most legislation refers to odour in terms of nuisance, which is usually accepted as requiring control of emissions to ensure that they are not offensive beyond the process boundary. It may therefore be helpful to consider the factors which would affect the assessment of an odour from the point of assessing its offensiveness.

It is possible to measure odour 'strength' but much more difficult to measure the subjective response to the offensiveness of an odour by a scientific method. Therefore, it is usual to assess offensiveness of odour by subjective sensory olfactory response of observers. The following matters should be considered when determining the degree of potential offence:

1. *Nature*—odours which would be generally accepted by the public as 'unpleasant' will generally be potentially offensive. For example, odours from a maggot breeding process would generally be accepted as unpleasant in comparison to odour from a food processing plant. In addition, the detection threshold for an odour is important in this respect as it will determine the likelihood of the odour being detected.
2. *Frequency*—odours which are released frequently or continuously from the process are likely to be determined to be offensive. This characteristic would often be assessed in conjunction with the odour's persistence in the environment.
3. *Persistence*—odours which are continuously released from processes or those which are emitted on a frequent basis but persist in the environment for a long period (that is do not readily disperse to a level where the odour is no longer detected) are likely to be judged

as offensive. It is possible to put forward a case that even the less unpleasant odours (such as food processing odours) may be offensive if the releases are continuous or frequent and persistent.

4. *Meteorological conditions*—as the majority of odour control techniques finally rely on dispersion for minimisation of odour effects, the meteorological conditions will be of prime importance. If conditions that are disadvantageous for dispersion are prevalent, odours may be detected even though the best available control methods are in use. Thus, in most cases, the detection of an odour by the process operator will result in a detailed process assessment to ensure that the process management and control is operating normally and to identify possible weather related effects.

In summary, the emission of odorous materials will, in most cases, result in a detailed process assessment and odour monitoring by relatively simple sensory means. If the odour problems are more difficult to identify, or if carrying out assessment of existing control measures or design of new control equipment, it may be necessary to carry out monitoring using extractive sampling and olfactometric methods of odour quantification. It must be understood at this stage that such quantitative monitoring will usually only determine relative 'strength' of an odour and the assessment of 'offensiveness' will still be a matter of personal sensory assessment.

Most odorous materials are detected at concentrations in air well below the levels at which they are hazardous, therefore the risk of health effects due to toxicity of the odour is generally insignificant. The only possible health effects created by odours are psychological. It is certain that when people begin to perceive odour it creates disturbance in their daily routine and may lead to the odour taking on an obsessive role in their daily life, which in turn can lead to stress and related psychological and physical problems. It could be hypothesised that odour is not harmful to health but is only a subjective response to small amounts of material by a sensitive receptor and is of a transitory nature. However, it must be accepted that odour can interfere with a person's enjoyment of their amenities, and no industrial process has the right to pollute air or cause material interference with 'common' resources like the air.

5.11   Legislation relating to odour emissions

In most countries, the control of odour emissions from food processing operations is a matter for control by reactive legislation (action being taken once the odour has been caused). The legislation is usually based upon the concept of nuisance, which can be defined as material harm, inconvenience, discomfort, damage or interference with an individual's or

a group of individuals' rights to enjoy their property and common amenities. In the case of nuisance controls, there is often a specified level of
action required by process operators to alleviate the nuisance. One such
approach which is used in the United Kingdom and Australia is that of
best practicable means (*BPM*). The best practicable means approach takes
account of controlling odour emissions and effects by means which are
reasonably practicable with regard to local conditions, financial implications and the current state of technical knowledge. This approach is not
drastically different to that taken for air pollution control based upon the
concept of BATNEEC.

There is an alternative approach used in parts of Australia and the
Netherlands based upon setting discharge limits for emissions from chimneys in terms of odour units (section 5.13) and specifying a chimney height
to ensure dispersion of odour to a level that will not cause offence. As
explained in section 5.13, it is possible to measure odour strength, although
the method does not take account of the 'offensiveness' or nature of the
odour.

The final regime used to control odour from food processing operations
is based upon land use planning. This system effectively seeks to minimise
odour-sensitive development near to potential odour sources. This results
in a distance around certain odorous process plants where development is
not permitted, the so called 'cordon sanitaire'. There is also strict control
over the siting of any processes likely to cause odour. In some countries
such as Germany, these distances are specified in regulations; most countries, however, rely on a less formal system.

5.12   Control of odour emissions

5.12.1   Introduction

One of the critical aspects of odour control is to ensure adequate containment and collection of odours. It is very difficult to prevent the emission
of odours from food processing plants by process change as, if the basic
process produces odour due to raw material characteristics, it is most
unlikely that this material can be changed. It is possible to reduce odour
generation by process optimisation and control. The following are some
of the principles of this approach:

1. containment of odours within process equipment by good design and
   extract ventilation where necessary;
2. good housekeeping and raw material handling practices;
3. maintaining equipment leakproof and spillproof as far as possible;
4. control and minimisation of cooker emissions;

5. containment of strong odour sources such as cooking emissions and treatment in odour control equipment;
6. prevention of fugitive loss, as uncontained emissions of this type are not capable of controlled dispersion.

In many cases, however, the only option available for effective control is the installation of odour control equipment.

5.12.2   Control techniques

There are several control techniques available for the minimisation and treatment of odour emissions from processes (Table 5.2). These techniques are largely for gaseous emissions. There may be odours associated with particulate phase emissions, for example fat from frying processes, and in these cases successful treatment has been achieved by the use of particulate matter control equipment, largely electrostatic precipitation.

Table 5.2 Gaseous emission and odour control options

Equipment type	Gases controlled	Efficiency (%)
Adsorption	VOCs and odours	>95
Thermal incineration	VOCs and odours	>95
Catalytic incineration	VOCs and odours	>95
Fibrous scrubber	Acid gases, VOCs and odours	>90
Moving bed scrubber	Acid gases, VOCs and odours	>90
Packed bed scrubber	Acid gases, VOCs and odours	>90
Plate scrubber	Acid gases, VOCs and odours	>90
Spray tower scrubber	Acid gases, VOCs and odours	>90
Sorbent injection	Acid gases	40–80
Biofiltration	VOCs and odours	>95
Spray drying	Acid gases	>90

The principles of the control techniques in Table 5.2 and a review of their applicability in food processing operations follows. It is difficult to offer definitive price guidance for this equipment as the price will depend upon the waste gas flow requirements and equipment availability. The costs given are for typical installation sizes.

Adsorption.   This is a process where the gas molecules are retained on a solid surface. There are several variations of this equipment, principally:

1. disposable cartridge filters for intermittent flows and low odour concentrations, the cost being dependent upon flow rates, but typically in the range of hundreds to a few thousand pounds in cost;

2. regenerating fixed beds where one bed is in adsorption mode and the other is regenerated, usually by steam stripping; this results in a secondary emission which must be treated;
3. fluidised bed systems where the bed is moved and regenerated outside the main reaction chamber.

The fixed and fluidised bed systems are effective for VOC emissions which can be recovered and re-used or burned, but are inappropriate for mixed odour streams as the regeneration leads to a secondary emission requiring treatment. The cost of fixed bed and fluidised bed systems is high, between £50 000 and £500 000. Disposable activated carbon cartridge filters have a limited use but suffer from the need for regular replacement, media degradation from fatty particles, risk of re-entrainment and breakthrough of odours once saturated, and final disposal concerns.

Thermal oxidation.   In this process, combustible gases and odours are oxidised by the application of heat. The advantage of this technique is that it can offer very high destruction efficiencies (often >99%), and is thus applicable for high odour strength emissions. It can be widely used as most odorous gases may be oxidised. The destruction efficiency is determined by oxidation temperature, time, turbulence and oxygen availability in the combustion zone. Temperatures typically of 800°C are required for efficient control of odours. There are several different oxidation systems available:

1. thermal oxidisers or afterburners where the waste gases are heated to >800°C by the use of support fuel. The amount of support fuel can be reduced by incorporating heat recovery to pre-heat incoming waste gases;
2. catalytic oxidisers where a catalyst is used to reduce the oxidation temperature, typically to between 350 and 400°C. The main problem with this type of equipment is the risk of catalyst coating or poisoning, which can lead to catalyst replacement costs of up to 20% of the original capital outlay;
3. regenerative thermal oxidisers such as the ceramic bed oxidiser. These units incorporate a simple system of passing the air into a pre-heated ceramic bed where oxidation is completed. The bed acts as a very efficient heat-exchanger and the cleaned air returns energy into the bed before discharge. The air flow is then reversed to utilise this stored heat. These units can offer 98% thermal efficiency and have an energy equivalent use of oxidising the odours at 30–50°C above the inlet temperature, offering savings of up to 95% running costs compared to the traditional thermal oxidiser.
4. another option is to pass odorous gases to existing boilers as combustion air, which is viable only where the boiler is on load continuously.

If the load reduces, the flame zone shortens and the destruction efficiency drops drastically.

Thermal oxidation technology offers extremely high odour destruction for a wide range of odorous emissions, and the low energy use of regenerative oxidisers offers greatly reduced running costs. This technology is the most suitable for high intensity odours. The typical capital cost of this technology would be between £50 000 and £400 000.

Absorption/scrubbing.   This technology is based upon the absorption of odour into a liquid system. The odorous gases must be brought into intimate contact with the liquor and must be provided with adequate residence time for the reaction to occur. In order to achieve the contact time, it is usual for odour absorbers to be of the packed tower type with packings ranging from plastic balls and rings to fibrous matting. The liquor is provided with chemical additives to promote treatment of the chemicals absorbed, typically controlled with acids or alkalis to maintain the pH of the liquor.

Odour absorbers have a wide usage, offer reasonable efficiencies for low to medium odour intensities, and are priced between £25 000 and £250 000. They require regular maintenance and dosing of chemical additives and have the disadvantage that, for some odours, it is necessary to have a number (two or three) of different stages dosed with different chemicals to treat the chemical species concerned. This multi-stage arrangement increases the price considerably towards the upper figure quoted.

Biofiltration.   This technique is based upon the oxidation treatment of odours by microorganisms and fungi supported in a biological media. The technique can offer high destruction efficiencies for certain odours, although it is less effective with certain organic compounds and must therefore be used with care. Prices range from £40 000 to £200 000. There are two basic types of biofilter:

1. Soil based. This comprises a network of air distribution pipes covered with about 1 m of soil. The soil must be maintained moist by irrigation to maintain the biomass.
2. Non-soil biofilters. These usually comprise a plenum chamber for the distribution of odorous gases, above which 1 to 2 m of biomaterial (such as peat, heather, wood bark compost, etc.) is supported. This system is usually provided with a humidifier to maintain the biomass moisture content

The critical points in design are to maintain the nutrient and moisture content, obtain good gas distribution in the bed, avoid consolidation and maintain the pH of the mixture. The one drawback is that the residence time required for gases in the biofilter is typically 3 to 5 min for soil biofilters and 30 to 90 s for non-soil biofilters. This results in large areas being required. Also, biofilters are not capable of handling hot gases as these destroy the biomass.

5.12.3   Dispersion of odours

Even with the application of sophisticated, high efficiency control equipment, it is often necessary to rely on dispersion of odours to finally reduce ambient concentrations below the odour detection threshold. The design of chimneys and selection of heights to ensure dispersion is a specialist task and is based upon mathematical models.

5.13   Monitoring of odours

As detailed in section 5.10, it is usually the offensiveness of an odour that causes the concerns and complaints. There are currently no scientifically credible techniques for quantifying the offensiveness of an odour. Therefore, the initial assessment of odour is usually based upon subjective olfactory assessment. It is possible to measure the concentration of target chemical species in a waste gas flow, but this can be misleading as it does not reflect any synergism or combination of effects of mixed chemical species.

The technique most widely used for the monitoring of odour is dynamic dilution olfactometry. A sample of the odorous gas is drawn into a non-reactive bag. The sample is then taken to an 'odour-free' laboratory and passed into the olfactometer. The olfactometer is an instrument which has a number of sniffing ports and facilities to mix the odorous gas with clean air to provide controlled dilutions. The diluted sample is then presented to a panel of six screened persons at the sniffing ports. The dilution range is varied until 50% of the panel can no longer detect an odour, and this is the number of dilutions to odour threshold of the sample. This effectively gives a numerical value for the strength of the odour based upon the number of times the sample had to be diluted with clean air before it was at its detection threshold; the higher the number of dilutions the stronger the odour. This technique is particularly valuable for identifying critical sources where there are a number of possible sources and also for the design of abatement measures and checking the effectiveness of any abatement equipment installed.

6 Water pollution in the food industry: sources, control and cost implications

A.D. WHEATLEY

6.1 Introduction

Effluent and waste are becoming very important aspects of food processing. Legislation on waste disposal is now more stringent and more
complex than it was a few years ago, charges are rising faster than other
costs. Environmental pollution is also a focus for public attention. In future
therefore management and staff in the food industry will need to be aware
of current environmental issues and legislative requirements. Factory
engineers will need to be able to cost different pollution control strategies
and be familiar with clean technology and treatment processes. These
therefore are the topics covered in this chapter with the aim of providing
a training and introductory guide to help with the development of policy.

6.2 Controls

6.2.1 Legislation

The highly publicised pollution issues such as global warming and the
accumulation of persistent micropollutants are international and legislative
decisions, by mutual agreement, and no longer the sole responsibility of
National Governments. Standards are being set by the UN, OECD and
by International Convention.

In Europe many of the environmental quality standards are being set by
the European Community. At present for example there are about 15 EC
directives in various stages of implementation which affect environmental
quality and indirectly therefore the installation and search for new technology. The Commission intends to encourage environmental protection
by further legislation and increased taxes on non-renewable resources.
This new legislation will continue to add to the food industries' costs for
pollution control and monitoring. Opinions differ as to the actual value of
these extra costs but in comparative terms the European Commission,
supported by some investment bank surveys, estimate that it will represent
between 2 and 3% of the gross national product of Europe by 1999. This
will at least double the existing costs for waste disposal. The food industries

therefore do need a highly professional approach to waste disposal and the environment.

6.2.2   International commissions and conventions

6.2.2.1   *The European Commission.*   The basic environmental policy of the European Commission is to promote recovery and recycling of waste materials. It aims to do this by applying three basic principles to waste disposal (Table 6.1). One of the other major aims of the EC's legislative programme is to ensure uniformity of standards between member states. There are objections to this approach because different discharge standards may be scientifically justifiable in different countries but while maintaining similar overall environmental qualities. In the United Kingdom, for example, rivers are short and fast flowing compared to many in Europe and therefore arguably capable of a greater degree of self-purification. Criticisms have also been levelled at the precautionary principle which may not provide good value for money in terms of environmental improvement or reduction in risk. These types of arguments, however, are not understood by public opinion. Within the European Community (EC) new legislation is initiated by the administrative Commission of the European Communities (CEC) in Brussels. These laws or Directives are, after suitable discussion and debate, approved by Council of Ministers (Representatives of National Governments) and made law. Prior to approval in the final form, draft Directives are circulated and published for discussion and amendment. Outlines of the Directives are published in the Official Journal (series L) and full details can be obtained from the appropriate Government Departments or Ministries, from Official Government sources (book shops), from EC Documentation Centres or from Commission Information Offices.

Once the Directive is approved by the Council of Ministers, it becomes binding on member states but it is left to the National Governments to introduce legislation conforming to the intention of the Directive and the legislation does not come into force until this is done. Directives usually set time limits for Governments to comply.

Table 6.1 European Commission pollution control philosophy

---

1. The polluter pays principle: the waste disposer should bear the cost of enviornmental restoration, e.g. conveyance treatment and monitoring

2. The proximity principle: waste, hazardous waste particularly, is best treated as close as possible to its source to avoid the generation of diffuse sources of pollutants

3. The precautionary principle: where there is a lack of toxicity or biodegradability data, maximum permitted concentrations of discharges should be set at the detection limits

---

At present there are about 15 major EC Directives (Table 6.2) in various stages of implementation which affect water quality and indirectly therefore the costs of effluent disposal in the food industry. The Directives can be divided into key groups affecting drinking water, natural waters, toxicity and persistence, environmental impact and competition (Table 6.3).

One of the most important characteristics of these Directives compared to most previous national legislation is the introduction of quantitative standards for a wide range of parameters. For example, the Dangerous Substances Directive (76/464/CEC) lists 129 substances which are particularly dangerous and therefore priority cases for control; this is known as List 1, the black list. The amounts of these chemicals which could be discharged were limited in two ways. The first was the uniform emission standard (UES) which specified limits by maximum concentration and total amount. The second defined an acceptable environmental quality standard (EQS) which has an upper environmental limit not to be exceeded. The Directives on surface water (78/659/CEC) are not as advanced but the oxygen depleting substances including nitrogen compounds will be covered. Fourteen chemical parameters are listed together with minimum sampling frequencies and analytical methods. It is likely that the Directive will also introduce ecological standards and two categories of water fisheries are defined; these are salmonid game fish and cyprinid coarse fish. The establishment of a coarse fishery will be the minimum for all surface waters. Sources of surface water for drinking are classified into three types, A1, A2 and A3, corresponding to different types of standard treatments (Directive number 75/440/CEC). Forty-six substances and parameters are listed with maximum admissible concentration (MAC) and guide levels (GL); 95% of samples must meet these values (Directive number 79/869/CEC). Surface water less than A3 in quality should not be used for drinking purposes. The drinking water Directive 80/778/CEC lists 60 substances with MAC. There is a further Directive on groundwater 80/68/CEC. This Directive bans the discharge of all List 1 substances contained in 76/464/CEC although exceptions are allowed after investigation. The dangerous substances Directive (76/464/CEC) also includes a list of potentially hazardous materials; List 2, the grey list. Discharges of List 2 substances to soil and potentially to groundwater therefore must be monitored and authorised by a national responsible authority (see also the section on UK legislation).

The biodegradability of chemical substances is covered by two groups of Directives. The problems of persistent detergents were recognised some time ago and a group of Directives (73/404/CEC, 73/405/CEC and 82/242/CEC, 82/243/CEC) specify a biodegradability of 90%. The sub-directives specify methods of analysis. The new substances Directives 79/831/671/548/CEC include a series of ecotoxicity and biodegradability

Table 6.2 Major EC Directives affecting water quality

(i) Drinking water

80/777/EEC　On the approximation of the laws of the member states relating to the exploitation and marketing of natural mineral waters

80/778/EEC　Relating to the quality of water intended for human consumption

(ii) Wastewater

91/271/EEC　Concerning urban waste water treatment

(iii) Surface and bathing waters

75/440/EEC　Concerning the quality required of surface water intended for the abstraction of drinking water in member states

76/160/EEC　Concerning the quality of bathing water

78/659/EEC　On the quality of freshwaters needing protection or improvement in order to support fish life

79/869/EEC　Concerning the methods of measurement and frequencies of samples and analysis of surface water intended for the abstraction for drinking in the member states (reference methods for 75/440/EEC)

79/923/EEC　On the quality required of shellfish waters

91/676/EEC　Concerning the protection of fresh, coastal and marine waters against pollution caused by nitrates from diffuse sources

(iv) Dangerous substances

76/464/EEC　On pollution caused by certain dangerous substances discharged into the aquatic environment of the Community

This Directive has given rise to several 'daughter directives'

82/176/EEC　On limit values and quality objectives for mercury discharges by the chlor-alkali electrolysis industry

83/513/EEC　On limit values and quality objectives for cadmium discharges

84/156/EEC　On limit values and quality objectives for mercury discharges by sectors other than by chlor-alkali electrolysis industry

84/491/EEC　On limit values and quality objectives for discharges of hexachlorocyclohexane, in particular lindane

86/280/EEC　On limit values and quality objectives for discharges of certain dangerous substances included in List I in the Annexe to Directive 76/464/EEC (covers DDT, PCP and CTC)

88/347/EEC　Amending Annex II to Directive 86/280/EEC relating to aldrin, dieldrin, endrin, isodrin (the 'Drins'), hexachlorobenzene (HCB), hexachlorobutadiene (HCBD), and chloroform

90/415/EEC　Amending Annex II to Directive 86/280/EEC on limit values and quality objectives for discharges of certain dangerous substances included in list I of the Annex to Directive 76/464/EEC

80/68/EEC　On protection of groundwater against pollution caused by certain dangerous substances

(v) Biodegradability

73/404/EEC　On the approximation of the laws of the member states relating to detergents

73/405/EEC　On the approximation of the laws of the member states relating to methods of testing the biogradability of anionic surfactants

82/242/EEC　Amending Directive 73/404/EEC

82/243/EEC　Amending Directive 73/405/EEC

86/94/EEC　Amending Directive 73/404/EEC

(vi) Sewage sludge disposal

86/278/EEC　On the protection of the environment, and in particular of the soil, when sewage is used in agriculture

91/375/EEC　Concerning the protection of waters against pollution caused by nitrates from agricultural sources

Table 6.2 (*continued*)

(vii) **Management and policy**

77/795/EEC[a]	Establishing a common procedure for the exchange of information on the quality of surface freshwater in the Community
83/189/EEC[a]	On laying down a procedure for the provision of information in the field of technical standards and regulations
86/85/EEC[a]	Establishing a Community information system for the control and reduction of pollution caused by the spillage of hydrocarbons and other harmful substances at sea
88/246/EEC[a]	Amending 86/85/EEC to include major inland waters
91/692/EEC[a]	On standardising and rationalising reports on the implementation of certain directives relating to the environment
92/446/EEC[a]	Concerning questionnaires relating to directives in the water sector
89/106/EEC	On the approximation of laws, regulations and administrative provisions of the Member States relating to construction products
90/531/EEC	On the procurement procedures of entities operating in the water, energy, transport and telecommunications sectors
90/682/EEC	Concerning the modules for the various phases of the conformity assessment procedures which are intended to be used in the technical harmonisation directives
92/13/EEC	Coordinating the laws and administrative provisions relating to the application of Community rules on the procurement procedures of entities operating in the water, energy, transport and telecommunications sector

(viii) **Other**

82/501/EEC	On the major accident hazards of certain industrial activities
85/337/EEC	On the assessment of effects of certain public and private projects on the environment
85/374/EEC	On the approximation of the laws, regulation and administration provisions of the member states concerning liability for defective products

(ix) **Proposed EC Directives**

COM(85)373	On dumping waste at sea
COM(85)733	On water quality objectives for chromium
COM(89)303	On the establishment of the European Environment Agency and the European Environment Monitoring and Information Network
COM(91)347	Amending 90/531/EEC

---

[a]A 'Decision' rather than a 'Directive'.

Table 6.3 The main areas of application of EC Directives affecting effluent disposal

(1)	Drinking water quality
(2)	Bathing water quality
(3)	Surface water quality
(4)	Dangerous substances
(5)	Biodegradability
(6)	Sludge disposal
(7)	Environmental impact
(8)	Wastewater
(9)	Procurement and utilities

standards for all substances produced in quantities greater than 100 tonnes per year. The tests assess breakdown in combination with sewage, in river water, in anaerobic environments and refuse. The tests are based on bottle tests, respirometry and simulation trials, e.g. soil columns and model wastewater treatment plants.

The sewage treatment directive proposes minimum treatment standards according to the size of population served and type of receiving water. Only about 45% of the sewage generated within the EC is treated. The United Kingdom, Germany and Holland treat more than 70% of their sewage while Greece, for example, has facilities for only 25% of its sewage (Figure 6.1). This reflects the degree of urbanisation. There are two main provisions in the proposed directive. The first is that sewage collection systems and sewers should be provided for all towns by 1998. A second requirement is that biological or equivalent treatment be provided for population equivalents exceeding 2000 when discharging to freshwater or 10 000 if the discharge is to sea. More stringent standards will be required if the receiving water is in a sensitive area. Criteria for designation of a pollution sensitive zone would be a risk of excessive algal growth (eutrophication) or water which is to be used for drinking. Standards for a sensitive area would include 5 mg/l total nitrogen and 1 mg/l total phosphorus (Table 6.4).

Member states may also identify areas of low risk of pollution which would not be adversely affected by stronger discharges of sewage. The proposed directive calls for experimental evidence that environmental quality will not be affected by these types of low quality wastewaters.

This directive will stimulate a significant market for sewage treatment in Spain, Italy, France and Greece. In the United Kingdom, there may be

Table 6.4 Requirements for discharge from sewage water treatment plants subject to Articles 4 and 5 of the Directive; phosphorus and nitrogen levels apply to discharges to sensitive areas that are subject to eutrophication[a]

Parameter	Concentration	Minimum percentage reduction
Biochemical oxygen demand (BOD$_5$ at 20°C without nitrification	25 mg/l O$_2$	70–90
Chemical oxygen demand	125 mg/l O$_2$	75
Total suspended solids	35 mg/l	90
Total phosphorus	2 mg/l	80
Total nitrogen	15 mg/l N	70–80

Source: Official Journal of the European Communities L135/40 dated 30.5.1991. Council Directive 91/271/EEC covering Urban Waste Water Directive.

[a]Standards are expressed as annual mean values for a population equivalent of 10–100 000; greater than 100 000, the standards are more stringent.

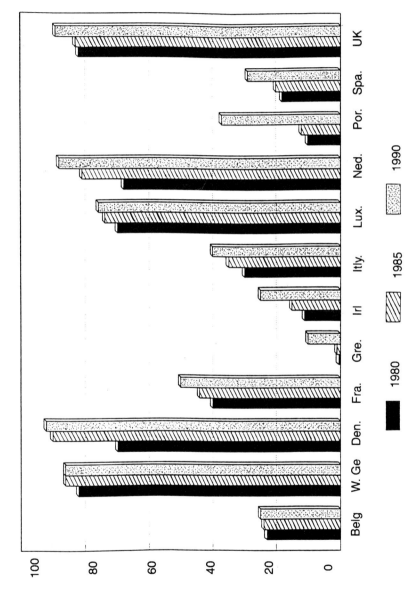

Figure 6.1 Rate of growth in the application of sewage treatment in Europe. Percentage of population with treatment.

up to 600 discharges of raw sewage to coastal waters through short sea outfalls. There is significant expenditure on replacing these short outfalls by simple treatments such as screening and settlement coupled to long sea outfalls. It can be shown by modelling and survey that these long sea outfalls do not cause significant pollution but whether this will be acceptable to public opinion remains uncertain and there will also be a significant number of complete sewage treatment works installed for coastal towns.

The sludge directive 86/181/CEC encourages the recycling of sewage sludge to land, whilst at the same time controls substances to avoid any harmful affects on soil vegetation or animals and the food chain. Treatment is therefore required or that the sludge be injected below the surface to avoid odour and reduce the potential for contamination by pathogens. Biological digestion is the treatment of choice, although in nitrogen sensitive areas this will be restricted by the risk of contamination of groundwater. The directive also requires monitoring and records to be kept of potentially hazardous material such as metals and persistent organics present in the sludge.

The environmental impact directive covers planning and new developments (85/337/CEC). It calls for a mass balance of all raw materials, products and wastes at processing sites. Details of the disposal routes for any wastes, their biodegradability and the environmental impact are required.

The procurement and utilities directive will apply to all water and effluent projects with a value of more than 400 000 ECU (about £265 000). Companies are required to publish basic information about these types of supply contracts in greater detail according to specified procedures, on contracts above 5M ECU (about £3.3M) in the *Official Journal of the European Community*. The aims of the directive are to encourage free and fair competition and to include specifications to European standards.

6.2.2.2   The Organisation for Economic Cooperation and Development (OECD).   This is a non-legislative system for cooperation on standards between North America and Europe. It has been a major influence on the EC policy.

The OECD has developed a number of standard biodegradability tests and produces regular state of the environment reports. The last report in 1985 noted considerable progress on oxygen balance and the microbiological quality in water. It suggested that new problems were likely to be caused by nutrients and eutrophication. It also called for more research on the transfer of pollutants to the sea, a theme taken up by other international organisations.

6.2.2.3   The World Health Organization (WHO).   Much of the WHO's work is associated with water supply and sanitation in rural countries. Eighty percent of all disease in the world is still linked to poor water quality. The European office, however, is concerned with long-term hazards associated with water quality. There are two currently important issues; one is the proliferation of new chemicals (about 1000 each year) which means that it is impossible to have precise data on their effect on the food chain or human toxicity. The other is the wide range of viruses that it is possible to identify in water as new methods of isolation have been developed. The evaluation of risk, extrapolation of data and the acceptance of risk are used to develop guidelines on drinking water quality. Many of these guidelines have subsequently been included in the CEC directives and national legislation.

6.2.2.4 The United Nations.   The United Nations Environment programme is involved with several regional seas and rivers programmes. One of the earliest which has served as an example was the Mediterranean programme ratified in Barcelona. Protocols were established which were designed to restrict the dumping of toxic or persistent substances (Annex 1) and to ensure treatment of less harmful but deleterious substances such as sewage and nutrients (Annex 2). The Barcelona protocol also included emergency procedures and restrictions on land-based pollution in the catchment area.

In 1987 the United Nations presented a report on methods of funding additional environmental quality improvements. The report was known as the Brundtland report after its chairperson, the Prime Minister of Norway. The report suggested that the present market prices for goods and services ignored the full costs of environmental protection and resource depletion since much of the cost associated with any subsequent environmental restoration was transferred to the whole community. An example quoted was that water customers were now paying the costs of removing nitrate pollution from groundwater caused by farming. The report recommended that the economic incentives for clean technology and recycling could be improved by changes in the tax structure with higher rates charged for pollution or valuable resource depletion. These suggestions were widely accepted and taken up by the OECD and the EC who have proposed changes to VAT. A carbon tax is predicted to ease the problems of global warming and to improve the economic position of renewable non-polluting energy sources such as surplus biomass from effluent treatment.

6.2.2.5 The North Sea conference.   There have now been two North Sea conferences, one in Braemer in 1984 and the other in London in 1988. These conferences consider all sources of pollution from land, ship and atmospheric fall out. The first conference in 1984 sought agreement to reduce the discharge of highly toxic and persistent compounds and to reduce the quantities of sewage and sewage sludge dumped to sea. The second conference focussed on nutrients. Algal blooms in the coastal regions of Denmark and Germany are now common. The most recent conference has also agreed to a ban on the dumping of sewage sludge in the North Sea. Traditionally the United Kingdom has used the North Sea for disposing of significant amounts of sludge but this has to end by 1995. This agreement will have an important effect on sewage and sludge disposal in the United Kingdom. Incineration is the favoured new method of sludge disposal in large urban areas but there are serious public concerns over stack emissions.

6.2.2.6   The Oslo Convention.   The Oslo Convention and Commission is a standing committee which investigates toxicity and persistence of substances disposed of to sea. The conference has called for participants to keep records on the types and quantities of these dangerous materials dumped at sea.

6.2.2.7   The Paris Commission.   The Paris Commission deals with pollution of the sea arising from land-based sources. It has the brief of monitoring and implementing the recommendations of the North Sea Conference and, like the European Community, it has legislative powers. In addition to the most dangerous (List 1) substances, it has produced recommendations on limiting oil discharges. Its most recent report has considered the potential role of anaerobic digestion to control land-based discharges to the sea (The Paris Commission, 1988).

6.2.3   National Policies

A recent publication by McLoughlin and Bellinger (1993) gives a brief review of the legislative procedures and pollution control laws of most of the industrial countries.

6.2.3.1   The United States.   The Environmental Protection Agency (EPA) is responsible for natural water quality in the USA. The EPA has an integrated pollution control mandate which includes control over atmospheric pollutants, solids waste management, hazardous waste management and natural waters. The EPA also has a research and development programme and is responsible for advising the President and Executive on necessary new legislation via the Council of Environmental Quality. The Council of Environmental Quality is composed of members of the Government Departments with environmental interests, e.g. Agriculture, Health, Transport, etc.

For particularly hazardous pollutants such as pesticides, radioactive waste and toxins, the EPA assumes responsibility for checking and enforcing standards. For most routine water quality standards the state authorities maintain standards, with occasional checks by the EPA. More details of the actual standards and parameters included in USA policy are included in a recent review edited by Corbitt (1989).

6.2.3.2   The United Kingdom.   Water administration in the United Kingdom is divided into three geographical areas: Scotland, Northern Ireland and England and Wales together. In Scotland, sewage treatment and water supply is the responsibility of nine regional municipal authorities. River protection and monitoring is controlled separately by river boards directly responsible via the Secretary of State for Scotland to central government. A recent policy review in Scotland has favoured retention of the existing system but to include the formation of three regional water authorities who are to include elements of privatisation by the participation of public companies in the management of water treatment plant.

In Northern Ireland, central government via the Department of the Environment for Northern Ireland is responsible for river and surface water quality. Sewage treatment is undertaken by the local authorities. England and Wales is divided up into ten multi-functional Water Companies who control water supply and sewage treatment. The ten Water Authorities of England and Wales were privatised as part of the 1989 Water Act.

Privatisation was overall government policy to reduce central and local government financing of certain services in favour of self-financing enterprises. In the period 1985–1989, both the operating costs and capital costs of the Water Authorities were reduced reflecting the restrictions on public sector borrowing. This led to a reduction in the rate of improvements in surface water quality and in some cases to a deterioration in river quality. To counteract this trend and provide a capital injection for the water standards called for by the EC Directives, the UK Government decided that the responsibility should be transferred to the private sector. The essential improvements which are needed to meet the requirements of EC Directives will, after privatisation, have to be met by increases in direct charges to the customer. These costs may be reduced as the water companies establish other sources of income. As part of privatisation, three new government agencies were set up to monitor the water companies:

1. A drinking water inspectorate, a quality unit within the Department of the Environment with responsibility for drinking water standards;
2. The National Rivers Authority (NRA) with responsibility for the protection of river water quality, groundwater and coastal waters;
3. The Office of Water Services (OFWAT) with a responsibility to regulate prices and oversee investments in infrastructure.

These arrangements were designed to avoid any conflict of interests concerning water quality and costs.

The National Rivers Authority raises a significant amount of its revenue from levies on abstractions and discharges of water. The largest customers are the new regional water companies (see Section 6.3 on costs). The disposal of sewage sludge to land and the licensing of sea dumping of sludges and waste has remained the duty of the Ministry of Agriculture, Fisheries and Food (MAFF).

Potentially hazardous processes and toxic wastes which might enter the water environment are the responsibility of Her Majesty's Inspectorate of Pollution (HMIP). HMIP approval and registration is required for a range of industries, mainly those for the manufacture of chemicals and materials which use potentially harmful reagents and processes. The HMIP takes an integrated approach to pollution control in order to minimise any adverse effects on the total environment, i.e. soil, air and water.

The HMIP is required to consult with the National Rivers Authority (NRA) for discharges to surface water. The NRA can require the inclusion of conditions, and may veto the authorisation if the release of substances into water will result in a failure to achieve published water quality objectives.

Recently, the Government has announced that it intends to set up an environmental protection agency which would incorporate all the pollution control functions of the NRA, HMIP and the waste regulation authorities (WDA). The WDAs are responsible for refuse disposal on behalf of local government. No time frame was set for these changes.

The regulation of water pollution is through three major acts.

1. The Control of Pollution 1974;
2. Environmental Protection 1990;
3. Water Resources 1991.

The Control of Pollution Act 1974 (COPA). The Control of Pollution Act came into force with the formation of the Water Authorities and succeeded a series of Public Health Acts 1910–1931 and Rivers Prevention of Pollution Acts 1951–1961. The important provisions of the Act are that all abstractions and discharges to sewer, river estuary or coastal waters require registration and consent.

The Act makes it illegal to cause or permit water pollution, and case precedence means it is not necessary to show either intent or negligence. The Act also includes powers to control the disposal of solids and other discharges likely to cause environmental pollution.

It included a provision to allow the Water Authorities and their successors, the Water Companies and the NRA, to recover the costs of waste treatment and pollution control and also to recover any expenses required to counteract a polluting discharge. The Bill also allowed for public access to information via a register of consents, analytical measurements and records of pollution incidents. The 1974 Pollution Control Bill did not include any quantitative or qualitative standards other than to restore and maintain good water quality but standards have been incorporated into the 1991 Water Resources Act.

The Environmental Protection Act 1990. This legislation, also known as the Integrated Pollution Control Bill (IPC) (1991), was the culmination of the investigations of three Government Committees on pollution in the United Kingdom. One was the twelfth and latest report of the Royal Commission on Environmental Protection and the second was a House of Commons Select Committee on the Environment (referred to as The Rossi Committee, after its Chairman) and a report on Contaminated Land. The bill also incorporates several European Community directives and agreements on sea dumping of waste into national law.

It includes the existing registrable processes of the Health and Safety at Work Act 1974 (which itself was derived from the Chlor-alkali Act 1938) but extends the coverage to all industries making discharges, not just the chemical industries. Inspection and registration will be controlled by the HMIP (Her Majesty's Inspectorate of Pollution) and the local authorities for non-hazardous industries. All emissions from the listed processes in the bill require a consent to discharge (issued by the HMIP or local authority). The consents are designed to minimise or render harmless offensive releases. They will include any limits for local or national environmental quality proscribed by the Secretary of State, the EC or other International agreements. The aim is to ensure the operator uses the best available techniques not entailing excessive cost (BATNEEC). The standards can impose limits on the concentration, amount emitted in any period and type of substance. Different standards may be set according to local circumstances. The HMIP or local authority will also have responsibility for enforcing these conditions.

A duty of care is included in the Bill in order to ensure that the waste is well managed. There are three main provisions: (i) the waste should be adequately described to allow proper handling and treatment; (ii) it must not be allowed to escape; and (iii) it should only be transferred to an authorised, licensed company. These responsibilities can be passed from registered group to registered group and so a producer is not strictly responsible for ultimate disposal.

Like the Control of Pollution Act, the Bill enables authorities to recover costs of implementing the new law. The HMIP's costs relating to IPC will be recovered by charges imposed for consents; approximately 70–75% of the total cost. It is also planned that the new system of authorisations will reduce monitoring costs by way of the system of prior approvals.

The Bill provides public access to information. The authorities are required to keep registers of consents and testing to which the public will have access. Information may be excluded from the Register if its inclusion would be contrary to the interests of national security or would prejudice commercial interests. The Integrated Pollution Control Bill has led to significant changes in the management of solid waste.

It was designed to reorganise waste regulation, disposal and collection authorities throughout the United Kingdom. The key proposal was the separation of the regulatory and operational functions of the Waste Disposal Authority (WDAs) by the designation of Waste Regulation Authorities (WRAs) and the creation of Local Authority Waste Disposal Companies (LAWDCs) which will then be obliged to compete with the private sector. This separation of functions was designed to minimise the scope for conflict of interest in the regulation of a local authority's own sites as compared with those of the private sector. The Bill introduced a new form of consent for solids waste disposal called a Waste Management Licence. This covered the deposit, treatment or disposal of controlled waste, defined by the Bill as 'household, industrial and commercial waste'. Licences include conditions relating to the waste, the precautions to be taken and treatments to be carried out. The WRA, which grants the licence, is given a wide discretion as to the nature of the conditions it may impose. The Secretary of State may add further regulations and conditions according to national policy which are to be included in a licence.

Water Resources Act 1991. The Water Resources Act superseded the 1989 Water Act which privatised the Water Authorities and set up the NRA. The act includes sections common to both COPA and IPC to cover pollution prevention, cost recovery and public registers.

Table 6.5 'Use classes' for controlled waters

Drinking water
Fisheries
Agricultural
Industrial
Water sports
Protected ecosystems

Additionally the Bill provides for the NRA to establish a system of statutory water quality objectives (SWQO) in the controlled waters, i.e. surface, ground and coastal waters. The quality criteria are to be based on use (Table 6.5). It also enables the designation of water protection zones to exclude certain industrial and agricultural activities which might prejudice groundwater quality, for example applications of fertilisers, pesticides and solvent use.

6.2.3.3   Other EC countries

Belgium. Control of water pollution in Belgium was reorganised between 1970 and 1975. The main Water Pollution Control Act was passed in 1971. It provided a legal framework to enforce wastewater purification and the protection of surface waters. Sixty-seven percent of Belgium's drinking water is obtained from groundwater and the 1971 laws provided protection and establishment of exclusive catchment zones. Three water authorities were formed in 1975 representing the three geographical regions: Flanders, Wallonia and Brussels. The water authorities report to a Minister of Public Health. Wastewater treatment companies were also set up at this time with three standards of treatment according to local conditions. There has been substantial investment in Belgium to increase the extent of sewage treatment (Figure 6.1) and industrial effluents have become subject to licences and charges which control wastewater disposal. Major improvements in waste treatment are still required to meet the EC directives.

Denmark. Water resources, supply of potable water and wastewater treatment are mostly the responsibility of the local authorities but with about a quarter supplied by private companies. Virtually all drinking water is groundwater and traditionally this has received very little treatment, usually filtration but rarely disinfection. Wastewater treatment requirements therefore are some of the most stringent in the EC. The Protection of the Environment Act 1973 prevents water pollution and stipulates that no wastewater, treated or untreated, may be discharged to surface water which is to be used for potable water supply.

Denmark has a 10-year programme, which started in 1987, to ensure that 98% of all wastewater is treated to at least primary standard. Sewage treatment works with a capacity in excess of 15 000 population equivalent and new plants greater than 5000 population must produce an effluent of less than 8 mg/l total N and less than 1.5 mg/l P. The cost will be passed on to the consumers. Dumping sewage sludge at sea is banned. The 10-year plan also includes restrictions on agriculture to reduce inputs of nitrogen, phosphate and organic matter to natural waters. Farms with thirty or more animals must provide nine months slurry storage, and crop rotation including pasture is required. The use of chemical fertiliser is now under review. The Danish Environmental Protection Administration has specified guidelines for agricultural use of sludge. These require that sludge be stabilised and then stored or sanitised before restricted use for cereals, parks, forests and land reclamation. The sludge must be ploughed in within 48 h of application on agricultural land.

France. The Water Law of 1964 is the main basis of water quality and pollution protection. The law includes a series of water quality objectives for the various types of river and sets a timetable for improvements to be made. The Act is usually used as a guide for managing water. Additions were made to the Act in 1971, 1976 and 1992 which specified quality by area and use, and also approved increased spending. An important addition was made in 1976 which required all discharges including sludge to be authorised and classified; the Installations Classées. The consents are granted according to what is considered technically and economically possible by an Inspecteur des Installations Classées. These decisions are taken nationally by the Ministry of the Environment. Water Policy is decided by the Service de l'Eau and the Service de l'Environnement Industriel, who exercise authority through a Conseil Supérieur des Installations Classées. The Ministry of Health is responsible for drinking water and the Ministry of Agriculture for the reuse of sludge. There are also regional policies based on six areas matching the main river catchments, each one managed by an Agence de l'Eau (Table 6.6). Their function through the Agences Financières de Bassin is to provide money for pollution control. They have the power to collect and levy charges on industry for discharges, based on decisions taken by the Installations Classées. The Agences de Bassin also make recommendations on water quality to the local municipal or department level.

In managing water treatment plant, both water supply and waste is the responsibility of these municipalities many of whom have set up joint boards and utility managements similar in style to the pre-1974 system in the United Kingdom. There are for example about 36 000 municipalities and about 14 000 water utilities. The municipalities or joint boards may run their utility themselves or delegate the operation to a specialist private water company. About 70% of the population are served by 65 private water companies but there are only five companies of size (Table 6.7). The municipalities or water boards retain ownership of the equipment but are also responsible for new investment. Enforcement of the standards is carried out at the department level. This is done by the Prefect (Commissaire de la Republique) who has authority over all services of the various Ministries in a department; he is an official of the central government.

Table 6.6 French Agence de l'Eau

Agence de l'Eau	Expenditure (Ffr M)	Population (M)
Adour – Garonne	10000	5.5
Artois – Picardie	6900	4.5
Loire – Bretagne	13000	11.2
Rhin – Meuse	8000	4.0
Rhone – Méditerranée-Corse	15000	12.0
Seine – Normandie	29000	17.0

Table 6.7 The largest private French water companies (Source: International Water Statistics, 1988)

Company	Population served (M)	Turnover (£B)
General des Eaux	24	12.3
Lyonnaise des Eaux Dumez	13	3.8
Société d'Aménagement Urbain et Rural Eaux (SAUR)	6.0	0.6
Group (CISE) Compagnie Internationale de Services d'Environnement	3.5	0.25

Germany. In Western Germany, water is managed by the municipalities, and drinking water and wastewater treatment have always been kept separate. In the east, there were 16 regional water utilities responsible for both water supply and wastewater treatment. To reach better water standards in eastern Germany quickly, the Federal Government is suggesting a new mix of associations of utilities and private company participation.

In Germany, central government provides a framework or model laws, but each Federal state retains freedom to modify or add to them through the local parliaments (The Laender). The basic federal or central law on water was set in 1976. This Water Management Act stipulates that all abstractions and discharges of water must be authorised and comply with Federal standards. Emission standards exist for 50 different types of industry as well as sewage works discharges. These are minimum standards and the Laender can impose stricter standards if it believes it is in the public interest (Wohl der Allegmeinheit).

Each Laender has slightly different arrangements for enforcing standards but a working group brings together representatives of each Laender to ensure consistency and dissemination of information. If standards do not exist for a particular type of industry, then there is provision in the Act for these to be based on as low a concentration of pollutants as possible using recognised technical equipment. The Federal law also includes a section which allows improvements and planning of overall water quality objectives. The Ministry of the Interior is responsible for the environment and water management. The Ministry of Agriculture has a coordinating role for fisheries and sludge disposal and the Ministry of Health is responsible for drinking water. There is a mandatory code of practice for sludge utilisation with lower limits for potentially hazardous materials than the CEC directive. This has encouraged more sludge incineration.

Greece. At present, only 25% of the population of Greece are connected to mains drainage. Most sewage is discharged to sea untreated. One-third of the population live in greater Athens which is at present building a sewage treatment system. The Ministry of Public Works is responsible for the construction of sewage works based on the advice given by the Ministry of Research and Technology as to the best types of treatment. The Ministry of the Environment is to set and enforce surface water standards whereas drinking water quality is controlled by the Ministry of Health.

Ireland. The central Government Ministry of the Environment is responsible for water pollution control and surface water standards. These water quality standards are enforced by the 87 local authorities using powers resulting from a Local Government Pollution Act 1977. An additional Local Government Act, Planning and Development is used to control industrial discharges. There are no Government guidelines on the agricultural reuse of sludge but there is advice from the Agricultural Research Institute.

Italy. Water supply and wastewater treatment in Italy are controlled by municipalities who, depending upon their size, can elect to manage their own equipment and resources, or form unions with other neighbouring local authorities or delegate responsibility to private companies. There are a large number of separate water undertakings and this has led to problems planning national resources and overcoming general pollution problems.

The first national legislation to control water pollution was passed in 1976 (MERLI Law 319), and was to be implemented by 1985, with the formation of a new Ministry of the environment. It proposed standards for discharges to sewer, surfaces waters and the sea. This law was coupled to a programme of investment to increase the amount of sewage treatment provided. At present only 25% receives full treatment. Further progressive improvements were planned. A general waste disposal law was passed in 1977 which included guidelines on the agricultural utilisation of sewage sludge and took into account CEC hazardous waste standards.

Luxembourg. In Luxembourg about 118 local communities, representing 20% of the population, distribute drinking water and treat wastewater. The remainder have formed joint utilities. Standards are issued by the Ministry's of Health and Environment generally in line with EC Directives. The municipalities are responsible for sewage treatment to standards issued by the Ministry of Public Health and the Environment. About 70% of wastewater is fully treated and industrial effluents discharged to sewers are controlled. Agricultural use of sludge is encouraged but there are no published guidelines; the agricultural reuse of sludge is according to the EC protocols.

The Netherlands. Water quality and pollution is controlled by the 1969 Surface Waters Pollution Act. The Act divided surface waters into two groups. The larger lakes, rivers, estuaries and coastal regions were made the responsibility of the Ministry of Transport and Public Works. The remaining waters were to be managed by the provincial government. In eight of the eleven provinces, Water Authorities were formed to control the local water basin. The law also included a provision for staged improvement plans for water quality, which would be reviewed every 5 years.

All abstractions and discharges are subject to approval by licence. All dischargers and abstractors pay at a level which varies according to the degree of pollution. The water law provides for the imposition of any reasonable limits necessary to protect the environment to be included in the consent. Exclusion zones restricting both industry and agriculture around drinking water aquifers are strictly enforced. The Government policy is that drinking water should be able to be produced by using only traditional methods such as coagulation and filtration. The geography of The Netherlands precludes much reservoir storage and effluent standards on the sewage industry and agricultural discharges are more stringent than the general EC standards.

An additional feature of Dutch policy is the Multi Year Programmes. The plans drawn up by the Ministry of Transport and Public Works provide a water quality framework for up to 10 years in the future. The plans assign priorities, and technical solutions, establish water quality objectives and forecast the likely budget.

Water supply in Holland is provided by provincial water companies. Water quality sampling and methods of analysis are included in a 1984 Waterworks Act. This is updated by amendment as new information becomes available. Guidelines for disposal of sludge to agriculture were published in 1980. These specify that only treated sludges should be used on pasture land and that sludge should not be applied to horticultural crops. Limitations are specified on the spreading rates and on potentially hazardous materials. There is a shortage of suitable land for agricultural reuse of sludge and this has led to a greater dependency on incineration.

Spain and Portugal. The water and wastewater needs of the majority of the population in Spain and Portugal are met by municipal authorities. There are differences according to the sizes of the communities with 20% private company participation in the larger populations ($>$10 000) and 50% participation in the smaller towns. Traditionally, sewage and waste has received only rudimentary treatment in Spain and Portugal but there is an ambitious project to build treatment works to meet the EC standards (construction work in hand to treat 50% of the population). Local authorities do have the power to control discharges and levy charges according to the degree of pollution. About 65% of drinking water comes from river water but the degree of pollution of river water in much of the Pyrenees and Central Spain is still high. Major improvements have occurred in the Mediterranean catchment.

6.3   Costs

6.3.1   Costs of disposal

The United Kingdom is one of only four countries in Europe with more than 80% of the population served by sewage treatment works. Sewers and sewage treatment works are therefore available for the disposal of food industry effluent in most regions of the United Kingdom. Usually treatability is improved by combination with domestic sewage. Dilution and buffering reduces the impact of clean downs and the supplementary nutrients available in sewage increases microbial growth rates. Some food wastes, e.g. fat, may lead to a deterioration in treatability because of high concentrations of cleaning aids, e.g. caustic soda or fat. The United States and all the countries of Europe therefore insist that discharges of effluent to sewer or the environment are licensed. This enables a consent to be issued listing maximum allowed concentrations (MAC) in the effluent. This type of registration prevents the release of chemicals which might damage the drains or inhibit or overload the treatment. It also allows for the recovery of treatment and monitoring costs and public scrutiny.

6.3.2   Consents to discharge

Materials which might immediately damage the drainage system by corrosion, for example strong acids or alkalis, are prohibited as are the common organic solvents such as alcohols, ethers and acetates. These could form explosive mixtures. There are strict limits on a second category of materials which could form corrosive products within the sewers by cross-reaction, for example sulphates and high temperature effluents. There are also restrictions on solids which would accumulate and block drains, e.g. fat. A further group of prohibited substances are those which would cause inhibition of the treatment processes or prevent the water companies disposing of the residues. These include fat, detergents, colour and very strong wastes as well as the more familiar list of metal, pesticide and organochlorines included in the red lists and black lists. Since privatisation and the establishment of water companies, licences to discharge to sewer are also contracts and water companies may wish to restrict any substance to suit local circumstances. Table 6.8 gives a typical list of commonly controlled substances and their permitted ranges.

Implementation of the EC directives discussed in Section 6.2 is expected to cost £30B between 1989–2000; this will double the cost of water. The Government Office of Water Services (OFWAT) has agreed with the companies a variable factor (the k factor) to be added to the retail price index to cover this capital expenditure. Between 1989 and 1991, this was between 5 and 10% above RPI.

Table 6.8 Typical UK consent conditions for discharge to sewer

Parameter	Value[b]
Temperature	$<40°C$
pH	5–9
Metals, total[a]	<30 mg/l
Cyanide	<1 mg/l
Phenol	<500 mg/l
Sulphide	<10 mg/l
Sulphur dioxide	<1 mg/l
Chlorine	<10 mg/l
Oil/grease	<100 mg/l
Insoluble tar	<60 mg/l

Source: Micklewright (1986).
[a]Totals of individual metals usually specified at 1–5 mg/l except Zn and Fe. Red list and heavy metals, e.g. Pb, Cd, Hg, set at detection limits.
[b]Maximum daily volume and maximum flow are also specified.

These increases in the costs of water over the next few years will give scope for advanced and complete waste treatment. All waste treatment processes are complex and their apparent cost effectiveness needs to be assessed to include factors for reliability maintenance and manning. Most of the UK food processing sites are too small to justify extensive treatment; for example, out of the 5000 factories in the United Kingdom, only about 150–200 generate effluent loads greater than 500 tonnes of COD per annum, the point at which treatment becomes economically attractive. There are a number of simple pre-treatment processes which even the smallest sites can utilise with advantage; these as well as complete treatment are described in this chapter.

6.3.3   Waste audits

Planning and a comparison between disposal options requires a thorough analysis of the waste generating processes. Waste audits are a systematic study of the mass balances of raw materials, products and waste. The sources and scale of the wastes from each production process have to be measured by flow and strength. The methods of analysis are standardised and published by the DoE; from this analysis, a report can usually be compiled which compares the effluent generating processes (Table 6.9).

This information will also be of value in fulfilling the terms of the EC Environmental Impact Directive which calls for a mass balance and declar-

Table 6.9 Waste audit information

1. Losses in terms of product and raw materials
2. The cost of disposing of this waste and an allocation to the department generating them
3. The selection and cost of treatment alternatives
4. Possible control procedures
5. Training on waste for key staff

ation of disposal routes for planning consents for large projects. These principles have been included in the UK land and registration procedures for the protection of groundwater and to provide a public register of historical land use. Environmental auditing is a useful system for raising awareness, ensuring legal compliance, limiting liability, assessing costs and identifying cleaner technology.

One of the aims of integrated pollution control is to promote a rethink of production processes to minimise waste. The onus will be on companies to justify publicly that they are using the Best Environmental Option (BEO) for waste disposal. At present, only the fuel and power industries are required to apply for registration but is anticipated that other industries including the food processing industry will eventually need to undertake eco-auditing.

6.3.4   Waste minimisation

Once the sources and quantities of waste have been established, then it is usual to find that there are methods of reducing water consumption and waste. Process re-design and re-organisation can also result in improvements in energy consumption, lower product losses, less accidents and spills, better public relations and reduced liability. There is a basic checklist to follow shown in Table 6.10.

6.3.5   Calculating the costs

The charge for treatment in Europe and the United States is based on the ratio of the organic strength of the food effluent compared to the local sewage and there are significant regional variations. There are further differences between countries in Europe. In Germany for example there is also an assessment of treatability and this is used to increase charges for poor biodegradability. In France there is also a standard charge for oxidising and removal of nitrogen; only the Anglia Water Company does this in the United Kingdom at present. The Anglia region has particular problems with an excess of nitrogen in ground and surface water.

The cost of disposal to sewer is then based on a formula similar in style to the UK (Table 6.11), known as the Mogden or NWC/CBI formula. The

Table 6.10 Waste minimisation procedures

1. *Material handling*: Material handling procedures should be designed to avoid damage contamination spoilage and to improve the quality of storage. If hazardous materials are used they should be kept separate and contained for the possibility of accident
2. *Control*: The aim of better control is to deliver precise amounts of raw materials, reactants, catalyst, physical change or water at exactly the right time. This avoids wasted energy, reactants and water. Improvements in monitoring and analytical equipment will be effective if they reduce waste.
3. *Product formulation*: Changes to an alternative cleaner raw material can reduce the amounts of waste produced and improve the quality of the product.
4. *Process modification*: Different processing operations may be used to avoid waste. For example, dry processing will reduce water consumption without affecting efficiency and quality. Very strong streams, i.e. fat, solids, etc., can usually be easily separated and disposed of differently
5. *Equipment design*: Changes in the design of existing machinery may also reduce pollution, without interfering with quality and efficiency, for example lower operating temperature, less water and less mechanical damage
6. *Plant layout*: Better integration of processes can reduce the amount of equipment and pipe runs, this usually means less cleaning. For example, heating and pumping operations should be in one location, to avoid unnecessary pipework
7. *Recycling*: Damaged raw materials or products can often be recycled without adverse effects. A common possibility is to use a high grade wastewater from cooling or final product washing, for a lower grade use such as primary washing
8. *By-products*: Some by-products can be recovered such as:

   a. Animal feeds
   b. Waste paper or card
   c. Fats and oils
   d. Fertilisers and land irrigation

   The simplest by-products are:

   a. Animal feeds
   b. Biogas and combustion of waste derived fuel
   c. Fats and oils
   d. Fertilisers

cost factors vary annually. Solids or sludge disposal charges have risen more steeply recently than oxidation charges because of sludge disposal problems. Urban Thames Water, for example, now charge more for solids than biological oxidation (Table 6.11).

6.3.6   Case studies

6.3.6.1 *Food industry.* A yeast processing company, which in 1988 was paying £132 000 per annum to discharge aerobically pretreated effluent to sewer, would be faced with a £0.5M charge in 1993 if the existing treatment was not replaced (as indicated in Table 6.12). These figures do not take into account inflation. Calculations (as shown in Table 6.13) indicate that significant savings could be made by the installation of either aerobic or anaerobic processes on site; the running costs of anaerobic digestion were

Table 6.11 Trade effluent charges 1992–1993

	Average regional strength		Charge factors						
	O_S (mg/l)	S_S (mg/l)	R (p/m³)	V (p/m³)	VB (p/m³)	VM (p/m³)	M (p/m³)	B (p/kg)	S (p/kg)
Anglian	426	371	6.68	10.46	2.02	5.19	0.42	11.39	5.61
Northumbrian	386	187	13.96	6.84	0.00	0.00	0.00	10.84	5.50
North West	389	234	7.30	5.90	0.80	0.00	5.50	6.40	4.30
Severn Trent	767	323	9.88	9.07	0.00	0.00	0.00	10.67	5.84
Southern	452	512	15.06	11.01	1.78	7.63	1.95	14.51	9.94
South West	767	487	22.42	22.69	0.00	0.00	3.94	36.58	25.38
Thames	445	336	5.54	6.81	0.00	0.00	0.00	10.74	13.68
Dwr Cymru	500	350	6.75	5.45	2.17	5.77	8.29	12.58	8.86
Wessex	802	313	5.56	8.95	0.85	5.13	9.65	19.81	11.45
Yorkshire	971	321	14.13		0.00	0.00	0.00	14.78	8.64
Northern Ireland	480	340	10.00	8.00	0.00	0.00	0.00	10.00	8.00

Total average charge is for average strength effluent. Trade effluents are charged using the following formulae:

$$C = R + (V + VB) + B\frac{O_t}{O_s} + S\left(\frac{S_t}{S_s}\right)$$

$$C = R + (V + VM) + B\frac{O_t}{O_s} + S\frac{S_t}{S_s}$$

$$C = R + (V + M) + B\frac{O_t}{O_s} + S\frac{S_t}{S_s}$$

C = total charge for trade effluent treatment
R = reception and conveyance charge
V = volumetric and primary treatment cost/m³
VB = additional charge/m³ where there is a biological treatment
VM = treatment and disposal charge for sea outfalls
M = treatment and disposal charge for designated long sea outfalls
O_t = the chemical oxygen demand (COD) of effluent after 1 h quiescent settlement at pH 7
O_S = COD of crude sewage after 1 h quiescent settlement
B = biological oxidation cost/m³ of settlement sewage
S_t = total suspended solids (mg/l) of the trade effluent at pH 7
S_S = total suspended solids (mg/l) of crude sewage
S = treatment and disposal costs of primary sludges/m³ of sewage

much lower than those of the aerobic process. Added to this was the potential benefit of fuel savings through use of the gas; these were likely to be greater than predicted due to the continuing rises in energy prices.

6.3.6.2 Installed plant starch waste example. Tunnel Refiners process maize and wheat flour to produce gluten and starch. A separate process is used to hydrolyse starch to produce various glucose syrups. The waste from these processes contains starch, sugars, proteinaceous material and

Table 6.12 Example of effluent disposal charges for a yeast processing company, Severn Trent area

Volume	$1000\ m^3/day$
COD	5500 mg/l
Suspended solids	400 mg/l

Cost of disposal (real cost)	
1988	311400

Projected	
1989	327170
1990	350100
1991	435250
1992	470100
1993	507700

Source: Adapted from Smith *et al.* (1988).

minerals from the corn and flour. An anaerobic digestion treatment system has recently been installed, as detailed in Table 6.14. The waste contains significant amounts of sulphur (SO_2, 100 mg/l) and ammonia (640–1700 mg/l total N).

The simple pay back on the capital of the plant was 1 year but there have been two unforeseen running costs. There have been some problems due to hydrogen sulphide (H_2S), with complaints being received about

Table 6.13 Example of the costs of anaerobic compared to aerobic treatment (discharge to sewer without treatment, £311 400)

Treatment type	New biotower, new foundations, option 1 £	Refurbishment of existing biotower, option 2 £	New anaerobic filter, option 3 £[a]
Capital	655200	523500	630000
Plant running costs and effluent disposal	224612	226000	143026
Annual saving	86780	85400	168297
Simple payback in years	7.55	6.03	3.74
Payback in years by tax computation for cash flow method	7.67	6.25	4.07

Source: Smith *et al.* (1988).
[a]The value of surplus gas (option 3), estimated at £12 000 p.a. in terms of coal equivalent, has been ignored.

Table 6.14 An example of an anaerobic plant treating starch waste

Reactor type	Anaerobic mixed flow contact process
Size	5710 m³
Biomass concentration	0.5% at optimum conditions
Clarifier volume	2500 m³ volume
Effluent flow	4678 m³/day
COD in	7000–8000 mg/l, max 20000
Total solids in	12000 mg/l
Total solids out	500 mg/l
Suspended solids	660 mg/l
Loading rate	5 kg COD/m³-day
	1 T COD/T Biomass-day
Daily load	4.8–28 T COD/day
COD removal	93% on total COD
pH_{in}	8.0
pH_{out}	7.0
Temperature	
Waste	37°C
Tank	30°C
HRT	29 h
R (recycle ratio)	0.34 (60 m³/h) 1:3 recycle to feed
Biogas production	4000–10000 m³/day
	av. 5000 m³/day, 0.38 m³/kg COD removed
Biogas use	Hot water generation
Capital cost	£1.75M, payback period 1.5 years
Location	Tunnel Refiners, South East London
Contractor	Biomechanics, built in 1986

odour and so the clarifier was roofed. The gas contains 1% H_2S and the effluent 1 mg/l. Ferric chloride is added to the effluent as it is discharged to sewer, and this precipitates sulphide as iron sulphide which helps to control the odour. It has also been noticed that when the protein content is high, this interferes with biomass settlement and density. Lime is used to improve settlement and to neutralise the waste. Lime is added at three points; at the equalisation tank, in the line from the equalisation tank to the digester, and into the digester. The resultant average total alkalinity is 1000 mg/l. Nickel and cobalt are also added as micronutrients.

6.3.6.3 Brewery waste. An expansion of the Watney–Mann brewery at Mortlake between 1987 and 1990 meant that changes would be needed to their on-site effluent treatment plant, which was a 10-year-old high rate biotower. Seven options were short listed, which compared discharging the whole flow untreated to sewer (option 1, Table 6.15) with several different treatment plants to remove 80–90% of the applied COD. The high rate biotower was designed to remove 70% of the applied COD at a flow rate of 2500 m³/day.

Conventional activated sludge was not considered as suitable because it had a poor reputation with strong industrial wastes. Other breweries

Table 6.15 Possible treatment options for brewery waste

Option	Description	Estimated capital cost (£000s)	Operation cost (£000s)	Cost (p/m³)
1	Discharge total flow to sewer		954	52.3
2	Discharge excess flow to sewer		774	42.5
3	Extensions to existing biotowers	895	465	25.5
4	Anaerobic filter and existing biotower	1113	388	21.3
5	Pure oxygen activated sludge and existing biotowers	1100	507	27.8
6	Completely new biofilters for existing and new flow	1480	467	25.6
7	Completely new pure oxygen activated sludge	1855	593	32.5

Source: Brooking *et al.* (1990).

reported difficulties with settlement, controlling dissolved oxygen and sludge return rates. Duplicating the existing biotower system would have been attractive because Watney–Mann had 10 years' successful operating experience with this system including overcoming an odour problem (option 3). This was, however, shown to be impractical because of the available space on site. Option 6, a new low rate biofilter, was ruled out on similar grounds. There was little experience with anaerobic treatment systems in the United Kingdom in 1986 and this was, therefore, judged to be unproven technology. A review of treatment methods at other breweries showed that pure oxygen activated sludge was in use at two other breweries in the United Kingdom where it had overcome the difficulties normally associated with activated sludge and was working well. Oxygen systems were readily controlled with extra capacity easily added by introducing more oxygen; this was well suited to the variable nature of the effluent. The oxygen activated sludge also had the additional advantage of being totally sealed and was therefore unobtrusive. Thus, option 7 combining the existing high rate biotower with a new oxygen activated sludge plant was chosen as the best combination of established technology, capital and running costs. The plant was built in 1988 and the first year's operating results are shown in Table 6.16.

The flow rate during 1988–1989 unexpectedly decreased (Table 6.16). This was because of changes in production. It meant that the biotower could be switched off and the whole load passed to the pure oxygen activated sludge plant; costs could then be compared. The oxygen activated sludge plant performed better than the biotower at the expense of slightly more sludge and the cost of the oxygen about £100 000 per annum. These costs were more than offset by the reduction in costs of discharge to sewer. In 1990, therefore, it was decided to demolish the biotower and provide extra oxygen capacity in the event of the anticipated increases in

Table 6.16 Design characteristics of new effluent treatment plant

	Design	Actual
Flow rate	4000	2269
Influent BOD (mg/l)	2000	–
Effluent BOD (mg/l)	100	95
Influent suspended solids (mg/l)	320	–
Effluent suspended solids	100	179
Power consumption (M/Wh week)	15.9	19.8
Sludge production dry solids (tonne/day)	3	1.2

Source: Brooking *et al*. (1990).

flow actually occurring. This had the major advantage of releasing land for further production developments at the site.

6.4   The characteristics and analysis of waste

6.4.1   *Wastewater composition*

Wastewater is the largest and most dilute of the three major categories of waste (Table 6.17). In the United Kingdom, there are about $9 \times 10^6 \, m^3$ of domestic wastewater, $7 \times 10^6 \, m^3$ of industrial effluent and, if rain and infiltration water are added, this gives a total of about $18 \times 10^6 \, m^3$ each day for treatment (Figure 6.2). About 5000 sewage works serve 80% of the population, 1000 of these serve populations over 10 000 and 17 take the waste of over 300 000 (Table 6.18).

Wastewater is contaminated with organic matter and bacteria some of which may be potential pathogens. The traditional aims of wastewater treatment have been to remove organic matter and reduce the number

Table 6.17 Quantities of waste in Europe 1986 (the quantities were increasing at the rate of 3% per year)

Millions of tonnes	Type of waste
120	Household waste
950	Agricultural waste
160	Industrial waste
300	Sewage sludge
250	Mining industries
170	Demolition and building waste
120	Consumer durables, cars, electrical goods, etc.
130	Others

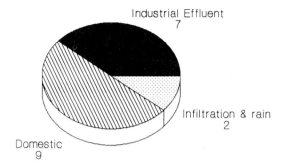

Figure 6.2 The UK's daily effluent treatment (M tonnes), the largest controlled industrial process in the United Kingdom.

of faecal organisms to allow the wastewater to be discharged into the environment without adverse effect.

Municipal wastewaters contain excreta, household wastes, industrial effluents, and storm run-off. They are usually the most complex of the wastewaters containing a wide range of suspended and dissolved materials, and different types of microorganisms. The range of contaminants and the pollution load is defined by a number of tests designed to assess these physical, chemical and biological characteristics. The methods of analysis used are similar throughout the world. In the UK they are published by

Table 6.18 Sewage works in England, Wales, Northern Ireland and Scotland in 1978 with a design dry weather flow greater than 100 000 m³/day

Name of sewage plant	Water authority or river purification board	Dry weather flow (000s m³/day)	Population (000s)
Beckton	Thames	912	2250
Crossness	Thames	505	1550
Minworth	Severn Trent	384	1050
Davyhulme	North West	314	714
Mogden, Isleworth	Thames	439	1330
Deephams	Thames	171	685
Stoke Bardolph	Severn Trent	146	465
Blackburn Meadows	Yorkshire	128	466
Derby (Raynesway)	Severn Trent	108	210
Knostrop (High Level)	Yorkshire	150	481
Finham	Severn Trent	112	339
Maple Lodge	Thames	113	434
Avonmouth	Wessex	160	500
Rye Meads	Thames	78	322
Dalmuir	Strathclyde	219	440
Dalmarnock	Clyde	136	300
Belfast (Duncure Street)	Northern Ireland	110	530

Source: The Water Data Unit (1979).

the Department of the Environment, in Europe they are appended to European Directives and in the USA they are jointly published by the water institutions. The analyses are then used to design the most suitable combinations of treatment equipment. The greatest pollution load for food, domestic, agricultural and a wide range of other industrial waste-waters is caused by their organic content. The organic material in waste stimulates the growth of bacteria and fungi naturally present in water which then consume dissolved oxygen. Normally the biologically generated oxygen demand in natural waters is less than 2 mg/l (BOD) and the most usual sign of extensive water pollution by sewage, industrial effluents or agricultural waste is therefore a reduction in dissolved oxygen.

The organic content of the wastewater is determined by three commonly used tests: chemical oxygen demand (COD), total organic carbon (TOC), and biological oxygen demand (BOD) (Table 6.19).

In rivers and streams, the water undergoes continuous mixing and turbulence and some oxygen (i.e. 2 mg/l) can be replenished (Figure 6.3). The original standards for discharges to rivers in the United Kingdom were set to avoid increasing the BOD of the river above 4 mg/l. In lakes, the water is static and higher standards are required. If the BOD exceeds 4 or

Table 6.19 Tests for organic carbon

Test	Method	Use
COD	Sample is oxidised with boiling chromic acid. The amount of organic carbon is equivalent to the chromic acid reduced. Test takes 3 h	Very common test used for all of wastewater to assess total organic carbon. Apparatus and techniques available in most laboratories
TOC	Sample is ignited and the carbon dioxide produced measured by infrared. Very rapid test, 5–10 min	Used by the larger laboratories with large numbers of samples. Requires specialised expensive equipment. Is becoming common as a process monitoring instrument
BOD	Sample is incubated with a culture of microorganisms. Their metabolic rate is measured by oxygen consumption over 5 days and is proportional to the biodegradable organic carbon	Very common test, used for all types of waste to assess biodegradability. Equipment simple, but requires some understanding of microbiology. Some automated equipment available
PV (permanganate)	Sample is oxidised by permanganate over 4 min or 4 h. The amount of organic carbon is equivalent to the permanganate reduced	Many of the organic compounds are not oxidised by the mild conditions and the test has largely been superseded by the COD. Is useful for field work, apparatus simple

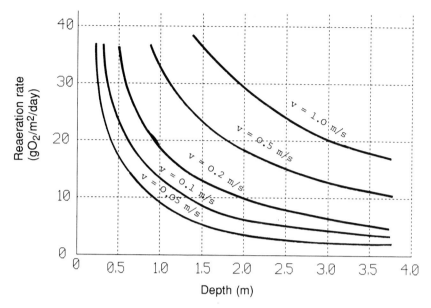

Figure 6.3 Oxygen replenishment in rivers and streams according to depth and velocity.

5 mg/l, then changes in dissolved oxygen will occur. More recently it has become recognised that an average BOD value may be insufficient to protect the natural ecosystem of the receiving water and standards have been restated in terms of 95 percentile compliance values. The EC urban wastewater directive due to come into force from 1998 onwards defines discharge limits in terms of a maximum allowable concentration (MAC) in an average sample. Standards are also stated on COD values but the COD test is not very precise at low concentrations (i.e. <100 mg/l) and BOD or TOC is to be preferred.

Another important very common constituent of wastewaters are solids. Suspended solids are a source of organic matter, they interfere with light penetration in receiving streams and settleable solids precipitate and cover the natural habitat of the benthic or bottom dwelling invertebrates and algae. Measurement of suspended solids is by filtration or light scattering (Table 6.20).

For design purposes, a number of average values have been developed from experience to describe the daily pollutant load per person (Table 6.21). Water consumption depends on income with the UK at 130 litres per head per day, above average for Europe but less than Germany where 200 litres per head is normal and the United States where consumption may be as high as 500 litres in the warmer states. To design waste treatment plants it is usual to double these consumption figures to include for infiltration, storm drainage and expansions in population.

Table 6.20 Classification of solids found in domestic wastewater[a]

Total 700 mg/l	Suspended 200 mg/l	Settleable 100 mg/l	Organic 75 mg/l	Mineral 25 mg/l
		Non-settleable 100 mg/l	Organic 75 mg/l	Mineral 25 mg/l
	Filterable 500 mg/l	Colloidal 50 mg/l	Organic 40 mg/l	Mineral 10 mg/l
		Dissolved 450 mg/l	Organic 160 mg/l	Mineral 290 mg/l

[a]Dry weights determined by warming at 105–110°C until constant weight. Inorganic content measured by heating to 650°C and weighing the residue. Settled samples settled for 20 min. Filtered samples filtered by GFC paper (1.5 μm).

Except for sewage, very few wastewaters have been analysed in detail but all the major components of food wastes, carbohydrate, fat and protein, can be fermented to carboxylic acids in the anoxic or anaerobic conditions of the drains and sewers.

Other pollution problems have become apparent in recent years particularly from inorganic pollutants and persistent or recalcitrant materials. Nitrogen in most of its various forms is a good example. Many food agricultural domestic wastes contain significant amounts of organic nitrogen as protein or urea. These are rapidly converted to ammonia by the anoxic conditions in drains. Ammonia is very toxic; 2 mg/l are sufficient to eliminate most fish and 1 mg/l has an effect on invertebrates. If effluents are to be recycled for public supply, then residual ammonia can generate hazardous by-products during chlorine sterilisation such as the chlor-

Table 6.21 Average daily sewage loads used by sanitary engineers for design

Wastewater (l/h per day)	230
Solids in sewage (g/h per day, 30% water)	200
Oxygen required for treatment (g/h per day)	60

amines. Effluent treatment can be designed to oxidise ammonia to nitrate but there are also problems with excessive concentrations of nitrates.

There are two potential health problems associated with nitrate. Firstly, it may interfere with the oxygen carrying capacity of the blood in infants (known as infantile cyanosis, methaemoglobinaemia or blue baby syndrome) and secondly, nitrate can, under certain circumstances, be reduced to potentially mutagenic nitrosamines in the stomach.

The World Health Organization (WHO) has recommended a limit of 50 mg/l nitrogen (as nitrate) in drinking water and this has been included in the European Community drinking water directive (80/778/CEC).

Nitrate accumulation in the environment has generated a further difficulty because in combination with phosphate, nitrate can lead to nutrient enrichment and excessive algal growth (eutrophication). These algae are unsightly but may also cause taste, odour, oxygen depletion and rarely microtoxin problems if the water is to be reused for domestic supply.

Phosphorus is often the limiting plant nutrient for the growth of phytoplankton (algae and aquatic plants). For example, 1 mg of phosphorus can generate 100 mg of algae (as dry solids) and eventually, on degradation, 140 mg of oxygen demand.

Phosphate like nitrate is residue from the biological oxidation of organic matter but about half is also derived from domestic and other detergents. Restrictions will be imposed on the release of nitrate and phosphorus to surface waters in the future (EC Directive on wastewaters in sensitive areas). There is no really effective and efficient method of removing phosphate from effluents at present which does not generate large quantities of sludge. The most cost effective method of reducing phosphates in water might be a voluntary code to eliminate phosphate in detergents. There has been a special ban on phosphate detergents in Switzerland since 1986 because most sewage discharges are to lakes. Results show (von Gunter and Lienert, 1993) that this is successful but there has also been other benefits including significant reductions in organic matter and therefore metals normally solubilised by the reducing conditions in lake and stream muds.

The accumulation of other inorganic salts, for example sodium chloride and calcium and magnesium, is also likely to cause problems in arid and semi-arid climates where water is recycled many times. Satisfactory methods of recycling these inorganic materials which do not generate other residues are also necessary.

Another common problem with wastes is that they may contain significant quantities of metals. There have been dramatic improvements in the amounts of metals released into the environment partly brought about by the recession of old heavy industries but also because of the imposition of more rigorous control by authorities. Some problems remain, for example metals in landfill leachate and zinc from cosmetics in domestic sewage.

These will require further restraint by voluntary recycling or code of practice.

Zinc, copper, nickel and boron are phytotoxic; their effects are additive and there are risks of accumulation in the food chain. Cadmium, lead and chromium are more mobile and there is a direct risk from the consumption of contaminated food. Cadmium causes the most concern because it is readily absorbed by plants and hence into the food chain. There are other potential risks from mercury, molybdenum, arsenic, fluorine and selenium. Most of these elements can also be derived from aerial deposition as well as applications of surplus sludges to soils and leachate contamination of water. Routine monitoring of soil is necessary to ensure total inorganics are kept within safe limits.

Modern and more sensitive chemical analysis has also revealed some accumulation of persistent organic micropollutants in the environment. The major areas of concern at the moment are the pesticides, organic solvents and the residues from plastics such as the polychlorinated biphenyls, and dioxins. These types of chemical are in common use by industry and agriculture and there are standards to prevent them entering general mixed wastes (red list and black list substances, see Section 6.2).

Future practice to be included in present European and US legislation will also call for better identification of persistent organic micropollutants by test work prior to licensing and use of new chemicals.

Many dyes and colours and some modern detergents are also only poorly degraded by conventional waste treatment processes. These two types of compounds have, however, been biodegraded under carefully controlled conditions and these less toxic but more concentrated organic pollutants are likely to be the most amenable to short-term biotechnological solutions.

6.4.2   Microbiological characteristics

Domestic wastewaters contain a large number of enteric bacteria (between 10^3 and 10^6/ml). There are also a wide variety of other organisms present, including the fungi, protozoans, nematodes and viruses. There are about 40 potential pathogens that are water-borne or can contaminate water (Horan, 1990), and wastewater treatment processes are effective at reducing numbers of bacteria by between 50 and 90% (Table 6.22). It would be usual to disinfect treated sewage effluent if it was to be used immediately for irrigation (WHO, 1973). Treated sewage effluent is also routinely chlorinated in the United States prior to discharge to surface waters but in Europe there is concern about the persistence and hazards associated with residual chlorinated organics. Other disinfectants are less persistent and not as cost effective. The excreta of infected individuals, discharges from abattoirs and run-off from grazing land provide a constant source of

Table 6.22 Summary of pathogens removal by various sewage treatment processes

Organisms	Stage in the treatment process[a]	Primary sedimentation	Trickling filter with primary and secondary sedimentation	Activated sludge with primary and secondary sedimentation	Oxidation ditch with sedimentation	Septic tanks	Land application or slow sand filtration as tertiary treatment	Anaerobic digestion (30–40°C)
Enteric viruses	A	10^3–10^5	10^3–10^5	10^3–10^5	10^3–10^5	0–10^9	10–10^4	May survive over 3 months
	B	10^2–10^5	10^2–10^4	10–10^4	10–10^4	10–10^3	0–10^2	
	C	0–30	90–95	90–99	90–99	50	99–100	
Salmonellae	A	10^3–10^4	10^3–10^4	10^3–10^4	10^3–10^4	0–10^9	10–10^3	May survive for several weeks
	B	10^2–10^3	10^2–10^3	10–10^3	10–10^3	0–10^8	0	
	C	50–90	90–95	90–99	90–99	50–90	100	
Shigellae	A	10^3–10^4	10^3–10^4	10^3–10^4	10^3–10^4	0–10^9	10–10^3	Unlikely to survive for more than a few days
	B	10^2–10^3	10^2–10^3	10–10^3	10–10^3	0–10^8	0	
	C	50–90	90–95	90–99	90–99	50–90	100	
Escherichia coli	A	10^6–10^8	10^6–10^8	10^6–10^8	10^6–10^8	10^7–10^9	10^4–10^7	May survive for several weeks
	B	10^5–10^7	10^5–10^7	10^4–10^7	10^4–10^7	10^6–10^8	0–10^3	
	C	50–90	90–95	90–99	90–99	50–90	99.99–100	
Cholera vibrio	A	10–10^3	10–10^3	10–10^3	10–10^3	0–10^8	0.1–10^2	May survive for 1 or 2 weeks
	B	1–10^2	1–10^2	0.1–10^2	0.1–10^2	0–10^8	0	
	C	50–90	90–95	90–99	90–99	50–90	100	
Entamoeba histolyica cysts	A	10–10^4	10–10^4	10–10^4	10–10^4	0–10^5	10–10^3	May survive for 3 weeks
	B	5–10^4	5–10^3	5–10^3	5–10^3	0–10^5	0	
	C	10–50	$50?$	$50?$	$50?$	$0?$	100	
Hookworm ova	A	10–10^3	10–10^3	10–10^3	10–10^3	0–10^4	10–10^2	Ova will survive
	B	10–10^2	10–10^2	10–10^2	10–10^2	0–10^3	0	
	C	$50?$	50–90	50–90	50–90	50–90	100	
Ascaris ova	A	10–10^3	10–10^3	10–10^3	10–10^3	0–10^4	0–10^2	Ova will survive for many months
	B	1–10	0–10^2	0–10^2	0–10^2	0–10^3	0	
	C	30–80	70–100	70–100	70–100	50–90	100	
Schistosome ova	A	1–100	1–100	1–100	1–100	1–100	1–10	Ova may survive up to 1 month
	B	1–10	1–10	1–10	1–10	1–10	0	
	C	$80?$	50–99	50–99	50–90	50–90	100	
Taenia ova	A	1–100	1–100	1–100	1–100	0–10^3	0.1–50	Ova will survive for a few months
	B	0.1–50	0.1–50	0.1–50	0–50	0–50	0	
	C	50–90	50–95	50–95	$50?$	50–90	100	

[a] Number of organisms: A, in raw sewage; B, in treated effluent; C, removal % numbers of organisms per litre.

Table 6.23   Indicator organisms commonly used to detect faecal contamination

Test	Method	Usage
Faecal coliforms	Generates gas and acid from the fermentation of lactose peptone media. Test performed at 37°C and confirmed at 44°C	Most commonly used test, occasionally produces false positives, but very sensitive and most useful indicator
Faecal streptococci	Growth in a sodium azide, glucose and bromocresol purple media with acid production. Test performed at 45°C	Some streptococci are exclusively human and can be used as confirmatory after the coliform test
Clostridia	The reduction of sulphites to sulphide in litmus milk media. Incubated anaerobically at 37°C	It is used to indicate intermittent pollution in the absence of other indicator organisms

Source: The Bacteriological Examination of Drinking Water (HMSO, 1982).

these potential pathogens. Faecal contamination of water and potential risk is indicated by the isolation of harmless bacteria which are reliably present in excreta. Three different groups are commonly used (Table 6.23).

There is a continued health risk from pathogens in recycled waste. There are few reliable data on the infective doses of the traditional bacterial and protozoan pathogens nor is there an easy method of determining viability; classical culture techniques are not suitable indicators of the potential to cause infection. Even less is known about the survival and persistence of viruses. There is therefore a need to develop test procedures for the rapid identification of all types of potential pathogens including newly evolved strains.

6.4.3   Biological indicators

Changes to the natural environment, such as pollution, cause alterations in the ecology of rivers and streams. All the major biological groups are affected and have been used as biological indicators of pollution. The benthic or bottom dwelling macroinvertebrates are the most popular because their habitat and low mobility means they are rapidly affected by pollution. They are abundant and easy to sample and identify which also makes them suitable for qualitative analysis. Several biotic indices of water quality have been developed for different habitats based on species diversity and abundance. Standard methods of analysis have been published (Heliwell, 1978). The principal influence on ecology is an alteration of the dissolved oxygen and three broad divisions of organic pollution and

Table 6.24 The saprobic zone system of biological indicators of pollution

Zone	Dissolved oxygen (mg/l)	Species
Oligosaprobic	8–9	Salmonid fish, stone flies and may flies
Mesosaprobic	5–7	Cyprinid (coarse) fish, caddis fly and freshwater shrimps
Polysaprobic	1–2	Tubificial worms, chironomids, leaches

consequent dissolved oxygen have been recognised (Table 6.24, Figure 6.4).

6.4.4   Measuring treatability

To avoid damage to the environment, sewers and sewage works discharges of industrial effluents are by licensed agreement in all the European countries and the United States (see Section 6.2). The hazardous nature of some substances are now quite well known.

The dangerous substances directive (76/464/CEC) lists 129 substances which are particularly dangerous and therefore a priority for control (the black list). Attempts have been made in the United Kingdom to set priorities for restricting the release of some of these compounds; the procedure used is based on four criteria shown in Table 6.25. In the United States, the EPA is responsible for controlling a similar group of substances (see Corbitt (1989) for more information).

Using these procedures, 23 substances were selected for priority action in the UK red list. They were all on the original EC list 1 except chloroform and carbon tetrachloride which did not show either high toxicity or accumulation by the DoE procedure. A further 23 substances were identified as possible red list candidates after further test work. Many of the substances on the red list are pesticides originating from very diffuse sources because of their use.

Table 6.25 Restricted substances and the major criteria used to classify them

Acute toxicity tests
Chronic toxicity tests
Bio accumulation
Quantities produced in the United Kingdom

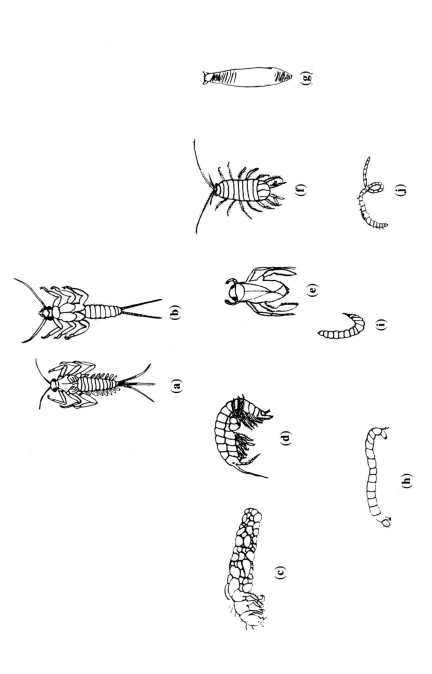

Figure 6.4 Ecological indicators of pollution. (a–b) Typically oligosaprobic invertebrates; (c–g) mesosaprobic invertebrates; (h–j) invertebrates associated with significant pollution, i.e. polysaprobic. (a) *Chloropera torrentium* (stone fly); (b) *Baetis rhodari* (may fly); (c) *Stenophylax* (caddis fly); (d) *Gammarus pulex* (fresh water shrimp); (e) *Corixa dorsalis* (water boatman); (f) *Asellus aquaticus* (water louse); (g) *Polycelis felina* (flat worm); (h) Chironomid larvae (filter fly also known as blood worm); (i) *Psychoda alternata* (filter midge); (j) *Tubifex tubifex* (sludge worm).

In practice, most synthetic compounds (xenobiotics) have been found to be biodegradable but there are four common problems in effluent:

1. chlorinated solvents;
2. biocides and pesticides;
3. detergents;
4. ammonia and sulphur.

These compounds can be tolerated at low concentrations but trials and test work are appropriate if these type of materials are known to be present.

For a number of wastes, treatability data are available for the design of treatment plant without intermediate laboratory and pilot studies. This is true of domestic wastes and many food waste applications where suppliers have already installed such plant at several similar factories using common design principles. There are still many wastes for which treatability data are not available or where the processing operations are significantly different.

The most frequently encountered problems with food wastes compared to domestic wastes are a lack of nutrients, variability and persistent toxins. Many of these difficulties can be predicted and overcome by laboratory treatability trials before design. Such tests are essential if there are any doubts about the characteristics of the waste.

Treatability trials are conducted at three scales:

1. bottle tests (250 ml reactors);
2. laboratory scale (5–10 l reactor site); and
3. pilot scale (10–20 m^3 reactor size)

6.4.4.1 *Bottle tests.* The bottle tests (OECD die away tests) measure microbial activity or substrate uptake under standardised and ideal conditions. They can be used to measure biodegradability and identify toxins compared with well characterised substrates such as glucose and yeast extract and standard microorganisms taken from a sewage works. The tests in common usage are biological oxygen demand (BOD) and biological methane potential (BMP). The ratios of BOD and BMP to COD (chemical oxygen demand) give an indication of biodegradability because the COD test measures all the organic carbon. The COD to BOD of starch wastes for example is about 1:2:1, of dairy waste 1:5:1 and for domestic sewage around 2:1.

6.4.4.2 *Continuous simulation trials.* Continuous culture trials in larger reactors (10–15 l) can use the real waste as a substrate and be run continuously for several months to identify nutrient deficiency, toxicity and reliability problems. These difficulties are not usually apparent from the initial analysis. The laboratory study can also investigate competing reactor types and likely process loading rates.

There are some standard test units for continuous culture work (Department of the Environment, 1979) but these are not really suitable for food effluents. The standard activated sludge models (see Section 6.5) for example are the Husmann or Porous pot; these recommend synthetic totally soluble substrates and do not effectively measure settlement. Model activated sludge units with sludge return can be workshop made and are more suitable for continuous trials. Similarly, the standard percolating filter model is a rolling table (Gloyna et al., 1952) whereas a model rotating biological contractor (RBC) is easier to construct and a better model of a percolating filter.

A laboratory study can never totally simulate the conditions at full scale due to the highly variable nature of industrial effluents. On site pilot trials are to be recommended in addition to laboratory studies whenever there are doubts concerning treatability. Advantages include more representative data and better information on operating problems with industrial scale ancillary equipment. Factory staff can also be familiarised with the process. It is important that pilot plant is of a realistic size to allow reasonable extrapolation to full scale. This normally means a reactor 10–20 m^3 in size. Most contractors will offer potential customers treatability trials at cost or with a discount against eventual equipment purchased. This type of arrangement reduces the independence of the advice given.

6.4.5 Sector review

The food industry is the largest water user in Europe and the USA. Average water consumption in the food industry expressed as water to product is 10:1 (Table 6.26); for the chemical industry it is about 5:1 and about 2:1 in paper and textiles. The hygiene and quality controls required in the food industry lead to a high water usage and few opportunities for recycling.

Most of the UK food processing sites are too small for economic on-site treatment. There are, for example, about 5000 food processing sites, but only 150–200 have loads greater than 300 tonnes per annum, the point at which treatment becomes attractive. For cost effective anaerobic treatment, wastes also need to be warm and strong (e.g. >20°C and COD >3000 mg/l). Treatment plants are common in the four largest sectors (Table 6.27).

1. Dairies
2. Breweries
3. Sugar and starch processing
4. Distilling and fermentation

Table 6.26 Strength and wastewater generated in the food industry

Industry	Strength (typical BOD) (mg/l)	Water to product ratio (l/unit of product)
Dairy	500–750	12:1
Butter and cheese	1500–2500	3:1
Distillery	1500–2000	20:1
Brewery	500–1500	8:1
Maltings	2000–3000	15:1
Food canning	100–1300	10:1
Frozen peas	1000–2000	12:1
Chips and other vegetables	1000–1500	20:1
Chickens	600	30:1
Slaughterhouse	1000–2000	20:1
Sewage	250	130 per head

6.4.5.1   The dairy industry.   The dairy industry is currently the largest single source of industrial effluent in Europe. Sites are often rural and discharge to municipal sewers is impossible. The milk industry spends about £60M a year on effluent treatment, with 50% being spent on sludge disposal; some of these costs could be avoided by different treatment. A typical European dairy processes 500 m^3 of milk per day and generates a similar volume of effluent. The waste is from the washing of tanks, evaporators and transport. Average strengths of dairy effluents can vary from 1000 to 5000 mg/l COD. Those effluents from dairy products, e.g. cheese, evaporated milk, etc., which are warm and strong are ideal for anaerobic treatment. Traditionally and prior to 1950 most effluent plant was modelled on sewage treatment and based on percolating filters. Percolating filters eventually became blocked with growth, excessive amounts of inorganic precipitates or media breakdown. The successor to filters for domestic wastes, conventional activated sludge, proved very difficult to operate because of the warm temperatures, ease of fermentation and surplus sludge production. Plastic media filters then became the favoured form of treatment but these tower structures often gave problems with odour. More recently, low rate extended aeration with standby oxygen injection has been used more successfully.

Typical problems with the treatment of dairy waste are the high concentrations of fat, protein, shock loads and cleaning agents. Highly alkaline cleaning aids based on caustic soda are used which can raise the pH to toxic levels. A two-stage balancing/neutralisation process is essential; stream separation of the caustic clean downs will also be beneficial. An ideal treatment process would include fat separation, flow balancing, dump tank and two-stage biological treatment. The first biological stage should be a fixed film process followed by extended aeration or percolating filters. Dilute wastes COD approximately 1–2000 are suitable for this type of treatment; stronger wastes would benefit from a third anaerobic

Table 6.27 Survey of effluent treatment in the food industry

Industry	Sector comparison by size				Effluent characteristics					
	Production (000 tonnes)	Sales (£M)	Added value (£M)	No. of employees (000s)	COD (mg/l)	SS (mg/l)	Volume (M³/annum, 000s)	Cost (p/m³)	Water usage to produce ratio	No. of sites surveyed
Meat and meat products including poultry	495	3046	174	103	2468 500–8632	712 75–4500	135 26–482	26 17–60	10 10	10
Oils and fats	523	568	955							0
Milk and milk products	1600	4045	855	42	4500 80–9500	820 24–4800	280	54	1.5/1.0	100
Fruit and vegetables	1657	1035	223	36	3500 1617–11147	500	175 14–633	25 1.3–79.0	15/20	6
Potato products					2360 2300–2500	656 329–900	414 373–600	6.0 4.7–58.0	20/30	4
Bread, biscuits, confectionery	2000	2669	1142	139	5076 275–9500	3144 215–7960	40 14–88	4.2 1.3–12		2
Sugar and syrups	2260	1042	219	7.9	2200 1400–3000	250 200–300	365	24		1
Cocoa, chocolate, confectionery	838	1718	683	62	9500 19000–30000	500 75–1500	150 3–1000	45 6–113	4	12
Starch cereals		1202			1855 1300–2575	394 300–670	223	29		1
Brewing	280		1072	55	2105 1500–3500	837 598–1294	441 77.7–1909	4.3 1.1–7.2	4 1.5–10	9
Malting					2195 1500–3910	189 184–220	81 68–93	7.5 4.5–14.2		3

Source: Gorsuch (1986).

pre-treatment step. There are ten full scale anaerobic plants in Europe, three in France, two in Holland, two in Ireland and one each in the United Kingdom, Germany and Spain.

6.4.5.2   Starch wastes.   Starch is used in snack foods, ready meals, biscuits and desserts; it is produced from maize, rice, wheat and potatoes. The effluent is strong (COD > 10 000) and warm, 20–25°C, too strong for aerobic treatment but ideal for anaerobic digestion. A high proportion of the COD is colloidal solids. These solids reduce biodegradability and favour solids tolerant processes, i.e. the contact process. There are seven anaerobic plants, three in the United Kingdom, two in the Netherlands and one each in Belgium, Ireland, France and Germany. Four are based on UASB reactors, three on contact digesters and two on filters. Operating data on one of the UK contact digesters treating starch waste have been published regularly (Butcher, 1988). The most common problems with starch wastes are the slow breakdown of solids and low concentrations of additional nutrients. Two-stage treatment with separate prehydrolysis and balancing (10–20 h retention) is a common method of overcoming treatability problems. More dilute wastes (i.e. COD < 2000) favour aerobic processes directly but solids tolerant fixed film processes would still be preferable as the first stage. A typical treatment process would be screens, flow balancing anaerobic treatment or high rate fixed film followed by extended aeration activated sludge.

6.4.5.3   The sugar processing industry.   The sugar industry is a major water consumer with usage rates between twenty and thirty times the product produced. The industry has had to take steps to conserve water and most processing factories now have extensive recirculation. This generates a concentrated effluent, well suited to anaerobic pretreatment followed by aerobic polishing. The sugar industry in Europe is based on beets; it is rural and seasonal, and requires on site treatment. The largest volume of wastewater is from washing and rinsing the beets. The wastewater contains between 10 and 20 g/l COD and deteriorates rapidly. Lime is used to counteract the acidity and prevent malodour. Lime is used extensively in sugar processing and is generated on-site at the larger factories (Huber and Metzner, 1986). The lime also precipitates solids, reduces corrosion and allows some of the water to be recycled. Surplus waste wash water is combined with other clean down solutions and condensates for dilution before treatment. The waste is still strong (COD 3–10 g/l) with total carboxylic acid concentrations up to 6 g/l. The pH, however, is usually between 5 and 6 because of the lime treatment. The alkalinity and calcium in the lime aid anaerobic treatment. The biomass in the anaerobic digester flocculates around the lime and promotes settlement in the contact and UASB processes. A disadvantage of lime is that it accumulates during the season thus reducing the space in the digester for active biomass. It also causes pipe scale. Solids tolerant digesters, the contact process and UASB reactors are essential. The anaerobic treatment of sugar wastes has been very successful; there are 20 plants in Europe, most with aerobic extended aeration final treatment before discharge to a water course. This combination is now established as the best treatment for this type of waste.

6.4.5.4   Confectionery/soft drinks.   Much of the waste from the confectionery industry is sugar based and CODs are large (5000–10 000 mg/l). The wastes are from cleaning, they are periodic and usually hot. Both aerobic and anaerobic treatability are low because of acidity and lack of additional nutrients. The chemical costs required to correct these problems means that dilution and mixing domestic sewage is frequently the best method of treatment. There are occasions, however, when because of the strengths of the waste, some form of pretreatment is required by the controlling authorities. Three anaerobic treatment plants have been built recently, one of which is in the United Kingdom. Running costs for alkalinity and nutrient additions have been high. Long retention time, i.e. contact digesters (retention times > 5 days) and extended aeration (retention > 5 days), are preferred if treatment is inevitable.

6.4.5.5   Breweries.   Brewing is the second largest source of industrial waste after dairy effluents. Breweries are also large and can show economic benefit from on-site effluent treatment. Unlike the dairy industry most breweries are urban and do have the option to discharge to mains drainage and many do to avoid the complications of running an effluent treatment plant. Wastewaters are weak (COD 500–1500 mg/l), with a neutral pH and cold; they are best treated aerobically (Figure 6.5).

Aerobic treatments have been successful and include two oxygen activated sludge plants. Increased water and effluent charges will encourage further applications. More efficient water usage may also make wastewaters more concentrated and improve the energy balance for anaerobic digestion. Small anaerobic digesters could then be utilised on stronger warmer process streams ignoring most of the cool wash waters for direct discharge to sewer or combined aerobic treatment.

6.4.5.6   The distillery and fermentation industry.   Distillery wastes are frequently very strong (COD values 10 000–60 000 mg/l, solids 10 000 mg/l). Water consumption is on average 10:1 (water to product) but volumes are smaller than either the dairy or brewery industries. Many distilleries particularly in the United Kingdom, where they are also small and rural, have been able to dispose of effluents by land irrigation or discharge to sea. A small Scottish highland distillery for example will

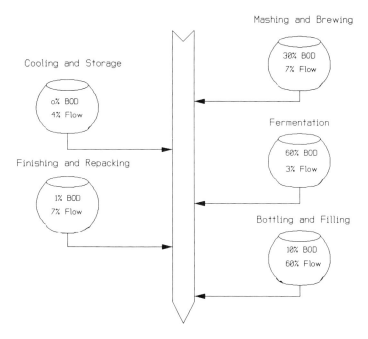

Figure 6.5 Typical soures of waste volume and load from a brewery.

produce only 500 m^3 of effluent a week. Large industrialised distilleries, however, have major waste disposal problems. One French cognac producer, reported in the literature, generated 10 000 m^3 of effluent a week (see Section 6.1), equivalent to the waste from a population of 0.5M. In these circumstances, on-site treatment is inevitable and there is extensive experience of waste treatment and by-product recovery within the distilling industry.

Wastewaters have previously been treated aerobically but only after dilution with other wash waters and recycle. Aerobic effluent treatment plants have always been difficult to operate because of the acidity of the waste, high temperatures and high oxygen demands. Robust biological filters have always been used as the first stage of treatment and usually worked very well (Smith, 1986). Distillery wastes are ideal for anaerobic treatment; there are few alternatives. The sector has the largest number of installed anaerobic plants (25–30) most of which are in Italy and France.

Distillery and fermentation wastes from molasses contain high concentrations of sulphate. Typically sulphate concentration is between 3000 and 8000 mg/l. Sulphate is reduced to sulphide under anaerobic conditions and the sulphide is toxic and malodorous. These types of effluent are unsuitable for anaerobic treatment.

6.4.5.7 Vegetable processing.   The vegetable and fruit processing industry, like the dairy and sugar industries, are rural. They may, like the sugar industry, also be seasonal although many process different crops at different times of the year. Effluents, however, are dilute and cold. This has favoured aerobic treatment. Typical treatments are high rate biofiltration followed by extended aeration activated sludge (Figure 6.6).

There are two exceptions, potatoes and peas, and both of these have easily soluble starches and produce a higher strength waste. Anaerobic digesters have been built at eleven potato and potato snack factories. They are mostly the sludge blanket UASB type or CSTR to cope with the high concentrations of colloidal solids from potatoes.

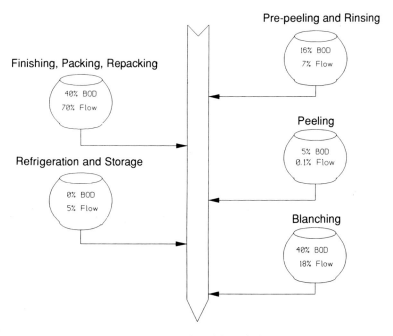

Pre-peeling and Rinsing

16% BOD
7% Flow

Finishing, Packing, Repacking

40% BOD
70% Flow

Peeling

5% BOD
0.1% Flow

Refrigeration and Storage

0% BOD
5% Flow

Blanching

40% BOD
18% Flow

Figure 6.6 Sources of waste volume and load from fruit and vegetable processing.

Pea processing wastes are also strong (COD >4000 mg/l) and could be treated anaerobically. However, the season is so short, 10–12 weeks on average, that the capital costs of anaerobic treatment compared to aerobic treatment are uncompetitive.

Vegetable wastes often contain significant amounts of large solids and primary treatment is used. A typical vegetable effluent plant therefore would consist of screening, mud separation, balancing, settlement and two stage biological treatment.

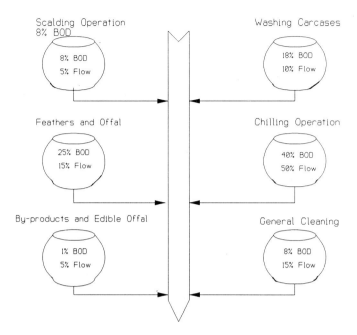

Figure 6.7 Sources and strength of wastes in chicken processing typical of meat processing operations.

6.4.5.8 Meat processing.   Meat processing wastes are significantly different from other food processing wastes. They are very strong, containing grease, blood and faeces. Significant amounts of recalcitrant organic matter, straw and hair are also present (Figure 6.7).

The wastes frequently include high concentrations of biocides and disinfectants such as hypochlorite. There are also problems arising from malodours and low temperatures. These are, therefore, very difficult wastes for any form of treatment and good separation of the various process streams is the best form of waste management. Only solids-tolerant, long retention time reactors are likely to succeed and the best treatment option, where possible, is dilution and mixing with domestic sewage. Two stages of screens may be necessary followed by flow balancing flotation and settlement. Two or three stages of biological treatment may then be necessary starting with anaerobic digestion and finishing with extended aeration activated sludge.

6.4.6 Conclusions

In principle, food industry wastes should be treated easily. In practice, there are a number of difficulties despite the fundamentally biodegradable constituents. The main problems are the high strengths and temperature compared to domestic sewage. Cleaning aids and sanitisers cause further problems. The high strengths of the waste also normally makes them deficient in additional nutrients particularly nitrogen and alkalinity.

Analysis and characterisation of the effluent is essential prior to any decisions on a process design for a waste treatment plant.

6.5 Pre-treatments

6.5.1 Preliminary treatment

Food processing effluents are a complex mixture of floating, settleable, suspended and dissolved materials. Complete treatment therefore requires a combination of physical, chemical and biological processes (Figure 6.8). Biological processes can deal with both suspended and dissolved or colloidal materials but normally it is cheaper to remove easily settleable or floatable material physically or chemically. Biological treatment usually costs two or three times as much as physical separation processes but there are occasions when the cost of the disposal of the separated solids is more expensive than capital and running costs associated with oxidising them biologically (in for example biological filters, extended aeration discussed

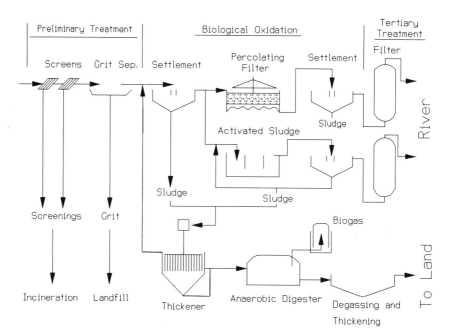

Figure 6.8 Schematic of sewage treatment.

in Section 6.6). The cost of sludge and solids disposal is getting more expensive because of increasing restrictions on the traditional land disposal. Some pretreatment prior to biological or secondary reactors is essential, otherwise there is always a risk of packaging and other debris damaging or blocking mechanical equipment. Pretreatment is also necessary if there are recalcitrant or toxic materials present, for example high pH due to caustic cleaning. These may be made more treatable by chemical neutralisation.

6.5.1.1 Flow balancing.   It is usual for food industry wastes to vary in strength and flow and drainage has to be designed to be large enough for periodic storms and changes of flow. Designs include for a 4:1 peak for up to 10 m³/h and for about 2:1 for flows greater than 20 m³/h. Biological treatment can cope with a wide range of loads including some shocks, but most equipment works more efficiently when the flow and load are controlled. It is cheaper to balance surges than design the biological reactor for maximum load. Water authorities frequently specify a maximum flow rate as well as the total amount of effluent to be discharged to sewer and flow balancing may be required to conform to these consent conditions. Flow balancing also has the advantage of evenning out the chemical composition of the waste and it is quite common for water authorities to specify a range of maximum allowable concentrations (see Section 6.2). The two most common difficulties associated with food wastes are pH and fat. Water authorities usually insist that the fat should not exceed 150 mg/l and the pH should be between 6 and 9. Excessive fat can interfere with oxygen transfer. A wide range of food industries require some form of balancing and fat removal to achieve these standards consistently. Sudden discharges of very strong streams, such as lost product, sludge returns or hazardous discharges (e.g. caustic cleaning), should be collected in a separate dump tank. They may usually be slowly reintroduced back into the main stream for combined diluted treatment.

Balancing tanks are designed with a constant forward flow and an emergency overflow to treatment; they usually have a holding capacity of up to a maximum of one day's average flow. The design of the right sized balance tank is difficult since too long a storage has an adverse effect on aerobic treatment. The usual problem is septicity, as the effluent is stored, natural microbial activity occurs and the dissolved oxygen is depleted. This is accompanied by a drop in pH (down to a minimum of 3.5) and bad smells associated with the sulphides and amines. Balance tank design depends on the effluent analysis and flow measurements described in Section 6.4. If there are high sulphate concentrations in the effluent from hard water, or sulphuric acid from boiler water treatment or from flocculants, then balancing tanks will need to be smaller, require roofing and extra air.

Some of these problem can be overcome by mixing, particularly with air, which then also counteracts the septicity. It is essential to be able to control the amount of air introduced since there is virtually no way of calculating how much will be required to avoid anaerobic conditions. Some effluents particularly those which contain an active inoculum such as the yeast in brewery effluents and lactic acid bacteria in milk wastes have high oxygen demands (>20 mg/O_2 solid per h). Major seasonal fluctuations in load or flow would require standby plant.

6.5.1.2 Anaerobic treatment. In the case of anaerobic biological treatment, there are fewer problems associated with balance tank design. Pre-acidification in an anoxic balancing tank can be beneficial, leading to accelerated hydrolysis and solubilisation. The balancing tank then becomes the first stage of a two-stage design. One reactor is for acid fermentation and solids breakdown, the other for methanogenesis from the solubilised solid waste.

For some industrial wastes, adequate pre-hydrolysis will be essential, for example, those from the starch and paper industry which are predominantly colloidal. Up to 3000–4000 mg/l total volatile acids can be obtained at retention times of up to 2 days. The pH after this first stage of the anaerobic process will be about 4–5.5, but if the wastes generate surplus alkalinity in the second stage anaerobic reactor, then the system can tolerate acid feeds. In practice, it is useful to have some form of pH control between the first stage, or the balancing hydrolysis tank, and the second stage, the anaerobic reactor. Between the two stages is the most useful point to control pH and make chemical additions to the waste. Anaerobic pre-acidification tanks will always need to be roofed.

Sludge scum and foam formation are common difficulties with both balancing tanks and acidification reactors. Methods for their removal need to be incorporated into the design; this can be a simple draw off.

6.5.1.3 Screens. Screens are designed to strain out large pieces of debris such as feathers, rags, string, plastic film, cardboard and other packaging material as well as any stray raw materials or product. Normally the minimum aperture size is 1–5 mm; smaller sizes block too quickly even for continuous cleaning. Sedimentation or flotation can be used for smaller particles.

It is prudent to install a simple form of screen for even apparently solid-free wastes such as dairy effluents to prevent packaging materials accidentally getting into the biological reactor and ancillary equipment. Some wastes, for example, meat processing waste and vegetable waste, may need coarse and fine screens because of the quantities of large debris. Coarse screens have spacings of 25–50 mm.

Screening of food processing effluents, notably the meat and vegetable industry, can remove significant amounts of the polluting load. The recovered screenings may be used in animal feed or otherwise they need to be landfilled or incinerated.

A variety of proprietary self-cleaning screens are available based on bars, mesh and wedge wire.

Bar screens. These are the simplest type of screen with parallel bars at between 30 and 60° to the flow. If the effluent is comparatively clean, then they can be 'home made' and manually raked. If there is a significant solids capture, then purpose built units are necessary with automatic brushes or rakes. The rakes protrude through the grid bars and are scraped clean at the top of their travel (Figure 6.9). The smallest bar screen is 10 mm and small particles, paper film, etc. pass easily through them.

Mesh screens. For finer screening, e.g. 5 mm, mesh sieves or wedgewire are used. There are three common types: brushed sieve, disposable bags and drum screens. In the brushed sieve (Parkwood type, Figure 6.10), the effluent flows over a partly cylindrical screen, and passes through slots or holes into a collection sump or channel beneath. The solids collecting on the perforated plate or mesh are swept away by revolving brushes into a separate collection channel and are periodically flushed into a skip.

For low solid loads, disposable filter bags have been introduced. Various mesh sizes are available and the bags are effective at removing plastic, cardboard, string and fat balls. Typically the bags will last from 4 to 6 weeks.

Figure 6.9 Typical bar screen arrangement.

Figure 6.10 Brushed screen type arrangement.

There are also different types of rotating drum screen available. The effluent enters the centre of the drum and passes out through the slowly rotating mesh covered drum. Water jets are used to keep the mesh clean. Traditionally, drum screens have been used for final straining of biologically treated effluents which avoids the worst problems of screen blinding which would occur with raw wastes. They are efficient at removing solids but are more complex than the fixed screen types.

Wedgewire screens. Wedgewire screens are popular for food industry effluents because they offer fine screening and are largely self-cleaning. The name is derived from the shape of the parallel bars used; the wider space is on the screened side to avoid blockage. There are three basic types: parabolic, cylindrical and inclined to the flow.

The parabolic wedgewire is 2 m high with a top feed and weir box to achieve good distribution across the width of the screen (Figure 6.11). The wedgewire bars are transverse to the flow and the effluent cascades down the parabolic curved surface driving the solids off at the bottom by impact and gravity. The effluent passes through the wedgewire openings. A disadvantage of the parabolic screen is that there is a significant head loss, 3–5 m, through the screen. This usually requires pumping.

The alternative types are either semi-cylinders (rotamat and rotascreen),

Figure 6.11 Parabolic wedge wire screen.

Figure 6.12 Inclined wedge wire screen.

or moving inclined screens; both are designed to fit into an open channel. The cylindrical screens lie at a shallow angle in the channel and screenings are removed and drained as they are lifted by a rotating internal archimedean scroll conveyor. The inclined moving wedgewire screens are cleaned by water jets at the top of their travel (Figure 6.12). In both systems, the screenings are discharged by a chute into a skip.

Cost. It is usual for screening and preliminary treatment to represent about 5–10% of the capital costs of total treatment, but for running costs to be high (20% of capital per year). Typical unit costs are between £10 000 and £40 000.

6.5.1.4   Grit removal.   Vegetable processing wastes require mud and soil removal to reduce wear on pumps and mechanical equipment. Large quantities of grit and soil can be removed from root crops such as sugar beet and potatoes. The separation process relies on the denser mineral particles settling at a much faster rate than organic solids. Effluent velocity is controlled to about 0.3–0.5 m/s in special channels, chambers or hydrocyclones. The deposited grit is sucked or scraped from the separator and landfilled. Grit separation is also a standard feature of domestic sewage treatment, it removes road grit. The grit collected may need washing with final effluent to prevent odour.

6.5.2   Primary treatment

6.5.2.1   Settlement.   Settlement is most useful for the removal of solids larger than 10 mm. Sedimentation of vegetable and meat processing wastes can remove 35% of the polluting load by precipitation of 60% of suspended solids. Particles less than 1 mm will not settle by gravity. Soluble and colloidal wastes such as from the soft drinks or dairy industry are unlikely to benefit from settlement without the addition of chemicals.

Theory. Traditionally, settlement was modelled on the density difference between the particles and water, the velocity of flow and temperature, i.e. Stokes' Law. It has since been shown that the concentration of the suspension has a marked effect on settling rate. Various modifications to Stokes' Law have been published to take account of the interference by particle, particle interaction and water retention. Most of the changes were empirical to take account of the results of tests in vertical tubes. Six effects were observed:

1. that large particles were settling relative to a suspension of smaller ones so that the effective density and viscosity of the fluid are increased;

2. the upward velocity of the fluid displaced during the settlement of a concentrated suspension is significant and the apparent settling velocity is therefore less than the actual velocity relative to the fluid;
3. there may be significant cooling from the surface of the tank which can set up eddy currents and circulation;
4. the velocity gradients in the fluid close to the particles were increased as a result of the change in area and shape of the void spaces;
5. the smaller particles tended to be dragged down by the motion of the large particles and settlement was accelerated;
6. flocculation and aggregation occurs and the effective size of the particles are increased.

These results make prediction of the rate of sedimentation of mixed particle sizes difficult. Agitation and stirring also increased the rate of settling. The stirring releases bound water held in place by the thick sediment at the bottom of a tank. During these final stages of settlement, liquid is squeezed and held in a packed bed of particles.

Four types of settlement behaviour are now commonly referred to:

1. settlement according to classical Stokes theory dependent on density difference;
2. settlement of flocculant particles with increased velocity compared to theory.

These are the predominant mechanisms in primary settlement but two other conditions exist where there is significant hindrance of settlement in concentrated biological suspensions such as activated sludge:

3. hindered settlement (or zone settlement), for example, occurs when a stable suspension settles as a unit and there is a reduced velocity compared to theory due to inhibited water displacement (interparticle forces hold the suspension together);
4. compressive settlement is similar and caused by the particles being mechanically supported by each other; compression and consolidation of the particles then takes place. This occurs at very high solids concentrations, i.e. in sludge consolidation tanks and sludge thickening in the bottom of settling tanks.

Design. Laboratory studies could be used to measure likely settling velocities but scale-up factors such as wall effects, turbulence and short circuiting limit their usefulness. Settlement tanks are designed to produce quiescent conditions. This is achieved by generating a low velocity, uniform flow and by preventing resuspension of settled particles.

Most tanks are circular because this makes scrapers cheaper and more reliable but rectangular tanks are common at domestic sewage plants to reduce land area. Deep hopper bottom tanks have been used in the past to eliminate a scraper mechanism completely and reduce sludge production by anaerobic re-solubilisation. These tanks do not work because of poor sludge consolidation and anaerobic fermentation causing rising sludge. They are also expensive because of the cost of excavation. The best tanks are usually 2 m deep with a 1 in 5 to 1 in 10 slope to the base.

Loading rate. Typical loading rates are shown in Table 6.28. Reduced loading or increased retentions may have adverse effects due to anaerobic fermentation, i.e. a fall in pH, gassing and malodour. Additional features are usually incorporated into the tank to reduce the possibility of turbulence and short circuiting. One of the main features is a diffuser drum for dissipating the feed over the plan area of the tank.

The diffuser drum occupies about 30% of the depth of the tank (Figure 6.13) and slots are often cut into the base of the drum to reduce bottom scour. The diffuser drum is galvanised or plastic to prevent corrosion. A bottom scraper ensures the sludge is collected into a hopper at the centre of the tank. The gentle stirring from the rotating scrapper prevents solids accumulating on the tank walls and assists with flocculation. A corrosion resistant material, usually galvanised steel, is used for the scraper fitted with plastic or rubber replaceable blades. The bottom of the tanks are reinforced concrete with a 5–10° slope to the central sludge hopper. Sludge accumulating in the hopper of the tank is removed periodically by the hydrostatic head through a screw threaded bell valve to be combined with the scum. The bell mouth allows inspection of the sludge during decanting to avoid drawing off clean water during desludging. A scum baffle and upper scraper are also necessary with fatty wastes to collect floating material. Scum and fat are then removed by a slot valve. An adjustable peripheral overflow weir is also required to ensure an even flow through the tank and compensate for later tank movement. It should be corrosion resistant, i.e. plastic.

Traditionally settlement tanks have been built of reinforced concrete. These are too expensive and too large for most industrial applications. Standard size prefabricated tanks are the most common. Smaller tanks are made of plastic, larger tanks from enamelled steel. Buoyancy valves are required if the tank is below the ground.

Table 6.28 Settlement tank design

Type of waste	Retention time (h)	Surface load (m^3/m^2 per day)
Meat processing	2–3	45
Vegetable	2.5	25
Cannery	4	40
Typical	4	40

Figure 6.13 New settlement tanks showing diffuser drum and scraper.

6.5.2.2 Flotation.   A wide range of food processing effluents contain fats and oils. Most of the greases and oils are readily biodegradable provided that they are soluble or sufficiently dispersed to give a uniform concentration accessible to the bacteria. Most fats, oils and greases (FOG), however, tend to separate from the main effluent stream and solidify, blocking or blinding biological reactors and process instruments.

High concentrations of fat and oil can also interfere with gas transfer during aeration. The maximum concentration for aerobic treatment is 150 mg/l. Often this standard can be achieved by reducing the flow in a simple chamber and trapping the oil between underflow weirs. The oil floats to the surface by density difference. This means separation can take place in balancing, first stage reactors or settlement tanks. A scum baffle or boom is linked to the sludge scraping mechanism and fats, oils and floating sludge collected by a scum or slot valve.

Unfortunately, wastes also often contain detergents and surface active materials which can emulsify the oil and reduce the efficiency of separation. The efficiency of the separators can also be reduced by warm temperatures. There are three methods of overcoming this by flotation: fat traps, dissolved air flotation and inclined plate separators.

Fat traps. Fat traps are designed to produce a slow and gentle uniform flow through a tank. This allows density difference to bring the fat to the surface without disturbing any accumulated scum and sludge.

An even distribution of flow can usually be achieved by a baffle at the inlet to the tank. Slotted inlet pipes can also be used with baffles to assist the flow pattern. Pumping prior to the fat trap should be avoided or special care taken to use pumps that do not generate turbulence and emulsification.

Solids and sludge will accumulate in the tank due to settlement and it is essential to incorporate some form of drain valve. Ideally, this should be complemented by a sloping tank bottom (i.e. 1 in 5). In home-made interceptors, fat removal can be done manually but it is important to provide good platform access to allow this to be done easily. Removable and adjustable retaining baffles can also then be hung on the walls of the tank. Purpose-built units normally include a moving scraper on an endless chain with a trigger to activate a scum removal valve.

Dimensions and loading rates. Fat traps are designed according to general settlement principles. Typically, they have a length to width ratio of 2:1, a retention time of 10–40 min and a loading of 0.4 m^3/m^2 per h to 3 m^3/m^2 per h at maximum flow rate. Table 6.29 shows some typical examples from the literature.

Table 6.29 Some examples of loading rates to fat traps

Product	Retention time (min)	Surface loading (m^3/m^2 per h)
Meat processing	20	2
Margarine processing	20–40	3
Soap	40	1
Milk, butter and cheese	30	1
Milk processing	20	0.4

Dissolved air flotation. Common problems with fat containing effluents are precipitation and emulsification due to pH, temperature, pumping and detergents. In these circumstances, gravity separation with a simple trap rarely gives satisfactory results and assisted flotation has to be used. Dissolved air flotation relies on the introduction of supersaturated water into the effluent. There is a hydrophobic mutual attraction between the bubbles and the suspended particles and this leads to the flotation of the solids. The main advantage of dissolved air flotation is its speed. Flotation rates are two to three times those of gravity and tank sizes are much smaller. It also has the advantage of avoiding potential anaerobic conditions. The efficiency of the process like sedimentation is dependent on particle size but is also affected by bubble attachment and the efficiency of gas transfer. It is as a consequence, more complex and less reliable than simple gravity separation.

Two types of flotation systems, dispersed and dissolved flotation, have evolved more or less separately. In dispersed air flotation, the bubbles are generated physically. This is the oldest type of flotation developed at the turn of the century. It is extensively used in the metal refining industries. It is not suitable for effluent treatment because of the shear forces produced by mechanical agitation.

Dissolved air flotation is preferred and is based on the release of air from a supersaturated solution by pressure reduction. Two different methods of pressure release have been developed. The earliest was vacuum flotation where air dissolved under atmospheric pressure was liberated by reducing the surface pressure. In the second more common type, pressure is used to supersaturate the effluent and is then released to reprecipitate the dissolved air.

A small volume of treated effluent is recycled and pressurised to provide the supersaturated process water. This eliminates the necessity to aerate the crude effluent.

Table 6.30 Design characteristics of a flotation unit

Surface load	30–60 m^3/m^2 per day
	1–3 m^3/m^2 per h
Retention time	20–30 min
Recycle rate	25–100%
Pressure vessel	3–6 atm

Design. Design is based on upward flow velocity and retention time as in settlement, but additionally there is a need to define a minimum air to solids ratio. It is difficult to set the air to solids ratio and recycle ratio theoretically and optimum conditions are often defined empirically from pilot trials. In most cases, however, because of the variability of bubble attachment and gas transfer, purpose built units include considerable flexibility. Table 6.30 shows some typical design characteristics. Surveys of the dissolved air flotation have shown that reliability is poor and operation difficult. Operating costs have been shown to be higher than gravity separation. The relatively complex technology is not well suited to effluents nor to the frequent changes in character that occur. Typical capital costs are between £1 and 2/m^3 per year with running costs between 10 and 30% of capital per year. Performance from a well-operated unit is better than that from gravity separation (Table 6.31).

Inclined plate separators. These are settlement tanks containing a series of inclined parallel plates. The plates are corrugated to give the maximum amount of surface within the tank. Inclined plate separators have been introduced recently for the treatment of food wastes. There is so far little

Table 6.31 Some examples of the performance of ideal dissolved air flotation

Effluent Type	Influent			Effluent			% Removal		
	SS	FAT	BOD	SS	FAT	BOD	SS	FAT	BOD
Cooking oil	230	460	2900	20	25	94	91.3	94.6	96.9
Margarine	5000	3900	–	200	40	–	96.0	99.0	–
Cosmetics	15000	5405	24500	1800	485	5880	88.0	91.0	76.0
Laundry	3469	3014	–	281	475	–	91.9	84.2	–
Wool scouring	8700	4650	2820	81	20	268	99.1	99.6	90.5
Abattoir	7428	3110	–	712	97	–	90.4	96.9	–
Poultry waste	1690	331	1075	275	74	86	83.7	77.6	92.0
Gelatine waste	2680	2825	–	458	315	–	82.9	88.9	–
Jam/pickles	1350	–	790	270	–	315	80.0	–	60.1
Metal plating	1700	–	6170	127	–	3000	92.6	–	51.4

information on their performance. Pilot trials would be necessary or there would need to be comprehensive operating data on a similar waste before installation. Maintenance and cleaning costs will be high.

The principle relies on the mutual hydrophobicity of surfaces and particulates so that the particles adhere to surfaces despite high upward flow velocities. Solids that collect on the surface may then be retained long enough for coalescence and the larger particles to float to the surface or settle. This aggregation allows the tank size to be reduced. Retention times are 30 min and surface loadings increased compared to passive flotation ($2.5–3.0 \, m^3 \, m^2$ per h).

6.5.3   Chemical treatment

Chemical adjuncts can improve the performance of most of the physical and biological processes used in effluent treatment. Traditionally, the most extensive use of chemicals has been to correct pH and to improve settlement rates by increasing particle density. The chemical oxidation of waste is not difficult but even the cheapest oxidising agent, chlorine, is twenty times the cost of biological treatment. Another problem with chemical treatment is that it imposes an extra level of control by including dosing equipment. This increases running and maintenance costs. Chemical treatment is useful when problems occur, for example, due to shock loads and seasonal changes and it can be made available on standby.

6.5.3.1   pH neutralisation.   The two most common neutralising agents are sodium hydroxide and sulphuric acid. They are normally the cheapest reagents when handling is taken into account (£200/tonne). It is usual to purchase and use up to 50% solutions. Lime is a cheaper alkali but is very difficult to prepare because of its poor solubility. Commercial slurries are available but there are additional difficulties because of the large volumes of sludge generated and the formation scale. If anaerobic biological treatment is in use, then sulphuric acid may add too much sulphate. This can cause malodour and inhibition of anaerobic digestion. Phosphoric acid would then be the preferred acid.

6.5.3.2   Coagulation and flocculation.   Chemical treatment can improve settlement and flotation rates and can be used to upgrade existing solids/ liquids separation. In some cases where particle size is very small, i.e. 1–10 mm, then it is the only way to produce reasonable separation.

The process of particle destabilisation is very complex but can be simplified to three basic mechanisms:

1. Charge neutralisation by adsorption of counter ions. Most natural particles develop negative charge in solution and can be aggregated by positive counter ions. This process is frequently called coagulation.
2. Bridging of particles by polymer chains. Each polymer may attach itself to several particles causing aggregation. This process is frequently called flocculation.
3. Physical enmeshment and straining by large masses of precipitate.

The most important mechanisms in effluent treatment are bridging and enmeshment. The most common reagents therefore are polymeric such as polyacrylamide, aluminium hydroxide and ferric hydroxide. Sulphate salts should be avoided if there is a possibility of anaerobic conditions and therefore sulphide formation. Sulphides in effluents will lead to corrosion and malodour.

In most cases, it is not sufficient to simply add the aggregating agent because good contact between the chemical and particles are required. This means a separate rapid mix tank to completely mix the reagent with the waste (Figure 6.14). The precipitate or flocs when formed are also fragile but still need gentle mixing to ensure good enmeshment. This is

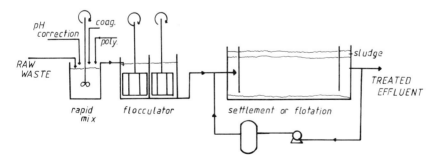

Figure 6.14 Typical flocculation system.

carried out in a second slow stirred tank (stirrer speed 1–2 rpm), before final settlement or flotation. A further difficulty arises because it is not possible to store the active flocculant and an activation or preparation step for the chemical is required. In the case of the synthetic organic polymeric materials, this means an additional rapid mix tank for dispersion (working solution 0.05–1%) and a slow mix tank for unravelling and ageing of the polymer. For aluminium and iron, dilution to a working strength of 1–2% is sufficient. Typically 1–5 mg/l organic polymers are required and/or 100–500 mg/l as Fe or Al. It is essential to use laboratory or pilot tests to establish the correct dose and combinations of flocculants.

A range of food grade flocculants are also available if the solids material is to be recycled, e.g.

1. cellulose;
2. starch;
3. lignosulphonic acid;
4. calcium polyphosphate.

They are not usually as efficient as aluminium, iron or polyacrylamide. The economics of chemical treatment have to be considered very carefully. Normally it is a simple cost benefit analysis for sludge consolidation or concentrated suspensions. For dilute effluents the running costs composed of maintenance, chemicals and sludge disposal counteract the benefit.

6.5.3.3 Oxidation.   Chemical oxidation can be justified when short-term problems arise such as a very short operating season, toxic wastes or a biological malfunction occur. It is a useful adjunct before biological oxidation when insufficient aeration is available. In these cases, it is usual to use pure oxygen, peroxide, or ozone although chlorine, permanganate and sulphur dioxide have also been used. In general, the sulphur compounds should be avoided if possible. Powerful oxidising agents, chlorine, hypochlorite and ozone, are commonly used to sterilise recycled effluent.

6.5.4 Nutrients

Few wastes, even food processing wastes, are balanced nutritionally and supplementation with nitrogen, phosphorus, trace metals and vitamins will improve performance. For successful aerobic treatment, it is usual to establish a carbon (as BOD), nitrogen (as inorganic nitrogen) and phosphorus (as inorganic phosphorus) ratio of 100:5:1 (see Section 6.6). In practice, if organic nitrogen is present as protein this can be used as a nitrogen source by the microorganisms. If only nitrogen is required, then it is usual to add urea. If both nitrogen and phosphorus are required then inorganic fertiliser (Nutraphos) is added.

Once the biomass is established then nutritional requirements are lower since most of the nutrients are recycled. Requirements can be controlled by ensuring there is a small residue of nutrients in the treated effluent, e.g. 1–2 mg/l.

The growth rate of anaerobic bacteria is lower than aerobes and nutritional requirements are less. Ratios of 300:5:1 are usual. The anaerobes are, however, vulnerable to shortages of transition metals iron, cobalt, nickel and manganese, because of the reducing environment and their precipitation as sulphides. These materials are available commercially and are commonly added to industrial digesters. Additional nutrient will also benefit aerobic treatment as complex nutrients or as biaugmentation. Iron additions can also be an effective method of counteracting mild sulphur toxicity in treatment by removing sulphide from solution.

6.5.5 Conclusions

Preliminary treatment such as screening, balancing, settlement and flotation will often be beneficial compared to the discharge of untreated effluent. Preliminary treatments are essential prior to biological or chemical treatment to prevent damage and clogging. The more complex preliminary processes such as flotation and chemical flocculation are difficult to operate and maintain. These extra costs need to be considered when calculating the benefits of treatment.

6.6 Aerobic biological treatment

6.6.1 Introduction

The most common types of treatment for removing organic matter from food industry effluents are aerobic (with aeration) and anaerobic (no oxygenation). Providing aeration for strong wastes, i.e. with a COD in excess of 5000 mg/l, is expensive. Roughly 1 kWh is required for each kg of BOD; also the efficiency of aerobic growth means that there are more surplus solids to dispose of than from the equivalent anaerobic process (Figure 6.15). Disadvantages of anaerobic treatment are that it is slow and is unable to produce a high quality treated effluent. Anaerobic treatment can only be a pretreatment process. In some areas of the world where land is relatively cheap and factories rural, for example some parts of the Americas and the Pacific basin, then long retention time natural process lagoons or lakes are possible. These types of treatments are not attractive in Europe because of the cost of land, odour potential and flies.

Aerobic biological waste treatment reactors are normally open-topped mixed microbial cultures which also acquire a diverse population of grazing

Table 6.32 Types of fixed film bioreactor

Percolating
Biological or trickling filters
Biotowers
Rotating biological contacts (RBC)
Submerged biological filtration
Biological aerated filter (BAF)
Expanded and fluidised beds (FB)

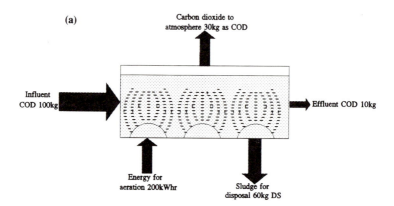

(a)

Carbon dioxide to atmosphere 30kg as COD

Influent COD 100kg

Effluent COD 10kg

Energy for aeration 200kWhr

Sludge for disposal 60kg DS

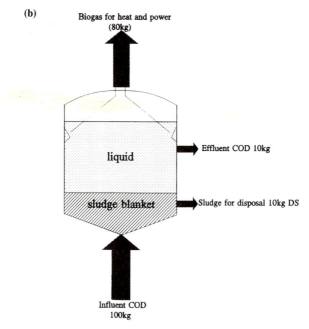

(b)

Biogas for heat and power (80kg)

liquid

Effluent COD 10kg

sludge blanket

Sludge for disposal 10kg DS

Influent COD 100kg

Figure 6.15 A comparison of the mass balance of carbon utilisation in (a) aerobic and (b) anaerobic processes.

Table 6.33 A simple comparison of the features of activated sludge and percolating filters

	Activated sludge	Percolating filters
Capital costs	Low	High
Land area	Low	High
Energy requirement	High for mixing aeration impossible without power	None, if necessary gravity flow, reaction distributor
Sludge production	Large amounts, high water content difficult to dewater	Small volume, higher solids content, well stablised
Hydrostatic head	Small for bioreactor but pumped sludge return equivalent in volume to feed	Head loss though media normally 2–3 m
Maintenance	Cleaning of diffusers, blowers monitoring equipment; not very robust, mechanical failures	Distributor needs cleaning daily; sturdy, few difficulties with breakdowns
Control	Requires skilled operation and monitoring, liable to upset and poor settlement	Simple but little turn up or control possible
Environmental	Few odours but may produce microbial aerosols can be noisy; no flies	Odour problems common and severe fly problem in local vicinity in summer
Seasonal	Not really affected by season or weather	Affected by temperature, poor nitrification in winter and seasonal, usually spring, discharges of solids
Waste	Sensitive to changes in nature of waste; industrial effluents usually cause a deterioration in settlement; foam is also a problem with fatty or detergent containing waste	Industrial effluents treated easily, able to withstand changes in loading; no problems with settlement or foam
Treated effluent quality	Good when working well, flocculates and removal of solids to a low concentration	Not as good effluent quality, difficult to achieve very high removals of solids
Nutrients	It is possible to remove nitrogen and phosphate by advanced control	Not possible to remove either nitrogen or phosphate by changes in operation

organisms. There are two basic types of treatment: plug flow fixed film systems (known as bacteria beds, percolating, biological or trickling filters) (Table 6.32) and completely mixed flocculant processes or activated sludge. The earliest type of reactor was the trickling filter, which developed directly from experiments carried out on the treatment of sewage by percolation through soil containing a graded biological support medium usually clinker, slag, stone, or gravel depending on local availability. They are easy to maintain, incur low running costs, and have a plant life of between 30 and 50 years. Percolating filters have proved to be very reliable and 70% of European and US treatment plants use this type of system. The alternative is activated sludge which is a mixed process, aerated and stirred by air diffusers or surface paddles. The retention time in the aeration tank is between 6 and 15 h after which the effluent is separated from the active sludge by settlement (2 h), and most of the sludge is returned to mix with the incoming effluent. The process is more efficient than percolating filters and is able to treat ten times as much waste; it is therefore cheaper to build. Activated sludge is, however, more difficult to operate and maintain, it also incurs higher running costs due to the mixing and aeration. The largest sewage works in Europe are activated sludge plants. Table 6.33 compares the advantages and disadvantages of the two processes.

Experience has shown that the plug flow fixed film process is more robust than activated sludge and is better suited to industrial wastes, particularly those containing only slowly biodegradable components. The plug flow means that the slowly biodegradable components may be retained and held for long periods in the biofilm. This gives more time for breakdown and also means that potential toxins are not evenly spread throughout the reactor. A second advantage is that fixed film reactors are not dependent on successful settling of the biomass. Surveys have shown that most activated sludge plants suffer from poor settlement at some stage and this is particularly true when dealing with food processing wastes.

6.6.2   Percolating filters

The basis of reactor design is to provide an environment in which the waste, the organisms responsible for purification, and air for aerobic treatment are brought into contact. The initial step is adsorption of the substrate onto the biological surface; typically 50% of the substrate is colloidal. This is followed by breakdown of the adsorbed substrate by extracellular enzymes and absorption of dissolved material into cells and biomass growth. Biological filters immobilise the biomass responsible for treatment on an inert support medium, either stone or plastic. The wastewater is sprayed over the surface of the filter by nozzle or moving

Figure 6.16 A high rate plastic media biofilter treating dairy waste.

distributor and allowed to percolate down through the bed. Good distribution of the waste over the surface of the filter is very important to provide intimate contact with the biofilm covering the support. The most popular system is a circular filter to give a simple rotating distributor (Figure 6.16). The distributor arms are drilled at intervals to provide an even spread over the surface of the filter. Usually the force of the water issuing from the holes is sufficient to drive the distributor around and no power is required.

Cleaning the distribution holes is one of the major maintenance problems with biological filters. They may require cleaning two or three times a day with a poorly screened effluent.

Two other important features of biological filter design are the surface area of the media, which governs the amount of biomass, and the space between the support media. The voidage of the media controls the ventilation, and therefore oxygen available for microbial growth, drainage and discharge of solids. Ventilation through the media is assisted by the temperature difference between ambient and the wastewater. There is a continuous cycle of biofilm growth and detachment taking place, partly due to autolysis and partly due to the action of the grazing organisms. The debris or humus flushed from the biological filter is collected in a final settling or humus tank.

In the spring, with the first increase in ambient temperature, very large amounts of biofilm and debris, which have accumulated during the winter, can be dislodged by the grazing organisms. This can cause overloading of the humus tank (Figure 6.17).

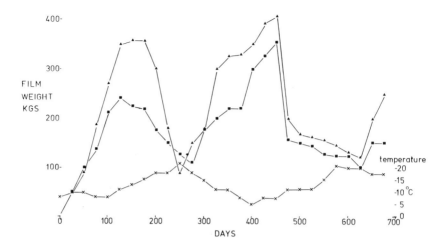

Figure 6.17 Seasonal changes in film weight on Flocor E, 150m²/m³ (■) and Flocor M, 200m²/m³ (▲).

6.6.2.1 Process design. Early in the development of the percolating filter, it became apparent that the loading rates were limited by excessive growths on the media. The voidage became filled with biomass and the filter was blocked or ponded. Treatment efficiency is in principle proportional to the amount of biomass. Increases in process intensitivity increase the amounts of active biomass and the requirements for aeration per volume of reactor.

The amounts of waste which could be treated and the aeration or ventilation required to ensure reliable treatment were at first established empirically in 1908 (Royal Commission) but there have been continuous experiments to improve the process. Tests in 1931 for example (O'Shaughnessy, 1931), noted that BOD removal was first order and that dilution by recycle led to better mixing. With recycle for dilution, there was a more even spread of biomass through a reactor. Measurements on biomass showed that the biomass was in two distinct zones. The system was plug flow and the surface of the filter received and removed the greatest amount of the applied substrate. The most active organisms were in the top 0.5 m of the bed known as the heterotrophic layer (Figure 6.18). Below this was the autotrophic zone where the bios was mostly debris and humus from the upper more active layers. The material occurred in flocculated deposits rather than as prostrate slime adhering closely to the support media as in the case of surface growth. There is little BOD removal in these layers, but considerable autotrophic nitrification. Higher hydraulic loads such as from recirculation increase efficiency by dissipating the load deeper into the bed. Dilution of the waste by recirculation also reduces the strength

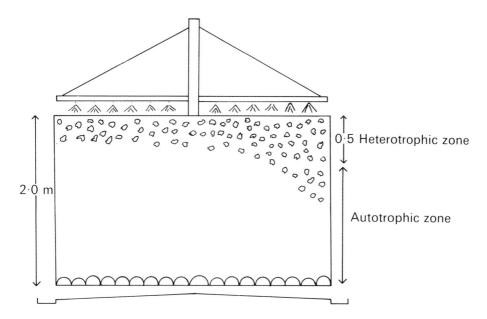

Figure 6.18 Ecological zones in biological filtration. First published in Wheatley (1984) and reproduced by permission from Intercept Press.

of the waste, reaerating it and recycling valuable nutrients. Wishart and Wilkinson (1941) described other experiments where they successfully controlled biomass by washing a winter blocked filter with treated effluent. They suggested a scheme of alternating double filtration (ADF) where the waste load normally applied to two filters in parallel was instead fed to two filters in series. Biomass accumulated in the first filter as it received and consumed virtually all of the BOD load. The order of the filters was then reversed before the first filter ponded. The original primary filter then received treated effluent which had passed through the new primary filter. This procedure resulted in rapid autolysis and consumption of the starved biomass. ADF enabled filters to be operated at more than twice the usual loads with fewer problems of blocked media. The best frequency of alternation was found to be weekly and ADF became the common method of operating large biological filters.

Other work used similar principles (Table 6.34). Hawkes and Shephard (1972) and others showed that slowing down the distributor on a biological filter also improved performance by encouraging an even spread of biomass through the filter depth. A recent technique is double filtration with different sized media. The first filter in the series of two contains a large medium (150–300 mm) to accommodate more biological growth, but at a lower BOD removal efficiency (about 70%). The second filter contains conventional media (50–75 mm) and completes the removal of organic

Table 6.34 Methods of operating percolating filters

Single filtration
Recirculation
Alternating double filtration
Low frequency dosing with electric drive
Two stage filtration with high rate primary filter
Plastic media filters

waste to 95% (Table 6.35). Overall the loading is higher. Traditionally, single pass percolating filters were 1.8 m (6 ft) deep, to achieve 95% BOD removal from domestic sewage. Recirculation and higher loadings meant 2–3 m deep filters for 95% BOD removal. The advantages of double filtration led to the introduction of plastic media. The two characteristics of media which most influence biological treatment efficiency are the specific surface area available for biological growth and the voidage for ventilation and drainage. Plastic materials can be moulded into shapes with optimum surface area and voidage. To be effective, however, the much greater surface area needs to be uniformly wetted. Two types of plastic media are used, modular self-supporting blocks or random rashig rings (Figure 6.19). Much taller biological filters were possible with the light weight plastic filter media and simple prefabricated cladding on a concrete base could be used for the self-supporting modules. The modular synthetic media have specific surface areas of $100-150 \, m^2/m^3$, about the same as 50 mm blast furnace slag.

Filters were built up to 6 m high (biotowers) and high rates of recirculation usually between 6 and 10:1 were used to generate complete mixing and ensure adequate utilisation of the available surface. The high rates of treatment (Table 6.34) with plastic media enabled major savings to be made and the process became widely used to treat strong industrial wastes.

The random plastic media are shaped with corrugations or vanes to promote an even flow pattern over the higher specific surface; up to $250 \, m^2/m^3$ are available. Lower recycle rates (e.g. 2 or 3:1) could then be used and some plug flow retained. Like the modular media, random plastic filters can then be taller, i.e. 2–4 m and utilise cheaper methods of construction, mainly prefabricated, coated, steel tanks. Unfortunately the cost of plastics has risen sharply recently and there are now fewer advantages to using plastic media.

6.6.2.2 Rotating biological contactors (RBC). A common problem with biological filters is the frequent blockage of the distributor holes. The rotating biological contactor or RBC was a development which overcomes this difficulty. A series of plastic sheets are rotated through a tank of the wastewater (Figure 6.20). About 40% of the surface area is submerged. RBCs or biodiscs have similar ecology to biological filters, but make more

Table 6.35 Typical biological filter loadings

Type of filter	BOD load (kg/m^3 per day)	Hydraulic load (m^3/m^2 per day)	Retention time (min)	BOD removal (%)	Conversion of BOD applied to sludge (%)
Septic tank unattended system	0.05	1–1.5	100–200	95	5
Low rate traditional	0.05–0.1	1–2	60–90	95	15–20
Mid range double filtration ADF or recirculation	0.01–0.05	2–5	30–60	85–90	20–50
High rate filtration	1–2	5–10	10–20	50–70	50–90

(a)

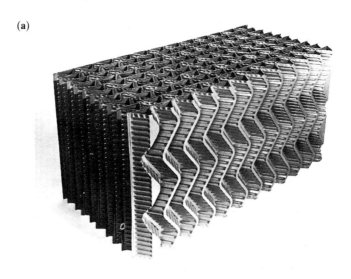

(b)

Figure 6.19 The main types of plastic media. (a) High rate modular medium 'Flocor E', module size 1200 × 600 × 600 mm. (b) The new random medium 'Flocor RC' prior to loading into the experimental filters. First published in Wheatley (1990) and reproduced by permission of the SCI.

efficient use of the support which is alternately completely wetted and then aerated. The slow rotation of the discs, 1–2 rpm, ensures uniform concentrations of substrate and dissolved oxygen. The tank beneath the discs can be baffled to produce a plug flow of waste and then nitrification can be achieved. To consistently remove 95% of the applied BOD, the maximum organic loading rate is 5 g BOD/m^2 of specific surface per day (Pike *et al.*, 1982). This is about five times the load on a biological filter to achieve the same standard. RBC plants are compact and have become very popular as

(a)

(b)

Figure 6.20(a) Rotating biological contactor (RBC) with (b) close up photograph of the support media. First published in Wheatley (1985) and reproduced by permission of the SCI.

a package plant for small flows. Typical prefabricated units are 1.5 m in diameter by 2 m long but larger units have been built for food industry wastes up to 5 m in diameter by 8 m long. Applications to food effluents have not been very successful. The treatment of strong wastes is limited by oxygen transfer and experiments have been conducted with forced aeration of the effluent tank (Wilson *et al.*, 1988). Maintenance problems have also been encountered, the rotating shaft and bearings are subject to a very corrosive environment. The shaft and discs of the RBC must be kept turning at all times, otherwise biomass accumulates in one position and imbalances occur. This can distort and damage the shaft and media.

6.6.2.3 Submerged filters. Totally submerging the biological support media significantly improves the efficiency of use. Fluidised beds, for example, combine the advantages of the percolating filter process with those of activated sludge. Biological fluidised beds are able to retain about five times the concentration of microorganisms compared to conventional plant and significant savings in capital cost are likely. The support particles (sand or plastic) can be much smaller than in percolating filters because there is no risk of clogging. The supports are expanded and kept well mixed by aeration or oxygen injection combined with effluent recycle often 4 or 5:1. Bed expansion is 20–25%. Most of the work reported on fluidised beds is from laboratory or pilot scale tests, the majority are for the anaerobic treatment of waste. Difficulties have been encountered with keeping the bed at the correct expansion; there are no aerobic examples in the food industry and widespread application may depend on better and new control systems.

A different and more robust high rate fixed film process is submerged filtration or biological aerated filter (BAF). There is no intention to expand the carrier bed in submerged filtration; the system works rather like sand filtration and includes periodic backwashing. The forced aeration and fine carrier gives a high rate of performance and solids retention so that most BAF units work without a clarifier.

BAF units work well as simple filters and as a consequence, process air requirements are less than for mainly biological processes such as activated sludge (about 1.5 kg O_2 per kg BOD) but because there is less oxidation, sludge production is high, 0.8–1 kg DS per kg BOD removed (Table 6.36).

The solids accumulate in the filter until eventually they reach a critical concentration. This is monitored by head loss through the system. The filter is then cleaned by backwashing and air scouring. Repeated backwashings are used until the system is clear and free of solids. The wash water has to be collected and balanced before recycling to avoid hydraulic surges. Volumes of wash water used are between 2 and 8% of flow rates. The wash water is returned to the front of the treatment plant for primary settlement.

Table 6.36 BAF loading rates compared to conventional percolating filters and activated sludge

	To achieve 90% BOD removal (kg/m^3 per day)	To achieve 70–80% nitrification (kg/m^3 per day)
Trickling filters	0.1–0.4	
Activated sludge	0.3–0.6	
BAF	0.7–3.0	
Nitrifying filters		0.6
BAF nitrification unit		0.6–1

Table 6.37 UK and some French operating BAF units

Location	Capacity (m³/day)	Standard SS/BOD (mg/l)	Start up
North Brierley (Bradford)	10000	10/10	1990
Silchester, Gloucester	14000	10/7	1991
St Austell, Cornwall	25200	35/25	1993
Nimes	70000	30/30	1991
Monaco	31000	15/20	1990

Both upflow and downflow units are available; the process air can be both co- and counter current. Downflow systems are thought to work with less dispersion and mixing. They are therefore claimed to have advantages for nitrification and for avoiding clogging of the distribution systems. Upflow systems with greater mixing can work at higher loads; they are also less odorous because only treated effluent is exposed. In downflow systems, there is potential to strip volatile compounds from the raw waste above the media (see Stephenson *et al.*, 1993 for a table of proprietary processes).

There are about 50 full scale BAF plants in Europe, 20 of which are in France where the two large French Water Companies market rival processes. In many cases, these plants have been built indoors to avoid odour and aerosol problems in urban areas. This is possible because of the small plan area that BAF occupy. There are about 5 plants in the United Kingdom used mainly as a tertiary type nitrification system for domestic sewage (Table 6.37). Ammonia can consistently be reduced from 20–30 mg/l to 1–5 mg/l (Lilly *et al.*, 1991). In the United States, the process has also been shown to be a cost effective method for the production of high quality effluents at smaller works where activated sludge is difficult to operate (Bishop and Kinner, 1986).

Sand shale and gravels are the most common support media but plastic media both modular and random have also been utilised. In the case of the modular media, air is injected through diffuser plates beneath the pack to provide mixing and aeration; separate clarification is necessary. Hydraulic retention times in BAF units are between 30 and 100 min.

6.6.3 Activated sludge

The large areas of land required for percolating filters and the capital costs mean that activated sludge is the preferred type of treatment for loads greater than 8 tonnes of COD per day. Activated sludge is a completely

Figure 6.21 A diffused air activated sludge plant treating dairy waste.

mixed process with biomass recycle after settlement. The development of colonies of flocculated bacteria are crucial to allow the successful separation of the biomass or sludge by settlement. There are two basic methods of aeration, diffused air or mechanical surface aeration.

The most common type of diffuser is a ceramic air stone fixed on the base of the tank. The rising bubbles also serve to mix the tank. Oxygen transfer efficiency from bottom diffusers has been measured to be better than surface aeration because bubble size can be controlled (Figure 6.21). There may, however, be problems keeping the diffusers clean; they can easily become clogged with fat and scale, and may need frequent cleaning. Another difficulty with diffusers is that to achieve good overall tank mixing requires more aeration than would be required for effective waste treatment alone. Coarse diffusers are also used for industrial wastes or in individual tanks to enhance mixing. Diffusers are now available made from light synthetic plastics which enables them to be withdrawn from the tank and cleaned without taking the tank out of service (Table 6.38).

There are a number of proprietory surface aerators, many with draft tubes to ensure good mixing. The oxygen transfer characteristics of mechanical aerators can be varied by adjusting the rotor height. Surface aerators are simpler and easier to maintain than diffused air, but are mostly used by the smaller works because of the lower oxygen transfer efficiency and increased costs.

6.6.3.1 Process designs.   A number of different activated sludge process designs have developed (Table 6.39) mostly aimed at reducing energy demands and to improve settlement. A common method of design is

Table 6.38 Characteristics of some available aerator systems

Aeration system	Typical transfer efficiency (%)	Transfer rate (kg O^2/kWh)	
		Standard[a]	Field[b]
Diffused-air systems			
Fine bubble	10–30	1.2–2.5	0.7–1.5
Medium bubble	6–15	1.0–1.6	0.6–1.0
Coarse bubble	4–8	0.6–1.2	0.3–0.9
Turbine sparger system	10–20	1.2–1.4	0.7–1.0
Static-tube system	7–10	1.2–1.6	0.7–0.9
Jet	10–25	1.2–1.4	0.7–1.4
Pure oxygen systems			
Mechanical surface aeration	79	–	1.4–1.8
Venturi systems	90	3.0	1.5–2.5
Turbine sparger	80	1.2–2.4	1.2–1.5
Impeller systems			
Low speed surface	10	1.2–2.0	0.7–1.3
Low speed surface with draft-tube	10–20	1.2–2.0	0.7–1.3
High speed floating aerator	10–20	1.2–2.0	0.7–1.4
Rotor-brush aerator	10–20	3.0	0.7–1.3
Bayer turmbiologie	90	5.0	–
ICI deep shaft	90	–	–

[a]Standard shop test under controlled conditions (ASCE, 1984).
[b]Average of field data available.

tapered aeration which is intended to match microbial oxygen demand with aeration. Most activated sludge plants are plug flow and the oxygen demand at the outlet is much less than the inlet, so aeration can be progressively reduced along the length of the tank. This is accomplished by using fewer diffuser domes in the base of the tank towards the outlet. A similar modification for use at surface aerated plants is step aeration which introduces some waste at intervals throughout the length of the tank. Aeration of the returned sludge without the addition of more waste is also used to encourage the bacteria to utilise any stored nutrient. The activated sludge is then able to assimilate greater amounts of substrate or waste when reintroduced into the main treatment tank. This process is known as contact stabilisation. Oxygen availability in the activated sludge process can be increased by using pure oxygen instead of air. There are two proprietary systems, one system uses completely sealed tanks and is very similar to conventional activated sludge. Surface mixers are used and the head space above the liquid is enriched with oxygen either from a storage tank or from on site production. The second system uses an open tank with external recirculation pumps to keep the tank mixed. High pressure oxygen is injected into a venturi throat on the outlet side of the pump.

Table 6.39 Design and performance of activated sludge

Type of activated sludge	Substrate loading, $F:M$ (kg BOD/ kg MLSS per day)[a]	Biomass concentration, MLSS (g/l)	Hydraulic retention time (HRT) (h)	Biomass growth rate, doubling time or solids retention time (SRT) (days)	Removal of organic matter, BOD removal (T)	Organic loading rate (kg BOD/m³)	Biomass growth rate surplus for disposal conversion to sludge (%)[d]
Extended aeration	0.02–0.06[b]	4–10	100+	10+	95+	0.1–0.2	5–20
Conventional design practice	0.2–0.5[b]	3–4	10–20	5–10[c]	95	0.6–1.5	25–50
High rate treatment	1.0–2.0	4–5	5–10	2–5	70–75	4–10	50–75

[a] Assumes 80% volatile or organic suspended solids.
[b] These are averages; reactors need not to be plug flow so initial loading rates are much higher, i.e. up to 100.
[c] To achieve microbial nitrification which is a different group and slow growing organisms minimum solids retention is 10 days.
[d] Often expressed as kg dry solids/kg BOD removed.

This dissolves the oxygen at high pressure. Oxygen utilisation efficiency is further increased by releasing the oxygenated mixture through outlet nozzles in the base of the tank. Pure oxygen plants are able to work with a larger biomass concentration and therefore higher loads than conventional plants. The capital costs of the plant are lower but the running costs higher. The process is ideal for strong seasonal wastes.

A totally different method of increasing oxygen solubility is to increase the hydrostatic pressure in the reactor by building tall reactor tanks. The best known of these is a tube sunk between 50–100 m into the ground. The process is called the 'deep shaft'. The shaft is 0.5–2 m in diameter and divided into two concentric tubes. The waste is introduced into the inner, downflow section, together with the recycled activated sludge and process air. In the outer upflow section, bubbles of dissolved gases are released as the pressure decreases and this reduces the density of the circulating water. It is this difference in density between the water in the downflow and upflow tubes that produces the circulating force for the shaft. The velocity generated is much higher than the rise rate of the air bubbles in the downflow section and the air is carried down. Dissolved oxygen and turbulence in the shaft are high which permits a high concentration of very active biomass to be obtained. To avoid flotation the treated effluent has to be vacuum degassed before settlement. The system has low running costs but can be very expensive to build because of the structural costs.

A slightly different approach to reduce these construction costs has been to utilise tall above ground tanks. The tower tanks are 20–30 m high in protected welded steel. Air is injected through an array of draft tubes arranged around the base of the tank or at high pressure directly into a multiport waste inlet manifold. The technology has been used successfully on chemical wastes and was pioneered by Bayer. There is one unit in the United Kingdom working on ICI chemical waste (McCann, 1993).

An unwanted consequence of intensifying aerobic waste treatment using the activated sludge process has been an increase in the amount of surplus biomass (sludge) to be disposed of. Extended residence times, e.g. >10 days, and low loads can be used to aerobically digest or autolyse most of the biomass produced. This process is known as extended aeration, the oxidation ditch being the most common example. The oxidation ditch was originally designed to be a maintenance free, cheap to run, system for small communities. They are oval shaped shallow ditches (Figure 6.22), run at a very low load and without primary settlement. Mixing and aeration is provided by a horizontal brush paddle at one or both ends. They incorporate separate settlement of the treated wastes and recycle of the sludge as normal.

6.6.3.2 Nutrient removal.   Most large domestic activated sludge plants now recover some energy by anoxic denitrification. The heterotrophic

(a)

(b)

Figure 6.22 (a) A typical oxidation ditch with (b) a close up of the turbulence caused by the rotor.

bacteria in activated sludge are able to utilise nitrate for respiration in the absence of oxygen. In a conventional activated sludge plant, at least 50% of the flow is recycled and this is enriched with nitrate from the oxidation of ammonia and organic nitrogen. Therefore, if the first portion of a plug flow activated sludge plant is made anoxic or has no free dissolved oxygen, then the high substrate concentration will encourage the microorganisms to use nitrate instead of oxygen for their respiration. Waste treatment will continue, without the cost of aeration. The transient exposure to anoxic conditions has no adverse effects on the process and there is the added benefit of removing nitrate as nitrogen gas (see the section on pollution damage). In practice, up to the first 30% of the activated sludge tank (i.e. about 4–5 h) can be anoxic and by increasing the proportion of recycle, 70–80% of the nitrate in the final effluent can be removed.

There has also been research which shows that a totally anaerobic stage (i.e. without oxygen and nitrate) can be used to increase phosphate uptake by the microorganisms.

Some nutrient removal will be required in sensitive locations in the United Kingdom to meet the new EC Urban Waste Water Directive (see Section 6.2). There is very limited UK experience of this technology but proprietary process designs have become established in South Africa, Australia and the United States. All of these designs use biological phosphate removal within a multi-stage activated sludge plant. A three-stage plant is the common approach with an anoxic zone, an anaerobic zone and finally a reaeration zone. It is the totally anaerobic zone which is necessary to encourage phosphate uptake. The theory behind the design is that normally aerobic bacteria can derive some energy from polyphosphate storage compounds (volutin granules) while their aerobic metabolism is blocked. In doing so the organisms will become phosphate deficient so that on re-aeration they absorb and store much more phosphate in 'luxury uptake'. Good denitrification is important to ensure anaerobic, rather than anoxic conditions, in the phosphate removal stage. In a typical activated sludge plant with a 1:1 recycle, then only about 50% denitrification should be achievable. Cooper *et al.* (1977) observed 57% nitrate removal in a standard plant. Increased recycle rates are necessary to improve denitrification but carbon to nitrate ratios of 3:1 (BOD NO_3) are necessary and the BOD must be readily degradable. Increased recycling will improve the degree of mixing and therefore encourage poor sludge settlement. The totally anaerobic environment of the phosphate removal step will also lead to settlement problems. Nutrient removal plants are therefore notoriously difficult to operate which has led some to suggest sidestream processes with chemical back up (Upton and Churchley, 1993). Adapting the activated sludge plant for nutrient removal will present major design and operational challenges for the future.

6.6.3.3 Sludge settlement.   The degree of mixing and organic loading have been found to exert a major influence on activated sludge settlement. The better the mixing the greater the exposed microbial surface to substrate and oxygen. The well mixed activated sludge process is therefore able to support a larger population of actively growing bacteria per unit volume of bioreactor than traditional percolating filters. It has also become evident, however, that good mixing which leads to low residual substrate concentrations can lead to poor settlement.

The microorganisms that grow in wastewater treatment processes are selected by their ability to degrade various substrate components in the waste, their ability to grow in oligotrophic environments and their retention within the system by bioflocculation. The ecology is also influenced by reactor design. The activated sludge process is totally aquatic while percolating filters utilise a thin film of effluent flowing over the surface of the bios.

The reduced ecological diversity of the activated sludge process compared to percolating filters contributes to the process instability, increases sludge production, reduces the resilience to shock or variable organic loads and makes the process more difficult to manage (Hawkes, 1963). The bacteria are the basis of both processes and the *Zoogloea* (gram-negative, non-sporing, non-motile, capsulated rods) are assumed to be the most important group and responsible for much of the treatment. There are still some doubts as to whether the *Zoogloea* are a defined group, polymorphic, or a strain of *Pseudomonas* which develop a slime layer because of the particular conditions in the process (Pike, 1975). Classical microbiology by media isolation does not give any information on which are the important bacteria in a wastewater treatment plant. A very wide range of bacteria can be isolated from wastewater but few of these are actively growing. Many of the bacteria in fresh sewage for example are enteric including some potential pathogens. These bacteria have no role in the treatment process and their numbers fall rapidly (Pike and Carrington, 1979). The organisms which colonise treatment processes are derived from aerial inoculation and infiltration water. *Zoogloea*, *Pseudomonas*, *Chromobacter*, *Achromobacter*, *Flavobacter* and *Arthrobacter* are thought to be the principal groups (Pike, 1975).

Experiments have shown that only a small proportion of the sludge floc or slime layer is actively growing, but most of the biomass can still carry out biochemical reactions via extracellular enzymes and biophysical adsorption (Pike and Carrington, 1972; Bishop and Kinner, 1986). The production of extracellular bacterial polymer is a most important feature of the activated sludge process. The detailed chemistry of the polymer is complex but it is predominantly polysaccharide. A number of soil and aquatic bacteria produce extracellular polymer as a response to oligotropic (nutrient limiting) conditions. The extracellular polymer has evolved as a binding agent primarily to collect or fix to solid substrates but also to adsorb dissolved materials at the surfaces.

In a well settling sludge, at least 25–30% of the total biomass is thought to be extracellular polymer. Bacterial polymers are not as strong polyelectrolytes or resistant to shear as polyacrylamide polymers, for example, but the overwhelming concentration makes activated sludge an effective binding agent for most of the solids in the wastewater. Other bacteria, stalked protozoans, detritus and debris can all be observed adsorbed on to the polymeric floc. Soluble and hydrated inorganics are also bound to the floc by the slightly negative surface charge from the carboxyl and amine groups present in the polysaccharide and proteins of the polymer (Brown and Lester, 1979).

Significant growth of bacteria filaments beyond the floc structure can cause settlement problems. The filaments prevent coagulation of the individual bacterial flocs by stopping close contact between them. Water is then held between the flocs rather than being squeezed out, sludge density is reduced and there is no consolidation. This condition is known as bulking, the deterioration in settlement is linked to the filament length protruding beyond the floc structure. Twenty-two morphologically different filamentous bacteria have been observed (Eikelboom, 1975) and a simple key system has been developed to identify them (Chambers and Tomlinson, 1982). The most commonly occurring ones are shown in Table 6.40. The organisms are not well characterised and many of the bacteria are identified only by number. It seems likely that some are the same polymorphic organism (Postgate, 1989). Traditionally most filamentous organisms were identified as *Sphaerotilus* or the sulphur bacteria and older texts refer only to these. The causes of bulking are an active area of research, but there are five common triggers: low dissolved oxygen, low pH, septic wastewater, nutrient deficiency (e.g. N and P) and low loading rates. Each results in problems from a different group of organisms. Low dissolved oxygen is associated with *Sphaerotilus*; septic effluent with *Thiothrix* and the other sulphur bacteria, low nitrogen and phosphorus with *Sphaerotilus*, low pH with the fungi and *Microthrix* 021N and 0041 with low loading rates. The floc forming bacteria have the ability to rapidly absorb and store nutrient compared to the filamentous bacteria. To avoid filamentous bacteria, it is necessary to ensure that the activated sludge is rapidly mixed with the raw waste. This is designed for by a plug flow reactor or a pre-mix tank prior to aeration (known as a selector). The subsequent aeration at low substrate concentrations allows the substrate

Table 6.40 Common filamentous organisms in activated sludge

Organism	Frequency of occurrence
Microthrix parvicella	Very common
Type 021N	Very common
Type 0041	Common
Sphaerotilus natans	Occasionally
Beggiatoa	Occasionally
Leptothrix	Occasionally
Nocardia (actinomycete)	Occasionally
Fungi	Rarely

Source: Chambers and Tomlinson (1982). There are differences between countries, particularly warmer climates.

to be biologically oxidised and regenerate the absorption capacity of the floc. Filamentous bacteria are much more efficient at taking up nutrients at lower concentrations possibly because of their larger surface area. Therefore, completely mixed reactors which have a lower and uniform concentration of substrate promote filamentous growth. Measurements on the kinetics of the organisms has confirmed these observations. *Zoogloea* flocs have a higher maximum growth rate but a low substrate affinity, whereas filamentous organisms have a lower maximum growth rate but a higher affinity for the substrate.

Most activated sludge plants suffer from bulking or settlement problems at some time, particularly if treating industrial effluents; arguably the process is not suitable for industrial effluents for this reason. Much research has been conducted in this area unfortunately often with contradictory results (Table 6.41).

A floc loading term has been introduced to the design of activated sludge to take account of the degree of mixing. Like the *F:M* ratio, floc loading is a measure of the ratio of substrate to sludge solids but unlike sludge loading rate (or *F:M* ratio) it is the instantaneous loading occurring at the point where the substrate and returned sludge meet. Floc loading is the

Table 6.41 Controlling bulking

1. Process design	a. Loads between 0.3 and 0.6 kg BOD/kg per day
	b. Plug flow selectors or baffles to give nutrient gradients
	c. Floc load greater than 50 kg/BOD per kg per day
2. Redox	a. DOs greater than 2.0
	b. Avoid anaerobic conditions by excessive settlement or balancing
	c. High temperatures cause filaments by reducing oxygen transfer; fixed films should be used as a 1st stage
3. Character of waste	a. The most common industrial effluents, i.e. starch bearing wastes, generate filaments; use biofilms as first stage
	b. Poor nutrients also cause bulking add N and P
	c. Control to neutral pH
4. Chemical controls	a. Flocculants can improve floc density. Iron is most common, but also lime and polyelectrodes used successfully
	b. Chlorine and peroxide dosing have been used to reduce microbial activity to allow regrowth; regrowths and THM are problems
	c. Re-inoculation also gives temporary relief until regrowth overwhelms new inoculum
	d. Especially prepared enzymes and bacteria also give some benefit until regrowth and nutrients are lost from the system

ratio of substrate to returned activated sludge RAS. Typically, floc loading needs to be between 100 and 200 kg BOD/kg MLSS for a minimum of 10 min. It can be designed for by either the degree of mixing or selectors to induce a very high substrate concentration at the inlet. The technique of floc loading was successfully used to eliminate bulking problems at Halifax Sewage-Treatment Works (Jones and Franklin, 1985).

Stable foam formation is also a common problem with activated sludge plants. Present problems are not linked to synthetic detergents but the presence of natural surfactants such as the long chain fatty acids and proteins. These cause the accumulation of solids, air and liquid films at the air sludge interface. Activated sludge plants with foam also contain filaments. Fatty wastes (e.g. dairy), high temperatures, poor sludge recycle rates and high dissolved oxygen are contributory factors (Foot, 1992). The foam, if unchecked, quickly drys to form dense matts which are further stabilised by the opportunistic growths of a filamentous actinomycete within the foam and at the interface. This type of dense foam is dark in colour and known as chocolate mousse. Interestingly, stable foams were not recognised as a problem until 1970 and can be associated with low loading rates and nitrification and also possibly to the much wider use of long chain vegetable oils although this needs to be scientifically established. Foaming is always worse at high temperatures and is prevalent in warm climates and occasionally in gas mixed sludge digestion.

The stabilising actinomycetes are all from the genus *Nocardia*. The actinomycetes like the fungi are truly branched and themselves generate long chain fatty acids during growth to produce hydrophobic hyphae and aid bubble attachment.

Significantly *Nocardia* have not been isolated from any other environment, and it is possible that it is a polymorphic form of a standard activated sludge microbe (Horan *et al.*, 1988). *Microthrix* is also occasionally linked to foaming.

Unlike the filamentous bacteria, *Nocardia* is not a major difficulty in settlement because it does not extend far beyond the bacterial floc structure. Foaming is an operational difficulty because foam and solids can be carried over into settlement and be discharged with the final effluent. One of the simplest and best ways of controlling foam is to avoid its formation by water sprays on the aeration tanks and clarifiers. This prevents thick foam formation and the ingress of *Nocardia*. Spraying and antifoams are ineffective against stable foams. Thick foams can be reduced by increasing loading by reductions in sludge age or MLSS concentrations (Foot, 1992). *Microthrix* and *Nocardia* have rapid growth rates and sludge ages may have to be reduced to 1 or 2 days. These growth rates will often lead to an unacceptable final effluent quality and loss of nitrification but reductions in MLSS may improve redox and help oxygen transfer in warm weather even at much higher sludge ages.

6.7   Anaerobic biological treatment

6.7.1   Types of anaerobic digester

As with aerobic treatment there are several types of anaerobic reactor but unlike aerobic bioreactors the choice between these versions depends on the type of waste to be treated. The organics in domestic sludge and agricultural wastes are mainly as solids whereas the organic pollutants in food effluents are in solution or colloidal suspension. Effluents are therefore more amenable to treatment. Many of the internal structures within reactors used for the treatment of dilute wastes could not be used for wastes with a high solids content. Large amounts of solids would lead to clogging and blockage. Reactors for the treatment of sewage sludge and agricultural waste are stirred tanks or long retention lagoons mixed by the methane generation. Retention times are governed by the rates of solids hydrolysis. Rates of solids breakdown are rapid for up to 15 days' retention, but then become slower as the easily metabolisable carbohydrates, proteins and fats are exhausted. There is always an indigestible residue of fibre of between 10 and 30% of the volatile feed solids even at retention times greater than 30 days (see the IWPC design manual 1979). Typical retention times for solids and slurry digestion are between 12 and 20 days and this is sufficient for microbial growth to replace organisms passed out with the treated waste (Figure 6.23a). If there is no system for keeping or reusing bacteria, then the minimum retention time in the reactor is limited by microbial growth rate. The doubling time of the methanogens is 5 days and this is too long for a reasonable sized commercially viable anaerobic reactor for industrial effluents. Different reactors designs have therefore been developed for food wastes which hold back biomass within the reactor or which recycle the bacteria after separation. Biomass retention is then no longer dependent on liquid retention time and high bacterial concentrations can be obtained. Microorganisms are retained by the standard methods (Figure 6.23).

1. Physical separation of the biomass from the effluent by filtration or sedimentation. The active sludge is then recycled back to the completely mixed reactor. This type of anaerobic system is usually known as the contact stirred tank reactor or CSTR.
2. Retention and attachment of the bacteria to an internal support medium. The packing increases head loss and provides areas of low upflow velocity where bacteria can accumulate. This type of reactor is called an anaerobic filter; the flow of waste can be upward or downward.
3. Natural bacterial flocculation assisted by low upflow velocities to generate a sludge bed or blanket in the bottom of the reactor. This

type of reactor is known as the upflow anaerobic sludge blanket reactor or UASB. This type of biomass retention is unusual to anaerobic treatment and is made possible by the accumulation of inorganics.

4. The flow through a flocculated sludge blanket may also be horizontal and the biomass retention assisted by a series of baffles. The reactor is known as an anaerobic baffled reactor (ABR).

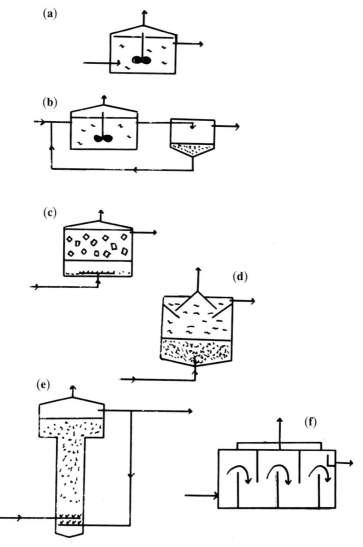

Figure 6.23 Types of anaerobic reactor: (a) see text; (b) CSTR; (c) anaerobic filter; (d) UASB; (e) fluidised bed; (f) ABR.

5. Attachment of the bacteria to small support particles and fluidisation of the particles by gas and effluent recycle. The particles and biomass can be completely mixed when the system is known as a fluidised bed or less vigorously mixed in an expanded bed.

Low rate large lagoons have occasionally been used for the anaerobic digestion of industrial and domestic wastes. The land use and lack of control makes them unpopular and they are not considered in detail in this chapter.

6.7.1.1 Sewage sludge digesters.   Anaerobic digesters for the treatment of domestic sludges and farm slurry are large, completely mixed, continuously heated tanks. The most important features of design are the efficiency of mixing, the effectiveness of heating, and because most of the substrate is solid, the solids retention time.

Mixing. Surveys of traditional concrete sewage sludge digesters (Swanwick *et al.*, 1969; Brade and Noon, 1981) have repeatedly found half the reactor ineffective because of poor mixing. Most problems were traced to blockage, fouling and corrosion of mechanical mixers. Mixing is required to ensure dispersion of the fresh raw sludge within the digester and to promote good contact between the waste and the bacteria. Mixing is also necessary to avoid dead zones, thermal stratification and grit and scum accumulation. Gas production within the digester causes some stirring, but this is usually insufficient for the complete mixing of sewage sludge digesters. Industrial digesters operating at high rates and which produce more than 1.5 times the volume of the digester in gas each day can be completely mixed by gas production (Tilche and Vierra, 1991). Reactors which operate at a very low load typical of rural digesters can also be self-sufficiently mixed by gas production. There are three methods of mixing sludge digesters: recirculation of sludge, recirculation of gas, and mechanical mixing.

External recirculation of the sludge, although easy to maintain, does not produce thorough mixing. The digester contents are turned over 'on block' rather than completely mixed, short circuiting and dead zones occur. Sludge recirculation is not used as the sole method of mixing and traditionally this is assisted by internal mechanical mixing. Sludge is sucked up a fixed tube by an impeller and sprayed out over the digester surface. This action avoids scum formation. Mechanical mixers are the most efficient type of mixer when new (Brade and Noon, 1981), but rapidly become choked with rags and eventually damaged by corrosion. Cleaning impellers is expensive and unpleasant. Current preferred practice is to use gas lift mixing. Gas is collected at the digester surface, cleaned, dewatered, and compressed. The gas is then reintroduced at the base of the digester. The

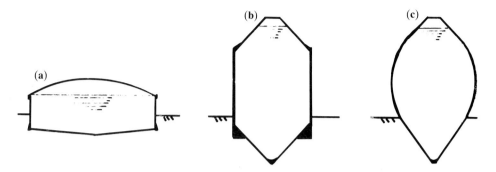

Figure 6.24 The shapes of digesters. (a) Anglo-Saxon, (b) European standard, (c) Teutonic. First published in Hobson and Wheatley (1992) and reproduced by permission of Elsevier.

gas may be injected into a vertical tube inside the digester which acts as a gas lift pump (confined gas lift mixing) or simply released at intervals around the base of the tank (unconfined mixing). Experiments have shown that unconfined gas mixing from evenly spaced distribution points around the base of a tall narrow tank gave the best dispersion and least scum (Rundle and Whyley, 1981; Baumann and Huibregtse, 1981). Unconfined gas lift mixing was also significantly cheaper than other types of mixing.

Many older digesters were too large for easy mixing, they were over $1000\,\text{m}^3$ in volume. Reactor shape was dictated by providing the largest volume at the cheapest cost. Reactors were large diameter shallow tanks. These were difficult to mix and were based on storage tank design rather than biological reactors. Standard prefabricated digesters based on silos have better aspect ratios and are better suited for gas lift mixing. Larger sizes can be provided for by several digesters. This modular approach has maintenance advantages as well, each digester can be serviced in turn without totally disrupting treatment (Figure 6.24).

Loading rate. Loading rates are defined by the rates of breakdown of the substrate, the solids in the sludge and growth rates of the mixed culture of anaerobic organisms. These can be used to fix the retention time of the digester. Design loading rates have been established empirically over time. It was observed from batch experiments that sludge digestion occurred rapidly during the first 10–15 days but then slowed down between 15 and 30 days. There was little further degradation beyond 30 days. The polysaccharide and cellulose polymers are the most abundant natural solids and polymers; they constitute the bulk of plant material and bacterial cell walls (Figure 6.25).

Most of these polymers are degradable quickly, i.e. within 10 days, but cellulose bound to hemicellulose and lignin is resistant to anaerobic breakdown. On average between 30 and 40% of the volatile solids introduced

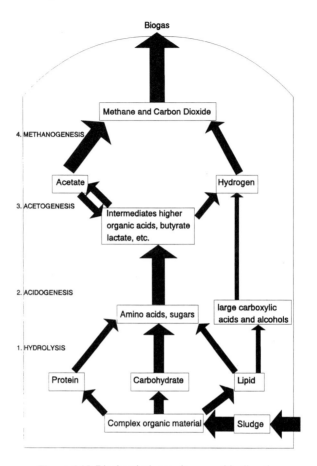

Figure 6.25 Biochemical steps in anaerobic digestion.

into a digester are lignocelluloses and degradation takes months even with ideal aerobic conditions. The rates of hydrolysis of the simple polymers such as the oligosaccharides and starches are rapid. Many older digesters were designed with retention times between 20 and 30 days or $0.2\,m^3$ reactor volume per person per day (Ministry of Housing, 1954). This was to achieve a 50–60% reduction in the organic solids in the raw sludges, and included a significant contingency for poor mixing and dilute feeds. Improvements in the design of ancillary equipment and the understanding of anaerobic digestion have enabled retention times to be reduced to 12–15 days (Noon and Brade, 1985). Typical loading rates are shown in Table 6.42.

Measurements on microbial growth rates have established that the doubling time for methanogens is about 5 days. This then is the critical

Table 6.42 Operating conditions of a domestic sludge digester

Parameter	Units	Typical value
Biomass VSS	mg/l	2000–6000
Loading rate	kg VS/kg VSS per day	1
Retention time	days	15
Performance removal of solids applied	% removal of VS	50–60

minimum retention time to avoid wash out (Henze and Harremoes, 1983). These figures were based on laboratory experiments with perfect mixing and ideal temperatures so in practice 12–15 days is a good design average to allow for imperfections in the process.

6.7.1.2   The contact stirred tank reactor (CSTR).   This was the first type of anaerobic reactor to be tested for the treatment of effluents. The reactor was developed from those used for sludge digestion and experiments were tried on very strong industrial wastes which were difficult to treat aerobically (Department of Scientific and Industrial Research, 1960). The principle of operation is like that of the activated sludge process. Active anaerobic bacteria are separated by settlement or filtration and recycled back into the reactor. Anaerobic bacteria do not produce much extra-cellular polymer and the anaerobic bacterial consortia do not precipitate as easily as aerobic activated sludge. Settlement is made worse by the warmth of the mesophilic effluent; this causes thermal eddies in the clarifier. Methane gas given off also makes the solids buoyant. In most designs, settlement is assisted by degassing and by filtration or inclined plates within the clarifier.

The bioreactor. Both mechanical and gas mixing are used for different proprietary CSTR systems. The more efficient the mixing system the greater can be the biomass concentration in the reactor. Solids contents up to 25–30 kg/m^3 can be achieved with gas injection compared to 5–10 kg/m^3 with mechanical mixing (Nahle, 1991). The power required for gas injection is between 5 and 10 W/m^3 for mechanical mixers between 2 and 5 W/m^3. Reactor design is based on the biomass loading rate; the optimal loading rate varies according to the characteristics of the waste (Table 6.43); typical loadings are shown in Table 6.44.

Degassing. There are four common methods of removing the biogas prior to settlement according to the proprietary system (Figure 6.26). Degassing units have a retention time of about 10–15 min, and the separated gas is collected. Most systems have a vacuum pump to assist separation.

Table 6.43 Typical organic loading rate for a mesophilic CSTR reactor

Load	0.5–2.5 kg COD/m per day
Retention time	1–5 days
COD removal	80–90%
Solids concentration	5000–10000 mg/l

Table 6.44 Examples of working CSTR reactors treating food wastes (taken from Nahle, 1991)

Type of effluent	Organic loading rate (kg COD/m³)	F:M (kg COD/kg TS)	COD removed (%)
Sugar processing	0.6–13.0	1.3–3.0	90–95
Distillery	1.5–2.5	0.2–0.25	90–95
Citric acid	1.3–4.0	0.2–0.3	75–80
Yeast production	3.0–4.0	0.2–0.4	77–80
Sauerkraut	1.5	0.4	96
Vegetable cannery	2.0–4.2	0.1–0.3	90–95
Pectin factory	1.7–5.3	0.03–0.2	88–93
Starch factory	3.6	1.4	65
Meat processing	0.8–4.8	0.5–1.1	90–95
Cellulose condensate	1.3–1.8	0.1–0.2	95–98

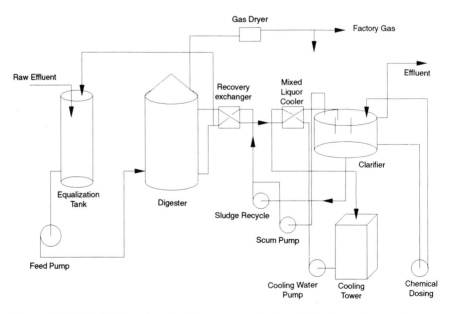

Figure 6.26 Typical process flow sheet for an anaerobic digester treating industrial effluent.

Settlement. Sludge separation and recycling during settlement is in most cases assisted by plate clarifiers. Settlement rates are significantly lower than aerobic biomass and upflow rates are designed at 0.1–0.2 m/h. The high concentration of inorganic materials in some wastes, from sugar processing for example, can improve rates of settlement; other wastes from polysaccharide oils or protein processing generate a poorly settling sludge. Clarifiers need to be roofed to avoid odour problems.

Applications. The absence of internal fittings make CSTR digesters suitable for the treatment of wastes with a high solids content. Loadings are usually modest but high COD removal efficiencies between 85 and 90% can be achieved easily because of the high degree of mixing. At typical retention times, 2–5 days, the reactor does not require close supervision and is quite resilient. The CSTR system is still cheaper than aerobic treatment because of the low sludge production and mixing energies. The CSTR is a common type of anaerobic reactor, much of its popularity is based on its similarity to conventional sludge digestion. Thirty percent of the industrial digesters in Europe are of this type and about half of them do not bother to recycle biomass and retention times are greater than 7 days. The most common application is for the treatment of distillery industry (30 full scale plants, 15 in Italy) (Pauss *et al.*, 1990). Treatment rates with this type of waste are low because of the lack of alkalinity and retention times are reported to be over 10 days. There are also a number of contact digesters that treat sugar processing wastewater; examples are shown in Table 6.43. Results from the treatment of sugar processing have also been published (Shore *et al.*, 1984; Smith, 1984). The plant treats half the total waste from a sugar processing factory during a 6-month season. The organic load is 2.5 kg COD/m³ per day at a retention time of 2.5 days. The digester is 6600 m³ with a 50 m³ flocculator and degasser; COD removal was reported at 86%. The treatment system was a success and three other digesters have been built at other sugar processing plants. Another good example is the performance of one of the earliest to be built for the treatment of starch processing wastewater (Morgan, 1980; Butler, 1984; Butcher, 1988). The starch waste had a COD strength of 2000 mg/l and the reactor was loaded at 2.5 kg COD/m³ per day with a retention time of 24 h. COD removal is between 70 and 80%. Biomass separation was assisted by a membrane filtration unit which filtered the sludge from the five 200 m³ digesters on rotation; this type of separation was used to improve performance compared to simple settlement.

Commercial systems. A common international design is a Scandinavian system, originally applied in the sugar industry; it is currently sold by Purac and known as the Anamet process. The digester is mechanically mixed and sludge separation assisted by a tower stirred flocculator prior to a lamella

Figure 6.27 An anaerobic CSTR reactor showing degassing tower, heat exchanger for cooling and settlement tank for sludge return.

plate settlement tank. Another widely used system in Europe and the United States is the French Degremont system. The digester is mixed by gas recirculation and is followed by a vacuum stirred tank degasser unit. Biomass separation is by a conventional stirred and scraped settlement tank. A third type of international design is that sold by Sulzer of Switzerland. The digester is mechanically mixed with a settlement tank incorporated into the top of the digester. Settlement and recycling of the biomass is assisted by lamella plates within the clarifier. The UK Biomechanics system used a combination of a falling film degasser and a heat exchanger to cool the biomass prior to conventional settlement (Figure 6.27).

6.7.1.3   Anaerobic filtration.   The difficulties associated with settling and recycling biomass in CSTR reactors led to an alternative approach to reactor design based on percolating filters. Bacteria were immobilised within a support medium to prolong solids retention time. Unlike aerobic filters but resembling BAF systems, anaerobic filters are both upflow and downflow. In both types of filter, the media is fully submerged. Downflow reactors have countercurrent gas and liquid flow, mixing is therefore intense and enhanced by recycle. Downflow reactors usually use orientated or tubular packings. Upflow filters use both orientated and random packing, recycling is also used but the upward flow velocities are lower compared to downflow filters. Upflow filters are usually cleaned with periodic flushes or desludging to dislodge accumulated biomass.

Packing materials. The packing materials are designed to retain biomass within the reactor. In the early upflow anaerobic reactors, the media were stone and gravels. These had low voidage and blocked with solids and biomass quite quickly (Young and McCarty, 1969). Plastic rashig and pall rings were then tried; this prolonged the time intervals between blockage but did not overcome the problem totally and increased flow rates were applied, using recycling to overcome the problem. Blockages still occasionally occurred and downflow filters were then tried. These down-flow filters worked at very high liquid velocities. Blockage and channelling has still been reported in some downflow filters but only when the waste contained fat, insoluble organics or a high concentration of solid material (Environment Canada, 1986). Present design practice anticipates some accumulation of solids and includes provision for desludging from the base of the reactor and from the media. The proportion of reactor containing packaging has also been reduced and is now typically between 60 and 75% (Oleszkiewz *et al.*, 1986; Oleszkiewz and Thadari, 1988). Solids may also be dislodged from the pack by temporary increases in upflow velocity induced by effluent and gas recycle (Camilleri, 1987; Ehlinger *et al.*, 1987). Once the solids have been removed, then performance is recovered.

Most downflow filters have used the modular sheet and block media (Figure 6.20) whilst most upflow filters have used the random ring type. Stone is no longer used except within low rate rural digesters; the voidage available for biomass accumulation is insufficient. The type of plastic material does not affect reactor performance; most surfaces can be colo-nised by bacteria. Nylon, polypropylene and polyvinylchloride have all been used as well as ceramic blocks and rings.

The media used must be mechanically stable and able to tolerate some long-term compression. Attachment to hydrophilic surfaces is very rapid. If the surface is hydrophobic, like the plastics, then the extracellular polymeric secretions of the bacteria and the general debris act as a bridge between the cell and the plastic. The function of the media is to retain biomass within the reactor but the predominant mechanisms are different in each type of anaerobic filter. In upflow anaerobic filters, most of the active biomass is held as flocculated granulated solids in the interstices of the medium. This type of accumulated solids are also the source of clogging problems (Wheatley *et al.*, 1988; Young and Dahab, 1983). Fine loose solids are also present, held in place by the upward flow velocity. The specific surface area available within upflow anaerobic filters is not as important as in downflow filters. In downflow anaerobic filters, there is little suspended solids and sludge within the medium. The important biomass is as a thin film firmly attached to and close to the contours of the media. Media surface area and orientation are more important than in upflow systems (Kennedy and Droste, 1986). Cross flow ordered media

Table 6.45 Some properties of typical media

Media description and name	Material	Weight (kg/m^3)	Specific surface area (m^2/m^3)	Voidage (%)
Flocor R random corrugated tube (50 mm × 50 mm)	PVC	90	250	95
ETA pack pall rings (75 mm × 75 mm)	Polypropylene	85	160	97
Furnace slag porous stone	Expanded ceramic with significant iron content	975	100	55
Flocor E regular sheet modules (1200 mm × 600 mm)	PVC	90	100	94
Cloisonyle, vertical vaned tubes	PVC	200	80	95

has been shown to perform slightly better than regular or tubular media and significantly better than random media even with larger surface areas (Adams and McKinney, 1989).

There have been a number of studies on the ideal characteristics of media for downflow filters. Rough surfaces have been shown to have more rapid start up and some ceramic materials which leached trace nutrients, such as red tile clay, performed better still (Murray and van den Berg, 1981). In practice, however, cross flow modular plastic media in combination with simple prefabricated reactor design usually offers the best value for money. There have been fewer investigations on the ideal characteristics of media for upflow filters. Larger media (>100 mm) would resist clogging better than the smaller materials (25–50 mm) but they may be more difficult to clean. More research is necessary on this topic. Examples of some typical media characteristics are given in Table 6.45.

Hydrodynamics and mixing. There is now a significant amount of operating experience on the performance of anaerobic filters. Further tests are required to provide models with a more fundamental basis but there is much empirical information which indicates that reactor hydrodynamics are the most important feature of design. Some comprehensive surveys (Young and Yang, 1989; Young, 1991) suggest that retention time is the most useful single indicator of performance when other conditions are constant. Typically, poor performance arises from dead zones and short circuiting within the reactor. The degree of mixing is an important influence on the retention time. The greater the mixing the less will be the amount of short circuiting and dead space. Upflow velocity and gas production control the degree of mixing. New upflow anaerobic filters behave as plug flow reactors but highly active filters are mixed by the gas production. Research has only relatively recently begun to consider critical upflow velocities produced by recycle and gas production. Early filter designs at low loading rates and without recycle, e.g. <1 volume gas/ volume of reactor per day did show plug flow behaviour (Dahab and Young, 1982; Wheatley and Cassell, 1985). Higher gas productions >2 volumes gas/volume of reactor per day showed mixed behaviour (Young and Young, 1988; Wheatley *et al.*, 1988). Downflow filters behave in a similar way, but because of the countercurrent gas and liquid flow, they are nearly always completely mixed (Hall, 1983; Samson *et al.*, 1985). The amount of dead space or degree of clogging are measured by the standard retention time techniques (Levenspiel, 1972; Wheatley *et al.*, 1988).

Recycle. Effluent recycle is beneficial, it provides better mixing and lateral distribution, and can assist with keeping the media clean. Recycle also provides extra alkalinity, nutrients and will dilute the concentrations of very strong wastes. Providing for the most appropriate recycle flow rate depends on reactor shape, gas production and media but it is usual to provide between 2:1 and 6:1. Reported upflow velocities vary with satisfactory performance reported between 0.2 and 7 m/h. In practice, upflow velocities need to be set to avoid wash out of the biomass which will depend on the degree of mixing and type of biomass; some versatility in pumping rates should be provided.

Distribution. Uniform distribution is also necessary to obtain optimum retention and performance. Typically, distributors are like cartwheels with a number of arms depending on the diameter of the vessel. The distribution holes point downwards into the bed with the diameter of the holes or number of holes profiles away from the inlet manifold. The recycle is introduced through a larger totally separate but similar system, slightly above the feed distributor. The distributor arms should protrude through the reactor walls to allow some possibility of rodding.

Applications. The simplicity and robustness of the anaerobic filter make it ideally suited to the treatment of soluble food effluents. Loading rates are much higher than those for CSTR reactors (Table 6.46). Despite these apparent advantages, the anaerobic filter is not as popular as the CSTR or UASB reactors; about 15% of the industrial anaerobic treatment plants in Europe are of this type (Wheatley and Coombes, 1991). The major worry is excessive biomass accumulation and blockage of the packed bed. At the moment, there are 32 anaerobic filters in Europe with about equal num-

Table 6.46 Typical operating conditions of an anaerobic filter

Organic load	2–10 kg COD/m³ per day
Retention time	10–50 h
COD removal	70–80%
Critical solids concentration in the feed	1000 mg/l

bers of downflow and upflow operation. Most are in France and all but two treat wastes from the agro-food industry. Nine have been built for the treatment of distillery wastes. Detailed information has been published on two (Camilleri, 1988; Racault, 1990); there are no reports of blockage. Young (1991) has published a list of upflow anaerobic filters in the United States and Canada. Most are for the treatment of food and distillery wastes although three have been used for the treatment of alcohols, acids and esters from the chemical industry (Witt *et al.*, 1979). Organic loads were found to vary between 0.2 and 16 kg COD/m³ per day with hydraulic retention times between 12 and 96 h. There are fewer downflow filters in the United States and Canada (Kennedy and Droste, 1991), but detailed information has been published on two. The performance and design of the downflow filter at Bacardi has been widely publicised (Szendry, 1983, 1986) and details on a dairy plant have also been reported (Environment Canada, 1986). The dairy filter used ceramic modular media and did block with fat after 2 years of operation. An extensive survey of laboratory and pilot studies on various types of waste has also been published (Bonastre and Paris, 1989).

6.7.1.4   The upflow sludge blanket reactor (UASB).   The problems due to clogging of the filter media in anaerobic filters, particularly the early mineral packings, resulted in investigations into methods of reducing the amount of media within the reactor. A high density granular sludge is needed which may then be retained within the reactor despite the gassing and upflow velocity of the waste. The development of this type of reactor has been very successful with applications for a wide range of food industry wastes and some experience with domestic sewage. There are about 200 full scale operating plants worldwide and it is the most popular type of high rate anaerobic reactor due largely to the research and development efforts of Lettinga *et al.* (1979) and two Dutch companies marketing the process.

Biomass granulation. Sludge granulation is a complex and unreliable process. To avoid problems, it is the usual commercial practice to use a large inoculum of granular sludge from an already operating plant. Inoculums of granular sludge between 10 and 15% of the reactor volume are used if available (Weiland and Rozzi, 1991). The hydrodynamics of the reactor, created by the distribution and reactor shape, are important in retaining the correct form of biomass. To maintain process efficiency, biomass settling velocities of 10 m/h are required. Measured velocities up to 90 m/h have been reported (Lettinga and Hulsoff-Pol, 1986). Granulation is a natural process and is due to a combination of microbial morphology, nature of the substrate and accumulation of inorganic salts (Dolfing, 1986). Formation of rapidly settling granules from an ordinary inoculum may take 50 days (Alibhai and Forster, 1986). The type of wastewater to be treated has an important role in the formation of granules. A satisfactory sludge blanket was formed from yeast processing, sugar beet and potato wastes but not with distillery, corn starch, abattoir or dairy effluents (Stronach *et al.*, 1986). Key elements in the feed substrate for successful granule formation are iron, calcium, phosphorus, ammonia, magnesium, aluminium and silicon (Kissel *et al.*, 1988). The process is similar to scale formation. These materials are readily available in root vegetable processing waters which contain some clay and soil. A large population of filamentous organisms, *Methanothrix* sp., are also important and may be associated with a high concentration of soluble components in the substrate, mainly acetic acid. Generally granular sludge will eventually develop from mostly soluble wastes (Lettinga and Hulshoff-Pol, 1991). If an ideal start up inoculum is available, then full process efficiency may be obtained within 1 month, but if a suitable inoculum is not available then the start up could take 6 months (Souza, 1986). Start up procedures used are similar to the other types of anaerobic reactor that is stepped increases in load of 0.05–0.1 kg COD/kg VSS per day assuming the pH and concentrations of carboxylic acids remain satisfactory.

Hydrodynamics and mixing. The shape of the UASB reactor, the upward flow velocity and the baffles inside the reactor are used to promote gas solid separation inside the reactor. The most important feature governing reactor height is the treatability of the waste and efficiency of granule formation. If the waste is soluble and a granular sludge has formed, then upflow velocities of 3 m/h can be achieved. Reactor heights can then be up to 10 m (Lettinga and Hulshoff-Pol, 1991). If the waste contains significant amounts of suspended COD and during start up when granulation is incomplete, then the biomass is usually present as a voluminous flocculant sludge. Under these conditions, upflow velocities need to be more modest, e.g. 1–1.5 m/h. Practically all wastes are heterogeneous and a good compromise reactor height is between 3 and 5 m (Figure 6.28).
    The distribution system also exerts an important influence on the upflow

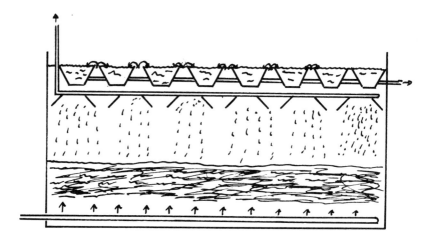

Figure 6.28 Typical UASB baffle and feed arrangement.

velocity and can be used to promote good contact between sludge and wastewater. The large plan areas of reactors enables a large number of small distribution points (usually one every 1–2.5 m). A particular problem with UASB reactors with a large number of small distribution points is clogging of the nozzles. Each influent system should be easy to clean and monitor.

The effect of gas production is more complex. Higher than optimum gas production will cause gulping and open paths through the blanket while a lower gas production will not encourage enough mixing within the blanket to avoid short circuiting through the dense sludge granules. It has been shown (Bolle *et al.*, 1986) that at typical gas and liquid velocities (1–1.5 m/h), then a sludge blanket height of half the reactor height is optimal. Lettinga and Hulshoff-Pol (1991) have provided a design guide for the appropriate numbers of distributors according to the gas production and organic loading rate.

Various designs of baffles inside the UASB reactor are used to promote gas/solid separation and therefore to retain the granules. The baffles provide extra surface area which reduces upward flow velocity and promotes biomass flocculation. The baffles are usually made of reinforced plastic so as to be light weight and corrosion resistant. Solids which collect in the cones should settle back into the reactor. Lettinga and Hulshoff-Pol (1991) have given a design guide based on waste characteristics. The gas solids separator usually occupies 25–30% of the reactor height, the baffles are set with an angle of between 45 and 60° and with an overlap of the plates of between 200 and 300 mm. There may be special problems with wastewaters that produce foam. Many effluents that contain oil and fat, such as dairy wastes, will foam when vigorously aerated in activated sludge or in a gas stirred reactor. Precautions against these foams blocking gas lines and outlet pipes are necessary. It is usually sufficient to install spray nozzles at the top of the reactor and above the baffles but in very tall reactors it may also be necessary to add a chemical antifoam to avoid clogging the UASB gas separator. In any event, maintenance of both the top and bottom of the reactor to remove scale, scum and grit will be necessary periodically.

Applications. The USAB reactor is the most widely used type of anaerobic reactor and there is a great deal of design and operating experience (Table 6.47). It has been very extensively applied to food processing wastes and there are about 50 plants in Holland with sizes between 100 and 1500 m³. There are five in the United Kingdom: Davidsons Papermill, Aberdeen, J. Sturge, Goole, citric acid waste; Caernarvon Creameries; General Foods, Banbury, and Coca Cola, Wakefield. The only common problems have been the cost of alkalinity and losses of solids. Wastes with a high proportion of insoluble COD (i.e. >15%) can give rise to poor granulation. Lettinga and Hulshoff-Pol (1991) give further details on recommended design loadings. These vary according to the amount and solubility of the solids in the waste. High concentrations of suspended solids cause problems by reducing the activity of the retained sludge, or lead to scum layers if the solids are fat. Prolonged and continuous entrapment of expanded flocculant sludge can lead to a spontaneous and sudden washing of the sludge by increases in flow, lasting about 1 hour, are recommended by the contractors (Lettinga and Hulshoff-Pol, 1991). If the waste does contain significant amounts of degradable suspended solids, then a two-stage system with separate solids hydrolysis would normally be used in the design of a UASB system.

Table 6.47 Usual design loadings of a UASB reactor at mesophilic temperatures

Load	2–15 kg COD/m³ per day
Retention time	10–50 h
COD removal	70–90%

6.7.1.5   The fluidised bed reactor.   The difficulties of biomass separation in completely mixed reactors and the loss of granulation or blockage in plug flow reactors can be overcome by a combination of the two types. This is the basis of the fluidised bed. Fluidisation of carrier particles within a reactor occurs at a critical upflow velocity which depends on the density of the particles and other losses within the vessel. This fluidisation point can be defined by standard equations for pressure loss (Levenspiel, 1972); it is usually between 10 and 30 m/h. The performance of fluidised beds depends on the carrier materials and the hydrodynamics of the reactor.

Media characteristics. Sand has been the usual support media for most fluidised beds but other natural materials such as anthracite and gravels have also been used. To reduce fluidisation velocities expanded lighter natural materials have been tried, for example, activated carbon, baked clays and porous ceramics. Synthetic materials can also be fabricated into porous structures with a low density and plastic carriers have included resin beads, reticulated foams, PVC and other types of synthetic beads. Diffusion into porous particles may eventually become limiting and the carrier may also break down with use. Much of the effectiveness of a fluidised bed compared to an anaerobic filter can be attributed to the smaller carrier particles which may be used without the risk of clogging. Start up has been shown to be much quicker with smaller particles and this was attributed to the lower liquid shear velocities with smaller particles (0.35 compared to 0.7 mm). Particle sizes are usually between 0.3 and 1 mm; smaller sizes are difficult to control and retain within the reactor, larger sizes are difficult to fluidise. Surface roughness, specific surface area, strength and stability will affect media performance as in anaerobic filters. The ideal physicochemical characteristics of fluidised bed particles have been investigated (Switzenbaum, 1983; Iza, 1991). The particles must be uniform in size and shape to obtain an even fluidisation or bed expansion throughout the reactor height. Some of these media properties do, however, change with the amount of biomass and that makes fluidised bed reactors difficult to control.

Hydrodynamics and mixing. The support particles are expanded and mixed by gas and effluent recycle. Sufficient recycle is required to cause some lateral mixing of the particles and avoid channelling. Bed expansion is typically 20–25% of the reactor volume. Obtaining uniform bed expansion is relatively easy while the carrier particles are homogeneous but becomes more difficult as they change shape and density during colonisation.

Distribution. The design of the distribution system, like the other high rate digesters, is a critical feature of the mixing characteristics. Many of the details of full scale distributors are included in proprietary designs or covered by confidentiality agreements and not therefore freely available. Small diameter reactors (1–2 m) can utilise an inverted cone with a downward pipe at the apex of the cone. Larger diameter reactors have used perforated plates, nozzles and square annular or star-shaped pipework.

Figure 6.29 An anaerobic fluidised bed reactor.

Reactor aspect ratio. To improve distribution and reduce the volume for recycle, fluidised beds are usually tall tanks with a 5 or 6:1 height to diameter ratio. A second larger diameter zone is usually incorporated within the fluidised bed for clarification. This is an increase in the diameter of the top 20–25% of the vessel (Figure 6.29). Foaming can be a problem with certain fat and protein containing wastes and if the fluidisation energy required is high. This may be counteracted by an antifoam agent and or an upper grid to avoid particle loss. Designs in the United States usually use a separate carrier or particle separator.

Applications. Biological fluidised bed technology has been extensively studied at laboratory and pilot scale but as yet there are few examples at full scale. The system has an important potential advantage in that very large concentrations of biomass can be achieved within the reactor without problems of blockage and channelling (40–100 kg VSS/m^3). Potential performance is therefore also high; typical organic loading rates are shown in Table 6.48.

Table 6.48 Typical operating conditions for a mesophilic fluidised bed

Load	2–50 kg COD/m^3 per day
Retention time	0.5–24 h
COD removal	70–80%

There are three commercial systems:

1. Gist-Brocades with plants in Delft, Prouvy, France and Monheim, Germany.
2. Degremont in France treating dairy waste (Iza, 1991) and in Spain for brewery wastewater (Oliva *et al.*, 1990).
3. Dorr-Oliver with 4–5 plants in the United States for the treatment of sludge heat treatment liquors and coke oven wastewaters.

There are no full scale anaerobic fluidised beds in the United Kingdom. Fluidised beds are very high rate processes and are therefore difficult to scale up and operate (Sixt and Sahm, 1987). More experience at full scale would be necessary before they could be recommended for food industry wastes.

6.7.2 *Materials of construction*

Most sewage works bioreactors and digesters are built from concrete. Capital costs were high, but the plant was expected to be operational for over 50 years. This was appropriate at a time when standards and technology were changing slowly and inflation was low.

One of the effects of the high capital costs of concrete digesters was to restrict the application of sludge digestion to the largest sewage works. There are 75 sewage works in the United Kingdom which serve populations greater than 100 000 (equivalent to a 2000 m^3 digester) and 95% of these use anaerobic treatment in concrete digesters. These large digesters are tanks of small height to diameter ratio and have flat, or very slightly sloped bottoms. For large digesters over 2000 m^3 in size, concrete is still the cheapest method of construction but with 80% of the UK population already served by sewage treatment, there will be few digesters of this size built in the United Kingdom in the future. A number of concrete digesters are being built in Europe. Continental digesters are much taller than most UK concrete digesters (Figure 6.24) and this tall thin shape is intended to make the digester contents much easier to mix by vertical motion. A steep conical bottom (45°) is also added to keep grit and scale in suspension for continuous removal. This type of tall digester needs to be well insulated because of the large surface area above ground and it is also very expensive to build; two or three times more than flat-bottomed digesters. This has led to a change in profile to an egg shape which can be constructed from successive ring segments to reduce the amount of shuttering and scaffolding, which was reported to reduce construction costs by 30% (Greeman, 1990). Two digesters at Dortmund, for example are 12 000 m^3 in volume and 24 m in diameter at the widest point. They were designed to treat screened, consolidated, primary (and secondary) sewage sludges at a retention time of 30 days. The digesters are mechanically mixed and sludge was drawn up a central draft tube and splashed over the surface of the digester liquid. The cost of construction was about £160/m^3; quoted UK costs for concrete digesters were £70/m^3. These figures were doubled by the costs of ancillary equipment.

Although some of the earlier farm digesters were made of concrete, it is generally too expensive and restricting for most industrial and farm use. Standard prefabricated tanks from other areas of farm and chemical work were preferred.

6.7.2.1 *Enamelled steel.*

At the smaller sizes, prefabricated tanks made from bolt-together, enamelled-steel plates, are 70% cheaper than concrete tanks. The glass-enamel coating and holes for piping, as well as the holding bolts, can be made during fabrication of the plates. This reduces on-site work and associated delays. Such tanks have been used for many years as grain silos, storage tanks for farm slurries and other liquids, etc., so there is significant experience of their construction and life span. The tank is built up on site from the shaped plates. The edges of the plates are sealed with mastic as they are bolted into the rings that form the tank. The bottom ring is grouted into a flat concrete base. The roof is of the same enamelled steel plates or plastic. Separate fixed or floating gas-holder roofs can be fabricated. The flat floors can accumulate grit, but manholes near the base can allow easy access and degritting. The tanks require insulation and this can be internal or, more generally, external. Layers of polyurethane or polyisocyanurate foams (50–100 mm) can be used or glass-wool (external only). All external insulations need a cladding or painting to waterproof the materials and to prevent birds or rodents attacking, or nesting in, the foam. The largest practical digester sizes are 1000 m^3, the limit being set by the maximum size of the steel-plate roof, but larger sizes could be built by reinforcing the roof, which may be subject to significant flexing with the varying gas production. Multiple tank systems provide for greater capacity, and have advantages over large single tanks in servicing and dealing with breakdowns. Increases in waste flow can be dealt with by adding extra tanks. Guaranteed plant life is 20 years compared to 40 for concrete.

The prefabricated stirred-tank digester has been very successfully applied to sewage, industrial and farm wastes.

6.7.2.2 *Steel tanks.*

Welded steel tanks have been used for larger industrial use greater than 2000 m^3 in volume. They are about 10% cheaper than smaller enamelled tanks and 20–30% cheaper at the larger sizes where multiple enamelled tanks would be needed. It is usual to coat the insides of mild-steel tanks with epoxy-rubber. Such coatings inside digesters can become detached or broken and liquid will get behind them. There are doubts as to whether coating is needed. Corrosion of the inside surface is now not thought to be a problem; the inside surfaces are found to be covered with a layer of black sulphide. Mild-steel digesters need insulation if they are running at above ambient temperature.

Stainless-steel has been proposed for digesters but its cost is too high for all except small, or pilot-plant tanks. Aluminium is unsuitable because of the high chloride concentration in the warm, digesting sludge. Galvanising provides satisfactory protection of steel tanks from the weather, but the rate of corrosion of galvanised steel in the digester liquid or the moist atmosphere above the liquid makes galvanising unsuitable for internal surfaces of digesters. Jointing of pipes of different metals or alloys can lead to corrosion.

6.7.2.3 Plastics.   Glass reinforced plastic (GRP) is corrosion-resistant and has been used for small digesters. There are difficulties with larger sizes because of its low strength, and the material is too flexible for large tanks without extra support. This can be overcome to a certain extent by excavation to sink the tank and backfilling, or the tank can be made into a horizontal tubular digester partly buried in the ground. GRP tanks are fabricated off-site and transported as a whole. This leads to an upper size-limited for complete tanks based on ease of transport, but larger tanks can be made up from moulded rings bolted or glued together on-site. To provide sufficient self-supporting strength, vertical digesters have to be tall and narrow and digesters up to $500 \, m^3$ (Figure 6.24) have been built in this way, but GRP digesters are no cheaper than enamelled-steel digesters at sizes above $200 \, m^3$. The costs of moulds for plastic digesters also means that 'one-off' tanks are hardly viable.

6.7.2.4 Gas-holders.   If the digester has a rigid roof then a separate gas-holder is needed. The most usual type is the floating-dome. The gas holder is stabilised as it rises and falls by guide rails and rollers. The bottom is a tank filled with water and gas is piped in above the water level to accumulate in the top tank which rises and falls with the gas volume. The bottom of the gas-tank is sealed in the water and the tank is stabilised by the guide rails. The gas tank may need counter-balancing by weights to produce the gas pressure required. Most gas appliances work better with a constant supply pressure. These gas holders are usually made of mild steel, but some small ones in GRP are available. A separate water-sealed gas holder or floating-roof digester has the advantage of acting as a safety valve if gas pressure is increased by failure in some other part of the system as excess gas will bubble out through the liquid seal if the gas production exceeds storage capacity.

Plastic or rubberised-fabric digester tops are used as gas holders mainly in continental Europe. However, so far as is known, large digester-top gas holders have not become common. Most plastic or rubber tops are used on small digesters; usually the trough in the ground type. The top may be sealed by fixing it mechanically to the edge of the digester trough, or the bottom edge may drop below the sludge level to give a water seal. Butyl-rubber or plastic bags are also used as separate gas holders. The bag or digester top is not usually inflated to stretch the fabric but to take up slack in a loose 'bag'. A uniform pressure can be obtained by having weights directly on top of the bag or operating through a system of levers. A number of designs were reviewed by Dohne (1980). Bags need separate safety valves to avoid overpressure and care has to be taken to see that fabrics are not torn or otherwise damaged. In hot weather, dark-coloured gas bags can get very warm and so gas pressure variations can be considerable.

All these systems store gas at low (50–150 mm or 2–6 m WG) pressure and the gas does not need to be specially cleaned before storage. The water in a water-sealed holder will scrub some impurities from the gas, so it is best changed each year. The capacity of the gas holder depends very much on the use made of the digester gas. If the gas is running a boiler or an engine virtually non-stop and this uses the available gas, then a gas holder of capacity only a few cubic metres will act as a gas ballast volume for a large digester. If the gas usage is intermittent, for example just working day use, then the gas produced at night might be stored for use during the day and the gas holder will have to be sized on the nightly gas production. In general, gas storage capacity should be as small as possible as steel water-sealed gas holders are as expensive as the digester tanks, and butyl rubber or other gas-impermeable fabric holders are similar unless they can be made in large numbers to one specification.

The medium-pressure gas lines need mechanical safety valves; low-pressure lines can rely on blow-off from water-sealed gas holders or U-tube water seals on the digester or even from condensate pots in the gas lines which remove water from the gas. The U-tube water seals can freeze in very cold weather so oil may be used in some cases or a strong glycol solution. Gas pipe runs are preferably lagged to reduce the possibilities of water freezing out of wet gas and blocking pipes or condensate traps. The bigger digesters usually have an automatic flare which burns off large excesses of unused gas and which is ignited when the gas holder is filled. Gas holders on the main lines should have pressure indicators to give some early warning of problems.

6.8   Sludge treatment

Effluent treatment processes generate solids. On average between 70 and 80% of the original organic carbon is converted to dry solids. In a vegetable processing plant, for example, about 30% of the original

COD might be removed by primary settlement to form a sludge and about 50–60% of the remainder converted into dry solids by the activated sludge process. These sludges are putrescible, highly polluting malodorous and offensive. They can also be hazardous because they adsorb and accumulate pathogens and toxins. Raw sludges are saturated with bound water and not easily dealt with by simple chemical or physical processes. Disposal of these sludges may represent half the cost of the total effluent treatment.

Sludge production per volume of effluent treated is increasing with the popularity of intensive aerobic processing (see Section 6.6) and the greater use of additional chemicals to attain more stringent standards. Further treatment of coastal discharges will produce additional sludge. Traditionally sludges generated from food effluents have been easy to recycle to land, they contain few materials which can be thought of as hazardous compared to sewage. It seems likely, however, that this task will become more difficult for the food industry as the water companies try to increase their use of these land outlets. In England and Wales, there are about 40M wet tonnes or 1M dry sewage solids to be disposed of each year; 16% of the sludge produced is tipped to landfill sites, 53% is used in agriculture, 7% is incinerated and 24% disposed of to sea (Figure 6.30).

The United Kingdom is the only major European country still using sea disposal. The sea has been an important UK method of waste treatment but it is to be phased out between 1995 and 1998 under an agreement made at the 1990 North Sea Conference. Incineration is regarded as the best solution to deal with this increased sludge load by two or three of the major

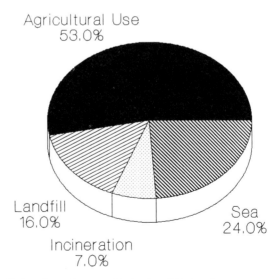

Figure 6.30 Sludge disposal routes, England and Wales. Source: Matthews (1992).

water utilities and it has been predicted that up to 40% of the sludge may be incinerated by the turn of the century (Hudson and Young, 1991). Sea disposal of sewage sludge is also banned in the USA.

6.8.1   Sludge thickening

Fresh or raw sludge is still largely water, some of which is biochemically bound to polymers or is intracellular but at least half the water is held only by hindrance within a sludge matrix structure. In most cases, removal of this loosely held water can significantly improve the economics of sludge treatment and disposal. The most common method of achieving this is by gravity or consolidation in purpose built tanks. Gravity thickening can double the solids content and for most food wastes this is often sufficient treatment prior to land disposal or for mixing with average sludge. Sludge thickening is not a simple process and is caused by the sludge compressing under its own weight. Water is thus squeezed out from between the solid particles. Sludges vary in their consolidation behaviour according to three characteristics:

1. the surface properties and charge; this will influence the degree of coagulation and interparticle attraction;
2. the origin of the solids; that is whether the solids are surplus biomass from biological treatment or primary solids from settlement; microbial biomass contains a higher proportion of bound water than primary solids because of intracellular water and polymer;
3. the age of the sludge can change these characteristics and lead to gas production as the sludge begins to break down anaerobically.

6.8.2   The design of thickeners

In principle, because of the variability of sludges, the design of sludge thickeners can be improved by test work and modelling (Hoyland *et al.*, 1989). In practice, for the average installation and for food processing wastes, prefabricated designs are available. Consolidation is envisaged as occurring when the irregular shaped and flexible solids are resting on each other. Further consolidation requires the interstitial held water to be displaced and for channels to be formed to allow the water to escape to the surface. Gentle mixing aids this process by promoting better flocculation and releasing gas and water. This type of mixing is carried out by a picket fence type agitator. Picket fences are a series of 50–60 mm diameter rods with about 150–200 mm spacings extending throughout the depth of the tank. It is important that the fence breaks the surface of the liquid to avoid the formation of a hard dry crust. The picket fence rotates slowly, 1–2 rpm or 3–4 m per min (Figure 6.31).

Figure 6.31 A standard prefabricated gravity sludge thickener with picket fence mixer.

A typical retention time for a gravity thickener is 2 days; solids can be retained for longer without too much deterioration due to flotation but there is little additional thickening. If the retention time is greater than 5 days, then in warm conditions there are often significant problems due to flotation. The shape of the thickening tank is important because the taller the tank the greater the solids thickness at the base but conversely the rate of thickening is lower than in a shallow tank because the path length of the escaping water is greater. Typically tanks are between 4 and 5 m high but are usually also fitted with multi-draw off points.

6.8.3   Sludge treatment

Currently the most common form of treatment is anaerobic digestion (Figure 6.32) but further sludge conditioning either by heating or chemical conditioning is possible but rarely economic compared to anaerobic treatment and agricultural recycling. Polyelectrolytes, iron, aluminium salts and lime are added to improve flocculation prior to mechanical dewatering. The most common dewatering processes are belt presses and centrifuges and less frequently plate and frame presses and vacuum filters. A further difficulty with these techniques apart from the chemical and power costs is control. The frequent changes in characteristics of biological sludges means that continued adjustments to the chemical dosing regime used are necessary. The most successful types of waste for further conditioning are those with a high fibre content such as vegetable wastes and paper wastes when solids contents up to 50% are achievable; otherwise 25–30% is more likely.

Anaerobic Digestion 60

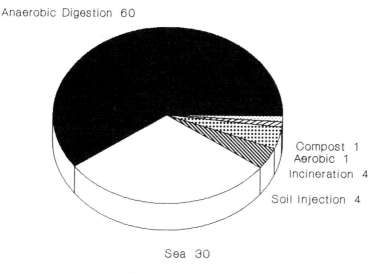

Compost 1
Aerobic 1
Incineration 4

Soil Injection 4

Sea 30

Figure 6.32 Treatment before disposal (%).

6.8.4   Sludge disposal

6.8.4.1   Incineration.   Incineration is not a common method of sludge disposal in Europe or the United States at present (Table 6.49) and this is due to its cost compared to the other routes. Traditionally, therefore, it has been used where there are particular difficulties with residual metals or organics from industrial effluents. Modern fluidised bed incinerators are

Table 6.49 Sludge disposal routes in selected countries

	000s (tonnes dry solids per year)				
	Total sludge	Agricultural use	Landfill	Incineration	Sea
United Kingdom	1500	615	350	66	450
Belgium	29	8	15	6	0
Denmark	131	57	39	35	0
France	850	234	446	170	0
Germany	2200	698	1290	196	0
Greece	15	0	15	0	0
Ireland	23	7	4	0	12
Italy	800	270	440	90	0
Luxembourg	15	12	3	0	0
Netherlands	200	127	55	7	11
Spain	280	173	28	0	79
Sweden	180	108	72	0	0
Switzerland	250	113	80	57	0
United States	4500	1395	1080	1215	810
Canada	500	[No information available]			

Adapted from Matthews (1992) and Vincent and Critchley (1984).

cheaper to build and operate compared to the current multiple hearth type and would be more popular but for the constraint of public confidence. Concern over emissions means that planning applications will require a public enquiry. Incineration is one of the few disposal routes which is predictable and versatile. It is not affected by weather and not dependent on others (e.g. acceptance by farmers); it can be turned up or turned off and this flexibility makes it popular with water managers.

In a multiple hearth incinerator, the sludge passes down through the furnace from top to bottom via a series of stages. The upper stages dry the sludge which is then autothermic by the time it reaches the lower combustion zones. Volatile organics are released in the upper drying regions and the air needs to be recirculated through the high temperature combustion zone at 800–900°C. Fluidised bed incinerators, recently introduced from Germany, are more efficient because of the much better mixing within the furnace. The sludge is fed directly into the hot combustion zone and needs to be pre-dried to at least 30–40% dry solids to be autothermic.

The main residues of burning sludge are carbon dioxide, nitrous oxides, sulphur dioxides and trioxides and the halogens and halides. All except the oxides of nitrogen can be removed by wet scrubbing with caustic soda. The nitrogen compounds are reduced by a catalytic after burner.

One of the main concerns with incineration are the formation of dioxins furans and other residues from reactions at the lower temperatures, i.e. 200–400°C. These temperatures will occur in flue gas equipment, heat recovery, etc.; the products of these reformation reactions may be more persistent and toxic than the original waste.

About 30% of the solids remain after incineration as ash; this is currently disposed of to landfill as a hazardous waste. In Japan where there is little available land there are a number of high temperature vitrification incinerators. Additional fuel is required to achieve these temperatures (>1000°C) and the final residue is a melted slag which has then been used for making jewellery, paving slabs and bricks (Tebbutt, 1992). Another novel approach is reductive hydrogenation of sludge at 400–450°C which gives a liquid oil or char (Campbell, 1989).

6.8.4.2 Agricultural use. This is the most popular sludge disposal method in the United Kingdom at present; about 65% of the sludge discharged to land is used as a soil conditioner. In the United States and large European countries such as Germany, France and Italy, landfilling is more popular (Table 6.48). Treated sewage sludge provides both plant nutrients and a soil conditioner from the lignin or humus content. In the United Kingdom, there have been national guides (Institute of Water Pollution Control, 1978) for the use of sludge on land since 1975 (Table 6.50). Many of these recommendations have been included in the more recent EC directive (see Section 6.2). Repeated experiments over the years have shown that 85% of the nitrogen and 50% of the phosphate can be

Table 6.50 Main provisions of the 1989 code of practice for agricultural use of sewage sludge (DoE, 1989)

1. To encourage recycling of sludge and an understanding of the benefits
2. Indicate the treatments available; all sludge must be treated to avoid pathogens and odour unless sub-surface injected
3. Provide standard methods for the analysis of sludges and soils
4. A list of the most likely sources of problems particularly metals and organics; to note the maximum application rates
5. Advice on the planting, grazing and harvesting constraints for particular crops
6. To note the type of records which need to be kept for auditing purposes
7. To give guidance on odour, run off, storage transport and application

taken up by growing plants from digested sludge (Table 6.51). A recent review of the benefits and hazards, using modern analytical methods, is given by Noguchi and Ito (1992).

Only small quantities of potassium and magnesium are present in sludge and these may have to be supplemented. Sludge is also a very good source of inert organic matter. About 30% of digested sewage sludge is fibre and this provides structure and voidage to the soil for ventilation. Much of the nitrogen in digested sludge is in the form of ammonia which, because of its solubility, can be lost during sludge dewatering. Thus, it is the water content of the sludge which governs its rate of application. Leaching losses in wet weather can be 75% of the nutrient content. This run off, or drainage through cracks in the soil in summer, can be a source of significant pollution.

Application rates therefore are varied according to conditions. Sub-surface injection is the best method of application; it relies on a special small chisel shaped plough which lifts the soil and injects the sludge via a feeder tube 25–50 mm below the surface. A light compactor presses the lifted soil back into position after the plough has passed. Application rates of 1.5–1.8 wet tonnes per hectare are possible with sub-surface injection and good ground conditions. Sub-surface injection avoids any problems due to odour, aerosols or pathogens on the soil surface. If the sludge is odour free and most food waste sludges are pathogen free, then the sludge may also be distributed by standard manure tankers or rain guns. Small standard manure tankers distribute the sludge via a simple fish tail nozzle

Table 6.51 Nutrient content of various types of sludge

Type of sludge	Nitrogen (% as N)	Phosphate (% as P_2O_5)	Potassium (% as K_2O)
Digested liquid sludge	0.2	0.2	0.010
Raw sludge (4% dry solids)	0.15	0.15	0.012
Sludge cake (20–40% dry solids)	1–1.4	1–2.0	0.09

Table 6.52 Metals in domestic sewage sludge (mg/kg dry solids)

Type of sludge	Dry solids (%)	Cd	Cr	Cu	Fe	Pb	Ni	Zn
Raw sludge Ex.1	1.9	20	90	315	13814	300	15	871
Raw sludge Ex.2	4.9	20	42	169	6651	206	15	568
Digested sludge	2.7	20	403	605	19355	454	81	1411

or spinning disc. Sludge is rarely odour free and rain or manure guns are not acceptable except in very remote areas. There are also problems with aerosol formation and spray drift onto neighbouring areas. The advantage of high pressure spray application is that it avoids all heavy transport on fields and therefore there is no risk of soil compaction.

A disadvantage of sewage sludge is that it may contain appreciable concentrations of potentially toxic materials. The best documented toxins in sludge are the heavy metals (Table 6.52). Metals added to soil are firmly bound by clay and organic matter and may remain in the soil indefinitely. The metals can be solubilised by acid conditions and the pH of the soil needs to be 7 or above. The concentration of toxic metals in sludges has decreased markedly over the last 20 years, both as a result of more stringent conditions imposed by water companies and also because of the decline in heavy industry. Cadmium, lead, mercury and chromium are highly toxic and need careful monitoring in soils and sludges. Cadmium accumulates in the leaves of plants and additions have to be restricted to 5 kg/ha per annum. Lead and chromium are less toxic since they are not taken into the edible parts of the plant (Nagouchi and Ito, 1992). It is not these metals, however, which are likely to limit agricultural use because they are now present at low concentration, but rather zinc and copper. Sewage sludge contains high concentrations of zinc (from galvanising and cosmetics), copper (from water pipes) and lesser quantities of chromium and nickel from stainless-steel cooking utensils. There may also be some lead from car exhausts (Table 6.52).

Fortunately, zinc is not highly toxic and if the soil pH is above 6.5, 20 kg/ha may be added annually. If the application is to grassland where it is not intended to grow arable crops for many years, or if the soil is calcarious with a pH above 7.0, then 37 kg/ha per annum may be added. Other metals which affect plant growth are copper which is twice as toxic as zinc, nickel which is eight times as toxic as zinc and boron which is 150 times more toxic.

Little is known about persistent trace organics in sludge since they are so variable. They depend on the nature of any industrial wastewater and, if present, steps should be taken to prevent them from entering the system.

In the long term, with changes in practice or with very clean sludges, the background metals and organics in soils are unlikely to be seriously affected by sludge application. The major limitation on the agricultural use of sludge is likely to be from the excessive applications of nitrogen adding to the nitrate burden of ground and surface waters.

6.8.4.3   Non-agricultural

Land restoration. There is scope for additional non-agricultural uses of sludges. The nutrients and organic matter in sludge have been shown to help the restoration of derelict and contaminated land (Hall, 1993). The biological breakdown of recalcitrant and toxic residues in old industrial and mining sites may be accelerated by co-metabolism, and enzyme induction. Applications of sludge bring about higher rates of general metabolic activity.

Forestry. Larger applications of sludge to forestry growth are possible than for simple agricultural use. Forests are usually grown on poor soil and in the United Kingdom, for example, the Forestry Commission uses 1.8 tonnes of fertiliser per hectare (Hall, 1993). Surveys have also shown that up to 20% of the Forestry Commission plantations may be within economical transport distances. Using sewage sludge for forestry is very popular in the United States, where transport distances greater than 100 km have been shown to be worthwhile after special pre-drying (Hall, 1993).

Landfill. This is a popular disposal route in the other large industrial countries of Europe (about 40% of the total) but in the United Kingdom it is used as a reserve for difficulties with agricultural use, i.e. due to the weather or unforeseen contamination. The future of landfilling is uncertain because of impending changes in the legislation (EC proposed Directive 91/C190/01). A disadvantage of landfilling of sludge is the high water content and consequent production of leachate although the water, nutrients, and inoculum of active bacteria increases the rate of degradation of domestic refuse. A number of the large water companies have invested in landfill sites to protect their continued use of this route as a standby facility (Hudson and Young, 1991).

Compost. At present there are only pilot schemes for composting sludges in the United Kingdom and Europe. In the United States, it is a popular process. There is renewed interest in the United Kingdom because of the public recognition of limited supplies of horticultural peat and the environmental damage caused by its extraction (640 000 tonnes per annum).

Composting is an aerobic process and it relies on the structural support of the solids to maintain openness and ventilation during the process. Straw, wood chips, shavings, bark and nut husks are commonly used to provide this building material. Straw, for example, will absorb three times its own weight of water and can be co-composted with liquid wastes such as sludges and farm slurry. The benefits of composting are similar to those of anaerobic digestion, these are the controlled decomposition and stabilisation of organic waste, odour control and the removal of pathogens. Composting is a successful process if the transport and operating costs can be overcome. In the United Kingdom, the most common use of composting is for mushrooming. Various demonstration schemes have been conducted on the large scale composting of animal and domestic wastes with straw, but there are insufficient financial incentives to make it competitive with peat which is also a better growing medium. The best results have so far been obtained with coir which is the high fibre residue from coconuts. The disadvantage of coir is its imported cost.

The best use of compost is as a soil conditioner. The humus and fibre content of compost make it suitable as a supplement to clay and sandy soils. Compost is not a good fertiliser; combined N:P:K are less than 3% and it is too bulky to transport. It has so far not been used for agriculture in Europe, but in Japan and the United States there are special projects to promote its use to avoid dependence on chemical fertilisers (USEPA, 1991). Premium uses, such as in landscaping, horticulture and land reclamation, are the most economic uses of compost; this type of use will be impossible for sewage sludge or domestic refuse because of the risks, although slight, of contamination with metals and organics. Food industry wastes are contamination free and could be used for horticulture; this could be a valuable outlet in the future.

Composting is a batch process and there is a succession from mesophilic to thermophilic ecology. The heat generated during the rapid growth of the bacteria and actinomycetes breaking down the smaller organic molecules raises the temperature to 40–50°C when a thermophilic population becomes established. The thermophilic fungi are efficient at breaking down cellulose. Temperatures frequently reach 70°C when the activity of most organisms becomes inhibited. These high temperatures are beneficial for the composting of animal and domestic wastes, since it assists the removal of pathogens.

Another consequence of the heating is that the wastes dry as composting takes place. This may limit activity once the moisture content falls below 25%. The moisture content and organic content of the starting materials govern the drying process.

Different techniques of composting have developed for different types of waste. The simplest technique is the open static pile. In this process, solid waste is collected in a pyramid about 2–3 m at the base and 1 m high. The pile is then periodically aerated by a perforated pipe at the base of the heap. Static pile composting can be carried out in the open, but it is more controllable if it is roofed or enclosed. An alternative method is to arrange the waste in long rows which are aerated by periodic mixing using special turning machines. This is known as the windrow process. There may be problems with dust and odour during turning. The aerial spores of the fungi growing in the compost, particularly *Aspergillus*, can be a potential hazard to the operators. Bioreactor composting systems have been used for domestic refuse in an attempt to reduce the land required for pile and row composting. Bioreactors are easier to control, but expensive and cannot be served from the value of the product. There are two basic types, an inclined rotating tunnel or a standard stirred tank (Anderson and Smith, 1987). Residence time in the reactor is 5–10 days, but this has to be followed by a maturation period of several weeks outside the reactor.

6.9   Conclusions

Greater environmental awareness is a major issue facing the food industry. Many people perceive industry as harmful and polluting (Liardet, 1991). Surveys also show that about 30% of the general public think that the environment and pollution are one of the most important problems that government has to deal with (DoE, 1992). The legislative response has been three key principles: integrated pollution control which is designed to lead to a fundamental rethink of production processes and encourage clean technology; the duty of care which is aimed at ensuring waste is disposed of in the best environmental way; and the urban wastewater directive which imposes limits on the amounts of a range of materials released into the water environment.

Overall, there are opportunities for reducing wastage and the costs of effluent disposal by a better understanding of the waste generating processes.

Simple pretreatments such as screening, balancing, settlement and filtration will in most food industry cases prove cost effective compared to the discharge of untreated material. Most complete effluent treatment systems are biological.

Waste treatment is the largest practical use of microorganisms. The diversity, volume and complexity of wastes means that there are few alternatives to this type of treatment. The size of the application coupled with popular demand for a better environment has continuously stimulated the development of more efficient processes.

A disadvantage of increasing microbial efficiency for waste treatment is biomass yield. This can result in the conversion of one problem (that is polluted water) into another (that of surplus sludge). A second problem is that more intense processes inevitably require better control and reliable sensors for wastewater are not often available.

Traditional processes, although they need space, have a substantial case history and most of the problems have been previously encountered.

Additional technologies such as membranes and physico-chemical oxidation such as photolysis and electro magnetic radiation will in future aid existing technologies to meet the new standards more consistently.

An outstanding constraint on existing high efficiency bioreactors is the ability to control them. New sensors and control models are an active area of research.

References

Adams, C.D. and McKinney, R.E. (1989) Anaerobic trickling filters: a new treatment potential. In *Proceedings of the 44th Purdue Industrial Waste Conference*. Ann Arbor Science, Michigan, pp. 1–12.

Alibhai, K.R.K. and Forster, C.F. (1986) An examination of the granulation process in UASB reactors. *Environ. Technol. Lett.* **7**, 193–200.

American Society of Civil Engineers (1984) *A Standard Measurement of Oxygen Transfer in Clean Water*. ASCE, New York.

Anderson, J.G. and Smith, J.E. (1987) Composting, in *Biotechnology of Waste Treatment and Exploitation*, eds. J.M. Sidwick and R.S. Holton. Ellis Horwood, Chichester, pp. 301–325.

Baumann, P.G. and Huibregtse, G.L. (1981) Evaluation and comparison of digester mixing systems. *J. Water Pollution Control Fed.* **54**, 1194–1203.

Bishop, P.L. and Kinner, N.E. (1986) Anaerobic fixed-film processes, in *Biotechnology: A Comprehensive Treatise*, eds. H.J. Rehm and G. Reed. VCH, Weinheim, pp. 113–176.

Bolle, W.L., van Breugel, J., van Eyberger, G.C., Kossen, N.W.F. and Zoetmeyer, R.J. (1986) Modelling the liquid flow in upflow anaerobic sludge blanket reactors. *Biotechnol. Bioeng.* **28**, 1615–1620.

Bonastre, N. and Paris, J.M. (1989) Survey of laboratory pilot and industrial anaerobic filter installations. *Proc. Biochem.* **241**, 15–20.

Brade, C.E. and Noon, G.P. (1981) Anaerobic sludge digestion – need it be expensive? I. Making more of existing resources. *Water Pollution Control* **80**, 70–90.

Brooking, J., Buckingham, C. and Fuggle, R. (1990) Constraints on effluent plant design for a brewery effluent treatment and waste disposal. *Int. Chem. Eng. Symp.* **116**, 109–126.

Brown, M.J. and Lester, J.N. (1979) Metal removal in activated sludge: the role of bacterial extra cellular polymer. *Water Res.* **13**, 817–837.

Butcher, G.J. (1988) Experiences with anaerobic digestion of wheat starch processing waste. *Int. Biodeterioration* **25**, 71–77.

Butler, G.A. (1984) Anaerobic digestion of starch process effluents at Tenstar Products, in *Anaerobic Treatment of Industrial Waste*, ed. J. Coombs. BABA, PO Box 7, Reading, UK.

Camilleri, C. (1987) Operating results from a fixed film anaerobic digester for pollution abatement and methane production from industrial wastes, in *Biomass for Energy and Industry, 4th EC Conference*, eds. G. Grassi, B. Delmon, J.F. Molle and H. Zibetta. Elsevier Applied Science, London, pp. 1338–1342.

Camilleri, C. (1988) Anaerobic digestion of food processing wastewater: industrial performance of fixed film technologies for methane recovery and pollution abatement, in *The 5th Symposium on Anaerobic Digestion, Bologna*, eds. A. Tilche and A. Rozzi. Monduzzi, Bologna, pp. 473–476.

Campbell, H.W. (1989) A status report on Canada's oil from sludge technology, in *Sewage Treatment and Use*, eds. A.H. Dirkzwager and P. L'Hermite. Elsevier, London, pp. 281–290.

Chambers, B. and Tomlinson, E.J., eds. (1982) *Bulking of Activated Sludge: Preventive and Remedial Methods*. Ellis Horwood for The Water Research Centre, Chichester.

Clescoi, L.S., Greenbury, A.E. and Trussell, R. (1989) *Standard Methods for the Examination of Water and Waste Water*, 17th edn. American Public Health Association, American Water Works Association and The Water Pollution Control Federation, Washington DC.

Commission of the European Communities (1989) *22nd General Report on the Activities of the European Communities*. CEC, Luxembourg, pp. 243–258.

Cooper, P.F., Drew, E.A., Bailey, D.A. and Thomas, E.V. (1977) Recent-advances in sewage effluent denitrification. *Water Pollution Control* **76**, 287–300.

Corbitt, R.A. (1989) *Standard Handbook of Environmental Engineering*. McGraw-Hill, ISBN 07-013158-9.

Dahab, M.F. and Young, J.C. (1982) Retention and distribution of biological solids in fixed-bed anaerobic filters. *Proc. 1st Int. Conf. Fixed Film Biol. Processes.* Kings Island, Ohio, pp. 1337–1351.

Department of Scientific and Industrial Research (1960) *Water Pollution Research: The Report of the Water Pollution Research Laboratory, 1955–1959.* HMSO, London.

Department of the Environment (1979) *Methods for the Examination of Waters and Associated Materials Analysis.* HMSO, London.

Department of the Environment (1982) The bacteriological examination of drinking water supplies. *Reports on Public Health and Medical Subjects No. 71.* HMSO, London.

Department of the Environment (1989) *Code of Practice for the Agricultural Use of Sewage Sludge.* HMSO, London, 20 pp.

Department of the Environment (1992) *The UK Environment Statistics.* HMSO Government Statistical Service.

Dohne, E. (1980) Bio Gas storage and utilization, in *Anaerobic digestion 1st International Symposium*, eds. D.A. Stafford, B.I. Wheatley and D.A. Hughes. Elsevier Applied Science, pp. 429–445.

Dolfing, J. (1986) Granulation in UASB reactors. *Water Sci. Technol.* **18**, 15–25.

Ehlinger, F., Audic, J.M., Vernier, D. and Fraup, G.M. (1987) The influence of the carbon source on microbiological clogging in an anaerobic filter. *Water Sci. Technol.* **19**, 261–273.

Eikelboom, D.H. (1975) Filamentous organisms observed in activated sludge. *Water Res.* **9**, 365–388.

Environment Canada (1986) *Anaerobic Treatment of Dairy Effluent.* Report EPS 3/FP/1 Environment Canada Ottawa.

European Commission (1991) Council directive concerning the urban waste water treatment 91.271/EEC. *Official Journal of the European Commission* May 21, 398–417.

Ferranti, M.P. (1987) Environmental biotechnology in Europe: community activities, in *Biotechnology of Waste Treatment and Exploitation*, eds. J.M. Sidwick and R.S. Holdam. Ellis Horwood, Chichester.

Foot, R.J. (1992) The effects of process control parameters on the composition and stability of activated sludge. *J. Inst. Water Environ. Mgmt.* **2**, 215–228.

Gloyna, E.F., Comstock, R.F. and Renn, C.E. (1952) Rotary tubes as experimental trickling filters. *Sewage Ind. Waste* **24**, 1355–1357.

Gorsuch, T.T. (1986) *Food Processing Research: a Report to the Priorities Board Ministry of Agriculture Fisheries and Food.* HMSO, 38 pp.

Greeman, A. (1990) Good eggs: a new concrete structural design for wastewater treatment. *New Civil Engineer* **10**, 14–17.

Hall, E.R. (1983) Biomass retention and mixing characteristics in fixed film and suspended growth anaerobic reactors. *Water Sci. Technol.* **15**, 371–396.

Hall, J.E. (1993) Recent developments in sewage sludge disposal and use. *Chem. Ind.* **6**, 188–191.

Hawkes, H.A. (1963) *The Ecology of Waste Water Treatment*, 1st edition. Pergamon Press, Oxford.

Hawkes, H.A. and Shephard, M.R.N. (1972) The effect of dosing frequency on the seasonal fluctuations and vertical distribution of solids and grazing fauna in sewage percolating filters. *Water Res.* **6**, 721–730.

Healey, M.G. (1984) Guidelines for the utilisation of sewage sludge on land in the United Kingdom. *Wat. Sci. Technol.* **26**, 461–471.

Heijnen, J.J., Enger, W.A., Mulder, A., Lourens, P.A., Keijzers, A.A. and Hoeks, F.W.J. (1985) Awendung der anaeroben wirbel schichttechnik in der biologischen abwasseinigung. *Wasser/abwasser* **126**, 115–130.

Heliwell, J.M. (1978) *Biological Surveillance of Rivers: A Biological Monitoring Handbook.* WRc Medmerham, 331 pp.

Henze, M. and Harremoes, P. (1983) Anaerobic treatment of waste water in fixed film reactors: a review. *Water Sci. Technol.* **15**, 1–90.

Hobson, P.N. and Wheatley, A.D. (1992) *Anaerobic Digestion: Modern Theory and Practice.* Elsevier, Barking, London, 288 pp.

Horan, N.J. (1990) *Biological Wastewater Treatment Systems and Operation.* Wiley, Chichester, 310 pp.

Horan, N.G., Bu'ali, A.M. and Eccles, C.R. (1988) Isolation, identification and characterization of filamentous and floc forming organisms from activated sludge. *Environ. Technol.* **9**, 449–457.

Hoyland, G., Dee, A. and Day, M.J. (1989) Optimum design of sewage sludge consolidation tanks. *J. Inst. Wat. Environ. Mgmt.* **3**(5), 505–5161.

Huber, L. and Metzner, G. (1986) *Examples of Industrial Waste Water Treatment in Biotechnology: a Comprehensive Treatise*, eds H.-J. Rehm and G. Read. VCH, Weinheim, pp. 269–305.

Hudson, J. and Young, G. (1991) Strategic role of anaerobic digestion in sludge management in Yorkshire, in *Anaerobic Digestion Seminar*, eds. G.E. Richards and P.B. Mistry. Harwell Press, Oxford, ISBN 07058-1645-1.

Institute of Water Pollution Control (1978) Sewage sludge 3. Utilisation and disposal. *Manuals of British Practice*. IWPC, Maidstone, Kent.

Institute of Water Pollution Control (1979) Sewage sludge 1. Production, preliminary treatment and digestion. *Manuals of British Practice*. IWPC, Maidstone, Kent.

Iza, J. (1991) Fluidised bed reactors for anaerobic treatment. *Water Sci. Technol.* **24**, 109–132.

Jones, G.A. and Franklin, B.C. (1985) The prevention of filamentous bulking of activated sludge by operation means at Halifax Sewage Treatment Works. *Water Pollution Control* **84**, 329–344.

Kennedy, K.J. and Droste, R.L. (1986) Anaerobic fixed film reactors treating carbohydrate wastewater. *Water Res.* **20**, 685–695.

Kennedy, K.J. and Droste, R.L. (1991) Anaerobic wastewater treatment in down flow stationary fixed film reactors. *Water Sci. Technol.* **24**, 157–177.

Kissel, J.C., Grotenhuis, J.T.C. and Zehnder, A.J.B. (1988) Computer simulation of granule growth in an upflow anaerobic sludge blanket reactor (UASBR) in *5th International Symposium on Anaerobic Digestion*, eds. A. Tilche and A. Rozzi. Monduzzi, Bologna, pp. 207–210.

Lettinga, G. and Hulsoff-Pol, L.W. (1986) Advanced reactor design, operation and economy. *Water Sci. Technol.* **18**, 12, 41–53.

Lettinga, G. and Hulshoff-Pol, L.W. (1991) UASB – process design for various types of wastewaters. *Water Sci. Technol.* **24**, 87–107.

Lettinga, G., Velsen, A.F.M., van Zeeuw, W.J. and Hobma, S.W. (1979) The application of anaerobic digestion to industrial pollution treatment, in *Anaerobic Digestion 1st International Symposium*, eds. D.A. Stafford, B.I. Wheatley and D.A. Hughes. Elsevier Applied Science, London.

Levenspiel, O. (1972) *Chemical Reaction Engineering*. Wiley, Chichester, pp. 253–325.

Liardet, G. (1991) Public opinion and the chemical industry. *Chem. Ind.* **4**, 118–123.

Lilly, W., Brown, H., Crabtree, H., Upton, J. and Thomas, V. (1991) The production of high quality effluents in sewage treatment by using the Biocarbone process. *J. Inst. Water Environ. Mgmt.* **5**(2), 123–133.

Matthews, P.J. (1992) Sewage sludge disposal in the UK: a new challenge for the next twenty years. *J. Inst. Water Environ. Mgmt.* **6**, 551–559.

McCann, W.C. (1993) The age of consent. *Water Environ. Mgmt.* **3**, 16–18.

McLoughlin, J. and Bellinger, E.G. (1993) *An Environmental Pollution Control Introduction to the Principles and Practice of Administration*. Graham and Trotman, London, ISBN 1-85 333-5770, pp. 249.

Micklewright, A.T. (1986) A review of the practice of trade effluent control and charging in the North West. *Water Pollution Control* **85**, 324–336.

Ministry of Agriculture, Fisheries and Food (1986) *Food Processing Research Consultative Committee. Report to the Priorities Board.* HMSO, London.

Ministry of Housing and Local Government (1954) *Report of an Informal Working Party on the Treatment and Disposal of Sewage Sludge.* HMSO, London.

Morgan, H. (1980) The development of an anaerobic process for the treatment of wheat starch factory effluent, in *Food Industry Wastes: Disposal and Recovery*, eds. A. Herzka and R.G. Booth. Elsevier, Barking, 246 pp.

Murray, W.D. and van den Berg, L. (1981) Effects of nickel cobalt and molybdenum on the performance of methonogenic fixed film reactors. *Appl. Environ. Microbiol.* **42**, 502–505.

Nahle, C. (1991) The contact process for the anaerobic treatment of wastewater: technology, design and experiences. *Water Sci. Technol.* **24**, 179–191.

Noguchi, H. and Ito, H. (1992) Long term experiments of applying sewage sludge fertilizer to agricultural land. *J. Inst. Water Environ. Mgmt.* **6**, 576–582.

Noon, G.P. and Brade, C.E. (1985) Anaerobic sludge digestion – need it be expensive, III. Integrated and low cost digestion. *J. Inst. Water Pollution Control* **84**, 309–328.

Oleszkiewz, J.A. and Thadari, V.J. (1988) Effects of biofilter media on performance of anaerobic hybrid reactors. *Environ. Technol. Lett.* **9**, 89–100.

Oleszkiewz, J.A., Hall, E.R. and Oziemblo, J.Z. (1986) Performance of laboratory scale anaerobic hybrid reactors with varying depths of media. *Environ. Technol. Lett.* **7**, 445–452.

Oliva, E., Jacquart, J.C. and Prevot, C. (1990) Treatment of brewery wastewater by methanization in fluidized bed reactors. *Water Sci. Technol.* **22**, 483–490.

O'Shaugnessy, F.R. (1931) Some considerations in the oxidation of sewage. *Proceedings of the Association of Managers of Sewage Disposal Works*, pp. 74–92.

Pauss, A., Depaepe, D. and Nyns, E.J. (1990) Review of AD plants in Europe, in *Euroenviron Anaerobic Digestion Workshops*, ed. G.E. Richards. Harwell, ISBN 0-7058-1608-7.

Pauss et al. (1991) Reactor design of anaerobic filters and sludge bed reactors. *Wat. Sci. Technol.* **24**(8), 193–206.

Pike, E.B. (1975) The aerobic bacteria, in *Ecological Aspects of Used-Water Treatment*, Vol. 1, eds. C.R. Curds and H.A. Hawkes. Academic Press, London, pp. 1–63.

Pike, E.B. and Carrington, E.G. (1972) Recent developments in the study of bacteria in the activated sludge process. *Water Pollution Control* **71**, 583–605.

Pike, E.B. and Carrington, E.G. (1979) The fate of enteric bacteria and pathogens during sewage treatment, in *Biological Indicators of Water Quality, a Symposium*, eds. A. James and L.M. Evison. Wiley, Chichester, pp. 20-1–20-32.

Pike, E.B., Carlton-Smith, C.H., Evans, R.H. and Harrington, D.W. (1982) Performance of rotating biological contractors under field conditions. *Water Pollution Control* **81**, 10–27.

Postgate, J. (1989) Microbial happy families. *New Sci.* Jan 21, 40–44.

Racault, Y. (1990) Treatment of distillery wastewater using an anaerobic downflow stationary fixed film reactor: performance of a large scale plant in operation for four years. *Wat. Sci. Technol.* **22** (1/2), 361–372.

Royal Commission on Sewage Disposal (1908) 5th Report. HMSO, London.

Rundle, H. and Whyley, J. (1981) Comparison of gas recirculation of systems for mixing in anaerobic digestion. *Water Pollution Control* **80**, 463–480.

Samson, R., van den Berg, L. and Kennedy, K.J. (1985) Mixing characteristics and start up of anaerobic stationary fixed film reactor. *J. Biotechnol.* **2**, 95–106.

Shore, M., Broughton, N.W. and Bumstead, N. (1984) Anaerobic treatment of waste waters in the sugar beet industry. *Water Pollution Control* **83**, 499–506.

Sixt, H. and Sahm, H. (1987) Biomethanation, in *The Biotechnology of Waste Treatment and Exploitation*, ed. J.M. Sidwick and R.S. Holdom. Ellis Horwood, Chichester, pp. 149–172.

Smith, L.J. (1986) The treatment of wastewaters from malting, brewing and distilling. *Water Sci. Technol.* **18**, 127–135.

Smith, M.O., Ferrall, J., Smith, A.J.T., Winstanley, C.I. and Wheatley, A.D. (1988) The economics of effluent treatment: a case study at Bovril. *Int. Biodeterioration* **25**, 97–105.

Smith, N. (1984) Anaerobic effluent treatment in British Sugar, in *Anaerobic Treatment of Industrial Waste*, ed. J. Coombs. BABA, PO Box 7, Reading, UK.

Souza, M.E. (1986) Criteria for the utilization design and operation of UASB reactors. *Water Sci. Technol.* **18**, 55–69.

Stephenson, T., Mann, A. and Upton, J. (1993) The small footprint wastewater treatment process. *Chemistry and Industry* **14**, 533–536.

Stronach, S.M., Rudd, T. and Lester, J.N. (1986) *Anaerobic Digestion Process in Industrial Waste Treatment*. Springer-Verlag, Berlin, 184 pp.

Swanwick, J.D., Shurben, D.G. and Jackson, S. (1969) A survey of the performance of sewage sludge digestion in Great Britain. *Water Pollution Control* **68**, 639–661.

Switzenbaum, M. (1983) A comparison of the anaerobic filter and anaerobic expanded/fluidised bed process. *Water Sci. Technol.* **15**, 399–413.

Szendry, L.M. (1983) Scale up and operation of the Bacardi Corporation anaerobic filter, in *Proceedings of the 3rd International Symposium on Anaerobic Digestion*. Boston, MA, pp. 365–377.

Szendry, L.M. (1986) The Bacardi Corporation digestion process for stabilizing rum distillery waste and producing methane, in *Energy from Biomass and Wastes VII*, Florida, 1983. The Chicago Gas Institute, pp. 767–794.

Tebbutt, T.H.Y. (1992) Japanese sludge treatment utilization and disposal. *J. Inst. Water Environ. Mgmt.* **6**, 628–632.

The Paris Commission (1988) Waste treatment approach and low waste technology convention for the prevention of marine pollution from land based sources. *Report from the 10th Paris Commission*, Lisbon, June 1988.

Tilche, A. and Vierra, S.M.M. (1991) Reactor design of anaerobic filters and sludge bed reactors. *Water Sci. Technol.* **24**, 193–206.

Upton, J.E. and Churchley, J.H. (1993) Process options for biological nutrient removal in activated sludge plants. Paper presented to Institution of Water and Environment Management at Leicester, February 1993.

USEPA (1991) *Technical Bulletin 430 981-011*: Composting processes to stabilize and disinfect municipal slewage sludge. Office of Water Program, Washington DC.

Vincent, A.J. and Critchley, R.F. (1984) A review of sewage sludge treatment and disposal in Europe, in *Sewage Sludge Stabilisation and Disinfection*, ed. A.M. Bruce. Ellis Horwood, Chichester, pp. 550–571.

Von Gunten, H.R. and Lienert, C. (1993) Water and ground water quality in Switzerland. *Nature* **364**, 220.

Water Data Unit (1979) *Water Data 1978*. Department of the Environment, Water Data Unit, Reading.

Weiland, P. and Rozzi, A. (1991) The start up, operation and monitoring of high rate anaerobic treatment systems. *Water Sci. Technol.* **24**, 257–277.

Wheatley, A.D. (1984) Biotechnology and effluent treatment, in *Biotechnology and Genetic Engineering Reviews*, Vol. 1, ed. G.E. Russell. Intercept Press, Newcastle upon Tyne.

Wheatley, A.D. (1985) Waste water treatment and by-product recovery, in *Topics in Waste Water Treatment*, ed. J.M. Sidwick. Blackwell, Oxford, pp. 68–105.

Wheatley, A.D. (1990) The treatment of industrial effluent. *Critical Reports in Applied Chemistry* **31**, 172–220.

Wheatley, A.D. and Cassell, L. (1985) Effluent treatment by anaerobic biofiltration. *Water Pollution Control* **84**, 10–20.

Wheatley, A.D. and Coombs, J. (1991) *Anaerobic Digestion: A Technical and Marketing Report*. CPL Scientific, Newbury, 330 pp.

Wheatley, A.D., Johnson, K.A. and Winstanley, C.I. (1988) The reliability of anaerobic digestion for the treatment of food processing effluents, in *Advances in Water Pollution Control Anaerobic Digestion*. Pergamon, Oxford, pp. 135–146.

Wilson, F., Hamoda, M.F., Islam, H. and Buranasin, P. (1988) The treatment of high strength vegetable pickling waste using the RBC process. *Env. Tech. Lett.* **9**(11), 1201–1212.

Wishart, J.M. and Wilkinson, R. (1941) Purification of settled sewage in percolating filters in series with periodic change in the order of the filter. *J. Proc. Inst. Sewage Purification* **1**, 15–38.

Witt, E.R., Humphreys, W.J. and Roberts, T.E. (1979) Full scale anaerobic filter treats high strength wastes. *Proceedings 34th Purdue Industrial Waste Treatment Conf.*, pp. 229–234.

World Health Organization (1973) Reuse of effluents: methods of wastewater treatment and health safeguards. *Technical Report Number 517*. WHO, Geneva.

Young, H.C. and Young, J.C. (1988) Hydraulic characteristics of upflow anaerobic filters. *J. Environ. Eng.* **114**, 621–638.

Young, J.C. and Yang, B.S. (1989) Design considerations for full-scale anaerobic filters. *J. Water Pollution Control Fed.* **61**, 1576–1587.

Young, J.C. and McCarty, P.L. (1969) The anaerobic filter for waste treatment. *J. Water Pollution Control Fed.* **41**, R160–R173.

Young, J.C. (1991) Factors affecting the design and performance of upflow anaerobic filters. *Water Sci. Technol.* **24**, 133–155.

Young, J.C. and Dahab, M.F. (1983) Effect of media design on the performance of fixed bed anaerobic filters. *Water Sci. Technol.* **15**, 369–383.

7 Cooling and temperature controlled storage and distribution systems

C.V.J. DELLINO and G. HAZLE

7.1 Introduction

This chapter is concerned with the effects on the environment of current and future techniques used to chill, freeze, store and transport food products. Simple cooling processes, such as the circulation of ambient air through warm products, have little or no effect on the environment; this chapter ignores them and concentrates on those processes that require the application of refrigeration.

7.2 Refrigeration

Refrigeration can be simply defined as any process that removes heat from where it is not wanted, and rejects it to a place where it can be tolerated. In its simplest form, this process is typified by a domestic refrigerator; where heat is extracted from the storage volume and dissipated, via a 'radiator' coil on the back, into the room air.

As heat will only flow from a warm source to a cooler one, the job of the refrigeration unit is to collect heat by providing a cold surface to attract it, gather it up and boost its temperature to a level that will allow it to leave the system. By far the most common 'heat sink' is ambient air, and most refrigeration systems use this convenient dumping ground, one way or another.

To move heat about in this way, by providing low temperature (at the cooler) and a higher temperature than, say, the ambient air, most systems use a volatile fluid (the 'refrigerant') that can be made to 'boil' at low pressure, thus picking up heat in the same way as a kettle takes heat from flame, and be condensed back to a liquid by giving up heat somewhere else.

To do this, the refrigerant is pumped around the system, by a compressor, and the work done by this compressor has to be paid for. Payment is made by the cost of the energy required at the compressor. The greater the temperature lift, between the cooled area and the heat sink, the more horsepower is required at the compressor shaft (Figure 7.1).

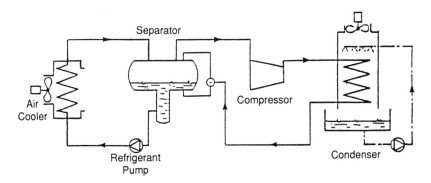

Figure 7.1 Simplified refrigeration plant circuit diagram.

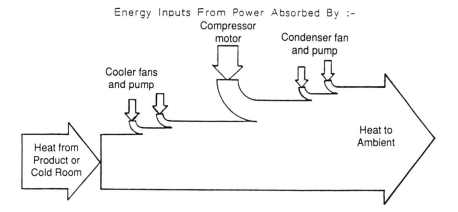

Figure 7.2 Extracted versus heat rejected by refrigeration plant.

Most of the energy used during this process is converted into heat and it, too, is ultimately rejected to the heat sink along with the heat taken up at the cooler. Most of the heat rejected from refrigeration plant condensers is low grade heat, that is to say, it is available at relatively low temperatures, around 30–35°C, and not much use for most heating requirements.

There are some exceptions to this but, in the main, condenser heat is most commonly just discharged into the air, or sometimes into surface water (Figure 7.2).

7.2.1   Cryogenic refrigeration

In addition to vapour compression systems, as described in the previous paragraphs, the food industry also uses 'total loss' systems of cooling such as liquid nitrogen and solid carbon dioxide. In these cases, ready-made 'cold' is purchased in the form of a liquefied gas or a solidified gas that will cool or freeze a product by taking from it the heat it requires to evaporate back to a gas. The gas then produced is never recycled, it just goes into the atmosphere. Whilst nitrogen is the main constituent of the air we breathe, CO_2 is not so welcome in our environment.

The energy required to produce these cryogenic substances, and to transport them, should be taken into account when considering the total impact of their use on our environment. In most applications, the total fossil fuel consumption to freeze with liquid nitrogen, as compared to freezing with a conventional vapour compression system, is very much greater. There will probably always be instances where the food industry will use cryogenics, in laboratory work, in the transport of small quantities of frozen products and highly specialised freezing processes. There are sound environmental and economic reasons for questioning their use in the average factory production line.

7.2.2   Energy use

From the foregoing notes, it is clear that industry will continue to cause concerns to anyone taking a responsible attitude towards the environment, as long as refrigeration plays a part in the food production and distribution chain. Industry must be seen to be among those with the 'responsible attitude', and one obvious area for re-evaluation is our attitude to energy use.

The environmental effects of inefficient energy use are twofold: we may pollute our local environment and also put avoidable loads on power stations (and cryogenic plants) who, in their turn, are discharging pollutants.

As far as cooling and temperature controlled storage is concerned, we use some liquid fuels (for example, in refrigerated vehicles) but, in the main, we burn up electrical energy that has been generated elsewhere, with varying effects on the environment, and it is in the reduction of electrical energy use that industry can make a significant contribution to improving the environment.

7.2.3   Energy costs and the food industry

The rise in cost of electrical energy to industrial consumers is indicated in Figure 7.3, which shows how the cost per unit (kWh) has risen over the period of maximum growth of the UK frozen foods industry. The costs shown are average figures and do not include special tariffs or standing charges.

It would be expected that the dramatic increase in such a basic cost would have concentrated the minds of cost-conscious managers; however,

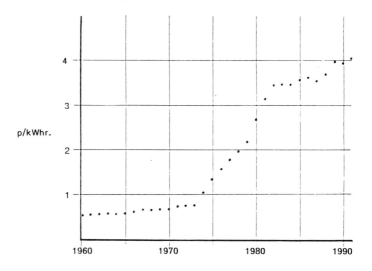

Figure 7.3 Average electricity prices to industrial users, p/kWh.

this has not been so. There seems to be two reasons for this. Firstly, their electricity bills have been one of their smaller accounts and, secondly, other prices have risen at much the same rate, thus keeping relative power costs in much the same position.

Producers of frozen foods have power costs (per ton of product) that are similar to their packaging costs, way down the table when compared to raw material and labour costs. Additional investment in automation and more efficient use of raw material has proved to be more attractive than improved energy efficiency.

As an illustration of the second point, relative power costs, Table 7.1 shows how the UK retail price index has moved over the same period, and gives an indication of the relative impact of energy price rises.

Although the electrical energy costs used in these illustrations are based on official data from UK sources, it may be assumed that similar uplifts will have occurred in the United States, and elsewhere, where electricity costs are geared to world fossil fuel prices.

There are, obviously, financial benefits from energy saving practices and one area of our industry has had a greater incentive to do so. The public cold store operators have electricity bills that are much more significant in their operating costs and it is interesting to see how their improved operating practices have reduced their energy costs per ton of product stored.

If we consider the period of maximum growth in their activities, from, say, 1965–1985, the one consistent factor has been the increase in store size.

Table 7.1 Relative cost of electricity to industrial users[a]

	A	B	C
1960	0.523	13.2	100.0
1961	0.551	13.6	103.0
1962	0.562	14.2	101.0
1963	0.572	14.5	101.0
1964	0.569	15.0	96.0
1965	0.595	15.7	97.0
1966	0.616	16.3	96.0
1967	0.631	16.7	100.0
1968	0.644	17.5	94.0
1969	0.644	18.4	89.0
1970	0.654	19.6	85.0
1971	0.721	21.4	86.0
1972	0.739	23.0	82.0
1973	0.742	25.1	75.0
1974	1.020	29.1	89.0
1975	1.344	36.1	95.0
1976	1.559	42.1	94.0
1977	1.790	48.8	94.0
1978	1.983	52.8	96.0
1979	2.190	59.9	93.0
1980	2.703	70.7	97.0
1981	3.133	79.1	101.0
1982	3.448	85.9	102.0
1983	3.465	89.8	98.0
1984	3.482	94.3	94.0
1985	3.589	100.0	91.0
1986	3.617	103.4	89.0
1987	3.528	107.7	83.0
1988	3.701	113.0	83.0
1989	3.988	121.8	83.0
1990	3.959	133.3	75.0
1991	4.084	141.1	74.0

[a]A, Average industrial electricity prices, p/kWh. B, UK retail price index, all items; 1985 = 100. C, A ÷ B and indexed to 1960 = 100. A and B are DTI figures.

The Year Book of the National Cold Storage Federation for 1965 shows that, of the major operators, the average cold store capacity was 200 000 ft^3 (5663 m^3). By 1985, however, similar statistics show the average storage module to have risen to 1 000 000 ft^3 (28 318 m^3). Over this period mechanical handling, plant design, materials of construction and store layouts have developed rapidly and an 'optimum' store evolved that has not changed very much since.

Figure 7.4 shows the effect of these design changes on the amount of energy consumed per ton of product stored, and how a cost-conscious sector of the industry has (albeit as a secondary effect) reduced environmental stress to some 35% of its old level.

There are many ways in which the environmental impact of the use of refrigeration can be minimised with regard to its use of electrical energy and much has been published on the subject. Good Practice Guides, Nos. 42 and 44 are a useful starting point for further reading on this subject. They are published by the Energy Efficiency Office of the Department of Energy.

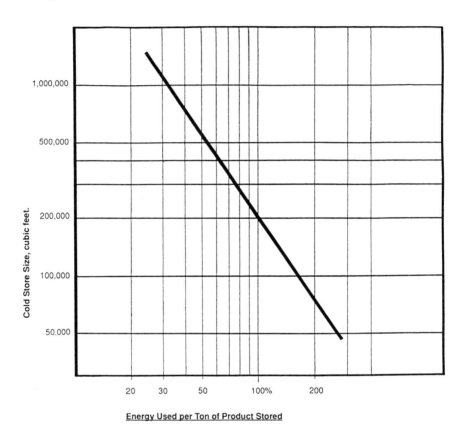

Energy Used per Ton of Product Stored

Figure 7.4 This graph illustrates the reduction in energy use, per ton of product stored as public cold stores grew in size. In 1965, the NCSF Year Book showed the average store to be some 200 000 ft^3 capacity and this is taken as datum. By the late 1980s (and little changed today), a typical cold store for frozen goods (−25 to −29°C) was closer to 1 000 000 ft^3.

Fuel economy has been considered first in this chapter because it will always be something that directly and indirectly affects our environment and should therefore be of permanent concern. A more 'high profile' but, hopefully, transient problem is the effect on the environment of the substances we use.

7.3   Global warming and the ozone layer

Some of the gases we use as refrigerants have been identified as being among those which, when released into the atmosphere, can alter the natural balance of the global environment. The two areas of concern are quite separate and, although the remedy is the same (do not release them!), it may be helpful to define the perceived dangers in each case. The processes are complicated, and well defined elsewhere, but the basic concerns can be set out as follows.

7.3.1   Global warming

Some of the energy received from the sun gets bounced back into space from the earth's surface. The earth's atmosphere has always contained the so-called 'greenhouse gases' that have acted like a well chosen blanket, keeping enough heat in the bed for us to be comfortable but allowing the remainder to escape. Of the man-made greenhouse gases, CO_2 is the most in evidence but, fortunately, it is not a very good material to make blankets from. The refrigerant R12, however, is some 7300 times more effective and, if we want to stay comfortable, our future actions should be obvious.

7.3.2   The ozone layer

Further out from our 'blanket' of gases, in the stratosphere, is another natural protective layer. This time it is more like sun-tan oil than a blanket as it protects us from the harmful effects of ultraviolet (UV) light from the sun. We know that small amounts of UV radiation can be harmful to plants, plankton and people. It can damage DNA, suppress our immune systems and cause cataracts and cancer. It is hardly surprising that international action is being taken to limit the depletion of this layer of ozone by man-made chemicals.

Unfortunately, many of our refrigerants come into this group. The destruction of the ozone is brought about by the presence of free chlorine in the stratospheric layer and, because they are so stable, the CFCs manage to get all the way there before they break down and release free chlorine. It can take up to ten years for them to get there and, having got there, the worst of them can remain active for another 100 years. It is hard to predict the effects of what we have already released, the Global Atmosphere Division of the UK Department of the Environment say '. . . it will not be until the second half of the next century that any significant improvement in the ozone layer is observed.' That prediction is based on the revised Montreal Protocol (see below).

7.3.3   What can we do about it?

The food chain, from farmers via processors to retailers, is a high profile target for the consumer and environmental watchdogs, and their viewpoints and findings are guaranteed to get wide media attention. After all, everyone eats!

Our ultimate clients, the consumers, are already showing awareness of environmental issues, and will continue to do so. It would seem important that the food industry is seen by the consumers as being 'on their side' in this respect. They will expect us to be pro-active in publicised areas of concern, such as global warming and the depletion of the ozone layer. Not only should we take steps that improve our impact on the environment, we must be clearly seen to be doing so.

Refrigeration is one of the technologies that has made considerable use of the CFCs and HCFCs that are now seen as being among the prime dangers to the ozone layer and global warming. These chemicals are now being phased out of production under the terms of the so-called 'Montreal Protocol', signed in 1987.

It is, perhaps, worthwhile to point out that the full name of this agreement is the 'Montreal Protocol on Substances that Deplete the Ozone Layer'; it is not concerned with anything else. This is important to consider when we look for alternatives to these substances. It is not beyond possibility that, should research show the need, other similar 'Protocols' could be signed to limit global warming, discharge of CO_2 or the use of other man-made chemicals.

The chemical industry that produced the CFCs in the first instance is now working on the production of new chemicals to be used as replacements. We know little about them, so far, other than that they will be significantly more expensive.

In using any alternative to the CFCs and HCFCs we must take into account the secondary environmental effects of their use by us on our sites. For example, a new refrigerant may be seen as totally benign in our plant room; but if it requires more horse-power to drive the compressors, there will be more CO_2 discharged at the power stations. Similarly, even if the power consumed is unchanged, the production process required to produce our benign refrigerant may, in itself, be found unacceptably energy expensive. In both these examples, a future 'energy tax' would change the equations to a considerable degree.

In making our choices of replacement substances, we should be pro-active, and not forget that the environmental pressure groups will have the same information as us and will be looking critically at how we tackle this problem.

7.3.4   CFCs and HCFCs

These chemicals have been used in refrigerated facilities in two main areas: as blowing agents in the production of insulating foam and as refrigerants in enclosed systems. Used in the production of foams, they have allowed insulation thicknesses to be reduced thus saving space and/or weight. Alternative production methods for the manufacture of insulation have always been available and reverting to them is not too difficult in the case of cold stores, as an extra few centimetres of wall thickness, or a bit more weight on the foundations, is hardly noticed.

This is not true of refrigerated transport, where every litre of transit space is important and every kilogram of unladen weight has to be paid for twice.

Apart from transport, therefore, it could be expected that the use of CFC blown foam will be avoided by a greater use of some of the original man-made insulants, such as expanded polystyrene.

It is in the matter of replacements for the refrigerants that the picture is less clear for the static refrigeration installation. The 'new' refrigerants are, at the time of writing notes, still under development and long-term testing for health and safety. The preliminary results are encouraging in some respects but some questions still remain. Much has been written and published on this subject and to repeat it in this chapter would be wasteful and, in view of the continuing developments, could even be misleading.

7.3.5   'Replacement' refrigerants

In hunting for new compounds to replace the refrigerants we use, the chemical industry is formulating new ones that have better characteristics regarding their impact on the ozone layer and their contribution to global warming.

The yardsticks by which they are measured have been given the names 'ozone depletion potential' (ODP) and 'global warming potential' (GWP) and these are useful in making comparisons between them. Table 7.2 shows the ODPs, GWPs and the approximate stratospheric lifetimes of the current refrigerants and the 'replacements'. The GWPs are based on a 50-year time horizon and the ODPs on CFC 11 = 1.0.

The table clearly shows the high risk values of the CFC group of refrigerants, the lower risks of the HCFCs and the limited risks associated with the HFCs. The Montreal Protocol will phase out production of the CFCs on a short time scale and the HCFCs on a longer one.

Missing from the table is R502 which is an azeotropic mixture of 49% HCFC 22 and 51% CFC 115, i.e. one good and one bad. R502 will, therefore, disappear with the CFCs.

Table 7.2 Refrigerant characteristics

	ODP	GWP ($CO_2 = 1.0$)	Stratospheric lifetime (years)
CFC 11	1.0	4100	55.0
CFC 12	1.0	7400	116.0
CFC 113	1.07	4700	110.0
CFC 114	0.8	6700	220.0
CFC 115	0.5	6200	550.0
HCFC 22	0.055	2600	15.2
HCFC 123	0.02	150	1.6
HCFC 124	0.022	760	6.6
HCFC 141b	0.11	980	7.8
HCFC 142b	0.065	2800	19.1
HFC 125	0.0	4500	28.0
HFC 134a	0.0	1900	15.5
HFC 143a	0.0	4500	41.0
HFC 152a	0.0	250	1.7

The most promising 'new' refrigerant (at the time of writing) is HFC 134a, which is in production and replacing CFC 12 in many new applications. Although it requires special lubricants, it is almost a 'drop-in' alternative on existing plant. Tests in retro-fit situations by SRCRA showed that, with cargo space at −18°C and +38°C ambient, there was a loss of refrigerating capacity of about 10%, but no significant loss in efficiency when changing from CFC 12 to HFC 134a. In other words, the compressors may have to be a little larger but no more power would be consumed to do the same cooling job.

Other replacements are being developed for the CFCs and R502, but most are 'cocktails' of gases that contain HCFC 22, so they, in their turn, will be vulnerable to its ultimate phasing out.

There is, however, one replacement for the CFCs and HCFCs that can be discussed with confidence. Just as cold store operators can return to the use of expanded polystyrene for insulating the store, so can they reconsider the use of ammonia to refrigerate it.

7.3.6   Ammonia as a 'replacement' refrigerant

Before discussing its future potential in our industry, it may be helpful to review the past role that ammonia (NH_3) took, and how its use has progressed alongside the man-made refrigerants (for simplicity, let us just call them CFCs).

Before the arrival of the CFCs, the most common refrigerants in use were NH_3, CO_2, SO_2 and methyl chloride. CO_2 required very high operating pressures and was confined, in the main, to those applications where an inert gas was essential, such as refrigerated shipping. All the others had 'nasty' characteristics of some sort, they were poisonous, explosive, irritant, inflammable and, sometimes combined these hazards. At the same time, plants were somewhat fundamental and leaky!

Under pressure from their enormous air-conditioning market, the American chemical industry came up with the CFCs, which at the time were seen to be the complete answer. At first, the CFCs penetrated the market at consumer level, household refrigerators, windowsill air-conditioners, display cabinets and so on. They soon moved into commercial applications, back-room storage at shops, central air-conditioning plant, refrigerated transport and distribution stores serving the (then) infant frozen foods market.

These new refrigerants were expensive, and any industry that used tonnage quantities had problems. Industrial users, such as dockside cold stores, ice-making plants, meat handlers and fishing ports, had every incentive to settle for NH_3 as their primary refrigerant. It was cheap, easily available, well known, and (of the alternatives) the least problematic. Most importantly, it was the most efficient in terms of horsepower input for refrigerating output. This created a divide that is still with us today.

As the frozen foods industry has grown over the last 30 years, so has the division grown between those who are 'comfortable' with NH_3 and those who are not. This applies equally to the users of refrigeration and the suppliers of plant. Those companies that had their roots in the old industrial market have different attitudes to NH_3 from those who are part of the later, retail developments. The big producers of frozen foods still rely, in the main, on NH_3 plants, as do the major cold store operators, who have similar histories.

The large CFC installations are, almost without exception, owned by companies that have moved to the 'industrial' scale from operations that were 'commercial' or even 'retail' in their original concepts. Naturally enough, those companies who cut their teeth on CFC charged installations are wary of NH_3; it does have disadvantages.

In today's climate, it is vital to recognise that NH_3 plants have changed dramatically from those that were around when the first CFCs came on the scene. The designers and contractors who supplied heavy NH_3 plant in the past soon learned how to build large CFC plants when they were required. The high cost of these refrigerants (and the difficulty of sensing a leak, when compared to NH_3) meant that systems had to be gas-tight to a degree that had not been justified before.

New techniques, such as weld-in-line valves, hermetically sealed pumps, capped valves, welded pipework and sophisticated shaft seals were used on industrial scale CFC plants, together with gas leak detectors. It did not take long for the 'ammonia men' to realise that they no longer needed to go about their business with eyes streaming and runny noses. The same gas-tight techniques are now applied to NH_3 plants. Further developments of small screw compressors and low charge plants have increased the potential application of NH_3 in areas where it has not been previously considered.

7.3.7 Ammonia and the environment

Owners and operators of refrigeration plants, generally, are very conscious of the effect of release of refrigerant into the atmosphere, regardless of which refrigerant. However, leaks do occur; always accidentally, sometimes from worn components, sometimes during service and maintenance operations. The harmful effects of CFC emissions is now recognised, but what about NH_3 release?

As a naturally occurring substance it has no effect on the earth's environment. Being twice as light as air, the gas disperses quickly and decomposes in the atmosphere in a few days. A liquid spill evaporates almost immediately (its boiling point at atmospheric pressure is $-30°C$) so it does not find its way into sub-surface water.

Its disadvantages are that it can explode, burn, choke, blind, and it smells. If we are going to give serious thought to why it is in such common use, and look at extending its use in industry, we must put these disadvantages in perspective.

It can be flammable in air. For this to be so, the concentration in the air has to be between 16% and 25%, but a developing leak can be 'smelled' at concentrations 1/20 000 of this, and the flashpoint would be well over 600°C. In practical terms the risk of fire or explosion is fairly small.

NH_3 has a suffocating effect and the smell may cause panic. The highest level for safe human exposure is about 25 parts per million (ppm) in air, but the fatal dose is calculated to be 30 000 ppm. There are no recurring toxic effects after human inhalation. NH_3 is highly soluble in water; eye irritation can be severe when leaks occur. The known risks in NH_3 use have caused it to be classed as a 'substance hazardous to health' but not a poison. By adopting techniques and practices that:

- keep it in the system;
- keep potential leak points away from people;
- automatically monitor potential leak points;
- keep total quantities in the system to a minimum;
- rapidly ventilate high risk areas (such as plant rooms);

most major users of refrigeration have been able to continue to use this highly efficient refrigerant. Not only is it by far the cheapest refrigerant to buy, its coefficient of performance (COP) (which is simply a measure of horsepower required to provide a certain cooling capacity) is better under most low temperature conditions than the alternatives.

Recognising that there will always be some areas, corner shops, vehicles, etc., where it will be impossible to introduce NH_3, there is every reason to look for a much wider use of this efficient, cheap and environmentally acceptable refrigerant.

7.3.8   Conclusions

The environmental impact of the cooling, freezing and temperature controlled storage sectors of our industry can be minimised by:

- energy efficient operation;
- heat recovery systems;
- responsible purchase of materials of construction;
- wider use of environmentally benign refrigerants.

But, above all, we need constant awareness of the overall effects of our activities and the potential future risks that we build into our operations by purchasing plant and equipment that could be seen as less than responsible.

7.4   Refrigerated transport systems

Primary and secondary distribution of perishable cargoes under controlled temperature conditions grew significantly during the 1970s and 1980s, largely under the influence of market forces. The major food retailers, led by the big-name supermarket chains, have, under the cost pressures of competition, striven to extend sell-by dates and times by retarding product deterioration.

In many cases, this has been forced on them by the mushrooming scale of their distribution operations, which requires product to be carried over longer distances, in vehicles of greater capacity, from larger and fewer depots. Many perishable foodstuffs, in consequence, now spend more time on the move than they did say 20 years ago.

In the summer months especially, vehicles with rudimentarily insulated bodywork, without refrigeration of any kind, which were traditionally acceptable for delivering dairy products, for example, within say a 50-km radius, are unable to meet the box-temperature expectations of today's competitively aware food distributor.

7.4.1   New legislation

Under the UK Food Hygiene (Amendment) Regulations, 1990 and 1991, specific temperature controls are laid down for a defined range of food products.

Part I

- soft cheeses (whether whole or cut) which have been ripened by the actions of moulds or other micro-organisms;
- cooked products (whether prepared ready for consumption or intended to be subject to reheating or further cooking prior to consumption) comprising or containing: meat, fish, eggs, substances used as a substitute for meat, fish or eggs, cheese, cereals, pulses, or vegetables;
- whether or not the food also includes other raw or partially cooked ingredients;
- smoked or cured fish; smoked or cured meat which has been cut or sliced after smoking or curing;
- desserts, an ingredient of which is milk or anything used as a substitute for milk, and which have a pH value of 4.5 or more;
- prepared vegetable salads, including those containing fruit;
- cooked pies and pasties containing meat, fish or any substitute for meat or fish or vegetables or cheese encased in pastry, except (in each case) those into which nothing has been introduced after cooking and which are intended to be sold on the day of their production or the day after that day;
- cooked sausage rolls, other than those intended to be sold on the day of their production or the day after that date;
- uncooked or partly cooked pastry and dough products containing meat, fish or any substance used as a substitute for meat or fish; sandwiches, filled rolls and other similar bread products containing: meat, fish, eggs, substances used as a substitute for meat, fish or eggs, soft cheese to which the regulation applies, or vegetables;
- cakes containing cream or cream substitute.

Part II

- cheeses which have been cut or otherwise separated from the whole cheese from which they were removed;
- relevant food which is of the description specified in paragraph 1(b) of the regulation ('cooked products') and which has been prepared for consumption without the necessity for further cooking or reheating;
- smoked or cured fish;
- smoked or cured meat which has been cut or sliced after smoking or curing; or
- sandwiches, filled rolls and similar bread products containing any of the foods mentioned in this section, unless they are intended to be sold within 24 h of their preparation.

In the UK, the foodstuffs listed under Part I must be kept at or below 8°C. Those under Part II must be kept at or below 5°C, but with a let-out clause for local delivery vehicles, defined as those not exceeding 7.5 tonnes gross (all up) weight, for which the 8°C temperature limit applies, dependent on a '12 h on board' time limit.

The specified temperature may be exceeded by up to 2°C for no more than 2 h, allowing for preparation, equipment defrosting and equipment repair.

Interestingly, the regulations (which strangely are not in force in Scotland) do not specifically require vehicles to be refrigerated, making allowance for short journeys made by vehicles which are loaded direct through a sealed chilled store doorway with a temperature 'safety margin' operating.

An EC Directive, broadly following the above requirements for the distribution of selected chilled foodstuffs now in force in England and Wales, is proposed.

In the United States, the USDA Food and Safety and Inspection Service is responsible for food safety. Storage temperature depends on product and manufacturer; typical temperatures for a public warehouse are 0 to −5°F; cooler is +28 to +38°F. Trucks must maintain the temperature of the foodstuffs as they come out of the warehouse. (Some manufacturers use paper that changes colour with a change in temperature and some bury thermometers in the shipment to make sure the temperature is maintained. The receiver will check the temperature at delivery.)

The UK Quick-Frozen Foodstuffs Regulations, 1990, lay down, with limited concessions covering short periods of time and local distribution, that quick-frozen foods must be kept at −18°C or below during transportation.

Thus, longer average journey distances and times have, along with new health and hygiene legislation, brought an increased requirement for controlled-temperature transport, boosting demand for refrigerated vehicles and related equipment, with resulting environmental implications.

A further less predictable fillip to those parts of the transport industry concerned with moving foodstuffs arose through the 1980s as the big supermarkets focussed their attention increasingly on fresh produce, i.e. 'fruit and vegetables'. Although it accounts for a relatively small percentage of turnover, it has become symbolic of product freshness and, by association, overall quality of a much wider range of products.

Freshness, both actual and perceived, has therefore become paramount. Shoppers' expectations have been raised accordingly, to the point where the small independent greengrocer, whose produce has traditionally been collected in the early morning from central markets using simple non temperature-controlled vans or covered dropside vehicles, is almost extinct.

Buyers of fresh produce for retailers now commonly deal directly with growers, both in the United Kingdom and further afield. In the case of green vegetables and indigenous fruit, they endeavour to establish a 'cool chain' extending sometimes from the field or orchard all the way to the supermarket shelf.

The move towards refrigerated transport for products traditionally carried at ambient temperature has not only put up initial vehicle cost, but refrigeration equipment adds to unladen weight, thus diminishing payload capacity, so that heavier duty vehicles or bigger fleets are implied for hauling the same tonne-mileage.

Whatever the measures taken to compensate for loss of overall vehicle carrying capacity, brought about through refrigerating hitherto ambient (or 'dry freight') fleets, the environmental impact is significant. There has unavoidably been an increase in exhaust emissions, from vehicle tail-pipes and from the small engines which drive most mechanical fridge units.

Emissions from vehicle engines, almost entirely diesels in a food industry transport context, are subject to progressively stricter legislative control. It is over 20 years since regulations concerned with truck and van diesel tail-pipe emissions first came under legislators' scrutiny.

British Standard BS AU 141a came into force in 1971, but it covered only visible emissions, i.e. the black smoke which in former days characterised the diesel engine as a species. The aim of the legislation was to avoid the unsightly appearance of lorries belching smoke as they ground their way up long hills. There was little thought to deleterious effects on health or on the environment.

It should be pointed out that in the 1970s, a much higher percentage of companies distributing food were the manufacturers themselves or alternatively the retailers, rather than contracted distribution specialists. Vehicle operators were only too conscious of the impression given by their vehicles to actual and would-be customers who noticed them in the street. And of course they and the contractors working for them remain so in the 1990s.

Accordingly, food-carrying vehicles were and are kept clean in the widest sense, including their exhaust emissions. The fact that 20 years ago most trucks were underpowered and needed to spend a high percentage of their running time developing full power, only served to aggravate the smoke problem, both at the time and in the longer term. This, in turn, made it difficult to maintain the conditions needed for clean combustion beyond the first few thousand miles.

By the late 1980s, vehicle emission concerns had grown beyond the mere negative aesthetics of a dirty smoking exhaust. Immediate effects on the health of plants, animals and, of course, humans as well as the longer-term greenhouse effect and global warming implications came within the ambit of the legislators' concerns and enactments.

Visible emissions, now referred to as particulates, comprising mainly solid or liquid carbon or hydrocarbon particles, together with three different categories of gaseous (invisible but polluting) emissions, are now subject to limiting European Community legislation, under Directives 88/77/EEC and 91/542/EEC.

Table 7.3 Limits for 1993 and later model year diesel heavy-duty engines

	g/brake horsepower-h	g/MJ
Hydrocarbons (petroleum diesel) and organic material hydrocarbons (methanol diesel)	1.3	0.48
Carbon monoxide	15.5	5.77
NO$_x$	50.0	1.9
Particulate	0.10	0.037

Controls on gaseous diesel exhaust emissions, oxides of nitrogen (NO$_x$), carbon monoxide (CO) and hydrocarbons (HC), were introduced in 1990. In 1992–1993 (in two stages) tighter gaseous emission limits, and for the first time a particulates limit, were applied, in so-called 'Euro 1' legislation. A further reduction in permitted levels of exhaust gas and particulate pollutants comes into force, again in two stages for 'Euro 2' legislation during 1995–1996.

In the United States, vehicle emissions are also subject to ever tightening control. Code of Federal Regulations (CFR) 85 deals with limits for engines. Limits on NO$_x$ have been cut by half since 1985; particulates have been cut from 0.6 g/brake horsepower hour to 0.1 since 1988 (Table 7.3).

All new trucks being put into service on the public road are now subject to emission controls. Those serving the food industry are affected no more nor less than any other vehicles in this respect.

There is in any case a measure of environmental controversy surrounding the emission requirements. The permitted NO$_x$ and particulate levels in particular come into conflict with each other in the sense that it is technically difficult to satisfy both without compromising fuel economy. While engine researchers are striving to reduce it to a minimum, some fuel penalty seems inevitable on the truck diesels of the late 1990s. If more fuel is burned then more carbon dioxide (CO$_2$) is released, making a possibly unwelcome contribution to global warming; CO$_2$ has not yet been added to the list of proscribed diesel exhaust pollutants.

On a refrigerated truck distributing food, a second albeit smaller diesel engine is likely to be found driving the compressor of the refrigeration equipment. As the law stands at present, that auxiliary power unit can emit unlimited noxious fumes into the atmosphere. It escapes completely the legislation controlling emissions from the vehicle's propulsive engine.

Because refrigeration unit engines are small, their output of pollutant gases and particulates is correspondingly limited. But EC discussions on the control of emissions from engines other than those powering vehicles on the public highway are proceeding, with off-road construction equipment, generator sets and large items of engine-driven industrial plant the main areas of attention. A tentative target date of the year 2000 for implementation of such regulations has been suggested.

It is probable that small 'donkey' engines of the kind employed in vehicle refrigeration units will be brought into the same category for emissions legislation purposes. Whether permitted pollutant levels will be related, as they are on vehicle diesels, to engine output (in horsepower or kilowatts) remains to be seen.

The cost in basic engine research and development, in other words in new technology, of reducing pollutant levels from small, relatively cheap, industrial diesels of the kind used to drive mechanical refrigeration units, will be disproportionately large. It might even be unacceptable, implying a need for exhaust after-treatment kits that can in particular filter out the particulates, although Thermo King claims to meet 'Euro 2' engine exhaust standards already.

A likely alternative development will be for mechanical fridge unit producers to switch to a different kind of engine, able to run on a more environmentally friendly fuel. Liquefied petroleum gas (LPG) was at one time considered the alternative fuel for auxiliary engines, as the many LPG-powered fork-lift trucks in warehouses and transport depots bear testimony.

However, attention is now turning to natural gas, of the kind piped into most households for heating and cooking, as an engine fuel. It is inherently cheaper to produce than LPG, needing no refinery processing, with all that implies by way of additional energy input. As such, in the context of the global energy equation, it is less wasteful of fossil fuel resources, and so more environmentally acceptable.

When natural gas is burned in an engine's combustion chamber, it produces far lower levels of proscribed pollutants. For practical storage and handling reasons, natural gas (chemical formula CH_4) has, for on-board use (powering the vehicles itself or a piece of auxiliary equipment such as an engine-driven fridge unit), to be at a considerably higher pressure than in one's domestic mains supply.

It can be 'fully' compressed to a liquid state, in which form it is commonly referred to as LNG. Because storage pressure is high, the volume occupied for a given usable quantity of fuel, and hence the tank capacity needed, is small. But those tanks have to be correspondingly heavy and expensive to withstand the pressure, with sophisticated and costly valve arrangements.

Natural gas in less 'concentrated' form, i.e. at about one-third the pressure and still in a gaseous state (known as CNG), is the increasingly favoured alternative to diesel fuel in environmentally sensitive applications. CNG-fuelled auxiliary engines for on-board vehicle refrigeration equipment are a distinct possibility in the medium- to long-term.

Unfortunately, for a given quantity of stored energy which can be equated to fridge unit engine running time, CNT tanks occupy something like 3.7 times the cubic space needed for diesel fuel. However, on most refrigerated vehicles, especially the heavier articulated outfits, there is ample space below floor level.

A high proportion of mechanical refrigeration units on temperature-controlled vehicles now incorporate an overnight mains electric stand-by drive. It is now established transport industry practice for trucks to be preloaded, with say Thursday's consignments, soon after their return back to base late on Wednesday afternoon, in readiness for an early departure.

Clearly the emissions and noise created by the auxiliary fridge unit engines, on perhaps 20 or 30 reefer vehicles lined up in a depot yard, running all night are unacceptable, not least to local residents. Plugging into the mains allows the fridge unit compressor to be switched from engine to mains electric drive. Noise is thereby reduced considerably and pollutant exhaust emissions from the auxiliary engines are avoided altogether. Environmentalists will point out that the mains electricity has to be generated in a coal-, oil- or gas-fired power station, which itself pushes noxious gases and particulates into the atmosphere.

The electric versus engine power environmental argument in any case hinges on economic issues and the economics are blurred by the differential taxes levied (or not) on various liquid, gaseous and solid fuels and by variations in electricity costs (a) for large versus small industrial consumers and (b) at night when overall demand for electrical power is low.

Mechanically driven vehicle refrigeration equipment and its accompanying auxiliary engine emissions, along with the environmentally damaging refrigerants described in the first part of this chapter, can be avoided altogether using fundamentally different forms of refrigeration, although again the global energy versus emissions balance sheet must not be ignored.

Cheap night-time electricity can be used to power passive (and silent) eutectic vehicle refrigeration systems, whose function can be likened to a domestic night storage heater in reverse.

A conventional refrigeration process is applied using the same kind of on-board compressor, evaporator and fluid refrigerants as those in a so-called mechanical system. But instead of the evaporator cooling a flow of air, being simultaneously blown into the loadspace, it cools a eutectic (low melting point) brine mixture contained in hollow, beams (or plates) mounted inside the vehicle body. Before the vehicle leaves the depot in the morning, the system is unplugged. 'Cold' is then progressively released from the beams into (or, as the technically pedantic would put it, heat is progressively extracted from) the loadspace.

The principle of gradual heat extraction means that eutectic systems can be seen as natural successors to the solid carbon dioxide and even ice-blocks placed directly in the loadspace of, respectively, ice-cream and fish-carrying vehicles in years gone by.

On the debit side, eutectic plate systems are heavy and they lack the operational flexibility needed to cope on large vehicles with prolonged door openings in warm ambient conditions.

Eutectic plates, although capable of holding a set box temperature for many hours, cannot achieve the rapid 'pull down' in temperature required, for health and hygiene reasons, once the doors have been closed before the vehicle gets on its way to the next drop.

Fast pull-down is an attribute of the other alternative to mechanical refrigeration, that is direct liquid nitrogen cooling, exemplified by BOC's Polarstream system. The liquefied gas is carried on board, under pressure, and released in a fine spray which immediately evaporates, a process that requires heat, that heat being extracted from the surrounding air in the vehicle loadspace. Cooling of the air is rapid, thereby arresting further heat gain into the product, which, by definition, has of course been pre-cooled in a cold/chill store.

Nitrogen is an inert harmless gas; it makes up about 80% of the air we breathe. For BOC and competitors like Air Products it is effectively a by-product of the production of oxygen. The energy input and consequent environmental cost involved in its manufacture is therefore difficult to quantify objectively.

Liquid nitrogen has obvious practical limitations. Where a vehicle is making multi-drops, so that there are frequent door openings, the system can run out of nitrogen; the on-board pressure tanks, like the CNG fuel tanks referred to earlier, take up significant space. The number of liquid nitrogen replenishment points around the country, enabling a vehicle to recharge its refrigeration system away from base, is undeniably limited.

For many refrigerated vehicle operators, away from their base depots for days or even weeks at a time, there is currently no viable alternative to mechanically driven compressor-evaporator refrigeration. Although the compressor might be driven by an auxiliary engine or by a land-based overnight electric stand-by motor, the process of refrigeration is the same.

A suitable substance, i.e. a refrigerant, is needed to circulate through the system. The chlorofluorocarbons (CFCs) used for many years are, because of their chlorine content, now universally acknowledged to be damaging to the earth's ozone layer. They also contribute to the global warming phenomenon.

A total ban on CFCs by members of the Montreal Protocol is scheduled for January 1995. This includes the EC and United States. They have already been replaced in most refrigeration equipment (static and vehicle-mounted) by a family of hydrochlorofluorocarbons (HCFCs) which, in simple terms, have some of their damaging chlorine replaced by hydrogen.

The range of HCFCs now available to equipment producers are much more environmentally acceptable than CFCs, although in absolute terms they vary considerably in their ozone depletion and global warming potential. They are also more expensive, by a factor of between 2 and 5.

Rival refrigeration equipment makers have in the last 3 years or so striven to 'brand' the new generation of refrigerants with what amounts to proprietary (rather than generic) designations, such as R22 and R69L. Claims of superior environmental characteristics are made for each new contender, under the influence of what the manufacturers see (although they might deny it) as a marketing (i.e. profit) opportunity, with all that implies in product cost.

Undoubtedly the new HCFCs are more expensive to produce than CFCs, but many environmentalists and food industry observers would like to see more collaboration between erstwhile refrigeration equipment and chemical company competitors, in developing an industry standard for refrigerants. Such a move would help contain the cost penalties now anticipated, while at the same time contributing to the 'greater good' of the environment.

Such considerations can be extrapolated into the next generation of refrigerants now being developed, the chlorine-free hydrofluorocarbons (HFCs), whose ozone depletion potential is nil, although their possible effect on global warming remains a concern.

In a transport and distribution context, the harmful effects of the older (and, in most cases cheaper) refrigerants on the earth's ozone layer are given an extra edge by the sort of operational hazards which could lead to an escape of the offending gas into the atmosphere.

Leaks, most obviously from pipe joints, are inevitably a greater risk on a vehicle than in a cold/chill store fridge installation. There are vibrations to contend with, not just from the vehicle and/or the fridge unit engine, but from all but the smoothest road surface. Repairs and maintenance also have to be carried out under less controlled conditions; sometimes away from home, possibly in a non-specialist contractor's workshop.

There is also the often unspoken, but real, danger of the refrigeration equipment suffering physical damage in an accident. A front bulkhead (or trailer front wall) mounted unit is in a vulnerable position in the event of a frontal impact. On those 'multiple box' installations, where the compressor and evaporator are several metres apart, the connecting refrigerant pipe-runs are often even more exposed to accident damage.

It should be remembered that the recent dramatic growth in vehicle refrigeration in the late 1980s has centred on chilled distribution, largely motivated by the need for retailers to project that 'image of freshness'. Volumes of frozen product (meat, fish and packaged vegetables) moved by road have grown less markedly.

Nevertheless, almost without exception, vehicles are specified for deep frozen food carrying. They have thicker insulation and higher capacity (in heat extraction terms) refrigeration equipment than is needed for chilled (down to 0°C) operation only. The reasons are economic.

Refrigerated vehicle buyers, in assessing total (i.e. whole life) vehicle running costs, are all too aware of residual values. With a frozen food carrying capability, preferably verified by the international ATP (Accord Transport Périssables) class C certification, a vehicle's secondhand value is greatly enhanced. Used reefers are invariably bought by small entrepreneurial carriers who need to be able to carry every category of perishable foodstuff, chilled, deep frozen and ambient.

The need to build in 'second owner appeal', which often prompts the choice of other truck features such as sleeper cabs, translates into a mandatory deep-frozen capability, which can only be readily achieved using the modern ozone-depleting refrigerants or their new more environment friendly, and much more expensive, substitutes.

If new vehicle refrigeration equipment could be specified for its specific purpose, then all those vehicles put on the road to distribute dairy products, fruit and vegetables and other chilled cabinet merchandise, could be equipped at much lower cost, while also incurring less payload penalty, with more conservatively rated refrigeration units containing less refrigerant.

In reality, many food carriers feel obliged to specify refrigeration equipment and bodywork which will give them the operational flexibility to carry either chilled or frozen produce, or even both, in a multi-compartment loadspace. This applies especially to the third-party transport sector, embracing food hauliers and contract distributors.

Ozone-depleting CFCs and HCFCs have traditionally been employed for a quite different purpose related to refrigeration, namely in the manufacture of foam slab or *in-situ* foamed insulation, principally polyurethane.

Alternative, more environmentally acceptable, foaming agents are readily available. Indeed water-blow urethanes are now in production, but their insulation properties per centimetre of material thickness are poorer. So too are those of older foam materials like expanded polystyrene and foamed PVC.

Expanded PVC has been favoured for some time where the insulation material is required to contribute significantly to the structural strength of the body shell. This applies especially in the case of a chassis-less refrigerated semi-trailer.

Compensation has to be made for inferior insulation properties in a cellular material employed in a vehicle body structure. The most obvious ploy is to increase thickness. In a cold store, an additional 10 mm of wall thickness is easily accommodated. On a vehicle, space is at much more of a premium.

Legal limits are set on vehicle dimensions, most pertinently on width.

For many years until the mid-1980s, a 2.5-m width limit applied through most of Europe. It meant that two metric (1200×1000 mm^2) pallets could be accommodated alongside each other, with their long sides across the vehicle, only by making the walls far thinner than a refrigeration engineer would recommend. In the United States, the width limit is 2.6 m (CFR 658).

Excessive heat gain through the sides of the body was compensated by increases in insulation thickness elsewhere, notably in the floor. However, this was not a thermally ideal solution, because the heat path through those thin side walls close to floor level led to 'hot spots' in the loadspaces. This was made worse when loads were jammed tight against the walls of the body/trailer, restricting the circulation of cold air from the fridge unit evaporator.

Compliance with ATP class C standards was, in many instances, marginal, although use wherever possible of the most efficient CFC-blown insulation material minimised these thermal performance shortcomings. Vigorous lobbying in Brussels and at national level by the Transfrigouroute reefer operators' organisation won a notable regulatory concession from the transport legislators. The permitted width of trucks carrying loads at controlled temperatures was increased, in stages, to the current 2.6 m limit. That extra 100 mm has seen the effective demise of the early 1980s 'thin wall' reefers, which were unloved for a variety of reasons, not least their questionable structural integrity.

Continuing research is needed to develop new foaming agents if we are to avoid a re-run, a decade on, of the thin-wall saga, with wall thicknesses having to be increased again, prompting refrigerated vehicle operators and manufacturers to agitate for another vehicle width concession.

In 1991, Exel Logistics set out a clear environmental policy in the United Kingdom, setting standards, monitoring performance and constantly searching for improvement.

Vehicles and vehicle equipment are identified as critical areas of concern in Exel Logistics' environmental policy declaration. Energy saving in terms of improved fuel consumption is a key element. A 15% fuel saving target over a 5-year period was set as part of the policy. To date a 5% saving has been recorded, and we are set to achieve 15% by 1996.

Exel Logistics drivers are now trained in driving for economy. They are shown that judicious use of the accelerator pedal and brake, along with good driving anticipation, can bring fuel savings without extending journey times.

After pioneering UK trials in 1988 on an extensively streamlined vehicle, which showed long-haul fuel savings of up to 20%, air management equipment is now widely fitted on Exel Logistics trucks.

Wind drag has been cut, particularly on those vehicles employed extensively on motorway running, where the fuel-saving benefits of improved aerodynamics are greatest. Exel Logistics also began a programme of fitting speed-limiters long before they became mandatory on new vehicles in August 1992.

There are also economic benefits to be obtained from fuel reduction of 20%, which we sum up under the heading 'saving more than the environment'.

As already acknowledged in this chapter, improving fuel consumption brings a directly proportional reduction in carbon dioxide exhaust emissions. Like CO_2, sulphur dioxide (SO_2) is a recognised pollutant yet to be proscribed by the legislators. Exel Logistics has nevertheless taken steps towards the cutting of exhaust SO_2, through a trial of a new experimental low sulphur fuel from the Swedish supplier Greenergy. A fleet of 25 Exel vehicles operated on behalf of Boots, the High Street chemist, were operated for 8 weeks on the new 'cleaner' fuel. Detailed findings from the trial were not available at the time of going to press, although subjective reactions from drivers and from Exel Logistics and Boots personnel were positive. The low sulphur content helps reduce particulates as well as SO_2.

Exel Logistics has instilled in its workforce of 16 300 employees a culture of concern for the environment which pervades all its operations. Although transport is the most environmentally damaging of its activities, reduction of waste in warehousing, general energy saving and recycling of materials wherever possible are now practised throughout the business.

Only by integrating transport policy into a broader environmental commitment can today's food distribution specialist make a true contribution to saving the environment.

8 Packaging options
S.E. SELKE

8.1 Introduction

The goal of this chapter is to examine packaging options, especially for food products, in light of their environmental impact, along with looking at current and projected changes in packaging, and the effects these may have on our environment. Although the entire life cycle of packages, from acquisition of raw materials through eventual disposal of the package, must be examined for a complete evaluation of environmental impact, in this chapter we do not discuss the impacts associated with disposal, since they are covered in a later chapter. Thus, we examine environmental impact due to the acquisition of raw materials, processing those raw materials into packaging materials and then to packages, and distributing the packages (filled or unfilled) to their users.

First, however, there are some necessary preliminaries. Packages exist because they perform certain necessary functions. An understanding of these functions is necessary in order to determine what packaging changes can or cannot be successfully adopted. In addition, it is necessary to have some basic background about packaging materials in order to evaluate the environmental impact of those materials.

8.2 Functions of packaging

Before evaluating the environmental impact of various packaging options, it is desirable to examine our reasons for using packages in the first place. After all, the package with the least environmental impact of all is the package that does not exist.

Lists of the functions served by packages of various types can be very long. For simplicity, it is possible to classify these reasons into three major categories: protection, communication and utility.

8.2.1 Protection

The protection function of packaging includes all those package attributes which act to protect the product from harm or damage from the environment surrounding it, as well as those attributes which act to protect the environment from harm or damage from the product contained in the package.

A basic protection function is containment itself. This allows the product to be moved from one place to another as a unit, and is obviously absolutely essential for products which are liquids, gases, or fine particles. It is hard to imagine how we might be able to have milk and corn flakes for breakfast, for instance, without both the milk and the cereal being contained in some type of package so we can get them from the cow and the cereal factory to our breakfast table.

For most products, some additional degree of protection beyond simple containment is also required. In our milk and corn flakes example, we wish to protect both foods from exposure to dust and dirt. We further wish to protect the milk from microorganisms, light, excessive heat, etc. We want to protect the cornflakes from exposure to moisture which will make them lose their crunch. This additional protection may be provided by the package itself, or it may be provided by modifications of the environment which the product and package inhabit, such as refrigeration. For example, we could prevent moisture gain by our cornflakes by maintaining the cereal in a dry atmosphere at all times, but we are more likely to utilize containment in a package that provides a barrier to the passage of water vapor. On the other hand, we are likely to utilize refrigeration to retard the spoilage of the milk, although we may alternatively use aseptic packaging techniques.

Protection from exposure to microorganisms and protection against excessive water gain are two common protective functions of packaging. Others include (but are certainly not limited to) protection against exposure to oxygen, shocks, vibrations, electrostatic discharges, ultraviolet light; as well as protection against loss of carbon dioxide, flavor compounds, organic vapors, etc.

If our product is toxic or hazardous in some other way, we are likely to use the package to provide some degree of protection against exposure to the product. For example, child resistant packaging is designed to protect small children from harm resulting from exposure to various types of products, including medications and toxic household products. The stringent regulations governing shipment of hazardous materials include restrictions relating to the packaging of these goods in ways that will minimize exposure of people and other aspects of the environment to these hazardous products, both during normal distribution and in the event of accidents.

An additional aspect of protection is those package components that are designed to deter tampering and/or to alert the potential user that product tampering may have occurred.

Protection, including containment, can be regarded as the most basic function of packaging.

8.2.2   Communication

Another set of package functions have communication to the potential user as their primary purpose. Many packages perform a wide variety of communication functions. The most basic communication function is to answer the question 'What is the product?' Often the identity of the product is conveyed through written words on the package. Other times it may be conveyed simply by transparency of the package so that the product itself can be seen and identified.

A variety of messages are legally required to be conveyed for many products, including such things as how much of the product is in the package, who is the product manufacturer, etc. Such legally required messages are often specified down to the minimum size print that may be used, and the place they must appear on the package. Other package communications are included because the seller wishes to convey certain messages to the potential consumer. These may include, for example, opening instructions for a blister package, or recipes and appetizing pictures on a box of spaghetti.

A significant communication goal for many packages is to convince the potential purchaser to pick that particular brand of product over the competitors on the shelf in the store. In addition to the package itself and its messages, the space the product occupies on the shelf also has communication value. It simply is easier for the consumer to see and be attracted to a product if it occupies more visible space.

As illustrated by some of the examples above, the communication aspects of the package are not necessarily printed words. Pictures, colors, shape and even package transparency can all be used to communicate to potential users. This is one reason why manufacturers of consumer goods are often reluctant to make major changes in package design; they risk losing the brand identity which is a major factor in their sales. Therefore, when significant changes are desired, they may be phased in gradually to facilitate their customers' ability to continue to easily recognize the product.

8.2.3   Utility

The utility features of the package are those that provide some degree of usefulness to people or entities handling or using the product or package. These can be as varied as a dispensing closure on a bottle of hand lotion, or a circle cut out of the backing of a blister package (a package that confines the product between a plastic bubble and a paperboard backing), to permit hanging the product on a display. In the first case, the utility is provided to the user of the product. In the second case, the utility is provided to the retailer. For some products, such as many aerosols, the utility provided by the package is essential to the proper functioning of the product. In other cases, the utility simply provides added convenience of use or handling.

8.2.4   Combination of functions

It should be recognized that package features do not always fit nicely into one of the three categories discussed above. Many package features perform more than one function. For example, a bar code on a product has both communication and utility functions. The oversize backing card on a tiny watch battery provides both communication and protection (in this case, primarily protection against shoplifting).

8.3   Package selection

There are almost an infinite number of combinations of package materials and package designs that could be considered for packaging a product. Most of these choices, for any given product, are impractical for one reason or another. Many will not do an adequate job of performing the functions that are necessary or desirable for the product. Others will be eliminated on cost grounds. The overall goal of package design is generally the selection of the package that will offer the greatest economic benefit to the producer of the product.

Thus, the package designer is trying to select an optimum package, balancing the cost of the package against the benefits (functions) the package will provide. A general rule is that the more the package does, the more it will cost.

In the area of protection, this can often be measured in a straightforward way. The more protection provided by the package, the more material is used, the more the package costs. On the other hand, the less the package does, the more the product is likely to be damaged. An economic relationship can be calculated, showing overall package and product system costs to be high at very high package cost, and also high at very low package costs due to high damage rates. The overall system cost will be lowest at some intermediate package costs where product protection is sufficient, and package costs are not excessive. The value of the product is a very significant variable in determining how much damage can be tolerated.

In the areas of communication and utility, determination of the optimum package is usually more complex. Here, the determining variables are often relationships between the packaged product and the product user's purchasing decisions. These decisions tend to be highly variable from one consumer or group of consumers to another, and can be extremely difficult to determine with any degree of certainty. Test marketing becomes extremely important, and a high degree of product failure in the marketplace is common.

It is impossible to cover, in the course of a single chapter, all the myriads of package designs that are available, or even the considerably smaller, but still large, number that are commonplace. Fortunately, the environmental impact of package alternatives is determined more by the basic package material or materials, than by the package type or style. Thus, our discussion is organized around the five basic package materials: wood, paper, metal, glass and plastics.

8.4   Wood

Wood in packaging is used primarily in pallets, with additional uses in crates, boxes, etc. Wood is a renewable resource, although utilizing it can lead to decrease in soil fertility, erosion, loss of habitat for wildlife, and other environmental impacts. Using wood also requires energy, for both harvesting and processing the wood.

The environmental impact of using wood packaging is, in large part, a subset of the environmental impact of using paper packaging. References to the impact of paper packaging are considerably more available in the literature than are references dealing with the impact of wood itself.

Boustead and Hancock (1981) provide an analysis of the energy required to produce a typical pallet, weighing 25.40 kg and containing 17.91 kg of softwood, 6.33 kg of hardwood and 1.16 kg of steel nails and wire. Total energy required was 1106.7 MJ (megajoules), and includes the feedstock energy for the wood. This total energy is broken down into 150.48 MJ for production of 18.81 kg of softwood, 3.19 MJ for sea transport of the softwood, and 6.25 MJ for road transport of the softwood. Production of 6.65 kg of hardwood consumes 53.20 MJ. Boustead and Hancock found published values for production of raw wood from standing timber ranging from 3.33 MJ/kg to 12.59 MJ/kg, and chose 8 MJ/kg as a representative average. The wood feedstock energy is 437.91 MJ, based on a 12% moisture content. Sawing and makeup of the pallet consume 418.96 MJ; 36.18 MJ are used for production of the steel products; and 0.52 MJ for their delivery. The difference between the wood weights required for production and the weight in the product represents an average of 5% waste. All energy values were based on the typical situation in the United Kingdom at the time of the analysis.

8.5   Paper and paperboard

Paper and paperboard are widely used in packaging, in forms ranging from corrugated boxes to glassine margarine wraps. In fact, it is estimated that about half of all packaging is paper and paperboard. The environmental impact associated with paper packaging includes impact due to harvesting and distribution of wood, pulping processes, paper and paperboard manufacture, converting operations, filling and sealing, and distribution.

8.5.1   Raw materials

The raw materials used to make paper and paperboard packaging are generally softwoods, although hardwoods are used in making corrugated medium (the fluted inner layer in corrugated board). As mentioned above, wood is, in principle, a renewable resource. Recycled paper is also an important fiber source.

8.5.2   Energy

Energy requirements for making paper and paperboard packaging are a function of transportation distances for raw materials, pulping processes used, papermaking machinery employed, thickness, and other variables. Energy required for conversion of the paper material into the finished product likewise varies depending on the package type being produced, etc. Calculations of energy requirements generally include the energy value of the wood raw material, as well as energy used during manufacture. As a rule, the energy associated with production of the packaging material is much greater than that associated with its conversion to packages.

One of the early reports of comparative energy requirements for packaging systems was published by the Midwest Research Institute in 1974 (Hunt and Welch, 1974). They reported energy requirements of 7.6 MJ (7515 Btu) for production of a paper gallon milk container, 0.65 MJ (612 Btu) for production of a paper gallon size produce bag, 0.34 MJ (324 Btu) for production of a 9-oz paper vending cup, and 0.89 MJ (847 Btu) for production of a pulp meat tray.

Gaines (1981) listed production energy requirements for various grades of packaging paper ranging from 58.8 MJ/kg (25 300 Btu/lb) for natural linerboard to 77.6 MJ/kg for bleached board (33 400 Btu/lb). Use of recycled fiber yielded energy savings of about 46.4 MJ/kg (20 000 Btu/lb). Corrugating medium, with a recycled content of 30%, had a production energy cost of 37.3 MJ/kg (16 050 Btu/lb). This energy requirement included the combustion energy of the raw material itself. Gaines further estimated that about 75% of the energy input is provided by wood and wood by-products, with the remainder being purchased energy. About 30% of the purchased energy was electricity, and most of the rest was oil and natural gas.

Bousted and Hancock (1981) found reported energy requirements for pulp production ranging from 29 to 31 MJ/kg. They chose 28.59 MJ/kg as a representative average, and selected 2% fiber loss as representative. Based on these values, they calculated that the production of 1 kg base paper from standing timber required 83.91 MJ, production of 1 kg of coated paper from standing timber required 99.95 MJ, and production of 1 kg of paperboard from standing timber required 102.85 MJ of energy. The energy requirement for producing paper sacks from paper was found to be insignificant compared to the energy required for producing the sacks themselves.

Fenton (1991) reported published values for energy requirements for Kraft paper bags ranging from 47.83 to 61.87 MJ/kg. Van Eijk *et al.* (1992) reported an energy requirement of 50.5 MJ/kg for production of PE-coated Kraft paperboard for the manufacture of cups (in the Netherlands).

More recently, the Tellus Institute (1992) reported energy requirements of 55.3 MJ/kg (47.57 MM Btu/ton) for corrugating medium to 89.8 MJ/kg (77.29 MM Btu/ton) for bleached kraft paperboard. These values also included the energy value of the incorporated wood. For recycled grades, energy requirements ranged from 40.1 MJ/kg (34.48 MM Btu/ton) for unbleached coated boxboard to 41.2 MJ/kg (35.46 MM Btu/ton) for recycled linerboard. The study includes analysis of energy requirements for each step of the production process.

Franklin Associates (1990) reported life cycle energy requirements for 9-in paperboard plates (1.04 MJ (984 Btu)), 4-in paperboard hinged containers (0.97 MJ (922 Btu)), and 16-oz wax and LDPE-coated paperboard cups (0.93 MJ and 0.76 MJ (878 and 718 Btu)). Of the total energy required, 95–96% was for the containers themselves, with 3.6–4.7% consumed by secondary packaging and then disposal energy was insignificant.

8.5.3   Other environmental impacts

Many studies, especially earlier ones, comparing environmental effects of various packaging materials, sum emissions across a category and simply report tonnage of air emissions and tonnage of water emissions. They then use these values to compare materials. This methodology cannot be justified, since there are major differences between pollutants of various chemical types in toxicity and other environmental impacts which are obscured by aggregation of data. Therefore such aggregated values are not reported here.

Effluents emitted during the manufacture of paper and paperboard packaging arise mostly during the paper manufacturing stage. The types and amounts of effluents emitted are highly process-specific, depending heavily on the particular pulping process employed, along with other process variables.

The Tellus Institute study (1992) provides a detailed description of the various stages of papermaking and the effluents associated with each.

Harvesting and transportation of the wood raw material can result in soil erosion if logging roads are improperly constructed, and in emission of particulates into the atmosphere if harvesting residues are burned. Washing of logs before debarking, a common operation, is estimated to result in 0.5–4.0 g of biological oxygen demand (BOD) per kg of wood (1–8 lb/ton), and in 2.5–27 g of total suspended solids (TSS) per kg of wood (5–55 lb/ton). The suspended solids are primarily silt. Debarking contributes 7.5–10 g of BOD and 25–50 g of TSS per kg of wood debarked (15–20 lb/ton BOD, 50–100 lb/ton TSS) if wet drum debarking is used. Hydraulic debarking results in lower emissions, 0.5–5.0 g BOD and 3.0–27.5 g TSS per kg (1–10 lb/ton BOD, 6–55 lb/ton TSS) (Tellus Institute, 1992).

Kraft pulping utilizes sodium hydroxide and sodium sulfide (added as sodium sulfate) as pulping chemicals. It is the most widely used pulping process for packaging paper and paperboard. The Tellus Institute study (1992) estimates that a third to a half of the BOD and TSS from a kraft mill arise from spills and wash-ups related to equipment breakdown, routine maintenance, power failures, shutdowns and start-up, and product grade changes. Air emissions include highly objectionable odors caused by emission of reduced sulfur compounds. The primary sulfur emissions are hydrogen sulfide, methyl mercaptan, dimethyl sulfide and dimethyl disulfide. Recovery of pulping chemicals is routinely practised, and in part involves combustion of the 'black liquor' effluent from the pulping digester, after it has been concentrated. The black liquor contains a substantial amount of organic matter, and its combustion provides process heat, as well as aiding in the conversion of the pulping chemicals back to desired forms (Tellus Institute, 1992).

The other major pulping process used for packaging paper is neutral sulfite semi-chemical (NSSC) pulping, which is the major process used in making corrugating medium. These plants emit particulates of sodium sulfate and sodium carbonate if spent liquor recovery systems are not used. They typically operate with a high degree of water recycling, so the effluent flow is low, but the BOD load in the effluent is high.

Controlled air emissions for kraft and NSSC pulping processes are summarized in Table 8.1. Water emissions from paper manufacturing processes are listed in Table 8.2.

When white paper or paperboard is desired, the pulp must be bleached to remove the brown color which naturally results from both kraft and NSSC pulping. Bleaching operations typically employ chlorine, chlorine dioxide and caustic. Energy use and emissions associated with these

Table 8.1 Controlled and uncontrolled air emissions from pulping processes (g/bone dry kg unbleached pulp)[a]

Emission type	Kraft (uncontrolled)	Kraft (controlled)	NSSC (uncontrolled)
TSP[b]	151.8	11.5	78.9
SO_x	2.89	2.36	11.6
NO_x	3.06	8.93×10^{-5}	0.95
VOC[c]	1.39	3.61×10^{-7}	0.157
CO	6.19	6.14	2.49×10^{-2}
Lead	1.06×10^{-5}	2.38×10^{-8}	2.51×10^{-4}
Methane	8.54×10^{-5}	1.93×10^{-7}	1.60×10^{-3}
Hydrogen sulfide	4.45	1.24	
Reduced sulfur compounds	3.44	0.61	
Sodium hydroxide	2.22	1.39×10^{-2}	

[a]Data derived from Tellus Institute (1992); controlled emissions for NSSC not available.
[b]Total suspended particulates.
[c]Volatile organic compounds.

Table 8.2 Controlled water emissions from production of kraft linerboard, corrugating medium and kraft paper (g/kg paper)[a]

Emission type	Liner	Medium	Paper
BOD5[b]	1.77	2.53	1.96
Suspended solids	2.32	4.09	3.83
Abietic acid	4.72×10^{-4}	1.05×10^{-3}	1.48×10^{-2}
Dehydroabietic acid	5.19×10^{-4}	3.77×10^{-4}	7.64×10^{-3}
Isopimaric acid	2.83×10^{-4}	1.88×10^{-4}	1.34×10^{-3}
Pimaric acid	4.72×10^{-5}	1.07×10^{-4}	2.87×10^{-3}
Oleic acid	1.79×10^{-3}	8.89×10^{-4}	3.41×10^{-3}
Linoleic acid	0.00	3.77×10^{-4}	0.00
Linolenic acid		9.44×10^{-4}	
Chlorodehydroabietic acid		6.46×10^{-4}	
Xylenes	0.00	5.39×10^{-5}	0.00
Benzene		5.39×10^{-5}	
Chloroform	0.00	0.00	0.00
Ethylbenzene		2.69×10^{-5}	
Methylene chloride	0.00	1.34×10^{-4}	3.59×10^{-4}
Naphthalene		0.00	
Isophorene	0.00		
Pentachlorophenol		2.69×10^{-5}	
Phenol	1.42×10^{-4}	3.77×10^{-4}	0.00
Bis(2-ethylhexyl) phthalate	1.42×10^{-4}	4.04×10^{-4}	8.94×10^{-5}
Butyl benzyl phthalate		0.00	
Di-n-butyl phthalate	4.72×10^{-5}	0.00	0.00
Toluene	0.00	5.39×10^{-5}	0.00
Trichloroethylene		0.00	
Chromium	3.31×10^{-4}	5.09×10^{-4}	1.07×10^{-3}
Copper	2.36×10^{-4}	6.74×10^{-4}	8.09×10^{-4}
Lead	2.36×10^{-4}	1.34×10^{-4}	1.43×10^{-3}
Mercury	1.18×10^{-6}	6.74×10^{-7}	2.24×10^{-6}
Nickel	2.36×10^{-4}	2.69×10^{-4}	4.48×10^{-4}
Zinc	3.16×10^{-3}	1.86×10^{-3}	7.24×10^{-3}

[a]Data derived from Tellus Institute (1992).
[b]Five-day biochemical oxygen demand.

processes are also reported in the Tellus Institute study (1992), and include chlorine gas, chlorine dioxide gas, chloroform, and sometimes sulfur dioxide. Bleach plants are reported to be the largest source of water pollution in a bleached board mill, contributing up to 40% of the BOD, 25% of the suspended solids, 70% of the color, and virtually all of the chlorinated organics in the waste stream. Bleaching chemicals are generally not recovered. It should be noted, however, that significant changes in bleaching operations are underway. These often involve changing from chlorine bleaching to bleaching with peroxides, and are resulting primarily from the need to reduce emissions of tetrachlorodibenzo-*p*-dioxins and tetrachlorodibenzofurans associated with chlorine bleaching. Therefore, some of the reported emissions are likely to soon be out of date.

After pulping, the fibers are subjected to a mechanical treatment known as refining before being made into paper. Various additives can be employed to impart desired properties to the paper or paperboard, and different types of pulp may be blended together. Common additives include sizing agents such as rosin and alum combinations, fillers such as clay, calcium carbonate, or titanium dioxide, and starch or synthetic polymers to enhance strength or performance. The actual formation of paper or paperboard from pulp generally employs either a fourdrinier machine or a cylinder machine. The pulp is used in a dilute form, generally only about 0.5% fiber and filler, with the rest being water. The 'whitewater' which leaves the machine contains substantial amounts of fiber, and is commonly reused. Slimicides, biocides, and defoamers are sometimes added to the water to inhibit growth of biological organisms in the water, and to reduce foaming. Much of the energy used in papermaking is expended to dry the paper from its typical 65% water content on leaving the press, to its final water content of about 6%. Air emissions during this process are insignificant compared to those during pulping. However, water emissions of many types result, as summarized in Table 8.2 (Tellus Institute, 1992).

Paper or paperboard for packaging use may be coated with a variety of materials. Environmental effects are determined by the particular coating and coating application techniques used. Typical effluents from production of polyethylene coated bleached kraft paper for paper cups are presented in Table 8.3 (van Eijk *et al.*, 1992). Franklin Associates (1990) also present data for atmospheric and waterborne emissions for hinged paperboard containers, paper plates, and wax-coated and PE-coated paper cups.

Solid waste resulting from papermaking is primarily residues from air pollution control devices and sludge from wastewater treatment (Tellus Institute, 1992).

Instead of utilizing virgin fiber, paper and paperboard can be made in whole or in part from recycled fibers. These materials must be repulped and cleaned before use, and depending on the application, may also need

Table 8.3 Effluents from production of LDPE coated bleached kraft paper for production of 1 kg cups (g/kg)[a]

	Paper	LDPE	Total
Air emissions			
Particulates	3.27		3.27
SO_x	13.06	0.08	13.14
NO_x	5.98	0.08	6.06
CO	3.27	0.05	3.31
Hydrocarbons	7.87	0.61	8.48
Water emissions			
BOD	3.00		3.00
Chemical oxygen demand	25.3		25.3
Suspended matter	1.84		1.84
Oils and fats	3.77×10^{-2}	0.02	0.06
Phenols		2.67×10^{-4}	2.67×10^{-4}
Dissolved matter	2.68	1.64	4.32
Organic substances		0.01	0.01
Fluoride	2.34×10^{-3}	6.67×10^{-5}	2.41×10^{-3}
Salts	44.9		44.9
Mercury	1.22×10^{-6}		1.22×10^{-6}
Chloride	18.7		18.7
Ammonia	1.08×10^{-3}		1.08×10^{-3}

[a]Data from van Eijk *et al.* (1992).

to be de-inked and/or bleached. However, for most packaging applications, de-inking and bleaching are not required. Typically, about 5–10% of the input waste paper ends up as waste for disposal. Typical emissions from production of paper and paperboard from recycled fiber are presented in the Tellus Institute (1992) study.

8.6   Aluminum

Aluminum is widely used in packaging for beverage cans, especially for carbonated beverages such as soft drinks and beer. Other major uses include semi-rigid packaging such as foil trays, pie plates, etc., and flexible packaging, where aluminum foil is often combined with other materials such as paper and plastics. Aluminum is also used in metallized paper and film. In flexible packaging applications, aluminum most often functions as a barrier layer.

8.6.1   Raw materials

Aluminum is produced from bauxite ore, which is mostly found in tropical regions. Bauxite consists of 40–60% aluminum oxide, with the rest of the material being iron oxide, titanium oxide and silicon oxide (Tellus Institute, 1992).

The ore is typically mined by open pit methods and is then crushed, washed, screened and dried, producing a relatively pure bauxite. The purified bauxite ore is converted to alumina by the Bayer process, which involves mixing the bauxite ore with lime, grinding it, and then mixing it with caustic soda. The resulting solution is pumped into large pressure tanks (digesters) where steam heat and pressure are applied, resulting in dissolving of the alumina in the caustic soda, forming sodium aluminate. Clarification and filtration of the liquid separates the aluminum solution from the impurities. Next the aluminum is recovered by precipitation as aluminum trihydrate. The crystals are filtered, washed, and then subjected to high temperatures to drive off the water, leaving pure alumina (Al_2O_3). Next the alumina is subjected to electrolytic reduction to pure aluminum and oxygen, generally using the Hall–Heroult method. In this process, alumina is dissolved in a molten bath of a fluoride electrolyte which contains cryolite, fluorspar and aluminum fluoride in an electrolytic cell consisting of a carbon cathode cell lining and a consumable anode made of petroleum coke and pitch. A high amperage, low voltage current reduces the aluminum to molten metal, which pools at the bottom of the cell. Oxygen reacts with carbon, sulfur and other impurities at the anode, forming carbon dioxide, carbon monoxide and sulfur dioxide. The molten aluminum is removed from the cells with a ladle or crucible, and is then cast as ingots. Alloying materials can be added during this step (Tellus Institute, 1992).

Aluminum can stock is made from aluminum alloyed with magnesium and manganese. A typical can body stock contains 0.8–1.3% magnesium and 1.0–1.5% manganese, while a typical end stock contains 4.0–5.0% magnesium and 0.2–0.5% manganese (Boustead and Hancock, 1981).

Production of 1 kg of aluminum ingot requires mining of approximately 0.16 kg of limestone, 2.75 kg of bauxite and 0.14 kg of salt. In addition, 0.55 kg of crude oil is required for the manufacture of coke and pitch (calculated from Hunt and Welch, 1974).

Aluminum for packaging use can also be produced from recycled aluminum, and in fact this is widely done. The difference in alloys for body and end stock results sometimes in the need to remove magnesium from body stock manufactured from a very high percentage of recycled cans. This process is known as demagging, and uses fluxing agents such as chlorine, aluminum fluoride, or aluminum chloride to remove magnesium and other contaminants (Tellus Institute, 1992).

8.6.2   Energy

Mining and initial processing of bauxite consumes approximately 0.59 MJ of energy per kg of bauxite produced (0.51 MM Btu/ton). Lime production consumes 5.70 MJ energy per kg of lime produced (4.91 MM Btu/ton). The Bayer process for alumina production uses 26.1 MJ energy per kg of alumina (22.5 MM Btu/ton). Reduction of the alumina to aluminum consumes 241.6 MJ/kg aluminum (208 MM Btu/ton) (Tellus Institute, 1992).

Processing of collected beverage cans into hot metal for recycling consumes about 9.60 MJ/kg (8.26 MM Btu/ton) (Tellus Institute, 1992), and thus represents a very significant energy saving.

Boustead and Hancock (1981) calculated the total energy required to produce 1 kg of aluminum can body stock in the United Kingdom as 346 MJ. Gaines (1981) calculated US energy consumption for production of aluminum beverage containers as 367 MJ/kg (158 000 Btu/ton) from virgin raw materials, and 132 MJ/kg (57 000 Btu/ton) if 100% recycled aluminum is used. Little (1984) calculated energy requirements for production of aluminum ingot from virgin raw materials as 204.5 MJ/kg, and from 100% recycled materials as 11.4 MJ/kg. For virgin aluminum, 69% of the energy was electricity, while for recycled aluminum, only 22.5% was electricity.

8.6.3   Other environmental impacts

Bauxite mining and processing of bauxite produces about 0.75 g total suspended particulate air emissions per kg bauxite produced (1.5 lb/ton), with emission controls in place, and not including emissions associated with energy production. Lime production has controlled emissions of about 21.4 g TSP per kg lime, 1.4 g NO_x/kg, and 1.0 g CO/kg. Production of caustic results in air emissions of 1.2 g chlorine/kg caustic, and water emissions of 7.04×10^{-3} g chlorine, 4.37×10^{-3} g copper, 2.14×10^{-3} g lead, and 3.30×10^{-6} g nickel per kg caustic. Alumina production results in air emissions of 19.2 g TSP per kg alumina. Production of 1 kg aluminum from alumina results in air emissions of 5.9 g TSP and 3.70 g fluoride, and water emissions of 1.91×10^{-2} g fluoride, 2.41×10^{-5} g benzo[a]pyrene, 4.23×10^{-3} g aluminum, 1.34×10^{-3} g antimony, and 5.74×10^{-4} g nickel. In all of the above, emissions associated with energy production are neglected (Tellus Institute, 1992).

Petroleum coke production is associated with a variety of air and water emissions. A summary of total emissions, as well as breakdowns by subprocess, is available in the Tellus Institute (1992) report.

Recycling of aluminum results in air emissions of 25.6 g TSP per kg aluminum, again not including emissions associated with process energy. Nearly all of these emissions are associated with demagging. Controlled water emissions for recycling processes were not available (Tellus Institute, 1992).

It should also be noted that during the electrolytic reduction of alumina, the carbon cathode lining of the cell becomes contaminated with fluorides, sodium, cyanide and other hazardous compounds, resulting in its classification as a hazardous waste (Tellus Institute, 1992).

8.7 Steel

The largest use of steel in packaging in the United States is in steel food cans. Steel is also used for beverage cans, drums, strapping and other forms of packaging.

8.7.1 Raw materials

The major raw materials required for the manufacture of steel are iron ore, limestone and coal. Iron ore is most often produced from open-pit mines. Much of the iron ore used is relatively low grade ore, containing 23–25% iron. A total of 10^2 tons of ore are required to produce 1 ton of iron pellets. Processing of the ore includes crushing, grinding and separation of the iron-containing particles from the rest of the material, either using magnetic separation or separation by density. The separated material is then pelletized by adding a binder and hardening the material in a furnace. The resultant pellets contain about 64% iron. Limestone is also produced in open-pit mines. Treatment includes crushing and screening. In some cases, the limestone is further processed in a cement kiln to convert the limestone to lime. Coal can be produced in either open pit mines or underground mines. It is cleaned to lower its ash and sulfur content, and then subjected to destructive distillation to yield coke. The coke is used in the blast furnace as both a fuel and an oxygen-reducing

Table 8.4 Raw materials used for production of steel in a basic oxygen furnace (g/kg steel)[a]

Material	Quantity
Pig iron	829
Scrap	320
Limestone	5
Lime	75
Fluorspar	8
Ferromanganese	11
Ferrosilicon	1
Aluminum	0.5
Pellets	3
Mill scale	8
Refractories	6.5
Oxygen	0.97 ft^3

[a]From Tellus Institute (1992).

agent. About 1.2 kg of mined coal is needed to produce 1 kg of clean coal, which then yields about 0.75 kg of coke. The blast furnace is fed with iron ore, coke and lime, producing molten iron (pig iron) and slag. Next, the pig iron is converted to steel, generally, for packaging uses, in a basic oxygen furnace. This furnace is charged with a combination of steel scrap and molten pig iron, and oxygen is supplied to oxidize impurities. After an initial heating period, lime and fluorspar are added to combine with the impurities and form a slag layer. Alloying metals are added, if desired, and the steel is then delivered for casting or ingot production. Table 8.4 summarizes the raw materials typically used for steel production (Tellus Institute, 1992).

For most packaging applications, provision of a non-corrosive layer to keep the steel from rusting is required. This is generally either a layer of tin (tinplate) or a very thin layer of chromium (tin-free steel, chromium type).

Steel scrap is routinely used in steel manufacture. Collected post-consumer steel cans are sometimes detinned before use, and sometimes used directly.

8.7.2 Energy

The Tellus Institute (1992) calculated the energy requirement for production of steel from the mix of ingredients listed in Table 8.4 as 22.8 MJ/kg (19.6 MM Btu/ton). Boustead and Hancock (1981) calculated the energy requirement to produce 1 kg of liquid steel in the United Kingdom from ore as 20.4 MJ, and that to produce 1 kg of hot rolled strip from ore as 30.67 MJ. Production of 1 kg of tinplate sheet from ore required 49.70 MJ, and production of 1 kg of tin-free steel sheet required 48.08 MJ. Production of 1 kg of steel strapping used 35.56 MJ.

Energy requirements to produce steel cans or other packaging materials from sheet are dependent on the design and size of the package. Gaines (1981) lists the energy requirement for the manufacture of 12-oz steel beverage containers with aluminum easy-open ends as 151 MJ/kg from virgin material, and 98 MJ/kg from recycled material. Little (1991) lists the total life cycle energy requirement for two-piece bimetallic 12-oz beverage cans as 102 MJ/kg, for two-piece, draw/redraw tinfree steel tuna cans as 108 MJ/kg, and for three-piece welded tinplate vegetable cans as 83.5 MJ/kg. These life cycle energy requirements include energy used in distribution and recycling, as well as manufacture, raw materials, etc.

8.7.3 Other environmental impacts

Air and water emissions associated with mining, concentration and pelletizing of iron ore are not available. Production of lime results in air emissions of 19.7 g TSP per kg lime produced, along with 1.3 g of NO_x and 0.9 g of CO. Production of coke from coal results in emissions of 1.48 g TSP/kg coke, 0.04 g benzene, 2.47×10^{-3} g POM, 0.22 g toluene and 0.02 g manganese. These emissions do not include emissions associated with required energy, or with coal mining. Coke production also results in emission of a long list of water pollutants. The Tellus Institute (1992) study contains a summary of the emissions associated with the overall steel production process, along with breakdowns by subprocess. Comparable values for steel production with 40% recycled content are also presented.

8.8   Glass

Glass packages are primarily bottles and jars. Because of the inertness, transparency, barrier and consumer appeal of glass, it is widely used especially for food and beverage products.

8.8.1   Raw materials

The primary raw materials for glass production are sand (or sandstone, silicon dioxide), soda ash (sodium carbonate), limestone (calcium carbonate) and feldspar (aluminum silicate). The carbonates are converted to oxides during glass formation, yielding a packaging glass with a typical composition of 70% silicon dioxide, 15% sodium oxide, 12% calcium oxide, 2% aluminum oxide, and 1% other ingredients. Cullet, recycled glass, is a necessary ingredient for efficient glass production.

The raw materials required to manufacture 1 kg of glass containers include 591 g sand, 181 g limestone, 84 g feldspar, 197 g soda ash, 100 g cullet and 13.8 g of other materials (Tellus Institute, 1992).

Limestone is generally quarried in open pit mines. Processing consists of crushing and screening, and results in about 90 g solid waste per ton of limestone produced (Tellus Institute, 1992).

Soda ash can be produced from natural minerals, or can be manufactured synthetically. All the soda ash used for glassmaking in the United States is natural, and the United States is a net exporter of soda ash. Natural soda ash is produced from trona ore, which contains 86–95% sodium sesquicarbonate. The ore is crushed, screened and calcined to form sodium carbonate, which is then purified, crystallized and dried (Tellus Institute, 1992). In the United Kingdom, all soda ash used is synthesized from limestone and salt (Boustead and Hancock, 1981).

In-house cullet typically constitutes 8.5% of the batch weight. The remainder of the cullet used comes from post-consumer sources. Current cullet use rates in the United States are about 25–30% for flint (clear) glass, 50% for amber glass and 70% for green glass (Tellus Institute, 1992).

One hundred percent cullet can be used for glass manufacture, although this is seldom done.

Processing of collected cullet for use includes size reduction and removal of contaminants. Color separation is, as a rule, required before crushing of the glass. The beneficiation process for cullet is designed to remove contaminants, especially aluminum, plastic and paper.

8.8.2   Energy

According to the Tellus Institute (1992), production of one kg of limestone requires 0.19 MJ of energy. Production of 1 kg of natural soda ash requires 9.98 MJ of energy. The total energy input for the manufacture of 1 kg of glass containers is estimated as 15.7 MJ (13.5 MM Btu/ton). Production of glass containers from 100% cullet is estimated to require 11.5 MJ/kg (9.92 MM Btu/ton).

Boustead and Hancock (1981) report the energy requirement for the production of synthetic soda ash as 14.23 MJ/kg soda ash. They report the average energy required to produce 1 kg of saleable glass containers from a mixture containing 20% in-house cullet, in the United Kingdom, as 22.2 MJ. Individual glass factories had energy requirements ranging from 18.03 MJ/kg to 29.39 MJ/kg. The effects of glass color on energy requirements were considerably smaller than the average variation between plants.

Gaines (1981) reports energy requirements for 12-oz beverage containers as 20.2 MJ/kg for virgin glass and 15.2 MJ/kg for recycled glass.

8.8.3   Other environmental impacts

The Tellus Institute (1992) study estimates emissions from glass manufacturing, using 10% cullet (in-house) and using 100% cullet to be as shown in Table 8.5.

8.8.4   Reuse of glass containers

Glass bottles, especially for carbonated beverages, are one of the very few types of consumer packages that have an extensive history of reuse. Although reuse of glass containers has become much less common, it still occurs to a significant degree in many places.

The environmental impact of reuse of glass packaging can be divided into three categories. First, because bottles designed for reuse need to maintain strength for a longer time and through more abuse, they must be made stronger initially than one-trip containers. Therefore, reusable glass bottles are heavier than non-reusable ones. This does not appreciably affect the environmental impact discussed on a weight basis, but makes a

Table 8.5 Controlled emissions from glass manufacturing (g/kg glass containers)[a]

Emission type	10% cullet	100% cullet
Air		
TSP	0.31	0.10
SO_x	2.09	0.96
NO_x	4.36	2.70
VOC	4.48	4.43
CO	0.33	0.15
Lead	8.34×10^{-4}	8.44×10^{-5}
Methane	0.015	0.005
Water		
Oil	4.69×10^{-4}	4.69×10^{-4}
TSS	4.69×10^{-4}	4.69×10^{-4}

[a]Data derived from Tellus Institute (1992).

considerable difference in per container impact. Gaines (1981) estimates that refillable bottles are, on average, 50% heavier than non-refillable ones, and therefore require 50% more energy to manufacture. It should also be remembered that increased size of the reusable bottles will in general lead to an increase in the size of any associated secondary and tertiary packaging, as well.

The second category of impact is that associated with the return system. Effects associated with transportation of the containers from the use site to the refill location are, in principle, no different from effects associated with transportation of containers from the production site to the fill location. In general, transportation effects are heavily dependent on the weight and/or volume of the packages, and on the distance involved, as discussed in Section 8.10. Gaines (1981) states that the marginal energy cost for reuse is low, since the non-refillable bottles must be transported to disposal or recycle, anyway. This argument is valid only as long as the distances are comparable.

The remaining category of impacts are those associated with the cleaning necessary to prepare the containers for refill. The cleaning cycle involves use of detergents and of significant quantities of water and energy. Detergents as well as product residues and dirt are discharged into the wastewater stream. Van Eijk et al. (1992) present an evaluation of the environmental impact of washing porcelain crockery in a dishwasher, a process that is similar (although certainly not identical) to that undergone by glass bottles. Gaines (1981) states that new glass bottles must also be washed, therefore decreasing the net effect of this aspect of the reuse cycle. However, Boustead and Hancock (1981) point out that returnable bottles need a hot detergent wash to remove labels and clean and sterilize the bottles, while non-returnable bottles require only a rinse. They calculated the energy required to fill non-returnable beer bottles as 64–84% of the energy required to fill returnable beer bottles, with the greatest difference for the smallest bottles. For soft drinks, the range was 57% for 6-oz bottles to 87% for 1-l bottles.

8.9 Plastics

Plastics have seen dramatically increasing use in packaging over the last several years, and indications are that this use will continue to grow. Switching materials to plastic packaging alternatives often permits significant source reduction (use of less packaging, by weight or by volume), as well as significant cost advantages. Unlike other packaging materials, it is difficult to assess the environmental effects of plastics packaging as a group, because various specific plastics have their own characteristics which can differ significantly from other members of the plastics packaging family. Therefore, in addition to some general discussion, we look in more detail at the major packaging plastics, including low and high density polyethylene (LDPE and HDPE), linear low density polyethylene (LLDPE), polypropylene (PP), polystyrene (PS), polyvinyl chloride (PVC) and polyethylene terephthalate (PET).

8.9.1 Raw materials

The basic raw materials for production of plastics are petroleum and natural gas. Natural gas yields ethane and propane for plastics production, while petroleum yields propane, butane, naphtha and gas oil. Propane and butane, combined, are termed liquified petroleum gases (LPG).

Natural gas is processed by removal of water and hydrocarbon condensate, removal of non-hydrocarbon gases, liquification and distillation. The hydrocarbon condensate is heavy hydrocarbons with five or more carbon atoms. The principal non-hydrocarbon gas found in natural gas is hydrogen sulfide, although nitrogen, hydrogen and helium are also found. Liquification and distillation are carried out to separate the hydrocarbons from each other. Up to 97% of the natural gas is methane. Heavier hydrocarbons are separated from methane by liquification. Distillation, or fractionation, of the liquified gases separates ethane, propane and butane from each other. Ethane is the major feedstock for manufacture of ethylene, and propane is used to produce propylene (Tellus Institute, 1992).

Processing of crude oil also involves separation of the oil mixture into a number of components. Because crude oil is chemically a more complex mixture than natural gas, its processing is also more complex. Preliminary processing of petroleum involves removal of water and suspended solids, and removal of dissolved salts in the oil (desalting). This is followed by a multi-stage distillation process, which produces, among other products, propane, naphtha and gas oil. Residuals from the distillation are sent through vacuum distillation and catalytic cracking, yielding naphtha and gas oil, among other products.

The four major petrochemical building blocks for production of packaging plastics are ethylene (used to make polyethylene, polystyrene, PET and PVC), propylene (used to make polypropylene), benzene (used to make polystyrene), and paraxylene (used to make PET). Ethylene and propylene can be made from liquified petroleum gases, naphtha and gas oil, as well as from natural gas. Benzene and paraxylene are manufactured from naphtha and gas oil (a small amount of benzene is made from coal) (Tellus Institute, 1992).

8.9.2 Energy

Onshore natural gas extraction and processing is estimated to require 0.793 MJ per MJ of natural gas produced, if a mixture of 50% sweet gas and 50% sour gas is produced. Sour gas has a hydrogen sulfide content greater than 0.25 grains per 100 standard cubic feet, and requires treatment with an amine solution to absorb the hydrogen sulfide. Processing of sweet natural gas requires only 0.310 MJ per MJ of natural gas produced, while processing of sour gas requires 1.132 MJ per MJ of gas. The drilling process requires 0.072 MJ per MJ of natural gas. The total energy input to produce 1 kg of ethane from natural gas is 91.3 MJ (78.58 MM Btu/ton). A total of 89.7 MJ of energy is required to produce 1 kg of propane from natural gas (77.22 MM Btu/ton) (the fuel value of the product is involved) (Tellus Institute, 1992).

Onshore extraction of petroleum requires 0.00148 MJ per MJ of crude oil produced. Production of propane from crude oil requires 51.8 MJ per kg of propane. Production of naphtha from atmospheric distillation requires 45.4 MJ per kg (39.04 MM Btu/ton). Production of naphtha from catalytic cracking requires 51.3 MJ per kg (44.15 MM Btu/ton) (Tellus Institute, 1992).

According to the Tellus Institute (1992) study, production of ethylene from ethane requires 110.7 MJ/kg, after credit for by-products is taken, and including energy content of the raw materials. For manufacture of ethylene from propane, 71.04 MJ per kg are required. If the raw material is naphtha, 61.32 MJ are required, and from heavy gas oil, 59.47 MJ. If a raw material mix of 25% from each source is assumed, an average energy cost of 75.64 MJ per kg of ethylene produced can be calculated, again including the energy value of the raw materials.

Production of propylene from ethane requires 110.7 MJ/kg, again including by-product credits and the energy content of the raw material. From propane, 71.08 MJ are required, from naphtha, 61.33 MJ, and from heavy gas oil, 59.47 MJ. If an average split of 2% ethane, 26% propane, 34% naphtha, and 48% heavy gas oil feedstock is assumed, the average energy required to produce 1 kg of propane is 63.95 MJ (Tellus Institute, 1992).

For production of benzene, the Tellus Institute (1992) calculated a split of 62% manufactured by catalytic reforming, and 38% by toluene dealkylation. Overall energy requirements were 67.47 MJ/kg. For paraxylene formation by catalytic reforming, energy requirements were 93.02 MJ/kg.

8.9.3 Other environmental impacts

A variety of environmental impacts are associated with natural gas and petroleum drilling and processing. Drilling wastes include drilling muds, drill cuttings, and drilling fluids. The American Petroleum Institute estimates the average amount of drilling waste per well as 5183 barrels (Tellus Institute, 1992). Pollutants in these wastes include a large number of compounds, in small concentrations. Air pollutants during drilling operations arise primarily from the large diesel engines used to power the drill, and include NO_x, CO, SO_x, volatile organic compounds and particulates. These emissions are generally uncontrolled.

Production wastes for oil and natural gas include water found in the oil or gas, along with water added during removal of the gas or oil from the well. As for drilling effluents, a large number of pollutants are found in small concentrations. Air emissions arise from fuel use, and from oil and gas separators, gas dehydrators and heater treaters (which remove water from crude oil). Other wastes include tank bottoms, separator sludges, cooling water and other miscellaneous wastes (Tellus Institute, 1992).

Processing of oil and natural gas also results in a variety of emissions, mostly in small quantities. Worthy of note are average emissions of 1.23 g SO_x per MJ natural gas produced (Tellus Institute, 1992).

The Tellus Institute (1992) summary of air pollutant emission factors for ethylene production includes controlled emissions of 0.084 g benzene per kg of ethylene. The only other significant air pollutant quantified was 8.34 g/kg uncontrolled emissions of volatile organic compounds (VOCs). A controlled emission value for VOCs was not available. For propylene production, air emissions of 0.50 g VOC/kg propylene were listed as uncontrolled emissions. For benzene production, 0.55 g VOC/kg benzene can be expected in uncontrolled emissions, along with 0.015 g toluene per kg of toluene used in benzene production. For production of mixed xylenes and paraxylene, 0.55 g VOC and 1.50 g xylene are emitted per kg of xylenes produced (Tellus Institute, 1992).

Water pollutant emissions for ethylene, propylene, benzene and xylene include a wide variety of compounds and are summarized in the Tellus Institute (1992) study.

8.9.4   *High density polyethylene (HDPE)*

High density polyethylene is the plastic resin most often used for bottles. Bottles and other containers are also the most common use of high density polyethylene in packaging. However, a significant amount of HDPE is also used in film applications.

HDPE is manufactured from ethylene at moderate temperatures (93°C) and pressures (20–48 atm) (Tellus Institute, 1992), using a catalyst. Polymerization processes can be either a liquid phase solution process, a liquid phase slurry process, or a gas phase process. HDPE manufactured with Phillips catalysts using a slurry process predominates, accounting for 58% of all HDPE manufactured. Ziegler catalysts and either a solution or slurry process account for 32% of production, and gas phase reactions account for 10% (Tellus Institute, 1992). For analysis of environmental impacts, the Tellus Institute study assumed 74% of HDPE produced by the slurry process, 16% by suspension and 10% in gas phase reactions.

Production of HDPE by the slurry process involves feeding ethylene, hydrogen as a molecular weight regulator, a diluent such as hexane and the catalyst into the reactor. Output from the reactor consists of polymer, diluent, off-bases, unreacted monomer, catalyst and waxes. The unreacted monomer and diluent are recycled back into the process. The solution

Table 8.6 Uncontrolled water emissions from HDPE, LLDPE and LDPE polymerization (g/kg product)[a]

Pollutant	HDPE	LLDPE	LDPE
BOD5	5.29×10^{-4}	2.17×10^{-4}	2.14
COD	7.04×10^{-4}	2.90×10^{-4}	5.74
Total organic carbon	6.39×10^{-4}	2.62×10^{-4}	3.27
Oil and grease			11.1
Total suspended solids	2.35×10^{-3}	9.64×10^{-4}	4.17
Total dissolved solids	2.10×10^{-2}	8.64×10^{-3}	4.73
Acenaphthylene			139
Benzene	2.52×10^{-5}	1.03×10^{-5}	2.48×10^{-2}
Benzo[a]anthracene	1.64×10^{-6}	6.74×10^{-7}	
Dimethyl phthalate			8.24×10^{-3}
Di-n-butyl phthalate			1.11×10^{-3}
Ethylene dichloride			4.76×10^{-4}
Phenol	1.84×10^{-6}	7.54×10^{-7}	1.46×10^{-3}
Toluene	4.04×10^{-4}	1.66×10^{-4}	2.36×10^{-2}
Aluminum	1.29×10^{-2}	5.29×10^{-3}	
Chromium			5.09×10^{-2}
Copper			2.36×10^{-3}
Lead			8.74×10^{-4}
Mercury			2.70×10^{-5}
Titanium	3.54×10^{-2}	1.45×10^{-2}	

[a]Data from Tellus Institute (1992).

Table 8.7 Controlled water emissions from HDPE, LLDPE and LDPE polymerization (g/kg product)[a]

Pollutant	HDPE	LLDPE	LDPE
BOD5			
COD			
Total organic carbon			
Oil and grease			
Total suspended solids			
Total dissolved solids			
Acenaphthylene			41.3
Benzene	6.64×10^{-7}	2.74×10^{-2}	7.44×10^{-3}
Benzo[a]anthracene	1.11×10^{-7}	4.57×10^{-8}	
Dimethyl phthalate			5.09×10^{-3}
Di-n-butyl phthalate			8.09×10^{-4}
Ethylene dichloride			2.16×10^{-4}
Phenol	2.00×10^{-6}	8.24×10^{-7}	8.79×10^{-4}
Toluene	9.09×10^{-6}	3.75×10^{-6}	7.19×10^{-3}
Aluminum	1.40×10^{-2}	5.79×10^{-3}	
Chromium			1.51×10^{-2}
Copper			7.09×10^{-4}
Lead			2.64×10^{-4}
Mercury			1.80×10^{-5}
Titanium	2.04×10^{-2}	8.39×10^{-3}	

[a]Data from Tellus Institute (1992); treated wastewater emissions not available for all effluents.

process is similar to the slurry process, but temperatures are higher so the polymer is dissolved rather than suspended in particle form. The gas phase polymerization polymerizes purified ethylene in the presence of a dry powder catalyst, a comonomer and hydrogen as a molecular weight regulator. Unreacted monomer and comonomer are recycled (Tellus Institute, 1992).

Overall energy requirements for production of HDPE are 92.5 MJ/kg, including the energy value of the HDPE. Process energy is 43.1 MJ, with the rest being material energy. One kilogram of polyethylene requires 1.02 kg of ethylene as raw material. The polymerization process itself requires 6.60 MJ steam and 8.71 MJ electricity per kg HDPE produced (Tellus Institute, 1992). An earlier estimate by Boustead and Hancock (1981) was that 107.76 MJ/kg are required to produce HDPE from crude oil, again including the energy value of the product.

Air emissions associated with HDPE production from ethylene are 16.7 g VOC, uncontrolled, per kg HDPE. Controlled air emission factors were not available. Water emission factors, uncontrolled and controlled, are presented in Tables 8.6 and 8.7. A complete set of controlled water emissions was not available, so these data are incomplete (Tellus Institute, 1992).

8.9.5   Linear low density polyethylene (LLDPE)

The primary use of linear low density polyethylene in packaging is in film applications, where it competes primarily against low density polyethylene. High density polyethylene and linear low density polyethylene are linear in molecular structure, while low density polyethylene is a branched structure.

Linear low density polyethylene is produced by processes similar to those used to produce high density polyethylene, but is a copolymer of ethylene and either 1-butene, 1-hexene, or 1-octene. Process equipment designed to manufacture either HDPE or LLDPE can, in general, also be used to produce the other, giving manufacturers what is known as 'swing capacity'.

The two primary methods for manufacture of LLDPE are gas phase and solution polymerization. In the Tellus Institute (1992) study, it was estimated that 63% of LLDPE is manufactured by gas-phase processing, and 37% by solution processing.

Energy requirements to produce LLDPE from ethylene and 1-butene by gas phase polymerization total 83.02 MJ/kg LLDPE (71.46 MM Btu/ton), including 75.87 MJ for 0.99 kg of ethylene, 2.9 MJ for 0.04 kg of 1-butene, and 4.24 MJ of process energy. The estimate for the 1-butene is low, since it does not include energy required to manufacture the 1-butene, only the energy content of the butene itself. Energy values for solution phase processing were not available, so were assumed to be the same as for gas phase polymerization (Tellus Institute, 1992).

Air pollutants from LLDPE production are primarily VOC, amounting to 25.4 g/kg LLDPE of uncontrolled air emissions. Again, controlled emission amounts were not available (Tellus Institute, 1992).

Gas phase polymerization of LLDPE results in no water pollutants. Solution polymerization results in water pollutants in essentially the same types and amounts as solution phase HDPE production, except that differences in the proportional use of each polymerization method must be accounted for. Amounts are shown in Tables 8.6 and 8.7 (Tellus Institute, 1992).

8.9.6   Low density polyethylene (LDPE)

The major packaging market for low density polyethylene is film, where, as mentioned earlier, it competes with linear low density polyethylene. Coating is another major market. Low density polyethylene is the oldest member of the polyethylene family.

LDPE is produced by polymerization of ethylene at relatively high temperatures (150–300°C) and pressures (1000–3400 atm) in an autoclave or tubular reactor. In addition to ethylene, a chain transfer agent such as hydrogen, and a free radical initiator such as oxygen or a peroxide, are added to the reaction vessel. When the product is removed, the unreacted ethylene is separated and recycled. By-products such as oils and waxes are commonly used as boiler fuel (Tellus Institute, 1992).

The total energy required to manufacture LDPE is 98.3 MJ per kg. Process energy amounts to 46.4 MJ, with the remainder being the energy content of the materials; 1.05 kg of ethylene is required to produce 1 kg of LDPE (Tellus Institute, 1992). Boustead and Hancock (1981) estimated energy required to manufacture LDPE as 21.01 MJ/kg from ethylene, or 104.89 MJ/kg from crude oil. To produce 1 kg polyethylene film from crude oil requires, by their calculations, 188.72 MJ. Fenton (1991) reported literature values of energy required to produce LDPE bags ranging from 74.44 to 116.27 MJ/kg.

The primary air emission from LDPE polymerization is VOC, in amounts of 8.73 g per kg LDPE in uncontrolled emissions. Data for controlled emissions were not available. However, 1.16 g benzene per kg LDPE are also found in uncontrolled air emissions (Tellus Institute, 1992).

Waste water from LDPE manufacturing is produced during removal of the oils and waxes from the unreacted ethylene, and when the pelletized LDPE is water-cooled. Water emissions for LDPE polymerization are also listed in Tables 8.6 and 8.7 (Tellus Institute, 1992).

8.9.7   Polypropylene (PP)

Polypropylene is used in packaging in the production of closures, as well as in containers and film. Nearly all the polypropylene used in packaging is a stereochemically ordered structure known as isotactic polypropylene. Polymerization processes generally also produce some undesired, unordered atactic polypropylene, which does not have desired properties and must be separated from the product.

The polymerization process for polypropylene may involve solution, suspension, or gas phase reactions. For purposes of analyzing environmental impact, the Tellus Institute (1992) study assumed a mix of 75% suspension polymerization and 25% gas phase polymerization. Polymerization processes can also be classified as high yield or low yield, based on the required ratio of catalyst to feedstock. Low yield catalysts are present in the polymer in high concentrations and must be removed, while high yield catalysts are present in low concentrations and do not require removal. High yield catalysts are the preferred method.

In continuous suspension polymerization with high yield catalysts, liquid propylene, hydrogen as a molecular weight regulating agent, a polymer suspension medium and a catalyst are fed into the reactor. Excess liquid propylene is used as a diluent. Polymerization occurs at a temperature of about 60°C and pressures of 20–27 atm. After the reaction mixture exits the reactor, unreacted monomer and atactic polymer are removed, and the isotactic polypropylene product is recovered. The process is the same for low yield polymerization, except that hexane or xylene are used as diluents, and the catalyst and diluent must be removed from the product stream (Tellus Institute, 1992).

In gas phase polymerization, the reaction vessel is fed with a mixture of propylene, hexane as a diluent, and catalysts. Unreacted monomer is recycled back into the reactor. The polymer product is recovered as a fine powder, which is then extruded and pelletized (Tellus Institute, 1992).

To produce 1 kg of polypropylene, 1.05 kg of propylene are required. Energy requirements for the polymerization process are 5.8 MJ and 6.3 MJ electricity per kg polypropylene produced. The total energy requirement, including material energy content, is 97.2 MJ/kg (Tellus Institute, 1992). By Boustead and Hancock's (1981) calculation, the energy required to produce polypropylene from crude oil is 114.12 MJ/kg.

As was the case for the polyethylenes, a major air emission during polymerization is VOC, in amounts of 36.7 g per kg PP produced in uncontrolled emissions. Other emissions include 36.7 g/kg NO_x and 1.50 g/kg total suspended particulates. Controlled air emissions were not available (Tellus Institute, 1992).

Water effluents are produced during diluent recovery, catalyst recovery and filtering of wastewater. Water emission data are available only for solution polymerization (which uses a solvent instead of a diluent), and are presented in Table 8.8. Gas phase reaction produces no water emissions. It is believed that emissions for suspension polymerization are similar to those for solution polymerization (Tellus Institute, 1992).

Table 8.8 Water emissions from solution phase PP polymerization (g/kg PP)[a]

Pollutant	Raw water	Treated water
BOD5	0.120	
COD	0.354	
Total organic carbon	0.154	
Benzene	4.02×10^{-4}	1.99×10^{-3}
Bis(2-ethylhexyl) phthalate	4.89×10^{-6}	5.84×10^{-5}
Chloroform	1.71×10^{-5}	2.05×10^{-4}
Ethylbenzene	2.34×10^{-3}	7.74×10^{-3}
1,1,1-Trichloroethane	1.10×10^{-5}	7.74×10^{-3}
Toluene	1.28×10^{-3}	6.19×10^{-3}
Chromium	1.95×10^{-3}	8.64×10^{-3}
Zinc	2.04×10^{-3}	8.99×10^{-3}

[a]Data from Tellus Instiute, 1992; treated wastewater emissions not available for BOD5, COD and total organic carbon; no explanation given for higher emissions for treated compared to untreated wastewater.

8.9.8 Polystyrene (PS)

Polystyrene is used in packaging in two distinct forms. A large amount of polystyrene in expanded form (foam) is used as cushioning material, either in shapes or as loose fill. It is also used in egg cartons, produce trays, etc. In non-expanded form (crystal), PS is used in lidding material, yogurt cups, produce trays, and a variety of other applications. High impact PS incorporates a comonomer, usually polybutadiene, to improve the impact strength of polystyrene, which, unmodified, is a relatively brittle material.

The basic chemical feedstocks used to produce polystyrene are ethylene and benzene. First, ethylene and benzene are combined, in a process known as alkylation, to form ethylbenzene. Next, ethylbenzene is dehydrogenated to form styrene. This process, carried out at 650°C in the presence of a catalyst, also produces a small amount of toluene as a by-product. Manufacture of 1 kg styrene requires 1.077 kg ethylbenzene, and produces 0.031 kg toluene by-product (Tellus Institute, 1992).

Polymerization of styrene can be done either with bulk, solution, suspension, or emulsion techniques. Bulk and suspension polymerization are most common. In bulk polymerization, mineral oil is added as a lubricant and plasticizer. Production of 1 kg of polystyrene requires 0.98 kg styrene and 0.03 kg mineral oil. General purpose (crystal) polystyrene is produced by both mass and suspension polymerization. Expandable bead polystyrene is generally produced by suspension polymerization. The blowing agent can be added before or after polymerization, although it is most commonly added after polymerization (Tellus Institute, 1992).

Production of 1 kg polystyrene from raw materials requires 88.6 MJ/kg, including the energy value of the materials, for production of general purpose (crystal) polystyrene by bulk polymerization. It is believed that suspension polymerization has slightly higher energy requirements (Tellus Institute, 1992). The bulk polymerization process itself uses 2.28 MJ/kg. Dehydrogenation of ethylbenzene to styrene consumes 12.18 MJ/kg polystyrene produced. However, alkylation of ethylene and benzene to ethylbenzene produces a net energy gain of 0.73 MJ/kg polystyrene, in the form of steam (Tellus Institute, 1992).

Van Eijk et al. (1992) calculate energy requirements for the production of polystyrene granulate, consisting of 50% high impact polystyrene and 50% general purpose polystyrene as 33.459 MJ/kg, in the Netherlands. Transportation of the oil required consumes an additional 1.045 MJ/kg PS, and transportation of the granulate to the forming facility uses 0.447 MJ/kg PS. Molding of cups from the granulate uses 12.948 MJ/kg PS, and transportation from the molder to the user requires 0.464 MJ/kg PS.

The air emissions of most concern in polystyrene production are volatile organic compounds (VOC), especially styrene and benzene, which are toxic. Table 8.9 presents air emissions for production of ethylbenzene and

Table 8.9 Air emissions from polystyrene production (g/kg PS)[a]

Pollutant	Ethylbenzene/styrene production		Polymerization	
	Uncontrolled	Controlled	Uncontrolled	Controlled
NO_x	1.96×10^{-2}			
VOC	16.5		1.65	
Benzene	2.55	0.939		
Styrene	5.19×10^{-2}	5.19×10^{-2}		

[a]Data from Tellus Institute, 1992; controlled air emissions not available for all categories.

Table 8.10 Water emissions from polystyrene polymerization (g/kg polystyrene)[a]

Pollutant	Mass polymerization		Suspension polymerization	
	Uncontrolled	Controlled	Uncontrolled	Controlled
BOD5	1.38		11.0	
COD	1.87		31.8	
Total organic carbon	0.794		10.5	
Total suspended solids	1.31×10^{-2}			
Aldrin	1.35×10^{-6}	1.39×10^{-6}	1.59×10^{-5}	7.94×10^{-6}
Benzene	1.04×10^{-2}	4.74×10^{-5}	1.30×10^{-3}	3.98×10^{-4}
Bis(2-ethylhexyl) phthalate	3.62×10^{-4}	1.39×10^{-4}	2.08×10^{-3}	3.98×10^{-4}
Butyl benzyl phthalate			8.74×10^{-5}	3.18×10^{-5}
1,2-Dichloropropane	9.19×10^{-5}	1.39×10^{-6}	3.98×10^{-4}	3.98×10^{-4}
Dimethyl phthalate	4.11×10^{-4}	1.39×10^{-4}	8.49×10^{-4}	3.98×10^{-4}
Ethylbenzene	2.38×10^{-2}	1.17×10^{-4}	9.10×10^{-4}	3.98×10^{-4}
Ethylene dichloride	2.70×10^{-5}	1.39×10^{-6}	1.59×10^{-4}	1.59×10^{-4}
Lindane (R-bhc-γ)	1.35×10^{-6}	1.39×10^{-6}	7.94×10^{-6}	7.94×10^{-6}
Phenol	6.04×10^{-4}	5.54×10^{-4}	7.14×10^{-4}	3.98×10^{-4}
Toluene	1.94×10^{-2}	8.09×10^{-5}	4.69×10^{-4}	3.98×10^{-4}
Chromium			4.61×10^{-4}	3.98×10^{-4}
Lead			2.39×10^{-5}	2.39×10^{-5}

[a]Data from Tellus Institute, 1992; controlled emission values not available for all categories.

styrene from ethylene and benzene, and for polymerization of styrene to polystyrene. The compounds listed as VOC are essentially all styrene. Batch-type polymerization has styrene emissions of 1.55 g/kg, while for continuous polymerization, the emissions are 1.75 g/kg. Suspension polymerization of expandable bead polystyrene produces air emissions of 9.29 kg VOC/kg polystyrene (Tellus Institute, 1992).

Both mass and suspension polymerization can produce a variety of water effluents. These are summarized in Table 8.10.

8.9.9   Polyvinyl chloride (PVC)

Polyvinyl chloride is used widely in blister packaging, and also has a number of other packaging applications, including bottles for potable water. Packaging consumes only a small portion of PVC production, since non-packaging applications such as pipe and siding are much larger markets.

Manufacture of PVC begins with chlorination of ethylene to yield ethylene dichloride. This can be carried out by direct chlorination, by oxychlorination, or, the process used most frequently, by a combination of these methods known as the balanced process. The chlorine used is produced from electrolysis of salt, which produces both chlorine and caustic soda, along with a small amount of hydrogen, from brine (Tellus Institute, 1992).

The next step in the process is dehydrochlorination of ethylene dichloride, yielding vinyl chloride and by-product HCl. In the United States, over 80% of all ethylene dichloride produced is used for synthesis of vinyl chloride, which in turn is used primarily for production of PVC.

Polyvinyl chloride can be produced by mass, solution, suspension, or emulsion polymerization, with suspension polymerization being by far the most common. The reaction is carried out in a dilute water suspension, under a nitrogen atmosphere (to prevent unwanted reactions with oxygen) (Tellus Institute, 1992).

Production of 1 kg of polyvinyl chloride requires 1.02 kg of vinyl chloride and 84.0 MJ of energy, including the raw material energy. The polymerization process energy is 4.32 MJ/kg PVC. Production of ethylene dichloride and vinyl chloride monomer consumes 0.46 kg ethylene and 0.58 kg chlorine, with a process energy requirement of 9.76 MJ/kg PVC. Production of the required amount of chlorine uses 12.52 MJ of process energy per kg PVC.

Air emissions from chlorine production, production of ethylene dichloride and vinyl chloride, and from PVC polymerization are listed in Table 8.11.

Controlled and uncontrolled water emissions associated with PVC polymerization are listed in Table 8.12.

8.9.10   Polyethylene terephthalate (PET)

The major use of PET in packaging is bottles for carbonated soft drinks. However, PET has been expanding fairly rapidly into other food and non-food markets, mostly in the form of bottles. PET films and coatings are also used in packaging.

PET is a condensation polymer, formed from ethylene glycol and dimethyl terephthalate (DMT) or terephthalic acid (TPA). Manufacture from DMT is more common, and produces methanol as a by-product. This polymerization process requires 1 kg of DMT and 0.7 kg of ethylene glycol to produce 1 kg of PET and 0.33 kg of methanol.

DMT can be produced by oxidation of paraxylene, or by esterification of terephthalic acid with methanol. Terephthalic acid is produced from

Table 8.11 Uncontrolled and controlled air emissions from PVC suspension polymerization steps (g/kg PVC)[a]

Pollutant	EDC/VCM production		PVC production	
	Uncontrolled	Controlled	Uncontrolled	Controlled
TSP			17.5	
SO_x			1.25×10^{-2}	
NO_x			100	
VOC	10.7		8.49	
1,3-Butadiene			2.10×10^{-4}	2.10×10^{-4}
Carbon tetrachloride	1.55	0.327		
Chloroform	1.82	3.65×10^{-2}		
Chloroprene			4.00×10^{-5}	4.00×10^{-5}
Ethyl chloride	4.89×10^{-3}	4.89×10^{-3}		
Ethylene dichloride	10.9	1.43	4.00×10^{-5}	4.00×10^{-5}
Hydrogen chloride			2.10×10^{-4}	2.10×10^{-4}
Propylene			6.99×10^{-5}	6.99×10^{-5}
Vinyl chloride	4.88	0.127	35.5	0.674
Vinylidene chloride			8.99×10^{-5}	3.24×10^{-4}

[a]Data from Tellus Institute (1992); controlled emission values not available for all categories.

Table 8.12 Uncontrolled and controlled water emissions from PVC suspension polymerization steps (g/kg PVC)[a]

Pollutant	EDC/VCM production		PVC production	
	Uncontrolled	Controlled	Uncontrolled	Controlled
BOD5	1.78		0.989	
COD	4.73		0.719	
Total organic carbon	1.42		0.124	
Total suspended solids	5.89×10^{-2}		1.75	
Total dissolved solids			0.819	
Acrolein			1.61×10^{-5}	
Bis(2-ethylhexyl) phthalate	6.44×10^{-5}	6.34×10^{-5}	1.67×10^{-4}	
Carbon tetrachloride		2.90×10^{-3}		
Chloroethane	1.64×10^{-5}	1.64×10^{-5}		
Chloroform	1.74	0.434		
1,3-Dichloropropene	8.44×10^{-5}	7.04×10^{-5}		
Di-n-butyl phthalate	4.04×10^{-4}	1.77×10^{-4}		
Ethylene dichloride	4.35	0.719		
Methylene chloride	2.82×10^{-2}	9.44×10^{-3}		1.32×10^{-4}
Pentachlorophenol	1.04×10^{-3}	2.68×10^{-4}		
Phenol			2.03×10^{-4}	
Tetrachloroethylene	3.66×10^{-3}	1.86×10^{-3}		
1,1,1-Trichloroethane				3.84×10^{-5}
Trichloroethylene	0.367	0.122		
Vinyl chloride	2.72×10^{-2}	6.84×10^{-3}	4.43×10^{-3}	5.49×10^{-4}
Chromium	1.22×10^{-3}	2.18×10^{-4}		
Copper	1.69×10^{-4}	3.62×10^{-5}		
Cyanide	2.52×10^{-5}	1.39×10^{-5}		
Lead				3.16×10^{-4}
Nickel	1.97×10^{-4}	6.99×10^{-5}		
Zinc				6.04×10^{-5}

[a]Data from Tellus Institute (1992); controlled emission values not available for all categories.

Table 8.13 Uncontrolled air pollutant emissions associated with PET production steps (g/kg PET)[a]

Pollutant	Paraxylene production	Ethylene oxide/ glycol production production	DMT	Polymerization
NO$_x$			3.00×10^{-2}	
VOC	0.346	5.24	19.8	9.69
CO			19.0	
Ethylene oxide		1.83		
Triethanol			0.130	
Xylene	0.944		7.09	

[a]Data from Tellus Institute (1992); controlled emission values not available for all categories.

acetic acid and paraxylene by oxidation in air. Production of 1 kg of DMT requires 0.63 kg of paraxylene and 0.38 kg of methanol, for the oxidation route (Tellus Institute, 1992).

Ethylene glycol is commonly manufactured by hydrolysis of ethylene oxide, although it can also be produced directly from ethylene. Ethylene oxide is produced by the direct oxidation of ethylene. Manufacture of 1 kg of ethylene oxide requires 0.9 kg of ethylene and 1.14 kg of oxygen. Manufacture of 1 kg of ethylene glycol requires 0.75 kg of ethylene oxide and 2 kg of water (Tellus Institute, 1992).

Production of PET from raw materials requires 122.7 MJ of energy per kg, including energy content of the materials. Oxidation of paraxylene uses 13.14 MJ/kg of PET produced, while the condensation polymerization reaction uses 6.16 MJ/kg (Tellus Institute, 1992).

Selected air and water emissions for production of xylene, production of ethylene oxide and ethylene glycol, production of DMT, and polymerization of PET are shown in Tables 8.13–8.16.

Table 8.14 Controlled air pollutant emissions associated with PET production steps (g/kg PET)[a]

Pollutant	Paraxylene production	Ethylene oxide/ glycol production	DMT production	Polymerization
NO$_x$				
VOC				0.534
CO				
Ethylene oxide		4.84×10^{-2}		
Triethanol			0.013	
Xylene				

[a]Data from Tellus Institute (1992); controlled emission values not available for all categories.

Table 8.15 Uncontrolled water pollutant emissions associated with PET production steps (g/kg PET)[a]

Pollutant	Paraxylene production	Ethylene oxide/ glycol production	DMT production	Polymerization
BOD5	4.99	20.3	0.339	4.36
COD	13.5	58.4	1.69	9.19
Total organic carbon	3.68	14.8	1.17	1.07
Oil and grease	3.11×10^{-5}	1.11		6.74×10^{-2}
Total suspended solids	0.939	15.9	3.39×10^{-3}	0.809
Total dissolved solids			2.35×10^{-2}	2.44
Acenaphthene		5.44×10^{-4}		
Acenaphthylene		1.12×10^{-4}		
Acrylonitrile				4.95×10^{-3}
Antimony				7.99×10^{-2}
Benzene	1.18×10^{-3}	0.123		
Bis(2-chloroisopropyl) ether		1.49×10^{-4}		
Chloroform	3.17×10^{-5}	2.13×10^{-5}		
2-Chlorophenol	4.48×10^{-5}			
2,4-Dimethylphenol	1.70×10^{-4}			
Dimethyl phthalate			5.09×10^{-3}	
Di-n-butyl phthalate			2.09×10^{-3}	
Ethylbenzene	5.34×10^{-4}	2.93×10^{-3}		6.74×10^{-3}
Ethylene dichloride		4.75×10^{-3}		
Fluorene		6.09×10^{-5}		
Methylene chloride	1.39×10^{-4}	1.15×10^{-4}		
Naphthalene	2.48×10^{-4}	1.32×10^{-3}		1.19×10^{-3}
Phenol	1.44×10^{-4}	1.07×10^{-3}	3.69×10^{-4}	0.704
Tetrachloroethylene		6.09×10^{-6}		
Toluene	2.42×10^{-3}	3.48×10^{-2}		
Vinyl chloride		4.13×10^{-4}		
Chromium	8.74×10^{-3}	1.21×10^{-5}		
Copper		1.18×10^{-4}		
Cyanide		6.99×10^{-5}		
Mercury			1.03×10^{-6}	
Sulfates		0.207		
Zinc	1.26×10^{-3}			

[a]Data from Tellus Institute (1992); controlled emission values not available for all categories.

8.10 Effects of transportation

The costs and the environmental impact of transportation are affected by both the weight and volume of packaging materials. Which is most significant depends on whether the truck (the most common transportation vehicle) or other vehicle fills up first, or reaches maximum weight limitations first. In general, vehicles will weight out first with heavy materials such as glass, and fill up first with light materials such as plastics.

Boustead and Hancock (1981) present energy cost calculations for road vehicles of varying types in the United Kingdom, for a full load, ranging from 9.61 MJ/vehicle-km (15.47 MJ per vehicle-mile) for vehicles of less

Table 8.16 Controlled water pollutant emissions associated with PET production steps (g/kg PET)[a]

Pollutant	Paraxylene production	Ethylene oxide/ glycol production	DMT production	Polymerization
BOD5				
COD				
Total organic carbon				
Oil and grease				
Total suspended solids				
Total dissolved solids				
Acenaphthene		1.53×10^{-6}		
Acenaphthylene		1.53×10^{-6}		
Acrylonitrile				1.55×10^{-3}
Antimony				3.43×10^{-2}
Benzene	3.29×10^{-4}	1.29×10^{-4}		
Bis(2-chloroisopropyl) ether		3.07×10^{-6}		
Chloroform	1.80×10^{-5}	1.53×10^{-6}		
2-Chlorophenol	3.66×10^{-5}			
2,4-Dimethylphenol	1.64×10^{-4}		1.29×10^{-5}	
Dimethyl phthalate			1.29×10^{-5}	
Di-n-butyl phthalate				
Ethylbenzene	1.65×10^{-4}	3.07×10^{-6}		2.10×10^{-3}
Ethylene dichloride		3.99×10^{-5}		
Fluorene		1.53×10^{-6}		
Methylene chloride	3.71×10^{-5}	1.53×10^{-6}		
Naphthalene	7.74×10^{-5}	3.07×10^{-6}		4.51×10^{-4}
Phenol	1.09×10^{-4}	7.94×10^{-4}	3.69×10^{-4}	0.270
Tetrachloroethylene		1.53×10^{-6}		
Toluene	1.98×10^{-4}	3.07×10^{-5}		
Vinyl chloride		1.53×10^{-6}		
Chromium	3.23×10^{-4}	1.23×10^{-5}		
Copper		1.16×10^{-4}		
Cyanide		3.68×10^{-5}		
Mercury			5.79×10^{-7}	
Sulfates				
Zinc	4.37×10^{-4}			

[a]Data from Tellus Institute (1992); controlled emission values not available for all categories.

than 1 tonne, to 27.5 MJ per vehicle-km (44.32 MJ per vehicle-mile) for articulated vehicles greater than 18 tonnes. When no load is carried, they say energy requirements can be reduced by a factor of 0.7. These energy requirements include energy consumed in supplying the fuel. Van Eijk *et al.* (1992) calculate an average energy cost for truck transport as 2.32 MJ/ton-km. Cross *et al.* (1974) estimated average truck transport energy consumption as 1.80 MJ/tonne-km (2.5×10^6 BTU/1000 ton-miles).

For rail transport, Boustead and Hancock (1981) calculated a total energy requirement of 1.50 MJ per tonne-mile for general rail freight, and 1.09 MJ per tonne-mile for circuit working freight trains. Sea transport is calculated to require 0.17 MJ per tonne-mile. Cross *et al.* (1974) estimate average rail transport energy as 0.58 MJ/tonne-km (0.81×10^6 BTU/1000 ton-miles).

8.11 Packaging trends

It is generally agreed that a powerful way to reduce the environmental effects of packaging is to use less packaging. Source reduction has a long history in the packaging industry, although, until recently, it was virtually always done for economic, rather than environmental reasons. Nonetheless, many of the packaging reductions carried out in order to save money have also reduced environmental impact. This trend is continuing. Examples include removal of outer cartons, changes from rigid to flexible packages, no-frills refill packages, and product concentration permitting smaller containers.

Another change occurring in the packaging industry is removal of target heavy metals (lead, cadmium, mercury and hexavalent chromium) from packaging materials, additives, pigments and inks. This development is being spurred on, in the United States, by legislation in several states which forbids all non-essential uses of these materials in packaging.

Packaging is also undergoing changes designed to permit increased use of recycled materials in packages. Such developments include multi-layer bottles, with a sandwiched inner layer of recycled plastic, for laundry detergent and fabric softener. Other design changes are aimed at facilitating the recycling of packages. An example is the PET/EVOH multi-layer bottle for ketchup, which is designed to fit into the beverage bottle PET recycling system.

It is not infrequent for packaging design changes that result in source reduction to also result in packages that are less easily recycled. Evaluation of the environmental trade-offs in such situations can be very complex. In general, it can usually be concluded that a significant degree of source reduction outweighs loss of recycling capability if recycling rates are low to moderate. If recycling rates are high, more specific information will be required.

It should be pointed out that the majority of the environmental impacts discussed in this chapter are listed on a weight basis. In comparing alternative packaging systems, the point of comparison should always be delivery of a standard amount of product. Thus, all per weight impacts need to be converted to a per package impact, and then to a 'per delivered product' impact. Only in this way can valid comparisons be made.

References

Boustead, I. and Hancock, G.F. (1981) *Energy and Packaging*. Ellis Horwood, Chichester.

Cross, A., Welch, R.O., Hunt, R.G. and Park, W.R. (1974) *Plastics: Resource and Environmental Profile Analyses*. Manufacturing Chemists Association, Washington, DC.

Fenton, R. (1991) *Grocery Bag Comparison*, Report No. 1. The Winnipeg Packaging Product, University of Winnipeg, Winnipeg, Manitoba.

Franklin Associates (1990) *Resource and Environmental Profile Analysis of Foam Polystyrene and Bleached Paperboard Containers*. Franklin Associates Ltd., Prairie Village, KS.

Gaines, L.L. (1981) *Energy and Materials Use in the Production and Recycling of Consumer-Goods Packaging*. US Dept. of Commerce, National Technical Information Service, ANL/CNSV-TM-58.

Hunt, R.G. and Welch, R.O. (1974) *Resource and Environmental Profile Analysis of Plastics and Non-Plastics Containers*. Midwest Research Institute, MRI Project No. 3714-D.

Little, Arthur D. Inc. (1984) *The Life Cycle Energy Content of Containers: 1984 Update*, Ref. 86046-03. A.D. Little, Inc., Cambridge, MA.

Little, Arthur D. Inc. (1991) *THe Life Cycle Energy Content of Containers: 1991 Update*, Ref. 67276. A.D. Little, Inc., Cambridge, MA.

Tellus Institute (1992) *CSG/Tellus Packaging Study*, Vols. I and II. Boston, MA.

van Eijk, J., Nieuwenhuis, J.W., Post, C.W. and DeZeeuw, J.H. (1992) *Reusable Versus Disposable: A Comparison of the Environmental Impact of Polystyrene, Paper/Cardboard and Porcelain Crockery*. Ministry of Housing, Physical Planning and Environment, The Netherlands.

9 Disposal of used packaging
R. WHITE

9.1 Introduction

Modern packaging has given the public what it was demanding, quicker shopping, less frequent shopping, more choice, lower prices, better hygiene; modern supermarkets could not function without the sophistication of packaging today. This has led to the 'throw away' society where the majority of packaging has become one trip and then thrown away. However, there is now a change taking place, governments in both developed and developing countries are introducing legislation which requires used packaging to be collected and reused or recycled. A growing concern about the amount of household waste being generated in the United States in the 1980s led to a vigorous spread of mandatory recycling laws covering producers and users of all packaged goods. The waste disposal problem and shortage of landfill sites for disposal of rubbish was highlighted when the mayor of New York arranged for a load of the city's garbage to be taken to the Caribbean and back. Whilst New York has a shortage of landfill sites, this is not generally the case elsewhere in the United States. In Europe, there are problems in the Netherlands and countries where the geology is unsuitable, but again many countries have more than adequate suitable landfill sites and so could continue present methods of disposal. Used packaging is perceived as one of the principal constituents of waste mainly because of its high profile. People are very aware of the high level of used packaging in their garbage bins but in reality, used packaging only represents approximately 1–1.5% of the total tonnage of waste produced in Europe each year. Used packaging accounts for a quarter by weight of household waste and a similar amount by volume of landfilled waste. Even if all packaging were removed, there would still be a waste problem.

However, the methods of waste disposal of the 1970s and 1980s were seen by sectors of the population as a waste of valuable resources and pressure has built up on governments to introduce legislation to enforce reuse and recycling of used packaging. This started in Germany where a minority disaffected with what they saw as excessive materialism was almost steered by Government towards packaging as an outlet for their frustrations. There were no easy answers to global warming, acid rain, the hole in the ozone layer, use of nuclear energy and packaging offered a suitable outlet. The Greens identified packaging as the cause of consumerism and boycotting plastics packaging was a way of demonstrating their feelings. Politicians recognising the political threat from the Greens began to urge consumers to avoid packaging if they wanted to contribute to a solution to the 'waste problem'. Industry was unwilling to challenge the arguments. The European Court of Justice ruled in 1988 that limitations on the free movement of goods were permissible if there was an appropriate gain in environmental protection. This was seen as a way of protecting locally manufactured goods against imports and led to demands for legislation in the name of environmental protection.

Germany was the first country in Europe to introduce legislation requiring all used packaging to be collected and reused and recycled. Incineration is not permitted although at the time of its introduction, up to 30% of household waste in Germany was being treated in this way and much of the energy created recovered in the form of hot water or electrical power. Subsequently other countries have introduced or are introducing similar legislation and there is draft European Commission legislation (EC, 1992), which it is anticipated will apply to all twelve countries by the late 1990s. All this legislation requires fixed high levels of material recycling to be achieved within designated time scales. There is debate as to whether each material should have a specific target level for recycling or whether an overall figure should be set for the level of packaging recycled. Some countries in Europe have introduced restrictions on certain materials; polyethylene terephthalate (PET) is banned in Germany for carbonated drinks and PVC bottles are banned in Switzerland. Gentlemen's agreements between industry and government have stopped the use of PVC in Sweden and led to restrictions on some forms of packaging in the Netherlands. Many of the restrictions are based on emotion rather than scientific fact. PVC for instance is seen as posing a carcinogenic hazard for the workers producing it, containing heavy metal salts which can leak out if it is put into landfill and harm the environment, and if burnt gives rise to dioxins. The reality is that modern polymerisation production techniques do not put workers at risk, heavy metal salts are not used in the material used for packaging and when the material is burnt, there is no evidence of dioxins being produced (PCOMI, 1992), but the incinerated gases must be scrubbed to remove hydrogen chloride and it is recommended that the material is burnt at very high temperatures up to 1200°C. PVC is one of the best packaging materials available.

There has also been pressure on governments and the food industry for safer, cleaner food. Packaging has played an important role in helping to provide this, but has also been subject to legislation that sets out what may and may not be used. In Europe, a directive on plastics in contact with foodstuffs (EC, 1990) sets out the monomers and additives that may be used and sets limits on the amounts that may migrate into the food under standard test conditions. These strict conditions rule out the use of post consumer recycled plastics because their content cannot be guaranteed. The legislation which states that the flavour of olefactory performance of the food may not be affected also rules out the use of recycled paper products for similar reasons.

In the United States, the Food and Drug administration does not allow the use of recycled materials in contact with foodstuffs except in the case of polyethylene terephthalate which has been broken down into its constituent monomers, purified and repolymerised. Food safety laws are in direct conflict with the recycling and reuse legislation and it is against this background that the collection, reuse, recycling, incineration and landfill of used packaging must be viewed.

9.2　Collection of used packaging

Used packaging is a lot of material often in small deposits spread over a very large area and is made up of a wide variety of materials some of which is contaminated with food and products that can be hazardous to human health thus making collection and sorting an expensive and difficult operation. The 'packaging flow' throughout the life of a product from manufacture to disposal is important because waste is produced at various stages in this life cycle. Whilst waste arising at various stages is important in the recovery process, the main volumes arise at the household or industrial level where the packed product is used. This environmental balance is described diagrammatically in Figure 9.1. The diagram for 'paper' (Figure 9.2) illustrates how complicated the material flow pattern is.

Most household waste is a mixture of used packaging (24%), other papers (29%), textiles, garden waste and waste food (25%), used diapers and many other unsavoury products. In most countries, this is collected by local authorities and either incinerated or landfilled. Systems are in operation to sort material and to remove anything with value. In Dunkirk, France, waste is collected and dumped on a conveyer where people on each side remove bottles, plastics, paper and cans for recycling. The stench is overpowering and workers can only stay alongside the conveyer for an hour before having a break. It is significant that a qualification to work there is that people must have been unemployed for a year. This type of sorting poses health risks for the people and the Danish Government has banned the hand sorting of mixed household waste. The economics of such operations in Europe are that they need a subsidy because the value of the products recovered does not cover the operational costs, but this probably ignores the savings on landfill. In lesser developed countries where labour is cheap, a local industry has arisen where unemployed scavenge the rubbish tips for anything that is recoverable and this has led to quite high recycling levels on plastic bottles, for instance in Egypt.

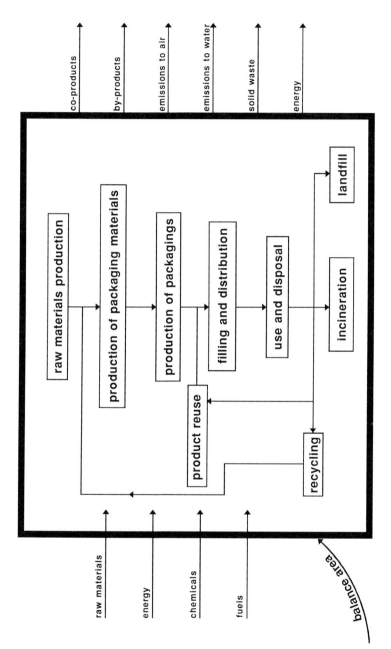

Figure 9.1 Packaging materials and environmental balance.

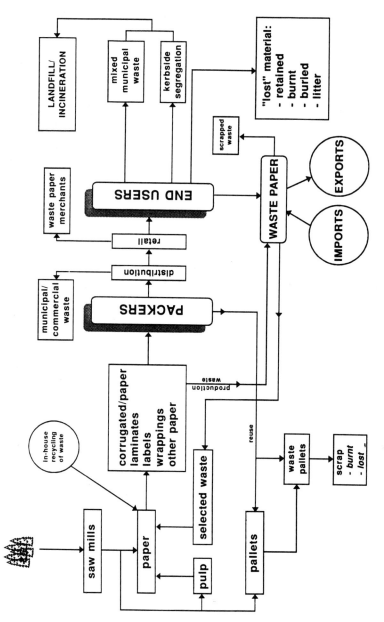

Figure 9.2 Materials flow chart for paper.

There are many other options to utilise the mixed material arriving at a centralised waste treatment plant, from energy recovery alone to combined materials recovery, energy recovery and compost systems. Many plants concentrate on producing waste derived fuel pellets and ferrous metals. The physical processing of the waste seeks to sort it into fractions by virtue of the different nature and characteristics of the various fractions. The material is first screened by passing it through a rotary screen and breaking it down into components. The second stage is magnetic extraction which can remove 90% of the ferrous products present. Better extraction levels are obtained if the material passes through hammer mills before passing over a magnetic belt. The final stage is to use ballistic separators, density separators and air classifiers to separate the waste into light and heavy fractions. Materials separated in this way tend to be heavily contaminated so that they only find low grade applications. Source separation schemes achieve higher levels of refinement leading to higher quality outlets. To compete, recycled materials must be able to achieve the same performance specifications as virgin raw materials.

Legislation has therefore centred on separating waste before it is mixed and becomes rubbish. It has aimed at taking out the valuable and easily sorted components of the waste. Glass and plastics bottles and metal cans can be separated and reused or recycled. Deposit systems are employed whereby a small charge is made when the product is purchased and a refund made when the used empty package is returned. Practice has shown that a deduction from the deposit must be made to cover the cost of collection and recycling. When recovery rates are high (approximately 75%), the value of deposits retained is insufficient to cover the cost of the collection and sorting process. Also the deposit has to be relatively high to overcome the inertia of people to persuade them to return the empty container. In Denmark, the deposit on some soft drinks is more than the value of the drink. Where hazardous products are concerned the container has a very high deposit to ensure that it is properly disposed of and does not get into the general waste stream of used packaging.

The other method of sorting and collection is known as kerbside collection where households are asked to separate waste into separate bins (plastic, paper, glass, metal, used batteries) and these are then collected and the products sent to recycling centres. Perhaps the best known scheme is the Toronto blue box scheme in Canada; but it is claimed to be too expensive and has almost bankrupted some local councils. The cost of recovery is not offset by the value of the materials recovered, especially at times of economic downturn where prices of international products like plastics and pulps are low in order that plants are kept operational. This makes it difficult to give any accurate costs for kerbside collection but published data for the United Kingdom (Cooper, 1992) suggests it could be as high as £130 per tonne for kerbside collection with the multi-materials collection schemes in the £40–80 per tonne range. One scheme in Greater Manchester provided households with a second bin for mixed recyclables, which was then delivered to a centre for sorting. However, the costs of sorting were found to be higher than the revenue generated and scheme was abandoned. The actual cost of collection had only increased marginally as the local authority changed collection schedules and the bins were supplied free to the council.

Although the collection costs were minimised, the cost of sorting was well above the revenue from the segregated waste even if the full cost of the landfill savings was credited to the scheme. The full cost of waste disposal is relatively high in Manchester so that where disposal is significantly cheaper, this form of segregation would be even more uneconomic.

9.3   Identification of materials for collection and sorting

The German and French packaging collection schemes require that the used packaging materials be marked in some way to indicate that the manufacturer/user has prepaid the fee for the collection of the used packaging. Perhaps the best known or most notorious is the green dot from Duales System Deutschland (DSD). DSD is a company which collects used packaging and sells it on to recyclers. It initially charged on the number of packs per year and their capacity but, based on the initial experience, the system has been changed to charge on a weight basis rather than volume and to have a scale of charges for various materials, plastics and laminated materials costing the most and natural materials the least. Once a packaging user has prepaid the fee, they are allowed to put a green dot on their packaging. A similar scheme but with a blue dot is planned in France. There are other schemes operating in Germany for the collection of other materials, e.g. corrugated cases, foil, etc., each of which carries its own symbol to signify that it will be collected by that particular organisation.

Many packs also carry a symbol indicating the material can be recycled and rigid plastic containers carry the mark with a number that identifies the polymer used in its manufacture and which aids separation prior to recycling.

9.4   Landfill

Landfill is the principal method of disposing of UK municipal (household) waste, with 90% of the waste being treated in this way. It comes bottom in the EC hierarchy of waste management options. The expression landfill broadly relates to any controlled operation where waste is deposited onto land. Over the years it has gained a bad reputation because of what can only be described as dumping of rubbish on land which is unsuitable or not properly prepared with the result that toxic materials have leached out, damaging the surrounding environment. There have also been cases where methane has built up in old landfill sites and been the cause of serious explosions. If properly exploited this build up of methane can be tapped and used as a source of energy. Modern landfill sites are now designed, engineered and managed to minimise the risk of these problems arising. There are, however, many sites that became operational some time ago and it is difficult to introduce controls retrospectively and to do so will give costs that will be passed on to the waste producer.

Landfill sites are managed according to the permeability of the geology under the deposited rubbish. The preferred method is to contain the build up of liquid in the site. The main sources of this build up is rain, surface and ground water, liquids in the waste or from its breakdown. Some water is lost through evaporation or taken up by surrounding plants but it is necessary to stop any water that could contain toxic materials leaching away from the site. This is done by either the geology of the site, e.g. a clay layer which is then covered with a plastic liner. On some sites where the underlying strata is permeable, clay is imported to form a base which is then covered with a plastic liner. It is good practice to pump out the liquid that builds up regularly, in order to prevent problems, although on some sites it is not always necessary.

As part of a good management policy, the materials placed in landfill sites should be controlled and toxic materials disposed of in other ways, such as controlled incineration. Used packaging does not present any hazard unless it has contained dangerous materials, e.g. medical waste, chemicals, pesticides and the safe disposal of these is now becoming a key issue with landfill increasingly not being an option.

Household waste, which is a significant percentage of used packaging, can be compacted in the landfill site but will settle in excess of 10% of the compacted volume due to biodegradation. The waste provides a source of nutrients for microorganisms which in the initial stage thrive in the presence of oxygen. As the oxygen is used up, the waste enters the methanorganic stage where the principal by-products are methane and carbon dioxide. As the gas can cause serious nuisance and hazards the site must be managed to allow it vent to atmosphere, or to bore a system of wells which draw the gas off for burning as an energy source.

Many governments are adopting the policy that the polluter must pay and as a consequence landfill costs will increase, due to the stricter controls and in an attempt to reduce the volume going to the sites. In 1990, the cost per tonne of landfill, ignoring transport, was £5–20 per tonne (Price, 1990). No clear picture of cost trends is available but in the medium term, costs are expected to increase 200–300% and incineration as a method of disposal will become more competitive reflecting the current situation in Europe where landfill is in the region of £130–170 per tonne.

The draft European Waste Directive limits landfill to 10% of the total packaging within 10 years of it becoming law. This would result in local authorities being very selective of the materials going into a site and may well be limited to the residues from incineration.

9.5   Composting

Methods of composting household waste are being examined; this requires the putrescibles and other suitable materials to be separated and composted under controlled conditions. The problems associated with the process are to ensure that all unsuitable materials such as glass are removed and that no toxic contaminants such as heavy metals are included.

It is a process in which microorganisms break down the materials in the presence of oxygen at elevated temperatures ($<50°C$) to give water, carbon dioxide, compost and heat. The microbiological activity heats up the compostable material and this composting stage is usually followed by a final stage at ambient temperature where the compost matures for several weeks. This is important to destroy any phototoxins formed in the initial stage, which would affect any plants grown in the compost.

The only used packaging which can be composted is paper products but they are not ideal material for the process, and there are more appropriate methods of disposal of used packaging.

9.6   Incineration

In some countries, such as Denmark and Japan, incineration is the main method of disposing of household waste. Denmark incinerates 75% of its waste and uses the heat generated to heat municipal buildings and homes. The amount of household waste incinerated varies throughout Europe; there are no incinerators in Ireland, Germany burns 30% of its household waste, although the packaging legislation does not allow packaging to be burnt. The proposed EC legislation allows for up to 30% of packaging to be incinerated provided the energy is recovered and the calorific value of the materials is greater than 13 mJ/kg (e.g. paper and cardboard) and provided it has no greater impact on the environment than the fuel it replaces.

The combustion of household waste is seen as an important source of fuel and reduces the volume by some 90% (US Government Advisory Association, 1989). There has been a rapid growth of energy recovery systems from municipal solid waste in the United States and there are plans in the United Kingdom to build waste to energy power plants under the Government's Non Fossil Fuel Obligation.

There are two main methods of combustion, one where the total waste is burnt and the second where it is converted to refuse-derived fuel. The combustion of waste leads to gaseous emissions which are closely controlled by law. There are also limits on the minimum residual lime, minimum oxygen levels and a minimum furnace temperature of 850°C. The design of the furnace is important in controlling the emissions which following the combustion stage are scrubbed to remove acid gases such as hydrogen chloride and sulphur oxides. Cyclones remove the coarse grit particles and electrostatic precipitation and filter bags remove the fine dust. Rapid cooling of the gases to below 300°C is essential to prevent dioxin formation in the post-combustion stage.

The estimated running costs of an advanced municipal waste incinerator with heat recovery is £45–50 per tonne.

Waste derived fuel pellets have already been mentioned. Typically the calorific value of such material is 18 mJ/kg compared with 27 mJ/kg for coal. However, there are problems with its use:

- clinker formation and boiler fouling;
- emissions of hydrogen chloride which require scrubbing;
- emission of particles high in metal chlorides which require to be controlled.

9.7 Reuse of packaging

The reuse of packaging rates second in the hierarchy of many governments when it comes to packaging legislation. Glass bottles have traditionally been collected and returned to the supplier for washing, inspection and reuse. The closed loop system used for milk and beer, where used containers can be collected when fresh supplies are delivered works well and many return trips can be achieved. However, with modern supermarket retailing, the systems are not geared to taking returns and the process has become less popular and the cost of recovery is often not justified. As a result, some governments have introduced legislation requiring retailers to take back empties and introduced deposit systems to encourage reasonable return rates.

Reuse systems focus on glass bottles, although plastic bottles are included in some countries, notably Germany and South Africa. Practice has shown that deposit schemes are successful, return rates of 90% or more are common. Once returned, the packaging can be reused or recycled.

The bottles have to be washed and inspected to ensure that they are safe for reuse. The washing procedure includes caustic/detergent washes and the effluent from such processes has to be disposed of safely. Energy requirements including transport of returns can be high.

Other packaging materials, such as pallets, are regularly reused and international collection schemes exist. Bulk containers for liquids and solids are now more widely used; these are generally designated for one product use to avoid contamination and the use of such containers is expected to grow.

Trials are being carried out in the Netherlands with bulk packs of detergents (bag in box) that are delivered to shops. The customer can either bring his own bottle for refill or obtain a new bottle from a dispenser alongside the bulk pack. When empty, the bulk pack is returned to the factory for refilling. The method is not new; Body Shop in the United Kingdom ran a similar project for shampoo. The main problem is product integrity as one cannot ensure that the bottles used by the customer are free of contamination.

9.8   Recycling

Many processes for the manufacture of packaging recycle in-house waste as part of the production process. The plastics industry for instance recycles 99% of its production scrap. This is clean material controlled in terms of purity, composition, etc. Post-consumer packaging waste is a totally different problem because it is often soiled with decayed food and could contain toxic substances and it is because the history of such material is unknown that it creates problems in recycling. Metals and glass present the least problems whereas plastics present the packaging industry with the greatest challenges.

The growing environmental awareness of society in the last 10 years, particularly in the industrialised societies, has led to a demand for more recycling to husband the world's resources. The reasons for recycling need to be examined to be sure that there is a net environmental benefit. Recycling does conserve raw materials (mineral and energy), reduces disposal costs and pollution effects such as emissions from incineration. However, there is no agreed method of evaluating these factors and until such times as a universally agreed method of life cycle analysis is developed, there will always be arguments about the merits and demerits of recycling and other methods of packaging disposal.

9.8.1   Recycling paper packaging

Packaging paper and boards are used for a wide range of products, primary packaging such as bags, sacks, cartons for frozen foods and dry goods, secondary packaging such as corrugated cases and transit packaging. It is also used in combination with other materials, e.g. plastics, aluminium foil when special properties or barrier resistance are required. Combining it with other materials makes it more difficult to recycle as these other materials (contraries) have to be separated from the paper fibres.

Paper packaging can be divided into three main categories:

- packaging papers;
- cartons;
- corrugated cases.

The material flows through the collection systems are complex as shown in Figures 9.3, 9.4 and 9.5. The collection of waste paper is dependent on efficient recovery and collection schemes where each different grade of paper is kept separate. In all, there are eleven different grades of waste paper (Table 9.1).

Different grading schemes are used in the United States and Europe. Each grade in whatever system contains a heterogeneous collection of waste paper. Groups 7–11 cover the packaging grades; these tend to be the lower quality materials and as there is a tendency to down cycle paper as a raw material, waste packaging will tend to finish up in a lower quality paper of board.

Having collected and sorted the waste paper, it is transported to a paper mill which will select the grade of waste required to make a particular type of paper or board. The material is pulped or slushed with large quantities of water to break the paper down into individual fibres, it is then passed through screens to remove contaminants centrifugally cleaned to remove grit and small solid particles. It is often treated with steam or other methods to disperse plastic materials and adhesives which cause problems in the paper making process. Having cleaned the material, the fibres are refined and then flow onto the paper making wire in the normal way.

The recycling process shortens the fibres each time they are processed so that after about four cycles, the fibres are too short to stay on the paper making wire and finish up as a sludge. Efforts are being made to find uses for this sludge including feeding into the middle ply in a multiply board where the first ply or layer of fibres on the paper making wire helps retain the fine particles. Where the fibres are combined with materials such as polyethylene a more complex pulping and cleaning process is required. For liquid packaging, board for instance, the cartons are put into the pulper and soaked at 60°C and agitated for 30 min. The slurry passes through a multi-stage cleaning system to take out the polyethylene and aluminium. The polyethylene is screened off using a mechanical process and the aluminium is removed using centrifugal force.

This stage takes around 20 min, depending how many times the slurry is screened; this can be up to three times to achieve the purest pulp possible. The pulp slurry is sent to the de-inking plant where soaps are

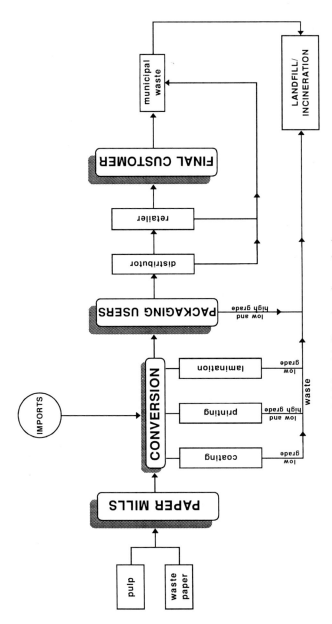

Figure 9.3 Materials flow chart for packaging papers.

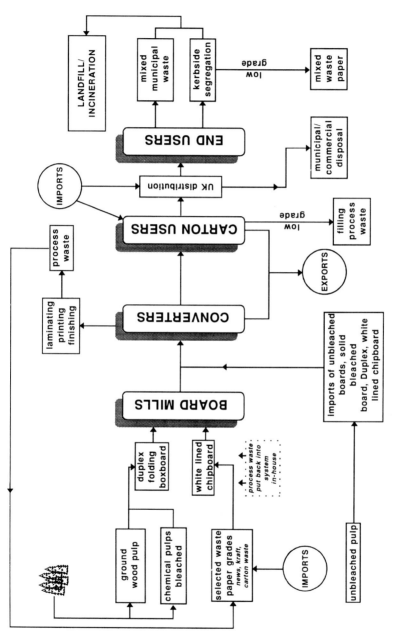

Figure 9.4 Materials flow chart for cartons.

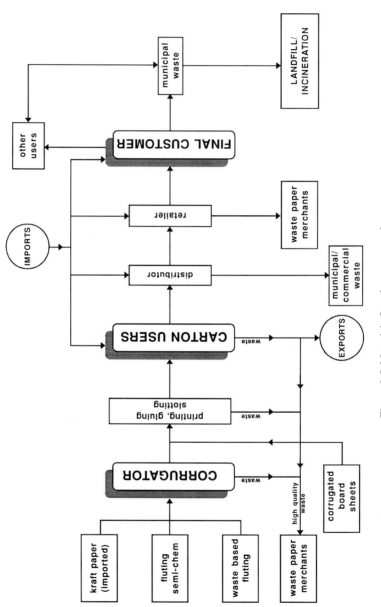

Figure 9.5 Materials flow for corrugated cases.

Table 9.1 UK waste paper grade structure

Group 1	Best white shavings, fine shavings, white and cream shavings, and white coated shavings
Group 2	White unprinted, white duplex and other mechanical wood pulp cuttings, slightly printed white card cuttings, best one-cuts, printed woody one-cuts, white and light tone shavings, white and coloured shavings
Group 3	White and lightly printed scanboard
Group 4	Ledgers, white and coloured heavy letter, white and coloured continuous stationery waste, white and coloured carbonless copy paper waste, quire, best white pams
Group 5	Over-issue news, once-read news, over-issue white and coloured woody pams, news and pams, telephone directories and soft covers, once-read woody pams
Group 6	Buff envelope cuttings, buff tabulating cards, coloured tabulating cards, light brown and buffs
Group 7	Double lined kraft and new KLS cuttings
Group 8	Container waste (old KLS)
Group 9	Mixed papers
Group 10	Coloured card
Group 11	Contaminated grades

Source: BPBIF.

added to soften the remaining ink particles. Air is injected into the solution and rises to the surface, carrying with it the ink particles. The ink is removed with the soap and foam and the clean fibre is concentrated ready for processing.

Whilst there is a very large use of waste paper worldwide, it is not recommended that packaging material made from it is used in direct contact with foodstuffs as it cannot be guaranteed free from toxic contaminants. With stricter food laws being introduced worldwide, waste paper materials can only be used in non-food contact outlets. As a result there is an increasing lobby that recommends that waste paper packaging should be incinerated with energy recovery and fresh trees used to produce food packaging material because trees are a renewable source of material and the forestry programme relies on harvesting the wood on a regular basis.

9.8.2   Recycling aluminium

The aluminium used in packaging is principally either in the form of cans or foil; the foil is usually combined with other materials to form flexible laminates used for either liquid or dry products. Figure 9.6 gives a brief outline of the flows of aluminium packaging.

The production of aluminium from bauxite, the naturally occurring aluminium mineral, requires large amounts of power (about 7.5 kWh for each pound of material produced (Aluminium Association, 1990)). Ninety-five percent of the energy is saved when new metal is made from used cans

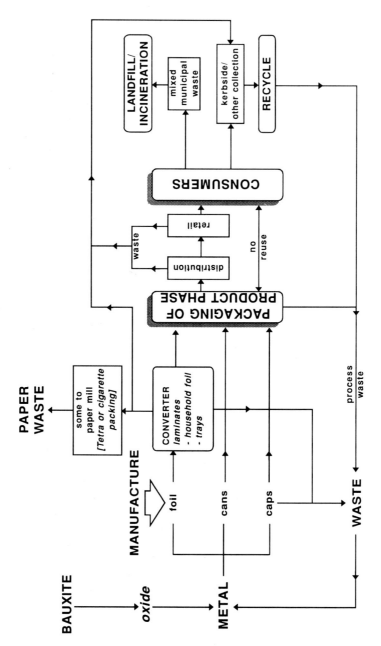

Figure 9.6 Materials flow for aluminium.

instead of raw materials. It is important to the economics of the recycling process that there is a regular and continuous supply of used cans through effective and convenient collection systems which provide the closed loop for the recycling process. Much publicity and deposit schemes have been used to raise consumer awareness of the need to recycle aluminium cans, and as a result it is considered a recycling success story. Recovery rates as high as 85% are recorded through these collection schemes. On collection the cans are crushed and baled for shipment to the recycling plant (Anon, 1992a). The material is first shredded into small pieces and passed through a magnetic separator to remove any steel present. A de-coating process burns off the paint and lacquer, the emissions from this process are recirculated and burnt with more fuel to preheat further batches of shredded cans, improving the energy efficiency of the process and reducing emissions.

The hot shreds of aluminium are then fed into melting furnaces where the composition of the molten metal can be alloyed to obtain the correct composition before casting into ingots. The ingots then go forward for the manufacture of new cans.

Aluminium foil poses much greater problems for recycling because it is usually combined with other materials such as polyethylene, paper, PET to name but a few. Currently there are no commercial methods available for separating the materials from these laminates although research work is being carried out. The only real alternative to landfill for these products is incineration. The one exception to this has been the separation of paper fibres from board foil polythene cartons for liquid packaging which is discussed elsewhere in this chapter.

9.8.3   Recycling of steel and tinplate

Food cans are principally made from steel or tin plated steel. Metal packaging represents about 8% of household waste (Anon, 1992b). The recycling of both tinplate and steel cans from the domestic waste stream has steadily increased in recent years. Collection of the cans is arranged either through can banks or more usually by the use of electromagnetic separation at the waste treatment plants (Anon, 1992b). Up to 80% of the available steel can be recovered. Once collected, the tin cans are cleaned to remove dirt, paper, plastic and aluminium and the dense pellets are de-tinned using an electrolytic process. The steel produced needs no further processing before its use in high specification steel making. The tin recovered can be reused to produce new tin plate for can making. The recycling of steel cans is also a recycling success story (Figure 9.7).

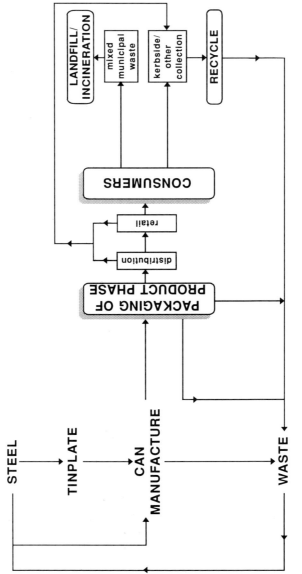

Figure 9.7 Materials flow chart for tinplate/steel.

9.8.4   Recycling of glass

The chemical composition of glass is largely unchanged by repeated reheating so the degradation processes that are associated with the reprocessing or re-melting of organically based packaging materials are absent.

Traditionally glassworks have used some 15–20% of broken glass or 'cullet' in their raw material mix but this proportion has increased dramatically. This is a direct result of industry policy in relation to the recovery of broken glass from waste, a desire to save energy because broken glass melts more readily than the mixed raw materials, and the all important attitude and response to customers.

The glass recycling industry in Europe has grown rapidly over the last 15 years. In the United Kingdom, the amount recycled has risen from 55 000 tonnes in 1980 to 372 000 tonnes in 1990 (Ogilvie, 1992). The glass industry has set a target of 50% recovery by the year 2000. This target will necessitate the reclamation of glass with good colour separation to enable much greater qualities of clear glass to be recycled (Figure 9.8).

From much of the world come reports of steady increases in recycled glass. Switzerland already uses 75% (Cornaz, 1989) recycled glass in new bottles and jars, and some 1.5 million tonnes have been collected by its Bottle Bank scheme (Anon, 1989a), which saves the Swiss Government some SFr20 million per year.

All containers produced by the German glass industry contain 50% cullet (Anon, 1989b) and the Netherlands reports (Anon, 1988) the same figure and claims to be Europe's leading glass collector. Japan (Ichiko, 1988) claims 9.2 billion containers incorporate 55% cullet. Average figures such as these indicate that many containers have in excess of 65% cullet and Swiss green container production (Anon, 1989a) is manufactured entirely from cullet.

The glass collected is generally contaminated with a variety of materials, e.g. metals, stone, cork, plastics and other materials not suitable for use by the glassworks. So it is necessary to clean the material, which has traditionally included handsorting but with increased volume being used automatic methods are being installed.

In the older method, the glass is put onto a conveyor and hand sorted to remove obvious contraries and oversize material, ferrous materials are then taken out by magnetic separator. Then the material is crushed in a hammermill followed by magnetic separator. The crushing operation gives cullet of a specific size. The material is then screened with an air classifier which removes light material such as paper, aluminium foil, cork and plastic. Some glass works employ a final hand sorting operation.

As the volume of cullet used and the specifications required by the glass works have increased, hand sorting has been replaced by electronic methods of detection and selection.

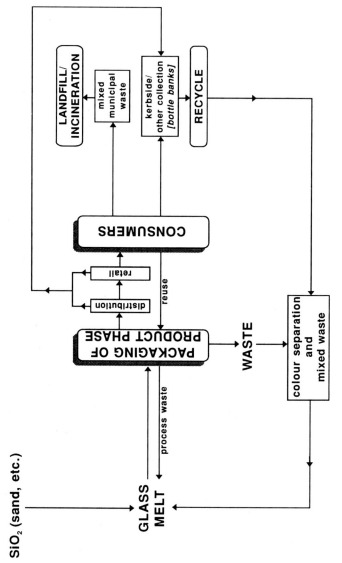

Figure 9.8 Materials flow chart for glass.

Separation of the coloured glass automatically presents the major problem to the industry. To do it efficiently requires the glass to be in large pieces, i.e. whole bottles which can then be separated into brown, green, clear and opaque by measuring the effect of a beam of visible wavelength light on the bottle, by measuring either the transparency or the reflectance. Once cleaned and sorted the cullet is fed into the furnace for reuse.

9.8.5   Recycling plastics packaging

Plastics packaging is lightweight and functional. It has replaced many traditional materials in recent years and the use of plastics has grown rapidly. The term plastic covers a wide range of polymeric materials which are made up from different base chemicals. They are divided into two types, thermosetting resins and thermoplastics. Packaging is mainly composed of the latter, which can be recycled. Some thermoset resins are used for bottle caps and these cannot be recycled and their use will decline as a result of legislation.

At least 13 different thermoplastic polymers are used either on their own or in combinations in packaging. The flow patterns are complicated as shown in Figure 9.9. For the inexperienced person, it is difficult to identify the materials and this is a major problem. A conventional numbering system has been set up for plastic containers so that the material can be identified (Figure 9.10). This covers the main materials used but does not take into account laminated materials. Also the system can only be applied to rigid containers or printed film.

For a material to be successfully recycled, it should not be mixed with other plastics. If polypropylene is mixed with more than 10% of high density polyethylene, the impact strength and other properties are substantially reduced. Other materials are incompatible if processed together, e.g. low density polyethylene and polystyrene, others, like polyethylene terephthalate, have to be dried before processing so it is essential for any recycling scheme to keep each plastic material separate to be successful. The most successful schemes have been those where the material can be easily recognised by the pack design, for example, plastic Coke bottles, high density milk bottles in the United States. Therefore, the emphasis during the collection process is to keep each material separate.

Mixed plastics can be recycled but it is necessary to add a compatibiliser which is a rubber based compound which acts as a binder for the plastic materials. This can add up to £200 per tonne to the cost of the material. The product can be used for fence posts and as a general wood substitute. One problem with the materials is that it can have variable properties due to variation of the constituents and recyclers of such material try to make it in large batches in order to establish a minimum performance level.

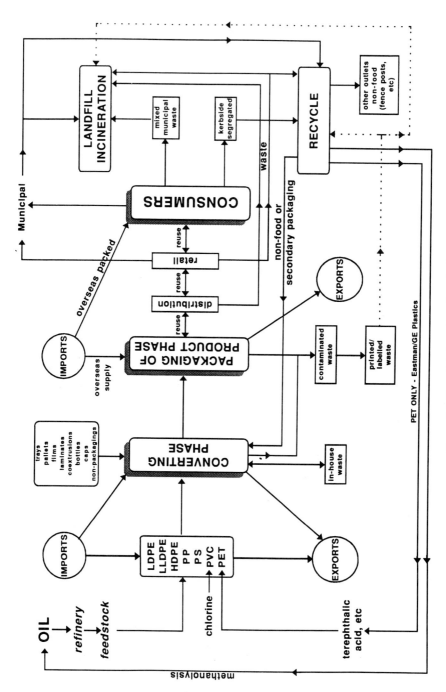

Figure 9.9 Materials flow chart for plastics.

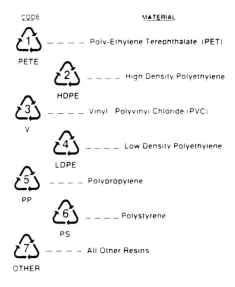

CODE   MATERIAL

1   — — — — Poly-Ethylene Terephthalate (PET)

PETE

2   — — — — High Density Polyethylene

HDPE

3   — — — — Vinyl Polyvinyl Chloride (PVC)

V

4   — — — — Low Density Polyethylene

LDPE

5   — — — — Polypropylene

PP

6   — — — — Polystyrene

PS

7   — — — — All Other Resins

OTHER

Figure 9.10 SPI plastics container material code.

In principle, the same recycling procedures are used for all the materials. They are sorted and in general plastic bottles are kept separate from films as the grades of polymers used for each outlet differ.

The bottles are granulated and the resultant material washed to remove labels, adhesives and other contaminants. The material is dried and passed through a cyclone to remove any metallic particles and grit. It is then extruded and chopped into small pellets and can then be mixed with virgin polymer or used on its own to make new bottles or other plastic components. A recent development has been to co-extrude the recycled material between two layers of virgin material which gives a bottle indistinguishable in appearance from one made of virgin material. The inner layer of virgin material also protects the bottle contents from possible contamination from the recycled material (Figure 9.11).

A similar process can be used for film where it is chopped into small pieces washed and cleaned and then re-extruded. As films are often heavily printed, the colour of the resultant product will be variable and can only be used for low grade outlets such as rubbish bags and carrier bags.

9.8.5.1 Low density polyethylene (LDPE). Main uses are plastic squeezy bottles, bags and carrier bags. If uncontaminated, the material can be recycled many times (tests up to 20 times have shown no deterioration (M. Shill, private communication)). Supermarket chains in the United Kingdom collect and recycle detergent bottles and carrier bags on a regular basis.

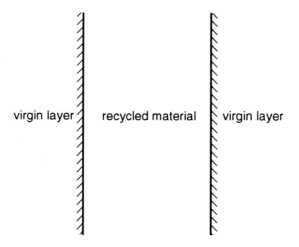

virgin layer   recycled material   virgin layer

Figure 9.11 Section through the wall of a co-extruded bottle.

9.8.5.2 High density polyethylene (HDPE).   Uses include rigid bottles and bags. The materials can be recycled many times provided they are not contaminated. Laundry detergent bottles and milk bottles are a major source of materials for recycling although it is difficult to remove the perfume of the detergent from the polymer or the smell of stale milk.

9.8.5.3 Polypropylene (PP).   Uses include closures, diary pot bottles but probably the main outlet is biaxially orientated film for wrappers and bags. The material can be recycled without problem provided it is not contaminated. Because it is mainly used in film and bags, it is costly to collect, little material spread over a large area.

9.8.5.4 Polyethylene terephthalate (PET).   PET is widely used for carbonated beverage bottles, ovenable trays and film; one of the recycling success stories. The material is clearly identified from the bottle labels and distinctive design so can be separated from the waste stream, granulated, washed and cleaned, dried and then reprocessed into base cups for new carbonated drinks bottles but more often into fibre fill for padded clothing and duvets.

9.8.5.5 Polyvinylchloride (PVC).   This material has been the focus of the criticism of plastics by many of the militant 'green' organisations. Twenty years ago the debate concentrated on the health hazards to which workers in PVC plants were exposed. Later the attention switched to the disposal of PVC and the dioxins that may be formed when it is burnt. Current scientific evidence shows that incineration of all chlorine containing materials can give rise to dioxins, but that if PVC is incinerated at high temperature and the flue gases washed and quickly cooled as previously described in this chapter, then it is a safe material to use. There will always be people who see PVC as an environmentally harmful material however carefully it is produced, however inert the chlorine content and however beneficial the application to which it is put.

PVC is one of the best packaging materials available; it is widely used for bottles, storage trays, thermoformed trays for modified atmosphere packed foods. It uses much less of our non-renewable petroleum resources than other thermoplastics, the chlorine used is derived from salt of which there are high natural reserves. PVC formulations can be tailored to different applications and it is more tolerant of contamination than is the case with some commodity polymers such as polyethylene and polypropylene.

The main source of post-consumer used PVC packaging is plastic bottles (there are some closed loop systems where trays used to collate and display goods on supermarket shelves are collected and returned for recycling) which are collected and separated from other plastic bottles manually (from the polymer identification codes (see Figure 9.10)). The chlorine atoms in PVC also give it a unique characteristic that enables it to be identified by automatic methods of sorting.

The PVC is cleaned and granulated and then moulded into long-term applications such as pipes, where it can replace new PVC.

9.8.5.6 Polystyrene (PS). Polystyrene is widely used in packaging; thermoformed for dairy pots and tubs and injection blow for talc bottles/dispensers. It is also used for caps and closures, and recent developments include biaxially orientated film. These outlets have attracted little attention from the 'green' lobby. However, another form of the material has been the focus of 'green' protest and that is foam polystyrene, which is used as a protective packaging for electronic and other products to stop impact damage. It is also used for take away disposable food containers and the litter these produce has been the subject of legislation. Originally, foam polystyrene was made using chlorofluorocarbons (CFCs) as the foaming agent. These are now banned under the Montreal Protocol to protect the ozone layer and other foaming agents are now used. As a result of the litter problem from fast food chains and the high profile of the material, recycling methods have been developed for foam polystyrene. The material is collected, cleaned, crushed and re-extruded for non-food outlets.

9.9   Multilayer materials

Co-extrusion technology has developed over the last 10 years to produce packaging materials with specific barrier properties. It has enabled producers to tailor make materials using thin layers of expensive materials with good barrier properties and produce a laminate which has good barrier properties and is economically viable. Some of the commercially available materials have up to seven layers of material and can contain up to four or five different polymers.

Opinion is divided on the feasibility of recycling such materials. Oxygen barrier is one property that these materials are required to exhibit and this is often achieved by using ethylene vinyl alcohol (EVOH) or polyvinylidene chloride (PVdC). The tendency is to use EVOH as PVdC cannot be recycled and as it contains chlorine, it is not considered acceptable by some organisations.

Because of the relatively small quantities of these materials, they could be recycled with films made out of the commodity polymers but as the market widens and because of the diverse range of materials, it may be necessary to find alternative ways of recycling these materials. The cost of recycling gives materials which are more expensive than virgin materials and whilst no overall accurate figures can be given, recycled materials will be more expensive unless subsidies or tax incentives to use them are introduced.

All the preceding recycling methods depend on mechanical methods of reprocessing the polymers. Because of the strict food laws in Europe and America, post-consumer plastics waste cannot be used in direct contact with foodstuffs because it cannot be guaranteed to be free of contaminants. The difficulties of sorting plastics and mechanically recycling mixed polymers has encouraged the industry to look at chemical methods of recycling used packaging. Whilst mechanical recycling should be seen as a relatively low cost, low energy solution, as long as markets for the recycled materials can be found, and should be seen as the first priority, the alternatives being developed would substantially contribute to increasing the amount of plastics recovered from plastics packaging.

Mechanical recycling produces similar material with generally a lower quality, chemical recycling leads to new materials with no quality compromise. The first commercially approved process is for PET where the material is broken down into its components which are then purified and repolymerised. At present it is only being operated on a relatively small scale but it is being claimed that on scaling up the process, it becomes economically viable. Recently, DuPont (Anon, 1993) has indicated that it may be possible to extend the process to polyethylene and polyamide (nylon) film structures.

Techniques have also been developed on a pilot scale to convert the mixed plastics into an acceptable hydrocarbon feedstock suitable for mixing with the feedstock currently used in polymer production. Contamination remains one of the problems of the process; these include heavy metals and chlorine from PVC. Work is also going on to convert the mixed plastics from post-consumer waste back into oil which can then be used to replace virgin mineral oil.

9.10   Biodegradable plastics

The industry has been pressurised to find ways of making plastics biodegradable because plastics do not break down into basic components or rot when put in landfill. None of the plastics in general use for packaging are biodegradable. However, the polyethylene used by Hi-Cone to make can carriers (the strips of plastic which are used to pack four or six cans together to form a multipack) has an additive incorporated in it so that after about 6 weeks' exposure to ultraviolet light, the plastic becomes brittle and breaks into small pieces. This is an embrittlement rather than biodegradation and is as a result of various green pressure groups accusing Hi-Cone of killing wildlife. There were supposedly instances of sea birds who were killed because they were strangled in the plastic rings. The claim was disputed by the company but they incorporated the additive in their material so that even if the can carriers were discarded as litter there would be no risk to wildlife.

The plastics industry has been careful to stress that if biodegradable plastics were available they could become a problem if they became part of the recycling systems because there would then be no guarantee on the life of the products made from recycled plastics.

Much research effort has gone into producing thermoplastics from naturally occurring materials. The first one to be marketed was ICI's Biopol which is completely biodegradable and is made from naturally occurring materials. At present only small quantities are available and it is very expensive. It can be made into film and bottles; bottles made from it are used in Germany for shampoo.

Several companies have developed biodegradable polymers from starch but these are not yet widely available. These materials should not be confused with starch-filled polyethylene which is used for carrier bags. These starch-filled materials are not biodegradable but when exposed to the elements, the starch is leached out leaving the basic polymer still present.

Biodegradable materials were principally seen as a solution to the litter problem but the answer to litter must lie in the education of people to take rubbish home rather than dumping it in the towns and countryside.

9.11   The way ahead

The field of recovery and disposal of used packaging is very dynamic because of the effects of legislation and restriction being imposed by governments and other organisations. The pressures are to reduce the volume of waste packaging and to recycle as much as possible. As already stated, this assumes that suitable outlets can be found for recycled materials. The economics of collection recycling and reuse are confused. There is no doubt that glass, aluminium and tinplate are viable materials to recycle and greater quantities will be collected and used.

Paper recycling is an established industry but is currently being overwhelmed by the amount of material available. Capital investment is required to use more material and the economics compared with other methods of disposal such as incineration may in the long run make this a more attractive proposition.

Plastics present the largest problem. Recycling is uneconomic compared with the use of virgin material; incineration may well be the long-term solution. The debate on the need to recycle, incinerate and landfill will continue until such time as an acceptable and viable method of total life cycle analysis is available for packaging that will give numerised data, enabling the correct choice to be made to produce a sensible balance of economics, environmental protection and packaging function.

References

Aluminium Association (1990) *Aluminium Recycling*. Aluminium Association, Washington DC, p. 6.
Anon (1988) Dutch bottle bank 10 years old. *Voedingsmiddelentechnologie* **21**(13), 11.
Anon (1989a) Farewell to Swiss glass recycling. *Verpackung (Zurich)* **44**(5), 22–25.
Anon (1989b) Increased in recycled glass. *Brauwelt* **129**(16), 631.
Anon (1992a) *The Can Makers*, Update No. 8, p. 8.
Anon (1992b) *The Can Makers*, Update No. 8, p. 1.
Anon (1993) *Packaging Week* 18 February.
Cooper, J. (1992) *Packaging and the Environment*, Pira International, p. 54.
Cornaz, J.D. (1989) The practical repercussions of the beverage regulation for glass. *Verpackung (Zurich)* **44**(5), 20–22.
EC (1990) EC Directive No. 90/128/EEC Plastics in contact with foodstuffs.
EC (1992) Proposal for a Council Directive on Packaging and Packaging Waste 92/C263/01. *Off. J. Eur. Commun.* 12 October.
Ichiko, T. (1988) Recycling of glass bottles. *JPI* **26**(12), 12–22.
PCOMI (1992) Plastics in municipal incineration, W. Freiesleben, European Centre for Plastics in the Environment, Brussels.
Price, B. (1990) *Hazardous Waste Management*, Financial Times Management Report.
Ogilvie, S.M. (1992) Glass cullet recycling offers opportunities for significant energy savings of up to 25% and reduced emissions as a result of fuel savings compared with manufacture from virgin materials. *A Review on the Environmental Impact of Recycling*. DTI, Warren Spring.
US Government Advisory Association (1989) *Resource Recovery Yearbook*. Government Advisory Association, New York.

10 Management accounting for food industry environmental issues

P.S. HARRIS

One of the most obvious features of any book dealing with environmental management is the fact that it appears naturally to comprise two parts: energy management and the rest. Energy management stands apart because CO_2 emissions to the atmosphere are not only a major contributor to environmental damage, they arise mainly from a single cause, energy use. The rest of environmental management is involved with emissions of other agents, some to the atmosphere, others to water courses, and arise from many sources.

There are clear differences between energy and the rest in terms of management. Energy is ubiquitous; all industry and commercial enterprises contribute something to CO_2 emissions, not all organisations emit all, or possibly even any, of the other agents. Energy, in the physics sense, is a conserved quantity through the laws of thermodynamics, the carbon dioxide associated with it is a conserved quantity through the laws of chemical stoichiometry. Environmental damage from CO_2 is in direct proportion to the energy taken in by the enterprise and recorded on energy bills. This is not the case for the other agents. Acid, base, toxic, allergenic and other properties are not conserved quantities; the damage from these emissions is not measurable from the inputs recorded on invoices of the chemical moieties from which they are derived.

Comparison of energy with the rest is useful because there exists a perception that energy management now has a respectably long history and has developed into a moderately coherent discipline. It is not unreasonable to expect that if management techniques apply to energy, there is a good chance they could be applied to the other agents. However, it is also pertinent to ask whether what energy management has to offer is appropriate or sufficient.

That is the essence of this chapter. It takes a challenging view of energy management. It explores the topic as a management issue, taking lessons from past successes and failures to establish the strength of the existing repertoire of energy management techniques. It examines the limits of our current capability to manage either energy or the environment. At risk of spoiling the narrative, the inclusion of the term *management accounting* in the title will be found to be an acknowledgement of a rapidly developing area of technique and skill of considerable promise to energy and environmental management, to complement the skills of engineers and technically trained people.

10.1   Lessons from history: the rise and fall of management accounting and energy management

10.1.1   Management accounting

It would be quite inappropriate to consider applying management accounting techniques to other areas of management without a consideration of what management accounting is and where its principal ideas came from, not least because of the recent internal wranglings in the profession.

Management accounting has its origins in the emergence of managed hierarchical manufacturing and service enterprises of North America in the 19th century (Kaplan and Atkinson, 1989). Then known as cost accounting, it took information on the vast numbers of financial transactions in these organisations and converted them to meaningful numbers; ratios of costs to revenues, such as cost per mile, revenue per square foot of selling space, etc. Cost accounting techniques were expanded in the early decades of the 20th century with the development of measures such as the return on investment (Kaplan and Atkinson, 1989).

There were further additions to the repertoire through the 1930s and 1940s but cost accounting became somewhat pedestrian in its development (Kaplan and Atkinson, 1989). It began to take on a change of name in the early 1950s and by the end of the 1950s, what is now known as management accounting was different in character, if one is to judge by the content of the textbooks of the day (Foster, 1971; Horngren, 1986). Whereas in the late 1940s the major emphasis was on inventory valuation and cost control, by the end of the 1960s management decision-making had overtaken cost control in terms of emphasis. If one looks at the student textbooks of today (Coates *et al.*, 1989; Kaplan and Atkinson, 1989; BPP/ACCA, 1992) and the concerns of management accounting researchers (Bromwich and Hopwood, 1986), there is an even greater emphasis on the role of management accounting in decision-making.

Management accounting is just beginning to emerge from a period of considerable turmoil created by a circumstance very germane to the issue of environmental management (Bromwich and Hopwood, 1986; Bromwich and Bhimani, 1989). This episode began in the late 1970s when a leading academic, Professor Kaplan of the Harvard Business School, set out to write a seminal text on advanced management accounting. However, within 2 years of publishing the first edition, he had severe misgivings (Kaplan, 1986) as to whether the repertoire of technique as it was then was very appropriate to new manufacturing practices based on

Just-in-Time, total quality, manufacturing resource planning (MRP), flexible manufacturing practices, etc. Eventually, a new edition of the book was published in 1989 (Kaplan and Atkinson, 1989).

Through the 1980s, the repertoire of technique broadened and management accounting became a much bigger topic. The training of management accountants gave more emphasis to numerical and analytical devices in which management accountants would be expected to be skilled (Coates *et al.*, 1989; BPP/ACCA, 1992), such as the basic mathematics of functions, solutions of equations, elementary differential calculus, linear programming, statistical concepts such as measures of location (mean, median, n-tile) and measures of spread, regression, probability, etc. It is this repertoire which is of special interest in the context of energy management because of the way the management accountant uses it to support decision-taking.

A key aspect of the crisis in management accounting is an aspect we might call the *Kaplan Problem*. Kaplan argues (Kaplan and Johnson, 1988) that 'Today's management accounting information, driven by the procedures and cycle of the organisation's financial reporting system, is too late, too aggregated and too distorted to be relevant for managers' planning and control decisions.' Kaplan argues that, in western economies, the need for annual financial reporting and the requirements of accounts to pass an annual financial audit places so great a burden on the organisation, of development and maintenance of information systems, that organisations are reluctant to set up other systems of management information to support aspects of management other than finance and they therefore look to other aspects of management to work with the same body of information, for which it may be entirely inappropriate. It is a key observation because the same reluctance applies to other activities that rely on information systems, such as energy and environmental management.

Western organisations are prepared to set up these information systems if the imperative is strong enough, however. This can be seen in one particular area, quality management. In addition to accepting the requirement for quality information systems, western organisations seem willing to adopt quite heavily prescriptive systems of management (BSI, 1987) which constrain traditional freedoms of management action and style. Significantly, almost exactly the same approach has been not so much developed as offered as a system for environmental management; British Standard BS 7750 (BSI, 1992) is very much modelled on BS 5750, the quality management standard (BSI, 1987), even the similarity of numbering is not an accident.

Kaplan also makes another extremely significant point, although it was probably seen by all but a few observers as rather obscurantist at the time. In an account of the application of linear regression, Kaplan drew attention to the limitations of the technique embodied in the *Gauss Markov condi-*

tions. To users of regression, they have been regarded as an obscure academic issue but they become important in the context of the application of one key technique, CUSUM, as we shall later see. A further key contribution to the development of management accounting, also probably considered less important at the time, was when Kirwan (1986) remarked that, working as a consultant, he makes the distinction between *control information*, by which he means regular and frequent information to compare actual performance with what it should be, and *study information* which is obtained by specific *ad hoc* investigations. In his search for better or more relevant techniques, Kaplan identified one particular candidate, activity based costing (ABC), which comprises an examination of where costs are added in the various stages of manufacture of a product or provision of a service as a guide to reducing cost, another idea central to the historical development of energy management.

10.1.2   Energy management

Energy management, the identification of energy as a resource to which a management strategy can be applied, distinguishable from other aspects of managing an enterprise, has its origins in the late 18th century with the work of Count Rumford (1802). Rumford used a qualitative approach to energy management based on the principle of 'instead of determining the quantity of heat lost in any given operation, I endeavour to find out how much less the same operation might perform with, by a more advantageous arrangement of the Fire and disposition of the machinery.' This he described in a series of essays published between 1796 and 1802. Although the approach now used in energy management tends to be predominantly the same, Rumford was compelled to use this route in a way we do not have to now because the key laws of physics which we take for granted had still to be discovered (the laws of conduction of heat, 1804; the first law of thermodynamics, 1842–1847; the heating properties of infrared radiation, 1800).

Energy management as an aspect of industrial management did not really take a leap forward until Oliver and Philip Lyle, of the Tate and Lyle sugar refining company, made an attempt to determine the heat balance of an operating sugar refinery in 1926 (Lyle, 1947, p. 570) prompted by the general strike and the announcement that the Government would subsidise production of sugar from domestically grown beet. These events together created an immensely strong imperative for the Lyle brothers to examine their largest cost after labour, energy. The approach they used was to measure the energy use of each part of the process and to use the first law of thermodynamics, *energy out = energy in*, to establish what energy could not be accounted for. They then used this insight into the process to locate areas of potential energy cost reduction, eventually in 1933–1934 finding up to 46% savings in the Plaistow Wharf refinery (Lyle, 1947, p. 572).

In 1943, the Minister for Fuel and Power asked Oliver Lyle to develop the techniques he and Philip had used in the sugar industry for application in a wider range of industries. In writing up the procedures, Oliver incorporated them in a larger manual, *The Efficient Use of Steam* (Lyle, 1947), in which he described in great detail how the principles were applied to a brewery, a laundry and another (unspecified) food based evaporative extraction process. In making his observations on the brewery, Lyle remarks that (p. 640) 'In this brewery 55 per cent of the steam is going about its private business unknown to the management. It is up to the management to find out what these private affairs are . . .'. The steam in question was making no active contribution to the production of beer and the essence of his approach was what Kaplan identifies as activity base costing. Lyle also developed the idea of *bogey*, the same term as used in golf, for measuring the performance of a process under a management which is 'uniformly steady but never overbrilliant', though it is no longer used.

Oliver Lyle's book became the bible of generations of process engineers. Philip Lyle, meanwhile, convinced of the value of linear regression wrote this up as a process handbook *Regression Analysis of Production Costs and Factory Operations*, which ran to two editions in the 1940s and was resurrected in 1957 (Lyle, 1957) having gone out of print, which is a testament to its quality and relevance. Lyle had picked up the technique from the cost accounting field and was familiar with concepts of control charts through Shewart's work in the 1930s (Lyle, 1957, p. 116). He was probably quite well briefed on the development and application of quantitative management methods in the United States in the 1940s (Lyle, 1957, p. 107), probably to an extent that is uncommon at this top level of companies today.

The Ministry of Fuel and Power were so impressed with the Lyles' methods and results that they set up a division to provide a service to industry to apply these techniques and the UK Government provided this as a subsidised service until 1972. The importance of this is that the approach came to dominate energy management thinking, not just in the United Kingdom but had an impact in much of what is now the Commonwealth. In 1954, the approach was described in a paper presented to the Institute of Fuel (Clegg and Walters, 1952) and acquired the name *energy audit*. This seems to have occurred through a confusion over the parallels between the energy balance sheet and a financial balance sheet. It has taken a long time for the confusion to be ironed out and only gradually has the energy audit proper begun to emerge.

In 1974, in response to the first oil crisis, the UK Department of Energy began once again to subsidise consultancy advice along the lines of the

Lyle analysis. This was at two levels: a very quick survey of the site in 1 or 2 days by a consultant looking for immediate areas of saving and an extended survey which might take some weeks and which would include some part of an energy balance. The UK Department of Industry also operated a programme of short surveys, the Industrial Energy Thrift Scheme (1983–1984), which carried out surveys of over 2500 industrial sites, including 337 in the food industry. This very much shaped the way consultants worked in order to maximise the subsidy and this also shaped the advice they gave. The survey schemes continued until 1988, when the subsidy was dropped. Although companies still use consultants for this kind of support, it is on a greatly reduced scale and in style is less influenced by the previous subsidy rules.

Experience with the energy balance and survey had shown that energy savings could be at two levels (Industrial Energy Thrift Scheme, 1983–1984; Walshe, 1992; Wilson, 1992):

- low cost or no cost housekeeping measures, correcting faults and eliminating wasteful custom and practice, which could be identified without making extensive measurement, implemented quickly and required little by way of financial approval,
- more substantial measures identified by more extensive measurement, requiring investment and appraisal.

Around 1979–1980, a new concept was introduced to energy management in the form of *monitoring and target setting* (M&T) in which information is collected on a regular basis and variances from an established pattern computed. The aim is then to manage energy by managing the variances. At about the same time, an operations researcher, R.J. Aird, at the University of Loughborough independently began to explore the application to energy of a group of techniques called cumulative sum or CUSUM techniques. These were already established in the area of quality control (Woodward and Goldsmith, 1981), although Aird was applying it to a slightly different problem, which we would now call parametric. The technique Aird developed (Aird, 1981) transformed the prospects for monitoring and target setting. M&T as a technique of first resort in the United Kingdom began to encroach on the primacy of energy surveys from 1988 with the ending of subsidies.

An important complementary development was the desktop computer and the computer spreadsheet around 1977–1978 and the IBM personal computer in 1980; computing power became affordable for companies and bigger consultancies. The computer spreadsheet was critical to the success of CUSUM because it is a lengthy calculation by hand and is errorprone. By 1992, there were many suppliers of computer software for energy monitoring and target setting (Pooley, 1992) almost all of which incorporate the parametric form of CUSUM.

Three important studies, however, cast doubt on the effectiveness of some key elements of the repertoire of energy management techniques up to this time. The first was a study commissioned by the UK Department of Energy from the consultants Armitage Norton (1981) which examined why companies were reluctant to invest in energy efficiency; energy efficiency investments with paybacks as low as 1 year were routinely disregarded. Even where investment opportunities had been identified, funding did not naturally follow. Armitage Norton (1982) were able to account for the cause of the problem as the way businesses naturally tend to classify investment in energy efficiency.

A second study carried out after subsidies for energy surveys ceased in 1988 (Walshe, 1992; Wilson, 1992) looked at how many of the recommendations of these were taken up between 1984 and 1989. The results showed that measures to realise 60% of the available savings overall had not been implemented (Anon, 1992). The key conclusion was that, although companies were ready and willing to take up recommendations that involved little or no cost, there was great reluctance to invest much, and in some industries anything at all.

In fact, there were far deeper problems with the energy survey (Cheriton Technology, 1992). In the form it usually took, the consultant would be commissioned to do a survey over a limited period of time and submit his findings in a report. Operational constraints would make some information harder to acquire than others and reports were a compromise between information necessary and sufficient to draw meaningful conclusions and what information could be realistically obtained. Consultants were inadequately trained to analyse management information in any depth and management data were often incomplete or unusable. The size and technicality of the report, and the fact that it often did not relate to anything else that regularly crossed their desk, did not positively encourage senior management to take an interest or ask questions.

After about 1984, monitoring and target setting became almost *de rigueur* the standard recommendation of the energy survey. The savings claimed from monitoring and target setting would typically be one of the largest areas of potential (Walshe, 1992; Wilson, 1992) and sometimes outstrip all other recommendations. What was seldom clear, however, was where these savings would come from or, more significantly, why monitoring and target setting would identify savings that had not shown up in the survey itself.

The third key study was of 100 organisations (Energy Efficiency Office, 1993a, p. 2) that had implemented energy monitoring and target setting of energy use in buildings. This showed that monitoring and target setting was working smoothly in less than 10% of the organisations contacted. One of the reasons was perceived to be that energy information is poorly integrated into broader management systems.

10.1.3 *Complementarity in energy management and management accounting*

This, then, is the background to the current state of energy management and management accounting. What is interesting about it is that if one sits back to think about the similarities between management accounting and energy management, management accounting as it has emerged in recent years offers solutions to many of the problems energy management has experienced. It is useful in this context to compare the skill base of the engineer, management accountant and technologist through the quantitative techniques incorporated in their professional training today (Table 10.1).

This shows that many of the quantitative methods which have in recent years been brought into the management accounting repertoire are already familiar territory to the engineer and technologist. What the engineer or technologist lacks is the training in law or audit method, the scientific method of investigation in which technologists are steeped is very different in both style and substance. From here, we may explore what the tools of management of energy and the environment are and for the management accountant, engineer or technologist to conclude for themselves the parts of their professional repertoire that already fit these requirements and to decide where they might develop their skills.

10.2 Classes of management information

At the root of the problems of both energy management and management accounting have been three problems:

- the cost of acquiring information and of maintaining information systems;
- the capability of the information in terms of the purpose it is used for; does it tell management what management needs to know?
- the integration of the management information system within the culture and style of the organisation.

These problems can only be tackled if we appreciate that not all information is the same. Different forms of information and different qualities of information have different costs. Each kind of information needs to be geared to the costs in relation to purpose. This is where the contribution of Kirwan (1986) is important. Kirwan said that he makes the distinction between *control* and *study information*. If we accept that there does indeed exist a taxonomy of types of information, it is worthwhile to consider expanding this to four (the cautious way this is phrased is to reflect the fact that the author has found few references to where anyone has

Table 10.1 Comparison of the basic skill repertoire of management accountants, engineers and technologists

	Management accountants	Engineers	Chemists/food technologists
Mathematics of functions	Basic level of skill	High level of skill	High level of skill
Solutions of equations	Basic level of skill	High level of skill	High level of skill
Calculus	Simple first order differential maxima and minima	High level of skill	High level of skill
Linear programming	Yes	Common	Unusual
Statistical concepts Measures of location, spread, regression	Yes	Yes	Yes
Probability	Decision trees Bayes theorem	Common	Different
Geometrical progressions	In context of discounting money values	Yes	Yes
Thermodynamics	No	Yes	Yes
Kinetics	No	Some	Yes
Chemistry (stoichiometry, toxicity)	No	Little	Yes
Systems analysis, auditing	Yes	Little	No
Law	Some	No	No
Investment appraisal	Yes	Yes	Uncommon
Economics	Yes	Maybe	Maybe
People and organisational theory	Some	No	No

thought much about how many types there are and four may not quite be an end to it).

1. *Summary information* is of a broadly indicative type, cheap to acquire or generate and revised occasionally to reflect long-term changes either in the organisation or in external factors. It is either information which itself changes only slowly or infrequently, such as the capacity of a production line, or is obtained by combining elements of variable information in a way that changes only slowly over time. Standard cost information, such as the average Btu per barrel for beer, which was the mainstream of cost accounting, is of this type.

2. *Control information* is regular and frequent information gathered to compare actual performance for the immediate past time period (day, week, month) to establish whether it is consistent with the established pattern and as a basis for immediate management action. It too must be cheap to acquire and use, but must be adequately precise and reliable for the purpose.

3. *Budget information* is information used as the basis of financial planning. In principle, energy is used to some particular end and the needs of that end determine the financial resources that need to be set aside to pay for it. The organisation has a financial management responsibility to oversee the balance of income and expenditure. Budgetting is the mechanism by which organisations project expenditure into the future and set aside funds to meet future financial commitments, such as energy bills. Budget information must be cheap to acquire, and must accommodate possible changes in projections about business prospects, i.e. revenue.

4. *Study information* is information gathered as a one-off exercise to support a specific management decision. It is usually information that does not already exist either as summary or control information but is generated by specific study techniques. The information may be mixed in terms of accuracy, precision or reliability and may be ephemeral. Typical examples in energy or environmental management are the results of an audit or survey or investigations to support financial appraisal of an investment.

The insight this gives is invaluable. It indicates that one of the causes of failure of the energy survey is that the methods used by energy consultants were mostly study methods but the product was often summary information which was unusable as a basis for control or budgets. In addition, the high cost and lack of specific goals of the survey meant that what information was gathered was determined by the cost of the exercise rather than utility of the information. The same could affect environmental management.

Having recognised that there are different classes of information, it is also important to ensure that the information is adequate for its purpose. There are four attributes of quality of information: accuracy, precision, resolution and reliability. Each of these has a precise meaning in information terms. Many managers in industry do not much worry about them because they do not encounter situations where the distinction is important.

To illustrate these, take a simple example of the measurement of electric current using a current transformer and an AC ammeter. The current transformer produces a current in a secondary circuit in exact proportion to a ratio of windings and the ammeter measures the current in the secondary circuit (this is how most electrical measurements are made in high voltage AC circuits). The current can be read from the dial such that, say, one can estimate the position of the pointer to the nearest half a division on a circular scale of 200 divisions (200°, divided into 1° divisions). Taking care not to introduce parallax errors, one could arrive at a measurement possibly *precise* to ±0.3°. Suppose now, however, that we discover that the current transformer has a windings ratio of 5:1 instead of 10:1. Now have a very *precise* number which is wildly *inaccurate* because what we read from the meter is far from the true current.

Now suppose that there are three meters located far from one another and attached to similar machines. There will be differences between the meters due to the variation of construction of each meter compared to the manufacturers' specification. Whether we could distinguish real differences between the current going through one machine and another could depend on whether each meter had been calibrated to a standard. The minimum detectable difference in current within these practical constraints is the *resolution*. Now suppose the measurement was made by a process operative who does not appreciate the importance of parallax, because parallax is not a word he has met before, and he does not write down the readings as he takes them but carries them in his head for a time first. Would we be happy to defend a lawsuit in a damages claim, rightly or wrongly, based on the meter readings? This is a measure of how *reliable* we thought the measurement to be.

In both energy and environmental management, these quality attributes in information are important.

10.3   Theory and empiricism in interpretation of measurements

A cornerstone of management accounting is the idea that the amount of a manufacturing resource is related to the output of a product. At its simplest, this is something one can take as common sense. Cost accounting has developed this concept in an effort to apply it to as wide a part of businesses as makes sense. It is relevant to energy management also but there are some key differences.

As normally described, absorption costing describes two kinds of revenue expenditure or costs: fixed costs and variable costs. Fixed costs are costs that go on irrespective of how much is produced and comprise rent, rates, space heating, offices, interest on capital invested, etc. Variable costs are those that increase in line with production such as raw materials, process energy, packaging and wages for operatives, etc. This distinction is important because it affects the average costs for different levels of production.

Where it is possible to classify costs uniquely to fixed or variable according to type (for example, rent is clearly a fixed cost and a key raw material would clearly be a variable cost), this is familiar territory to cost accountants. They work out total costs by first adding up the fixed cost items, which can be done from the financial records, and then adding to this the costs of variable items for any level of production.

$$\text{Total costs} = \text{fixed costs} + \text{variable costs} \qquad (10.1)$$

The solution is shown in Figure 10.1.

There are important consequences, however, when an individual item of cost has both fixed and variable components. Energy provides a prime

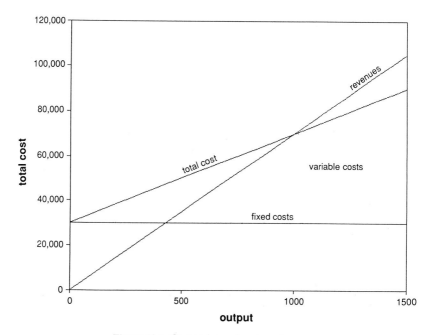

Figure 10.1 Comparison of costs and revenues.

example. In many processes there is an energy use which is incurred even at zero output through the standing losses of the oven or boiler and then variable energy use incurred for each additional unit of output. The only direct measure of energy we have at our disposal is the total energy input, we have no idea what part of this is related to production and what part is not; calculation from first principles is too unreliable. The same basic form of diagram still applies. Energy would be drawn on the y-axis, as the dependent variable, and production, the independent variable, on the x-axis. However, the procedure for determining the split between fixed and variable costs is quite different. The data represent the known total costs. The fixed costs are obtained by extrapolating the graph to zero production (Figure 10.2). The variable cost component at any level of production is now the total cost less this fixed quantity.

$$\text{Fixed costs} = \text{total costs} - \text{variable costs} \qquad (10.2)$$

If there is a contrast between Kaplan's approach to management accounting (Kaplan and Atkinson, 1989) and standard cost accounting (Whitehead and Upson, 1982; Mott, 1987), it is the emphasis Kaplan places on the techniques to solve equation (10.2) by regression. The form of graph most commonly encountered is that in Figures 10.1 and 10.2, consisting of a straight line with an intercept, although in practice there are variations on

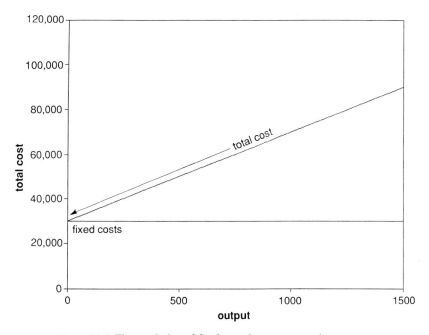

Figure 10.2 The resolution of fixed costs in an energy using process.

this through the impact of volume discounts on raw materials, cost of overtime as output rises over capacity, sales commissions, incremental additions of supervisory labour, bonuses, etc. (Whitehead and Upson, 1982).

For energy, the number of possible forms of relation are limited mainly by physical laws which govern energy transformations and, as such, are different from the common variants found in textbooks on cost management. Similarly, there would be expected to be differences for discharges of other agents such as nitrogen oxides, by-products, etc. determined by rules of stoichiometry (the chemical laws which govern relationships between reactants and products of chemical reactions). So far as energy is concerned, there are two ways in which this relationship between energy and production is important; one is the energy used in production, the other is where energy is used in buildings. The energy used in buildings is important in the food industry because about 17% of energy use, for example in the UK food industry (Crawford and Elson, 1982), is in buildings.

10.3.1   Relating energy to production and the weather

The energy required to heat a material, from physics, is

$$H_{1,2} = M\,C_p\,(T_2 - T_1) \qquad (10.3)$$

where M is the mass, C_p is the specific heat and T_1 and T_2 are initial and final temperatures. C_p may not be a constant but varies with temperature and can be regarded as constant if T_1 and T_2 are about the same for all measurements.

The energy required to melt or evaporate a material is

$$H_{change} = M\,L_{change} \qquad (10.4)$$

where M is the mass and L is the latent heat per unit of mass for the phase change concerned. If heating is accompanied by a phase change or a phase changing process requires some change in the temperature of the material before and after the phase change, then

$$H_{1,2} = M\,[C_{p,phase1}\,(T_c - T_1) + L_{change} + C_{p,phase2}\,(T_2 - T_c)] \qquad (10.5)$$

where T_c is the temperature at which the phase change occurs (the melting or boiling point).

For a process that produces a consistent product, T_1 and T_2 probably do not vary. If the product is always made from the same material, C_p and L_{change} do not change either. What is likely to vary is the mass of material processed in a given time and a graph of energy against mass of material processed for equal time intervals is a straight line of slope $[C_{p,phase1}(T_c - T_1) + L_{change} + C_{p,phase2}(T_2 - T_c)]$.

This is the basis of the empirical expectation that energy plotted against production is a straight line.

For buildings, a similar argument holds. The heat needs of a building are primarily determined by the need to maintain the temperature of the building by adding heat, through the boiler or other heating device, to offset heat lost through the fabric and ventilation. This can be expressed by Newton's law of cooling as follows:

$$\frac{dH}{dt} = U A (T_i - T_o) + C_p N V (T_i - T_o) \tag{10.6}$$

where dH/dt is the rate of heat input to the building, U is the thermal conductivity of the external fabric of the building usually expressed as the U-value, A is the external area of the building fabric, C_p is the specific heat of air, N is the number of changes of air in the period, V is the volume of the building, $(T_i - T_o)$ is the difference in temperature between the inside and the outside.

The rate of heat input to the building is related to the fuel input to the heating apparatus (boiler, heater, etc.) by the efficiency, η, of the heater. There are two terms in this equation but the temperature difference is common. For a permanent building, U and A are constants and are known. C_p is a constant and is known. N, the rate of air changes, is not a constant but it can be treated as approximately so. For a complex structure UA and C_pNV can be added up for all the component parts and represented by ΣUA and ΣC_pNV.

In a typical modern building under thermostatic control, the inside temperature T_i is a constant but the outside temperature T_o is always varying. Furthermore, the outside temperature varies both above and below the inside temperature. When the outside temperature is below the inside temperature, the building requires heat to be put in; when the outside temperature is above the inside temperature the building requires no heating. So we need to ignore solutions to this equation when $T_i - T_o$ is negative. Equation (10.6) relates to an instant in time, we need to evaluate it over an accounting period so we need to integrate. The equation then becomes

$$H = \frac{1}{\eta} (\Sigma UA + \Sigma C_p NV) \int_+ (T_o - T_i) \, dt \tag{10.7}$$

where the + signs means we are only interested in energy use when the temperature difference is positive. There is a measure of the weather that particularly suits the needs of the term $\int_+ (T_i - T_o)$ called the *degree day* (Cheriton Technology, 1992). Degree days in practice are measured from the daily maximum and minimum temperatures and an approximation formula (McVicker, 1946). They are available in printed tables for each geographical region (for the United Kingdom there are 18 regions with an observing station in each region) and a new figure is published each month by the Meteorological Office and by other commercial degree day services.

The importance of the degree day is that energy use of a building maintained at a constant temperature expressed as

$$H = \frac{1}{\eta} (\Sigma UA + \Sigma C_p NV) \times \text{degree days} \qquad (10.8)$$

has the form of a straight line when plotted as energy against degree days.

10.3.2   Linear regression

Why is it necessary to go through all this to establish that one expects a straight line? There are three reasons:

- the fact that the existence of a straight line relation can be ascribed to laws of physics greatly increases the confidence and reliability of any management system based on it;
- the circumstances that give rise to scatter and deviations from linearity become much more worthwhile management issues; and
- it facilitates the characterisation of the energy use pattern of a process or building by using the technique of linear regression.

A straight line also means that masses of accumulated data can be reduced to just two coefficients, which are useful as summary information and large numbers of sample data can be used to characterise with precision the current operating pattern.

However, there is an important aspect to regression which was not well enough appreciated until Kaplan and Atkinson (1989) reminded those of us who are not trained statisticians of it. Regression is based on a procedure for finding the coefficients of a straight line relation by minimising the sum of the squares of the differences between the points and the best fit line. It uses a rule from calculus that the first derivative of a function (obtained by differentiation) is zero when the function is at a minimum. Regression uses this fact to derive two simple equations which enable the least squares best fit line to a series of data points x', y' to be calculated:

$$c = \bar{y} - m\bar{x} \qquad (10.9)$$

and

$$m = \frac{\Sigma (x' - \bar{x})(y' - \bar{y})}{\Sigma (x' - \bar{x})^2} \qquad (10.10)$$

These are well known to users of regression. The symbol Σ means 'the sum of all such terms as', $\bar{x}$ and $\bar{y}$ are the average values of x' and y'. All the quantities in the equation are calculable from the data.

The key point, however, is that this procedure only works for the sum of the squares of the differences, not for any other error function. Using the least sum of the squares of the difference rather than, say, the least sum of just the differences has the potential to produce bizarre results because the further a point is from the line, the more weight the least squares method gives to it. To avoid this, there has over the years been formalised a set of conditions to which data must conform for regression to become a safe procedure. They are called the *Gauss Markov conditions* (Sen and Srivastava, 1989). In summary, they say that least squares regression is only a safe procedure if:

- the function (or law) to which the data conform, notwithstanding the variance, is linear;
- the error function is normal; and
- the data are *homoscedastic*; that is,
    - there is no variation of the underlying function with time;
    - the error function for y does not depend on the x variable.

A normal error function means that the errors are distributed evenly on either side of the true line according to the normal distribution error law. Energy violates this condition to some extent for two reasons:

- The first law of thermodynamics states that energy is conserved in all processes. A corollary is that the optimum energy input to achieve a given state is a minimum. To the extent that energy requirements to achieve a given state may vary, they should always be over and above this minimum.
- The second law states that spontaneous processes increase energy requirements. This means that systems left to themselves without intervention will tend to increase consumption rather than decrease it.

The laws of stoichiometry in chemistry state essentially the same about the quantities of chemical agents.

The key condition for scedasticity, however, turns out to be the variation with time because this is a difficult condition to meet for management information. It is a basic mission of management to attempt to improve performance over time, which is in contrast to the scientific origins of regression, which were to ensure experiments are reproducible over time. This is also a common cause of the breakdown of the second homoscedasticity condition. The second condition essentially means that the scatter is random about the line and is not greater in particular ranges of the x variable merely by virtue of the fact that the process is working in the range of that variable. Figure 10.3 shows a data set in which the range of the scatter appears to increase with the x variable. This is a common form

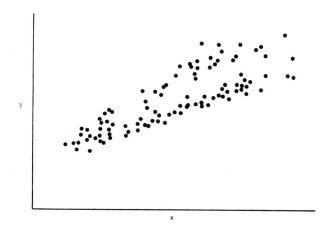

y

x

Figure 10.3 A heteroscedastic data set.

of heteroscedasticity in management information which occurs where a process has been modified over time to reduce both the production related and production unrelated consumption. This divergence of the scatter with increasing *x* is then common and expected. This will become clearer, however, once we have considered another key concept, CUSUM.

10.4   Interpreting time series information: CUSUM

CUSUM stands for CUmulative SUM deviation. It is a technique for measuring *bias in equal interval sequential* data. That is, if information is gathered at equal intervals on some aspect of a process or system, if there is then some change to an existing pattern of behaviour, CUSUM will detect and measure it. As originally developed, CUSUM only handled a single variable. The first use of CUSUM in the relationship between two or more variables for energy management seems to have been in 1980, or thereabouts, when Aird, then at the University of Loughborough, used it to examine the changing relation between the energy use of a building and degree days (Aird, 1981). This is now known as the *parametric* application of CUSUM.

There are now three distinguishable forms of CUSUM which have become recognised since about early 1990 (Cheriton Technology, 1992). These are:

- *univariant CUSUM* is the form of CUSUM usually described in textbooks on quality management and statistical process control. It looks at changes in time of a single variable, it is familiar to managers involved in quality control, is not used in energy management but may be important in environmental management.

- *parametric CUSUM* examines the changes in the way one variable changes its dependence on another. It is the form developed by Aird and it is the form commonly incorporated into energy monitoring software.
- *recurrent CUSUM* examines the changes in a pattern which repeats over time. It was developed for the monitoring of electricity use in buildings (Cheriton Technology, 1992).

The principles behind them are essentially the same; they differ only in the formulation of the baseline.

The simplest way to see the importance of CUSUM is to consider a simple example. Look at the energy consumption data in Table 10.2 and presented in Figure 10.4. This shows the production and specific energy use (energy per unit of production) for a process, call it an oven. The form of data presentation here is quite common practice in industry and across much of industry would be described as a simple, common sense approach to interpreting the data. The data appear in time series order and the graph uses the energy use per tonne to take account of the fact that energy use depends on the level of production.

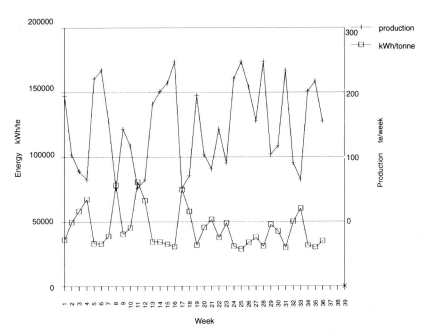

Figure 10.4 Production and specific energy compared.

Table 10.2 Energy and production data for an oven

Week	Production (tonnes)	Energy (kWh)
1	195	140726
2	104	103223
3	78	90764
4	65	87567
5	221	146600
6	234	154773
7	156	121575
8	52	81436
9	143	115586
10	117	105909
11	52	83916
12	65	86272
13	182	125892
14	202	138966
15	215	139922
16	247	152274
17	52	77788
18	72	82711
19	195	124317
20	104	94677
21	82	84628
22	143	108041
23	91	89115
24	221	136388
25	247	141428
26	208	141215
27	156	118319
28	247	152506
29	104	99267
30	117	99468
31	234	140188
32	91	91262
33	65	78248
34	202	128005
35	217	131003
36	156	109192

Now consider seven simple questions, the answers to which would be the main purpose of collecting this information:

- How many energy saving measures have been introduced?
- When did each take effect?
- How much energy has each measure saved?
- Are all the energy saving measures still working?
- Have any breakdowns been restored?
- How much energy will be required for a budgetted production of 120 tonnes a week in the next quarter?
- What further savings can be achieved?

In fact, although all this information is available from the dataset, it can only be accessed if the appropriate form of analysis is applied. CUSUM provides the simplest and most reliable means to do this.

CUSUM has two key steps:

- determine the underlying form of pattern;
- examine how this pattern changes with time.

At the outset there is a mutual interference between these two steps. The variations in time stand in the way of accurately defining the underlying pattern in the first instance, so the process tends to be an iterative one. How the steps in this iteration are performed in detail depends on the technology employed to do it. It tends to be done differently in a hand calculation compared to when it is performed on computer spreadsheets or in databases.

To do'it by hand, the first step is to plot all the data as energy against production on an x–y graph marking the points in some way to indicate their order in time (Figure 10.5). Then, starting with the first point, to pick out by eye the pattern followed by a series of consecutive points early in the dataset. This is easiest to do with a coloured pen, and tends to be more craft than science. In a data series where the trend has been to reduce energy consumption, the baseline pattern has been identified when all the remaining unmarked points lie to the right and below the coloured ones. A seasoned practitioner can get to this point in a minute or two. A line is

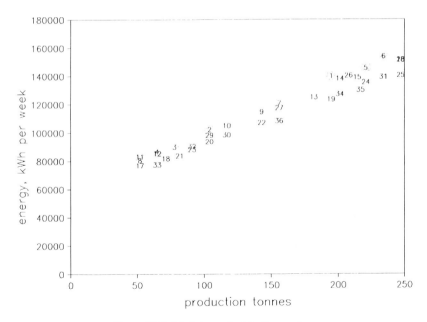

Figure 10.5 All data marked in time series.

then drawn through the points and its formula calculated in the form

$$\text{Energy} = m \times \text{production} + c \tag{10.11}$$

where c and m are obtained from the formula of the line. In this example, this line is

$$\text{Energy (kWh)} = 61\,360 + 394 \times \text{production (tonnes)} \tag{10.12}$$

This formula is now used to calculate a predicted consumption for each week by substituting the production for that week in the formula. The predicted consumption is subtracted from the consumption for each week to find the difference. The difference is summed for all the weeks up to the present to obtain CUSUM (Table 10.3) and CUSUM plotted against time (Figure 10.6).

The CUSUM graph has a characteristic form. The period that corresponds to the baseline hovers either side of zero, reflecting the fact that, if the pattern had not changed, the differences in actual consumption compared to the predicted consumption are small and random about zero. If nothing were to happen to change the pattern, then the line would continue to track about zero through the whole data set. If the pattern has changed then, from the time of the change, the differences will become consistently either negative (savings) or positive (increased consumption) and CUSUM, as the accumulation of these differences, will track either up or down the page. It will do this until something else alters the pattern when there will be another change in direction. In most cases, therefore, the graph of CUSUM against time produces a graph comprising a series of straight lines with sharp kinks at each event which changes the underlying pattern (Figure 10.6). Extrapolation of the individual segments of the graph to the current date provides a measure of the cumulative impact of the change.

Figure 10.6 shows that

- there have been two measures to reduce consumption, one took effect in week 12 and one in week 18;
- the first measure had saved 62 270 kWh and the second measure had saved 39 250 kWh by the time the second measure broke down in week 25;
- this second measure was restored in week 29 and by the end of the data series, the combined measures had saved 210 333 kWh.

It does not contain the information we needed on the budget but that is still available to us. Now look again at Figure 10.4. Can any of these assertions be supported from the data as presented there?

To pick out a baseline using a spreadsheet, one uses regression to establish the best fit to all the data, then compute CUSUM on this as a baseline formula. This produces a CUSUM plot which still has kinks and

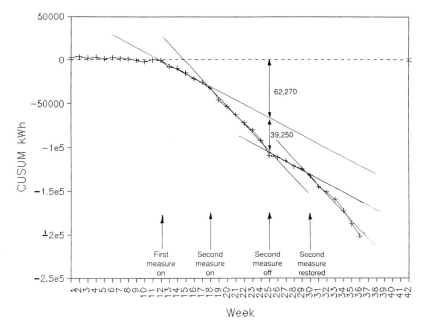

Figure 10.6 CUSUM for the oven.

straight sections in it but it will start and end close to zero (Harris, 1989). The baseline is the period between the start of the data set and the first change of direction of the CUSUM graph. This is replotted to find the formula for the pattern of this period only. CUSUM is then recalculated from this formula.

This describes the use of parametric CUSUM. Univariant and recurrent CUSUM differ only in the formulation of the baseline pattern. Univariant CUSUM takes as its baseline the average value of a single variable, parametric CUSUM uses a baseline prediction for each interval over a cycle; for example, if the cycle is an annual one, recurrent CUSUM uses as a baseline pattern a prediction for January based on the average of all the Januaries in the baseline period, a prediction for February based on all the Februaries in the baseline period, and so on for each month of the year.

10.4.1   CUSUM as the basis of control

The first uses of CUSUM for statistical process control and quality control were to provide a means to generate *control* information (Woodward and Goldsmith, 1981). The concept of CUSUM as a basis of control is very simple. The CUSUM graph comprises a series of straight sections sepa-

Table 10.3 Computation of CUSUM and the control chart for the oven

Week	Production (tonnes)	Energy (kWh)	Baseline Predicted (kWh)	Baseline Difference (kWh)	CUSUM (kWh)	Control chart Predicted (kWh)	Control chart Difference (kWh)
1	195	140726	138024	2702	2702	125360	15366
2	104	103223	102250	973	3675	92600	10623
3	78	90764	92029	-1265	2410	83240	7524
4	65	87567	86918	649	3059	78560	9007
5	221	146600	148246	-1646	1413	134720	11880
6	234	154773	153356	1417	2830	139400	15373
7	156	121575	122693	-1118	1712	111320	10255
8	52	81436	81808	-372	1340	73880	7556
9	143	115586	117582	-1996	-656	106640	8946
10	117	105909	107361	-1452	-2108	97280	8629
11	52	83916	81808	2108	0	73880	10036
12	65	86272	86918	-646	-646	78560	7712
13	182	125892	132914	-7022	-7668	120680	5212
14	202	138966	140580	-1614	-9282	127700	11266
15	215	139922	145690	-5768	-15050	132380	7542
16	247	152274	158467	-6193	-21243	144080	8194

17	52	77788	81808	−4020	−25263	73880	3908
18	72	82711	89474	−6763	−32026	80900	1811
19	195	124317	138024	−13707	−45733	125360	−1043
20	104	94677	102250	−7573	−53306	92600	2077
21	82	84628	93562	−8934	−62240	84644	−16
22	143	108041	117582	−9541	−71781	106640	1401
23	91	89115	97140	−8025	−79806	87920	1195
24	221	136388	148246	−11858	−91664	134720	1668
25	247	141428	158467	−17039	−108703	144080	−2652
26	208	141215	143135	−1920	−110623	130040	11175
27	156	118319	122693	−4374	−114997	111320	6999
28	247	152506	158467	−5961	−120958	144080	8426
29	104	99267	102250	−2983	−123941	92600	6667
30	117	99468	107361	−7893	−131834	97280	2188
31	234	140188	153356	−13168	−145002	139400	788
32	91	91262	97140	−5878	−150880	87920	3342
33	65	78248	86918	−8670	−159550	78560	−312
34	202	128005	140580	−12575	−172125	127700	305
35	267	131003	146712	−15709	−187834	133316	−2313
36	156	109192	122693	−13501	−201335	111320	−2128

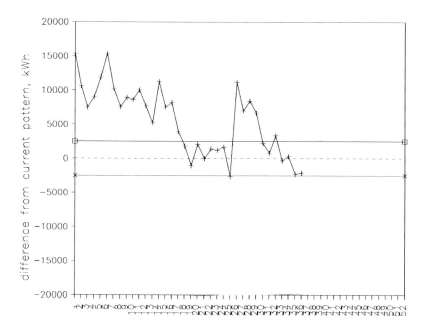

Figure 10.7 The control chart.

rated by kinks. The period up to the first kink represents the baseline. The period since the last kink represents the time over which the process or building has behaved consistently and represents the way, if no change has occurred since the last observation, the system works now. This period is called the *current pattern* period.

A *control chart* can be created by calculating the pattern of the data in the current pattern period, calculating the differences from the prediction from this formula and plotting the differences as a function of time (Figure 10.7). All that is required then is to set limits for the permissible variance before some kind of management investigation is required of out-of-limit variances. The function of the control chart is to create the means to manage by exception.

10.5   Variants in energy use pattern for buildings and processes

The straight line graph is the most common form of graph for buildings and processes and is the easiest to handle. Until the late 1980s, most of the promotion of monitoring and target setting of energy use in processes and building tended to assume it as a universal relation. However, this is not the case and there are many variants of it which are permitted by thermodynamic considerations and are commonly encountered in practice.

The straight line graph with an intercept means that there are two components to energy use:

- a production or degree day unrelated independent part, which goes on irrespective of how much is produced or how cold the weather;
- a production or degree day related part in which the energy use per unit of production or per degree day is a constant.

In a process, the production unrelated part is the energy used in a process when product is not going through. It comprises the heat losses through the process containment such as oven walls, the end losses in batch processes when the equipment heats up as in biscuit ovens, or the washing periods, in food processes in particular, for plant such as evaporators or heat exchangers. A straight line of positive slope indicates that the energy consumption per unit of output is a constant, which is expected from thermodynamics for a unitary process. In any processes there are inefficiencies, such as stack losses in ovens, condensate losses in steam based processes, which add to either the production related or the production unrelated consumption, or both, and need to be close to constant in proportion for linearity to be maintained.

10.5.1   Variants of pattern of energy against production

Some common variants which have been found in processes and can be attributed to theory (Harris, 1989) are shown in Figure 10.8. Type I is the basic form with a modest production unrelated demand. This has the formula

$$\text{Energy} = m \times \text{production} + c \tag{10.13}$$

It is probably the most common for processes overall. Type II is the same case but has no production unrelated demand. It has the formula

$$\text{Energy} = m \times \text{production} \tag{10.14}$$

This type is common in some very particular processes and industries, metal melting for instance, but is otherwise unusual. It happens in plant designed such that energy goes only into the product; that is, where there is no heating up or cooling down period for the plant and no structures to retain heat. It would therefore be expected in processes such as radio-frequency, microwave and infrared heating, some low temperature dehumidification processes, such as setting jellies in confectionery production, and one or two others.

Type II is unique in one important respect. It is the only case where it is possible to talk meaningfully in terms of specific energy use (energy use per kilo, per litre, per tonne or cubic metre) without reference to the production rate.

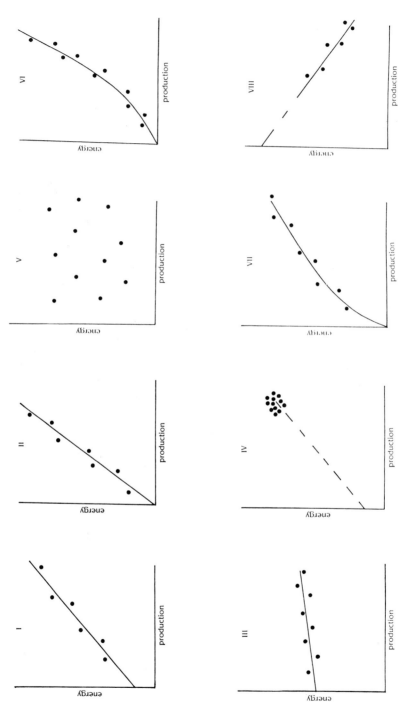

Figure 10.8 Types of baseline graphs for processes.

Type III is like the first type but just has a disproportionately high production unrelated demand. It also has the formula

$$\text{Energy} = m \times \text{production} + c$$

Type III processes must be regarded as inherently energy wasteful. This kind of relationship can indicate something very simple is wrong with the process. On a steam using plant, for example, this kind of baseline would be found if a steam trap were faulty. Water use often shows this form when there is a fixed leak. There are processes, however, where this type occurs even with no-fault conditions and these are candidates for positive action to reduce energy use.

Type IV occurs when there is a very narrow range of production rates; when production is nominally fixed. It is important here to determine the cause of scatter, both in the apparent production rate and in energy use. Often in this kind of process the production rate is fixed by the capacity of the plant and variations in throughput are due to discounting of rejects in the production variable (food products dropped on the floor, for example), variations in unit weights of output or compositional variations in the input. These latter may be deliberate or inadvertent. An important case is where the throughput is fixed by the rate of energy input; deep fryers in the snacks industry are an example. The energy use is fixed by the heat transfer in the cooking oil heating system; the main heat requirements are to evaporate water from the product and the rate of heat transfer determines the throughput of product.

In principle at least, Type IV processes are amenable to the closest control of energy use but it is important to consider which is the truly dependent variable. The line has been drawn dashed because from analysis of the distribution of points (regression) alone, it is not possible to reliably determine the production unrelated demand. If measurement of this were considered to be important, it would be necessary to measure energy use with the plant running with no production. Monitoring energy use in these circumstances might use one or two formulae depending on which is the truly dependent variable:

$$\text{Energy} = c + m \times \text{production}$$

where energy depends on the rate at which product goes through or

$$\text{Production} = \frac{(\text{energy} - c)}{m} \tag{10.15}$$

where the rate of throughput depends on the energy put into the process. The second of these is subtly, but importantly, different from the first. It means CUSUM would measure gains in production and the differences would measure gains or losses of production instead of energy. As a measure of productivity, this is often of far more interest to production management because small losses in production have greater financial implication than large losses of energy; for example, in the production of chip snacks, where energy costs are a mere 3–4% of total output value. However, because the cooker is both the principal energy using stage and is the stage that determines the entire output rate of the factory, a 1% change in cooker efficiency has 25 times the financial implication for output than it has for energy costs!

Type V appears to represent a case where energy and production are not related. Thermodynamic considerations lead us to expect that this cannot be so where energy plays a significant role in the process. Type V occurs in two main circumstances:

- where the time periods for the energy use and the production do not coincide because the information comes from different parts of the organisation and its collection is uncoordinated,
- where the energy use is not mainly dependent on the parameter used as the measure of output.

It is essential to ensure that the data are collected synchronously. This might sound a rather obvious precaution but the introduction of energy or environmental management represents the first time that information on energy, other process consumables, discharges and production in many firms have ever been brought together and examined in sufficient detail for this kind of mismatch to become apparent. It is not at all uncommon to find an engineering department that routinely changes steam meter charts on Monday afternoon but production is recorded from Monday morning to Friday (Sunday) night, simply because previously changing steam meter charts was a low priority job and Monday afternoon is a quiet time when routine 'unimportant' jobs could be tackled.

The second case occurs where the nature of the process is such that control of energy use is not coupled to the measure of output used. The most obvious example is drying processes where the energy requirements of the process are to drive off water but any existing system of production records is based on the material inputs and outputs of the residual solid. This applies to cookers, evaporators and stills as well as driers.

Type VI has the same characteristics as Type I except that it has a curved instead of a straight line. There are variants of it corresponding to Types II and III; that is, without the intercept and with a very high intercept. Type VI refers specifically to the case of a curve which increases in slope with increasing production; that is, production related energy use per unit of production increases with increasing production. It is rare with single items of plant but it is common in one specific circumstance; when several similar items of plant which are run in a merit order are monitored as a group. Manufacturing milk depots which have a high seasonal variation in liquid milk throughput are an example (Harris, 1986). The prediction formula has the form

$$\text{Energy} = (C_1 + M_1 \times \text{production}_1) + (C_2 + M_2 \times \text{production}_2)$$
$$+ (C_3 + M_3 \times \text{production}_3) + \ldots \qquad (10.16)$$

where 1, 2, 3, etc. refer to the production and values of m and c for each item of plant. The parameters m and c need to be determined for each different item of the plant; if the individual items are not metered, this can be done by multiple linear regression (Pooley, 1992) provided that the scatter for each is not great. If this proves not to be possible then the process cannot be effectively monitored without sub-metering.

Type VII has a curve but the slope decreases with increasing production. Again this is rare. It corresponds to the case where the efficiency improves with increasing throughput and is more likely with unitary processes than with whole sites (since it is not a merit order strategy). It can also include characteristics of Types II and III. (Some monitoring and target setting texts recommend the use of the form $E = bP^a$, however there is no physical basis for such a formula.)

Type VIII is another form that is generally rare but sporadically common. It is common in breweries, textile finishing and laundries and rare otherwise (Harris, 1989). It appears to defy thermodynamics in that as production increases, it uses less energy. It tends to occur where there is a high degree of internal heat recycling and only appears to be a straight line because of the limited range of production; the range of production in which the energy use rises with production may not ever be operated in practice because of operational design constraints.

10.5.2   Variants of pattern of energy against degree days

There are variants for buildings also, although the range of variants is very different, reflecting the very different underlying principles. It is important to appreciate these differences because the taxonomy of types is dependent on the thermodynamics of the underlying physical processes occurring in processes and buildings and the types encountered in monitoring emissions of other environmentally significant agents will create yet other taxonomies.

In processes, the principle is that the energy necessary and sufficient to achieve the desired change in the product is determined by the first law of thermodynamics. If the energy is not put in, this implies that the product in the state required does not come out. In buildings it is different. If the energy required to create a state (comfort levels, mainly) is not available, the user is likely simply not to be accepting the intended state but, maybe grudgingly, some other state. What is accepted is reflected in the energy use pattern. The key variants for buildings in the food processing sector are shown in Figure 10.9 (Cheriton Technology, 1992).

Type 1 is the common type, and would be described as a normal building. The straight line indicates that the degree day base temperature is appropriate, that the building operates a degree of thermostatic control and the heating equipment is adequate to meet the heat needs in the coldest weather.

Type 2 is where there is apparently no degree day unrelated demand. This type is rarer than might be imagined because it also depends on the degree day base temperature being exactly right. In fact, in the United Kingdom, most users of degree days use a standard base temperature of 15.5°C. This is only approximately correct for most buildings, and may be quite far out for some industrial buildings such as those in the food

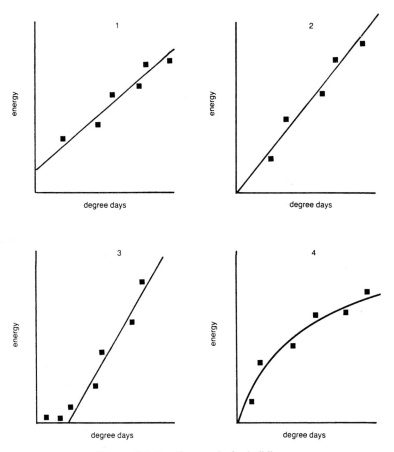

Figure 10.9 Baseline graphs for buildings.

industry, for raw material and packaging warehouses, in particular. In general, one should ignore the possibility of type 2 graphs; that is, never assume that the line goes through the origin.

Type 3 has an intercept on the degree day axis. It occurs when the degree day unrelated use is fairly small and either the degree day base temperature is too high or there is a level of degree days that needs to be achieved before the space heating is used, or both. It is caused either by the building being maintained at a constant temperature but far below the degree day base temperature or by there being a large internal heat gain, such as a process unit. Heat based processes housed inside buildings where there are many people requiring comfort heating in winter, at packing lines for example, makes this type common in the food industry.

Type 4, curved degree day baseline graphs for buildings are another case that is generally rare but sporadically common. This is the only common one. It indicates that there is a level of energy use above which greater degree days do not incur greater energy use. This is most likely because, although it may have thermostatic control, the heating system is undersized for the heat losses in severe weather, possibly because of undersizing of equipment, poor building fabric or excessive ventilation rates. The form of prediction formula is

$$\text{Energy} = c + m(1 - e^{-k \times \text{ degree days}}) \qquad (10.17)$$

where k is another empirical constant and $(c + m)$ represents an asymptotic value at the maximum energy input to the building. c is commonly negative. This type is common in the food industry, especially in warehouses where limited capacity heating systems are deployed just to take the chill off. Ineffective use of such heating systems, by running them at full capacity in the mild seasons, is commonplace.

It is likely that there are similar variants for relations between output or other factors of production and other aspects of environmental impact, such as discharges to water courses but the open literature contains very little by way of case history or empirical guidance, as yet.

10.5.3   Measures of production

A key consideration of monitoring of processes is the choice of unit used as a measure of output. It is important that the unit adopted is as close as possible to the fundamental determinant of energy requirements or environmental impact. The commonest are mass, volume, time and water content (Harris, 1989). More rarely it could be such units as surface area, number (when it refers to discrete objects), etc.

Most manufacturing organisations will already have some kind of system for monitoring production output tailored to its previous specific management needs. It is important to determine how suitable these measures of production are. There are two key considerations:

- does the measure of production measure all and only the material on which energy is expended?
- does the measure of production reflect energy requirements or environmental impact?

The first of these is a common trap; for example, in compound animal feeds, some feeds might contain flaked maize whilst others not, the relative proportions of these feed compositions have a very significant effect on the energy required for output overall and this could vary through the year. Similarly, it is common for manufacturers of a range of products to record production in some kind of 'standard statistical unit'. This is usually based on some general measure of resource requirements, often heavily geared to labour inputs (Kaplan and Atkinson, 1989). Suppose these were in the production of frozen convenience foods; more labour and added value may go into production of a filled deep-fried pancake than fish goujons, which thereby require more energy as a proportion of the standard statistical unit.

In terms of whether an existing or proposed measure of production is useful for monitoring energy there are two basic questions worth asking:

- is it sensible?
- does it work?

So far as it being sensible, does it have any physical basis, in terms of physics for energy or stoichiometry for chemicals. Volume is a reasonable production parameter where constant density makes it easy to relate to mass. When processes operate on constant mass flow rate, such as a large continuous evaporation plant, running hours can be a useful parameter but care needs to be exercised.

Broadly speaking, for most basic foods, measures of production are reasonably easy to find: e.g. litres for milk, beer, oils, ice cream; kilograms or tonnes for malt, vegetables, grain, snacks; number for processed poultry. The most important general class of process for which care needs to be taken for energy monitoring is that involving water removal. The thermodynamic requirement here is the provision of the latent heat of evaporation of water and energy is expected to be proportional to the weight of water evaporated. Correlation of energy use with output is only appropriate if the water evaporated is proportional to output, which is a rare and unlikely condition.

For example, take the case of potato crisps. The process is mainly to evaporate water from a potato slice at 20–30% solid content, 70–80% water to about 2% moisture, 98% solid. The slice then picks up oil from the cooker and incorporates this into the slice. The factors which create variability of moisture content in the potato also affects the oil take up.

After cooling, the slice is coated with flavour salt and weighed into the packet. The weighing technology used in the industry is so highly developed that the error in weighing the crisp and flavour salt into the packet is less than ±0.5% and the final weight of product is available to a very high degree of accuracy by counting the packets and estimating the overweight. This only represents part of the weight of product going through the cooker, however, because of waste and spoilage. Waste and spoilage represent a sufficiently small proportion of the product weight that quite crude weighing of the waste does not materially affect the accuracy or precision.

Even so, such is the natural variation in water content of the raw potato and the range of flavour salt density that correlating energy use with saleable output gives a far poorer correlation and a resolution that can detect a change in the cooker fuel consumption no smaller than perhaps ±10%. However, most snack producers now gather enough data on production for quality control purposes to enable a computation of the water evaporated on a weekly basis from the saleable weight, the mass of flavour salt used, the oil takeup of the cooker, the waste and spoilage, and the solids content of the potato (which is an important quality control parameter because the water content is an important determinant of the cooker settings to produce a crisp of consistent colour). Correlation of the energy use with mass of water evaporated is adequate to resolve variations of energy use with a precision of fractions of 1 or 2% using CUSUM (Harris, unpublished).

10.6   Relating energy use to efficiency

The characterisation of the pattern in terms of the parameters taken from a straight line or the type of behaviour indicated by the graph provide information as good as, often far better and more reliable than the information from a study exercise and far cheaper.

The slope of a graph of energy use against production provides a direct measure of the efficiency of the process. For example, the energy requirement of a process that evaporates water from a cold (20°C) raw material and produces an essentially cool product and releases the water as vapour at a cooker temperature of, say, 260°C is the latent heat of evaporation of water, 16.6 GJ per tonne water evaporated. The slope of the line of energy against water evaporated is in the same units and the efficiency of the cooker is the ratio of the latent heat of steam and the actual slope of the graph. For a potato crisp cooker this would be typically 45%.

It is important, however, to be aware of the difference between precision, accuracy and reliability in the context of efficiency measurements. CUSUM is a precision based technique, relying on readings from a single meter. It is quite capable of detecting changes in pattern of fractions of 1%. If it is applied to costs as represented in bills, the result is accurate to the extent that it reflects the information appearing in bills and is an absolute indicator of cost. However, if it is intended to compare energy use between two cookers, these will be based on different meters and differences in calibration of the meters will determine the extent to which any perceived differences in efficiency are real. It certainly will not be with the resolution that CUSUM can detect a change in pattern.

In the case of buildings, the slope of the line, if it is straight, is a measure of the rate of heat loss from the building. In Equation (10.8), it was seen that the slope is represented by

$$\frac{H}{\text{(degree days)}} = \frac{1}{\eta} \{\Sigma UA + \Sigma C_p NV\}$$

where A and U refer to the area and thermal transmittance of the fabric of the building. A has units of m^2 and U is characteristic of both the type of material and the arrangement of several materials in a structure. U is conventionally measured in W/m^2 per °C and is available in a wide variety of published sources for many types of materials and structures (CIBSE, 1986). C_p is the heat capacity of air, measured in kWh/m^3 per °C, N is the number of air changes and V is the volume measured in m^3. Simple conversion of U and C_p using dimensional analysis can bring these to the same units as the measured value of the slope of the line (Harris, 1989). All that is required is to gather information on the area and U-value of each type of fabric in the external structure of the building (walls, windows, roof, door fabric, etc.), find the product UA for each element and add them up, measure the volume and look up the heat capacity of air.

A difficulty is the fact that N is very difficult to measure (for difficult, for all practical purposes substitute impossible) but this only means that the result is an equation in a single unknown, N. It is then possible to compare the apparent ventilation rate, derived from the other known values, with occupational health requirements (CIBSE, 1986) and determine whether the rate observed in this way is a reasonable level of ventilation to support. In most industrial buildings it is too high, either because of unnecessary opening of loading doors, or overzealous or inappropriate use of mechanical ventilation.

10.7   Budget management

The current pattern derived from CUSUM is the most reliable summary of energy requirements available. It relates energy use to production and the weather. It is then possible from production forecasts and weather projections to forecast energy use into the future. The main reason for doing this is for budget purposes. In environmental management, some form of budget is a useful means to ensure that licence arrangements for permitted releases of pollutants can be complied with.

In many organisations, budget procedures for ancillary factors of production such as energy, water and discharges to water course are astonishingly crude; 'last year plus a bit', 'last year plus a bit minus what was not spent last year' or, even an arbitrary, 'last year less some'. A budget such as these is made without much regard for either levels of production or the way in which energy use has both production related and production unrelated components or is determined by the process design. Where this is the case, it is usually done with no sensible mechanism of releasing funds from budgets in surplus, or of avoiding undesirable deficits.

Once the energy use has been characterised as a current pattern by using CUSUM and regression, an energy budget can be managed not only with extreme precision, but a well managed energy budget can enable scarce opportunity funds, such as those created by a mild winter, to be channelled to secondary priorities in an orderly way.

10.7.1 Prescriptive and flexible budgets

How best to do this is found to depend mainly on the form of budget management that is appropriate. There are two forms, *prescriptive* and *flexible* (Cheriton Technology, 1992). In manufacturing industry, funding comes from sales revenues. There is a continuous flow of incomes and expenditures. The role of the financial year-end in a company is simply to set the date on which a balance sheet is drawn up to determine its balance of revenues and costs, its assets, liabilities and tax due. The important point is that the money in the organisation on the last day of the financial year is essentially the same money as that on the first day of the next financial year. In principle, it does not matter that a particular budget is underspent or overspent, budget procedures are a mechanism to enable management by exception and as a defence to protect the basis of product pricing decisions.

This can be usefully contrasted with, for example, financial management in the public sector and the use of licences to regulate discharges of pollutants, which are prescriptive. These are not related to revenue or output but are determined partly in abstract. The end of the financial year represents a time when, in principle, all the funds of the department or the authorisation in the permit or licence should have been used up. The first day of the new financial year or licence year endows the organisation with totally new funds or permission to discharge; neither the money nor the discharges are regarded as the same. If there is a residue at the end of one year this, in principle, is taken away; it cannot be drawn on in the next year and if the budget is exceeded there is, in principle, no money or permit for the extra, so financial budget holders and permit holders for releases of pollutants are expected not to exceed the budget agreed and in financial management to create no surpluses.

If the current pattern is characterised well enough, as it can be through the use of CUSUM and regression, the difference between actual consumption or discharge and the budget or licence can be continuously monitored and any surpluses or mounting deficits recognised quickly. It is found to be prudent to work on the basis of a budget which creates a small surplus and then, in the case of energy, to make a conscious decision on how to dispose of the surplus. This is valuable in the context of another problem to be discussed later, the Armitage Norton problem.

10.7.2   Capital return budgets

In the case of energy management, the key benefit, or imperative, has been to reduce costs; energy management in its present form was a creation of the response to rising oil prices in the 1970s. However, a problem is that energy savings on a significant scale also require investment. Environmental protection measures also require investment, although apart from areas where the polluter pays principle can be applied, the revenue cost reduction aspect may not be so rewarding.

In 1981, the UK Department of Energy commissioned a study by the management consultants Armitage Norton (1982) to explain why companies did not invest in energy efficiency. Their contribution is so valuable, it is worth expanding on in detail.

They argue that, in any business, there are two broad categories of expenditure (Figure 10.10):

- *revenue expenditure*, is money spent by the business which tends to yield its main benefit in the financial year in which it is spent, this includes such items as wages, fuel, raw materials, consumable chemicals, packaging, rent, etc.
- *capital expenditure*, is money invested in the business which, although it gives a benefit in the year in which it is spent, gives rise to an asset which makes a contribution to the business in subsequent years; this includes plant and machinery, buildings, research and development, etc.

This is standard accounting theory. These areas of expenditure are commonly handled separately in the financial accounting of a business. Armitage Norton argued that capital expenditure is then further subdivided, implicitly even if there may be no formal treatment of it by management in this way, into:

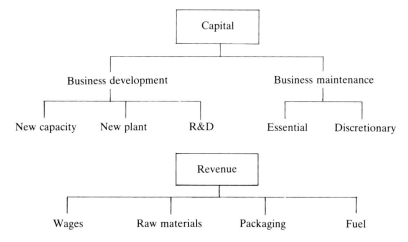

Figure 10.10 Classes of expenditure in a business.

- *business maintenance* capital expenditure, which is investment in plant and machinery to produce existing products for existing markets or existing customers and
- *business development capital expenditure*, which is investment to generate new business, new products for existing customers or to meet a wider customer base with existing products.

Business development capital expenditure is given a high priority in most businesses because it is seen as strategically important. It also requires substantial amounts of capital and thereby commands a high profile. Business maintenance capital expenditure is further subdivided, again implicitly rather than explicitly, into:

- *discretionary expenditure*, which is money the business may choose to spend or not and
- *essential expenditure*, which the business has to spend to stay in its mainstream activity.

Armitage Norton argued that the problem for energy efficiency measures is that it mostly falls in the area of *discretionary business maintenance capital expenditure* to reduce a *revenue* cost item. This tends to be given low priority and this kind of investment is left to compete for scarce *opportunity funds*, as they were called; the kind of funds which appear as unmanaged budget surpluses and windfalls. This creates what we can call the *Armitage Norton problem*.

To see how the problem arises, consider how businesses commonly go about assessing performance in a given area. Most businesses simply examine all the expenditures and revenues related to the part of the business under review. For revenue increasing projects, this is relatively easy because the invoices, and other records relating to costs and sales are readily available as part of the information required for the annual financial report. All that is required is to assemble the costs and revenues and compare them. If revenues greatly exceed expenditures, the business makes a surplus in that area and if expenditures exceed revenues it makes a loss.

This approach, however, is not possible where the capital expenditure is to reduce a revenue cost, such as improving energy efficiency. The only records that are routinely assembled by the Accounts Department are records of continued outgoings; the costs of the various measures taken, the salary and costs of the people involved and invoices relating to the fuel and electricity still being used. There are no records of income because energy efficiency, or any other form of cost reduction or of environmental protection, does not create income, it operates by retaining funds, it is one of the blind spots in financial information systems observed by Kaplan.

The solution, however, is very simple. All that is required is to find the means to measure, if not an income, the reduction in outgoings. The measured reductions can then be set out in the form of a *capital return budget* (Harris, 1986). A capital return budget compares the capital expenditure and reductions in revenue expenditure over the timespan of the investment programme. Its essential feature is that it makes visible the fact that capital expenditures in one year generate savings in subsequent years. It shows that, as the passage of time takes each measure past its payback, it transforms it from an expenditure to a net retention of funds.

The capital return budget overcomes the Armitage Norton problem of having to rely on opportunity funds because it creates its own virtual funds through the reduction in outgoings. Since this virtual fund is created by energy cost reduction activities and is known first to the energy management function, it gives this area of investment natural precedence. CUSUM provides the means to measure directly the reduction in the physical quantity of energy. This can then be valued by applying the price information and comparing with the capital and other costs required to achieve it.

This is clear from Table 10.4, which shows the typical form of a capital return budget for a factory. Its purpose is to bring out the fact that capital expenditures on single measures in one year give rise to savings which not only accrue over several years but extend beyond the year in which payback is achieved. The result is that:

- the main body of savings are from measures that have involved some capital investment, only a small number of measures have involved no outlay and the savings from these are often small;

Table 10.4 Capital return budget

	1988	1989	1990	1991	1992	1993 (est)	1994 (est)	1995 (est)
Costs								
Tariff savings	0							
Energy survey		4500	4600					
New burners				12000				
Steam system improvements					18000			
Building heating controls						16500		
Heat recovery							51000	
Total	0	4500	4600	12000	18000	16500	51000	
Savings								
Tariff savings	4500	4800	5100	5300	5500	5700	6000	6000
Energy survey: housekeeping	0	7600	2300	7800	7850	8010	8200	8200
monitoring			250	4380	3500	3700	3500	3500
New burners	0	0	0	1800	6500	6300	6300	6300
Steam system improvements	0	0	0	0	2500	2500	2500	2500
Building heating controls	0	0	0	0	4900	12000	12200	12300
Heat recovery	0	0	0	0	0	0	8900	16300
Total	4500	12400	7650	19280	30750	38210	47600	55100
Savings: costs for year	4500	7900	3050	7280	12750	21710	(3400)	55100
Cumulative surplus	4500	12400	15450	22730	35480	57190	53790	108890

- since the earliest items tackled first tend to be those with the shortest payback, the entire programme may well have been in surplus since the beginning and will continue to be in surplus even though measures still to be taken up have much longer paybacks;
- most importantly, the organisation can afford to invest in these longer payback measures because a surplus of funds has been generated from the investments made early in the programme.

The expenditure element of the table comes from the financial records of the expenditures made. Savings from measures taken to reduce the physical quantity of energy used can be evaluated from the CUSUM graph and from the current and past pattern of consumption. The CUSUM chart indicates the time of onset of a savings measure and indicates if a measure subsequently fails, is taken out or abandoned. The CUSUM chart also indicates, through the extrapolation of the baseline trend and the current value of CUSUM, the total savings to date. Where two measures take effect at the same time, or close to one another in time, CUSUM cannot resolve these, although it can determine the combined effect.

A feature included in Table 10.4 is a saving from building heating controls and modifications to a steam system prior to installation of the capital project. This is included in the example because it is quite a common occurrence (Harris, 1986, p. 50; NHS, 1991, p. 129); the task of examining energy consumption and possible savings in order to produce an engineering specification for investment in modifications to existing plant itself often provides savings that can be implemented at low cost even before the capital equipment is installed.

Reading the savings off the CUSUM chart is not very precise. Far greater precision can be achieved by comparing the detailed patterns of consumption. This also enables the savings from investments to be budgeted into the future. In the case of heating fuel, the baseline, the current pattern, or the pattern after any one change in pattern is given by a formula of the form

$$\text{Energy} = c + m \times \text{production}$$

There will be a value of c and a value of m appropriate to each pattern. To find the difference between one pattern and another, it is only necessary to find the difference in the c and m for the two patterns and to use these in a formula of the same form. This then quantifies the savings at any level of production.

10.8   The financial appraisal of energy saving and environmental protection measures

Energy efficiency and environmental protection measures eventually will create a need for the organisation to invest. If industry were to invest only in energy saving capital projects which have a better financial return than most other forms of investment they currently make, this would be a substantial contribution to reduction in emissions of greenhouse gases, such as CO_2.

The natural assumption would be that if an organisation can see a worthwhile investment project with a good return, it would find the capital resources and give the project appropriate priority. In practice, industry is very hesitant about investing in energy efficiency. There are three main barriers to be overcome:

- the low priority given in most organisations to energy efficiency, i.e. the Armitage Norton problem;
- ensuring that the standards of investment appraisal used are appropriate to the needs of the firm;
- ensuring the decision to invest or not is taken at the right level in the firm.

We will take it that the accounting mechanics of financial appraisal based on discounted cash flow are essentially familiar. One of the interesting aspects of financial appraisal is that it is an area with which engineers are reluctant to become involved but it is arguably an area which naturally falls to the engineer. The clearest statement of this I have ever seen is in Wilkinson Riddle's (1982) Accounting Level III where he says 'The accountant's role in this evaluation process is usually grossly exaggerated by textbooks. . . . The point is that many of these predictions (not all) will be made by non-accountants, the accountant's role being merely to translate these predictions into budgetted cash flows and accounts.' This is key. The accountant does not expect to have a key role in evaluating projects, the engineer may think that he does.

The point is that what appears to be the central feature of financial appraisal, the discounting of cash flows, is a very minor procedural aspect of it although it is the result of this part of it which gives the best yardstick of the perceived value of the project in the organisation. The bulk of work of financial appraisal really is the quantification of the costs and benefits that go into the cash flow statement, identifying what needs to be bought, what will be saved, what the alternative projects are. This is solely the province of the engineer and the technically qualified, quite outside the scope and judgement of the financial accountant. Only the decision on the project lifetime may not be an engineering decision.

Energy efficiency fares badly because the technical aspects of the appraisal are often done badly and the responsibility for this must rest with engineers who put them forward. There are four ways in which financial appraisal of energy efficiency projects goes wrong:

- the benefits arising from the project are underestimated, the project looks less attractive than it really is, fails the hurdles presented by management and is not proceeded with;
- the engineering options are not fully explored so the costs and benefits are not optimised;
- the costs are underestimated so that the project appears more attractive than it really is, it goes ahead, the actual costs then come to light and create a prejudice against future projects;
- the decision is taken at the wrong level; senior management posts financial criteria in terms of payback which are taken too literally and are not sufficiently indicative of the funds that are available.

These considerations are also important because, almost 20 years after the price changes which first brought energy management onto the corporate agenda, many organisations have not varied much the payback criterion on which they base investment. If they have funded what has met these criteria, much of the remaining potential for energy saving lies only marginally beyond the payback criterion. Investment is like an iceberg. If management is only allowed to see what lies above the water, they may never realise the size of the investment funds they need to set aside to offset unforeseen hazards and opportunities. Projects which fall outside the payback criterion should still go forward for senior management to turn down. Many company senior executives have never realised the energy saving potential because they have never seen a submission which sets it out.

10.8.1   Investment priorities

One problem for energy efficiency is the failure of organisations to see that energy efficiency not only ought to be considered alongside other investments in the firm, they need to be open to the idea that there are areas of energy saving investment that might be a natural priority area for investment. We can see this as follows. A food manufacturing business gets its income from its customers, who buy its products. Most businesses operate with a range of products and have many customers. They also have to work in competition with other firms providing similar products also seeking customers. Businesses prosper by ensuring that they provide the products that customers want at the right quality and price and ensuring that they have customers for the products they have the capacity to make. That much is obvious.

The most basic survival strategy for any business depends on maintaining existing business by retaining existing customers for the existing product range. There are two ways an enterprise can do this:

- by improving the product to keep it more attractive than the competition or
- by making it cheaper.

This is embodied in the concept of the *Ansoff Matrix* (Figure 10.11). The least risk strategy for any company is to maintain its competitiveness in its existing market place by reducing costs and maintaining, or improving, quality. It is commonly accepted that energy saving measures reduce costs but there are also many energy saving investments which also improve quality.

Each of these priorities requires a view from the enterprise on its need for investment and its longer term development. The right balance can only be achieved by looking at the product mix, the place of these products in their existing markets, including costs and margins, and the investment requirements created by market conditions. A significant contribution to this part of business strategy was made by the Boston Consulting Group when they combined market growth and market share in a simple diagram now called the Boston Matrix (Figure 10.12). The inputs to the matrix are the relative share of the firms products in a given market, which can be rated high or low, and the rate of growth of that market, which can also be rated high or low. The matrix has four boxes, to which the Boston Consulting Group gave names:

- a *star* has achieved a high market share and generates a large amount of revenue but the market is growing rapidly and the enterprise needs

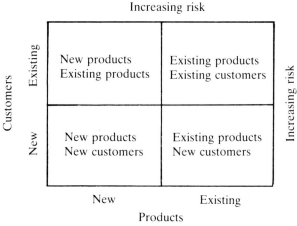

Figure 10.11 Ansoff's matrix.

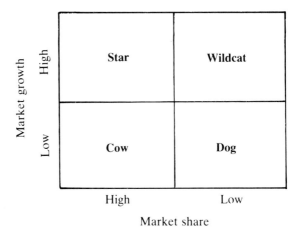

Figure 10.12 The Boston matrix.

to increase production to maintain its dominant position. The firm probably finds it is obliged to invest in this area.

- A *wildcat* does not have a dominant market position but the market is growing rapidly. A star that has received insufficient investment could become a wildcat. If the firm wants to gain or restore market share, it will either have to invest heavily or find ways and means of producing at much lower cost.
- A *cow* is a market leader in a static market. Often called 'cash cows', they require little product improvement or investment and often provide a high volume of profitable income and are a rich source of funds on which the enterprise needs to make little supporting expenditure.
- A *dog* is a product with poor prospects of generating funds and often is a drain on the resources of the enterprise.

Products have a natural life cycle. A successful product progresses from the wildcat through the star to the cash cow to the dog. The Boston matrix is valuable because it brings out that it is the *business maintenance* activities of an enterprise which create the resources for further investment, and which should therefore be a priority for investment funds, whether essential or discretionary; this is in contrast with the description given by Armitage Norton of how many businesses tend to place business maintenance as an area of low priority, priority for investment does not equate with the amount of investment, and a priority for business maintenance capital investment is cost reduction to maintain competitiveness in markets.

10.9   Environmental auditing

Audit awareness is a central feature of the skill repertoire of the management accountant. Nothing like it exists in the background of the training of the engineer or chemist but the concept of the environmental audit is now very much upon us (Anon, 1991). The first significant steps to make environmental audits and responsibilities a permanent part of the way of life of all UK commercial organisations were taken with the publication in 1992 of BS 7750, *A Specification for Environmental Management Systems* (BSI, 1992).

The document which finally emerged from BSI is very different from that which was originally envisaged (BSI, 1991) and is partly a product of circumstance. The standard is one of the fastest standards ever to appear from the BSI and the final specification is both very different from the draft specification circulated for comment and very similar to BS 5750, *The Specification for Quality Management systems*. The speed of preparation of the standard is probably very much to do with the gathering pace in 1990 and 1991 of firm proposals in the European Commission for environmental audit legislation and the actions it provoked from industry groups, especially the chemicals industry (Anon, 1991). The final document (BSI, 1992), largely modelled on the quality standard, is a compromise of speed and approach. Modelling it on the quality standard at least has the advantage that it is modelled on something that seems to work, if not for everybody, although how relevant it is to managing energy or the environment is still largely untested.

This is not the only management system that works, however. The chemicals industry, which has experience of auditing other management systems in other discretionary (or, rather, not prescribed) areas such as safety and occupational health, issued its own guidelines for auditing environmental management under its responsible care programme (Chemical Industries Association, 1991). Numerous other commercial groups have tried other approaches and published documentation, for example HASTAM (1991) in the United Kingdom.

The key point about any audit system is, apart from the procedural element to ensure that systems are in place, the audit needs to ensure that these systems are effective. There are two concerns here:

- does the information system, which is an essential focus of every proposed system of audit, have the powers of resolution to support the decisions required to manage the area of activity concerned;
- do the information system and the structural features of the organisation, its people and their responsibilities, function effectively.

In the case of financial auditing, this is highly developed and underpinned by the law of treasury (money in = money out) as a means to prescribe the forms used for balance sheets, although even this is not perfect (Davis, 1991). However, energy management is still almost entirely a discretionary activity and is conspicuously in a state of development and change. Environmental management is still discretionary in areas not covered by the Environmental Protection Act and other statutes and management techniques and disciplines have still to be developed in many areas. There is little point attempting to emulate financial auditing by establishing a high level which all organisations are expected to achieve, irrespective of their previous history. It would only serve to discourage the less than totally committed.

Management accounting has a great deal to offer here. The monitoring techniques described here (CUSUM, characterising the current pattern, the accommodation of the limitations of regression and the taxonomy of management information) are in large degree the products of management science applied to an area governed by thermodynamics. They provide a yardstick to determine the potential effectiveness of information systems, the cornerstone of an energy or environmental management system. What has been set out here is not a prescription for how information systems should be set up, or of how budget management has to be organised, but it is useful in identifying areas where there is potential for management systems to break down.

Apart from the procedures, there is also the need for the system to fit into the organisation in an effective way. Where systems are essential or statutory, it is entirely reasonable to expect organisations to adjust their culture and style to conform, in financial reporting for example, although even here things may not be perfect. Where activities are discretionary, it is more appropriate to expect the system to accommodate the culture and style of the organisation. The importance of this was recognised by Armitage Norton (1982) but acceptance of it by key institutions is only recent.

The Armitage Norton Report (1982) identified three aspects of an organisation which measure its commitment to energy management and efficiency. These were energy policy, energy management structures and energy reporting systems. The report set five levels of attainment in each of these. The Chemical Industries Association Guidance on Safety, Occupational Health and Environmental Protection Auditing (Chemical Industries Association 1991) takes a similar approach to environmental auditing taking 7 areas, 22 sub-areas within these and four or five levels of attainment. The important observation made at the time (Harris, 1984) was that, as important as developing these areas to a high level, this development should be in a balanced way; the development of policy and structure need to relate to one another; information, however well developed, is useless if the management structure is not geared to make use of it.

Recently, two contributions have extended this idea, both in the context of energy management in buildings (Energy Efficiency Office, 1993a,b). The UK Energy Efficiency Office (EEO) (1993b) has produced a report which provides a matrix diagram for organisations to compare their levels of attainment in six areas: policy, organisation, motivation, information systems, marketing (in the context of marketing energy (or environmental) management within the organisation) and investment. To use the matrix, one marks the level attained in each area and draws a line connecting them. This produces a diagram whose shape is determined by the state of development of the programme overall. Another, independently developed, matrix (Cheriton Technology, 1992) uses seven areas but the areas are different: policy, organisation, monitoring, targets, purchasing, budgets, investment (Figure 10.13).

There are key differences in approach between these. The EEO matrix places much more emphasis on interrelations between people in the organisation, where the Cheriton matrix is far more orientated to functions within the organisation. The difference this creates in practice is that the EEO matrix has policy as the key imperative and the imperative is internal to the organisation, the Cheriton matrix uses as the imperative the changing market in energy supply, which is changing in the United Kingdom as a result of the transfer of energy utilities from the public to the private sector and is an imperative external to the organisation. To make the matrix appropriate to environmental management would require the inclu-

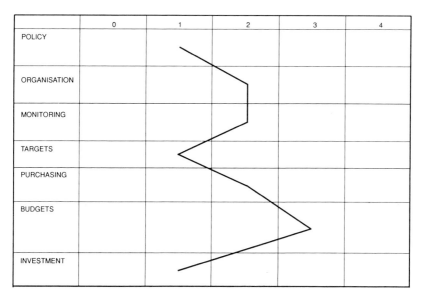

Figure 10.13 Levels of development in an energy management programme.

sion of a column for legal aspects, which would also introduce an external imperative.

What is found in practice (Energy Efficiency Office, 1993b) is that the particular view of the level of development in each area and the shape of the matrix overall is often influenced by who in the organisation draws it up, or whether it is drawn up by an external observer such as an auditor. This is valuable because the differences provide a focus for discussion and argument within the organisation and this adds greatly to the power of the device as a management tool.

10.10   Conclusions

In this chapter, the common ground that exists between management accounting and energy efficiency as they have been developed up to the present day are reviewed, picking up in particular areas where they may be individually weak but where combining recent developments in each enables a system of management for energy and the environment to be established which is stronger than anything which has existed hitherto.

There is no doubt that the criticisms of both management accounting and energy management which have been made over the past decade in no small measure make the combination of the two far stronger. Introducing some of the thinking that underlies management accounting can improve the power of the repertoire of the engineer in energy management. The solid rock of scientific principle on which energy management is based in the form of thermodynamics provides a testbed for management accounting and offers an area for management accounting to extend its sphere of influence in an area of immense importance for mankind. Environmental management, as the emergent discipline within which energy management probably belongs, is likely to benefit greatly as a result.

References

Aird, R.J. (1981) Using degree days to manage energy. *Energy Management* July, 7.
Anon (1991) Environmental audits are coming. *Chem. Br.* **27**, 493.
Anon (1992) *Energy Management* May/June, 22.
Armitage Norton (1982) *Energy Conservation Investment in Industry: An Appraisal of the Barriers. Energy Paper No. 50*. HMSO, London.
BPP/ACCA (1992) *Study Text, No. 2.6: Decision Making Techniques* (ISBN 0 86277 623 6).
Bromwich, M. and Bhimani, A. (1989) *Management Accounting: Evolution not Revolution*. CIMA (ISBN 0 948036 65 6).
Bromwich, M. and Hopwood, A.G., eds. (1986) *Research and Current Issues in Management Accounting, Proc. 4th Delloitte Haskins & Sells Accounting and Auditing Research Symposium*. Pitman, London.

BSI (1987) *British Standard Quality Systems*, BS 5750, Part 1 1987. British Standards Institution, London.

BSI (1992) *Specification for Environmental Management Systems*, BS 7750, British Standards Institution, London.

BSI (1994) *Specification for Environmental Management Systems*, EPC/50, DOC 91/53255, draft for public comment. British Standards Institution, London.

Chemical Industries Association (1991) *Guidance on Safety, Occupational Health and Environmental Protection Auditing*. Chemical Industries Association, UK.

Cheriton Technology (1992) *An Applications Manual for an Energy Management Accounting Scheme for Energy in Buildings*. Cheriton Technology Publications (ISBN 1 872157 01 7).

CIBSE (1986) *CIBSE Guide, Part A*. Chartered Institute of Building Services Engineers, London.

Clegg, L. and Price Walters, J. (1952) Fuel, heat and power auditing. *J. Inst. Fuel.* July, 136–145.

Coates, J., Rickwood, C. and Stacey, R. (1989) Control and Audit Management Accounting. CIMA (ISBN 0 434 90268 3).

Crawford, A.G. and Elson, C.R. (1982) *Energy Use in the Food Manufacturing Industry, Scientific and Technical Surveys, No. 128*. Leatherhead Food Research Association.

Davis, R. (1991) Auditing expectation gap must be closed. *Financial Times* 10 October, 13.

Energy Efficiency Office (1993a) *Organisational Aspects of Energy Management*, General Information Report 12. Energy Efficiency Office, London.

Energy Efficiency Office (1993b) *Reviewing Energy Management*, General Information Report 13. Energy Efficiency Office, London.

Foster, G. (1971) The decision making theme in expositions of accounting, unpublished MSc thesis, University of Sydney, 1971; quoted by Horngren (1986).

Harris, P.S. (1984) *The Armitage Norton Report*, Bulletin No. 44. Energy Users Research Association.

Harris, P.S. (1986) *Preparing the Company Energy Plan*. Energy Publications. ISBN 0 905332 46 6 (1 872157 00 9).

Harris, P.S. (1989) *Energy Monitoring and Target Setting Using CUSUM*. Cheriton Technology Publications.

HASTAM (1991) *Environmental Audit, A Complete Guide to Undertaking an Environmental Audit for your Business*. Mercury Books (ISBN 1 85252 100 7).

Horngren, C.T. (1986) Cost and management accounting: yesterday and today, in *Researches and Current Issues in Management Accounting, Proc. 4th Delloitte Haskins & Sells Accounting and Auditing Research Symposium*, eds. M. Bromwich and A.G. Hopwood. Pitman, London.

Industrial Energy Thrift Scheme (1983–1984) Sector Reports No. 32. Meat, fish, fruit and vegetable processing (1983); No. 42. Milling, mixing and edible fat processing (1984); No. 47. Confectionery (1984); No. 48. Baking (1984); No. 49. Dairy, alcoholic and soft drinks (1984). Department of Trade and Industry.

Kaplan, R. (1986) Quantitative models for management accounting in today's production environment, in *Research and Current Issues in Management Accounting, Proc. 4th Delloitte Haskins & Sells Accounting and Auditing Research Symposium*, eds. M. Bromwich and A.G. Hopwood. Pitman, London, pp. 103–115.

Kaplan, R.S. and Atkinson, A.A. (1989) *Advanced Management Accounting*, 2nd edition. Prentice Hall, Englewood Cliffs, NJ, p. 135.

Kaplan, R. and Johnson, H.T. (1988) Relevance Lost---The Rise and Fall of Management Accounting. Harvard University Press.

Kirwan, M. (1986) Management accounting in practice---a consultant's view, in *Researches and Current Issues in Management Accounting, Proc. 4th Delloitte Haskins & Sells Accounting and Auditing Research Symposium*, eds. M. Bromwich and A.G. Hopwood. Pitman, London.

Lyle, O. (1947) *The Efficient Use of Steam*. HMSO, London.

Lyle, P. (1957) *Regression Analysis of Production Costs and Factory Operations*, 3rd edition. Oliver & Boyd, London.

McVicker, I.F.G. (1946) The calculation of degree days. *J. Inst. Heat Vent. Eng.* **14**, 252–299.

Mott, G. (1987) *Managing Accounting*. Pan Business Management (ISBN 0 330 29727 9).

NHS (1991) *Energy Management Audit Guide*. The Audit Commission for Local Authorities and the National Health Service in England and Wales.

Pooley, J. (1992) *Computer Aided Monitoring and Targetting for Industry, Energy Efficiency Good Practice Guide No. 31*. Department of the Environment, London.

Rumford, Count (1802) *The Principles of the Management of Fire and Economy of Fuel*.

Sen, A. and Srivastava, M. (1989) *Regression Analysis, Theory, Methods and Applications*. Springer-Verlag, Berlin.

Walshe, N.M.A. (1992) Analysis of Baking Industry Extended Energy Survey Reports, 1984–1989, ETSU R61 and Analysis of Dairy Industry Extended Energy Survey Reports, 1984–1989, ETSU R62. Department of Energy, London.

Whitehead, G. and Upson, A. (1982) *Success in Accounting and Costing*. John Murray (ISBN 0 7195 3835 1).

Wilkinson Riddle, G.J. (1982) *Accounting Level III*. Macdonald & Evans.

Wilson, A.E.D. (1992) Analysis of Brewing Industry Extended Energy Survey Reports, 1984–1989, ETSU R66. Department of Energy, London.

Woodward, R.H. and Goldsmith, P.L. (1981) *Cumulative Sum Techniques*, ICI Monograph No. 3. Institute of Manpower Studies (ISBN 0 904744 12 4).

Index